Illustrated Paradox 3.0 Volume II

Paradox Application Language (PAL)

Debbie and Doug Stone

Wordware Publishing, Inc.

Library of Congress Cataloging-in-Publication Data
(Revised for volume 2)

Stone, Deborah L.
Illustrated Paradox.

Includes Indexes.
Contents: v. 1. Basic menu commands edition —
v. 2. Version 3.0, Paradox Application Language (PAL)
1. Paradox (Computer program) 2. Data base management
I. Stone, Doug. II. Title..

QA76.9.D3S754 1987 00.75'65 87-13290
ISBN 0-915381-94-X
ISBN 0-915381-93-1 (v. 1)
ISBN 1-55622-108-8 (v. 2)

1506 Capital Avenue
Plano, Texas 75074

Printed in the United States of America

ISBN 1-55622-108-8
10 9 8 7 6 5 4 3 2 1
9004

All inquiries for volume purchases of this book should be addressed to Wordware Publishing, Inc.,
at the above address. Telephone inquiries may be made by calling:

(214) 423-0090

Contents

Module	Title	Page
1	About This Book	1
2	An Overview of Paradox	4
3	Sample Session	6
4	Game Rules	8
5	=	17
6	@, ?, ??	21
7	ACCEPT	26
8	ADD	33
9	ARRAY	37
10	BEEP	41
11	CANCELEDIT	43
12	CANVAS	47
13	CLEAR	49
14	COEDIT	52
15	COPY	55
16	COPYFORM	62
17	COPYFROMARRAY	64
18	COPYREPORT	68
19	COPYTOARRAY	70
20	CREATE	74
21	CREATELIB	79
22	CURSOR	82
23	DEBUG	84
24	DELETE	90
25	DOS, DOSBIG	93
26	ECHO	95
27	EDIT	98
28	EDITLOG	105
29	EMPTY	108
30	EXECPROC	110
31	EXECUTE	112
32	EXIT	114
33	FIRSTSHOW	117
34	FOR, ENDFOR	119
35	FORMTABLES	124
36	IF, ENDIF	128
37	IMAGERIGHTS	133
38	INDEX	135
39	INFOLIB	139
40	KEYPRESS	141
41	LOCATE	143
42	LOCK, UNLOCK	148
43	LOCKRECORD, UNLOCKRECORD	151
44	LOOP	154

Contents (Cont.)

Module	Title	Page
45	MESSAGE	158
46	MOVETO	161
47	OPEN PRINTER, CLOSE PRINTER	165
48	PAINTCANVAS	167
49	PASSWORD	170
50	PICKFORM	172
51	PLAY	177
52	PRINT	180
53	PRINTER	185
54	PRIVTABLES	193
55	PROC, ENDPROC	195
56	PROMPT	199
57	PROTECT	201
58	QUERY, ENDQUERY	203
59	QUIT	211
60	QUITLOOP	214
61	READLIB	217
62	RELEASE	219
63	RENAME	224
64	REPORT	227
65	REPORTTABLES	233
66	REQUIREDCHECK	238
67	RESET	240
68	RETURN	242
69	RUN	247
70	SAVEVARS	249
71	SCAN, ENDSCAN	253
72	SELECT	257
73	SETDIR	259
74	SETKEY	263
75	SETMARGIN	265
76	SETMAXSIZE	268
77	SETNEGCOLOR	270
78	SETPRINTER	273
79	SETPRIVDIR	274
80	SETQUERYORDER	276
81	SETRECORDPOSITION	280
82	SETRESTARTCOUNT	282
83	SETRETRYPERIOD	284
84	SETSWAP	286
85	SETUSERNAME	287
86	SHOWARRAY	288
87	SHOWFILES	290
88	SHOWMENU	292

Contents (Cont.)

Module	Title	Page
89	SHOWTABLES	296
90	SKIP	298
91	SLEEP	303
92	SORT	306
93	STYLE	310
94	SUBTRACT	313
95	SWITCH, ENDSWITCH	317
96	SYNCCURSOR	323
97	TEXT, ENDTEXT	325
98	TYPEIN	329
99	UNPASSWORD	331
100	VIEW	335
101	WAIT	341
102	WHILE, ENDWHILE	345
103	WRITELIB	350

Appendix A — Terms And Definitions . . . 353
Appendix B — Special Keys . . . 359
Appendix C — Query Operators . . . 361
Appendix D — PAL Functions . . . 363
Appendix E — PAL Reserved Words . . . 383
Appendix F — Paradox Menu Options . . . 387
Appendix G — Paradox Network Overview . . . 389
Appendix H — Paradox Exercises . . . 391

Index . . . 403

Recommended Learning Sequence

Sequence	*Topic*	*Module*	*Page*
5	@, ?, ??	6	21
6	=	5	17
7	BEEP	10	41
8	CLEAR	13	49
9	DEBUG	23	84
10	ACCEPT	7	26
11	SLEEP	91	303
12	PAINTCANVAS	48	167
13	CANVAS	12	47
14	FOR, ENDFOR	34	119
15	TEXT, ENDTEXT	97	325
16	SETMARGIN	75	265
17	QUIT	59	211
18	EXIT	32	114
19	WHILE, ENDWHILE	102	345
20	IF, ENDIF	36	128
21	LOOP	44	154
22	QUITLOOP	60	214
23	MESSAGE	45	158
24	STYLE	93	310
25	SHOWMENU	88	292
26	SWITCH, ENDSWITCH	95	317
27	PLAY	51	177
28	RETURN	68	242
29	SETDIR	73	259
30	CREATE	20	74
31	EDIT	27	98
32	WAIT	101	341
33	EDITLOG	28	105
34	LOCATE	41	143
35	MOVETO	46	161
36	CANCELEDIT	11	43
37	REPORT	64	227
38	PRINTER	53	185
39	PRINT	52	180
40	VIEW	100	335
41	PICKFORM	50	172
42	SKIP	90	298

Recommended Learning Sequence (Cont.)

Sequence	*Topic*	*Module*	*Page*
43	SCAN, ENDSCAN	71	253
44	QUERY, ENDQUERY	58	203
45	SORT	92	306
46	INDEX	38	165
47	ADD	8	33
48	SUBTRACT	94	313
49	EMPTY	29	108
50	ARRAY	9	37
51	COPYTOARRAY	19	70
52	COPYFROMARRAY	17	64
53	SHOWARRAY	86	288
54	SHOWFILES	87	290
55	SHOWTABLES	89	296
56	SAVEVARS	70	249
57	RELEASE	62	219
58	COPY	15	55
59	COPYREPORT	18	68
60	COPYFORM	16	62
61	RENAME	63	224
62	DELETE	24	90
63	FIRSTSHOW	33	117
64	PROC, ENDPROC	55	195
65	CREATELIB	21	79
66	WRITELIB	103	350
67	INFOLIB	39	139
68	READLIB	61	217
69	CURSOR	22	82
70	SYNCCURSOR	96	323
71	PROMPT	56	199
72	REQUIREDCHECK	66	238
73	ECHO	26	95
74	PROTECT	57	201
75	PASSWORD	49	170
76	UNPASSWORD	99	331
77	IMAGERIGHTS	37	133
78	RESET	67	240
79	SETKEY	74	263
80	SELECT	72	257

Recommended Learning Sequence (Cont.)

Sequence	*Topic*	*Module*	*Page*
81	EXECUTE	31	112
82	EXECPROC	30	110
83	TYPEIN	98	329
84	KEYPRESS	40	141
85	RUN	69	247
86	DOS	25	93
87	OPEN PRINTER, CLOSE PRINTER	47	165
88	SETPRINTER	78	273
89	SETMAXSIZE	76	268
90	PRIVTABLES	54	193
91	SETPRIVDIR	79	274
92	COEDIT	14	52
93	LOCK, UNLOCK	42	148
94	LOCKRECORD, UNLOCKRECORD	43	151
95	SETRETRYPERIOD	83	284
96	SETSWAP	84	286
97	SETUSERNAME	85	287
98	REPORTTABLES	65	233
99	FORMTABLES	35	124
100	SETNEGCOLOR	77	270
101	SETRECORDPOSITION	81	280
102	SETQUERYORDER	80	276
103	SETRESTARTCOUNT	82	282

Module 1
ABOUT THIS BOOK

INTRODUCTION

Illustrated Paradox — Volume II describes Borland International's Paradox Application Language (PAL). It presents information about combining menu options with the PAL commands for writing specialized scripts (programs).

This book is designed for beginning users who wish to learn how to write and/or enhance their Paradox scripts. It is also for intermediate and advanced users who need a quick reference that contains script examples and explains the rules.

ORGANIZATION

In this book, you will find detailed descriptions of each of the PAL commands as well as examples that show you how to use them. Each Paradox command is described in a separate module. The modules are organized alphabetically.

To fit the broad range of users it addresses, this book is organized into small, easy-to-read modules. The modules include descriptions, applications, and illustrations that provide insight into how Paradox commands can be used in scripts to speed and simplify everyday tasks.

Many examples are presented in the Description, Applications, and Typical Operation sections of the modules. These examples are helpful to users at all skill levels.

The examples in this book can be used as models to design your own application solutions. They bring to light details that are otherwise buried in the material presented in the Paradox manuals. With the exception of Modules 1 through 4, each module in this book contains information that pertains to one specific Paradox command.

Module 2 is an introduction to the Paradox package. This module covers Paradox guidelines, terms, and techniques.

Module 3 presents the Sample Session for this book.

Module 4 presents an overview of Paradox and the keys which tell it what to do.

HARDWARE AND SOFTWARE REQUIREMENTS

Paradox operates on the IBM PC, XT, AT, or 3270 PC, or any 100% compatible computer. It requires the PC-DOS (version 2.0 or higher) operating system and a minimum of 512K of memory. Your system should be equipped with disk drives, and a printer if you want to print documents.

Before running the Paradox software package, you must install it. Select the set of instructions which meets your computer hardware.

Floppy Disk Installation These instructions use A and B to identify the two available disk drives.

1. Insert your DOS disk into drive A and turn on the computer.
2. When the A> prompt appears, insert the Paradox Installation Disk into drive B.
3. Type **B:install** and press **Enter**.
4. Follow the installation instructions that appear on the screen. For example, if you are asked if you want to continue the install, type **Y** and press **Enter**.
5. When you are asked for System Disk I, remove the Installation Disk from drive B, insert the disk labeled System Disk I, and press **Enter**. Type **Paradox** and press **Enter** at the A> prompt.
6. When asked for System Disk II, replace the disk in drive B with the one labeled System Disk II and press **Enter**.
7. When you are asked for your name and Paradox serial number, type them so they may be recorded on your disk.
8. The installation procedure is complete.

Hard Disk Installation These instructions use A to identify the floppy disk drive and C for the hard disk.

1. Turn on the computer.
2. When the C> prompt appears, insert the Paradox Installation Disk into drive A.
3. Type **A:install C:** and press **Enter**. Paradox tells you that files are being copied from the Installation Disk to drive C.
4. Follow the installation instructions that appear on the screen. For example, if you are asked if you want to continue the install, type **Y** and press **Enter**.
5. When you are asked for System Disk I, remove the Installation Disk from drive A, insert the disk labeled System Disk I, and press **Enter**. Again, Paradox tells you that files are being copied from drive A to drive C.

6. When asked for System Disk II, replace the disk in drive A with the one labeled System Disk II and press **Enter**. The last of the Paradox programs and files are being copied from drive A.
7. When you are asked for your name and Paradox serial number, type them so they may be recorded on your disk.
8. The installation procedure is complete.

Once Paradox is installed, you do not need to repeat the procedure unless the installation failed. Since the Paradox disks are not copy-protected, be sure that you create a proper number of backup disks and store the original disks in a safe place.

This is especially important if you are using a floppy disk system instead of a hard disk. If the floppy disks you are using to run Paradox become damaged, use the originals to make new copies. Always keep the set of original floppy disks and use only copies to operate Paradox.

WHAT YOU SHOULD KNOW

You should be familiar with your computer, its keyboard, and some of the commands available on your operating system. Also, a basic knowledge of using Paradox menu options and scripts is helpful. If you can do these things, you are ready to use Paradox Application Language (PAL).

Module 2
AN OVERVIEW OF PARADOX

INTRODUCTION

Paradox is an easy-to-use software package that helps you keep, organize, and report information (data). As with several other database software packages, there are two modes of Paradox. This book uses both modes to teach you the quickest and most efficient uses of the software.

The mode which is easiest to use provides a series of menus from which you select the option you want performed. Since menus are provided by Paradox to help you accomplish your work, this mode is called "menu driven."

All available menu options in the menu-driven mode are preset by Paradox. Each one is explained in *Illustrated Paradox—Volume I*. For example, the Main Menu appears across the top of the screen as in the following display.

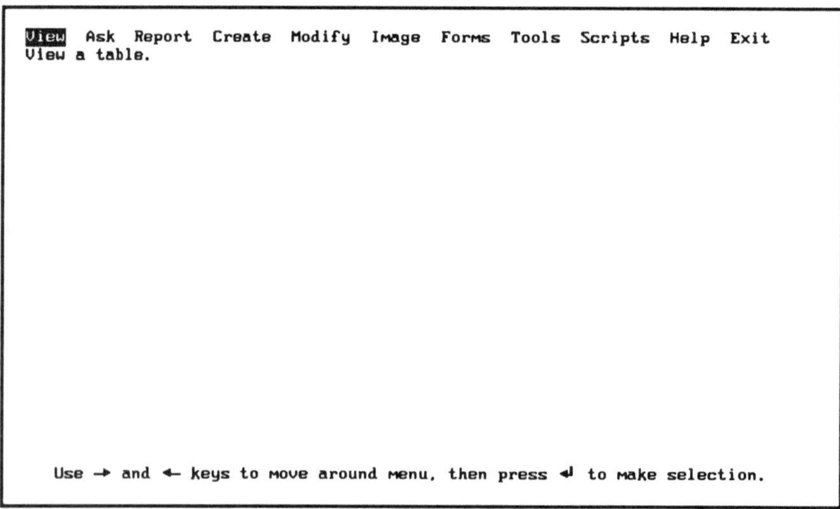

Press the arrow (cursor) keys to position the cursor on the option you want, read the message under the menu line, and press the Enter key. Paradox responds by asking for specific information (e.g., a table name), presenting another menu line of options, or performing the selected task.

The second mode is for "custom" Paradox applications. This mode lets you control the screen and the keyboard. Such control is accomplished by creating, saving, and running Paradox programs called *scripts.*

A script is a series of Paradox instructions. It may consist of specific options from the menu-driven mode and/or Paradox Applications Language (PAL) commands.

If you have recorded scripts in the menu-driven mode already, you know that tasks are completed faster with a script because you do not initiate each one individually. By running (playing) a script, you save yourself several keystrokes. When you tell Paradox to play the script, the computer follows the script's instructions without your guidance.

For example, the recorded script in the following display reads the Texas table, selects a report form, sends the report to the printer, and returns the cursor to an empty workspace.

```
Designing script C:\paradox3\zipcode                                   Script

....+...10....+...20....+...30....+...40....+...50....+...60....+...70....+...80
{Report} {Output} {TEXAS} {1} {Printer} {Scripts} {End-Record}
```

Use the menu-driven mode as much as possible to create small scripts which accomplish a task. Then, write other scripts which play the smaller ones. This building-block activity links the pieces together until your custom application starts to take form.

As the application reaches completion, the need for Paradox Applications Language (PAL) commands becomes more apparent. Use PAL to provide the application with Paradox-like menus, messages, and control. In other words, make your custom application menu driven.

WHY PARADOX?

Menu-driven applications are very easy to use.

Paradox provides menus that may be used for any Paradox database. As your experience and needs increase, you have the option of developing your own menus that are specific to the application.

Also, results are almost immediate. Develop a full application in just a few hours. Then, be ready to do your work.

If you know how to use menu-driven Paradox, you already know the importance of scripts. Start your learning experience with small scripts. Change and test them until you are comfortable with the menu options and PAL. Before too long, you will be writing scripts like a pro.

Module 3
SAMPLE SESSION

Since Paradox is a large program that spans several diskettes, it is difficult to run it from a floppy disk drive. Copy all diskettes into a subdirectory called PARADOX3 on your hard disk and run the install procedure. This program helps you identify the computer hardware.

To run a sample session, perform the following steps.

1. From the DOS C> prompt, type **Paradox3** and press **Enter**. After Paradox draws the introduction, a Main Menu screen is displayed and resembles the following.

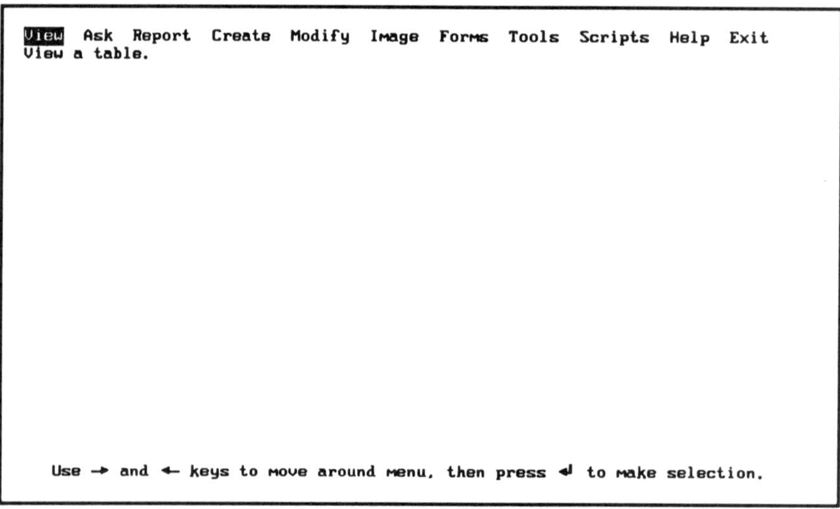

2. Each word along the top of the screen is a Main Menu option. Press the right and left arrow keys to move the menu bar from option to option. A brief description of each menu option follows.

View	Review or search the data kept in an existing table.
Ask	Set selection criteria for the data in the table.
Report	Create, change, print or display the data in a specified sequence.
Create	Identify the data kept in a table (fieldname, type, and length).
Modify	Change the data kept in an existing table.

Image	Change the column widths of a table while it is displayed on the screen.
Forms	Create, or change the way the data is displayed on the screen.
Tools	Options to empty, delete, or rename a table and its family of screens and reports.
Scripts	Create, edit, or run a Paradox program to perform several operations for the table, printer, or screen.
Help	Provides information about the currently selected menu option.
Exit	End the current Paradox session.

3. Position the cursor bar on the Exit option and press **Enter**. The Main Menu bar is replaced by another set of options asking if you want to end the Paradox session. Type **Y** to end the session and return to the DOS C> prompt.

Module 4
GAME RULES

DESCRIPTION

Learning to use a new software package is like learning a new game. You read the rules, play a few practice games, and then you play for real.

The rules for Paradox are easy to follow. Though there are several of them, you will catch on quickly as you experience your first few sessions. You can read this module straight through, or stop and press the keys when indicated as you read the text.

Be sure that you use the Paradox Installation disk to configure Paradox for your computer hardware. You need to do this only once.

Before beginning a Paradox session, make sure that your Paradox System I diskette is in drive A (or on your hard disk). Place a blank, formatted diskette in drive B. Type PARADOX and press the Enter key to begin your Paradox session.

After Paradox draws its introduction and presents the license agreement on the screen, change the disk in drive A to the Paradox System II diskette and press the Enter key. The Paradox Main Menu (similar to the following display) appears on your screen.

Each of the words along the top of your screen (workspace) is a Main Menu option. To select one of the options, use the arrow (cursor) keys to highlight the desired option and press the Enter key. A shortcut to accomplish the same thing is to type the first letter of the option.

When you select an option, Paradox either performs the requested task, provides a submenu of options, or asks for the name of the table, form, etc. that you want to use. If you select an option from a menu or submenu and then change your mind, just press the Esc key to return to the previous menu.

When you have tasks that must be performed regularly, record each menu option required for that task in one or more scripts. Like a program, a script is a series of instructions that tell Paradox what you want done. Each time the script is played, the tasks are performed.

Another advantage to using scripts is that the tasks repeat identically each time the script is played. With just a few keystrokes, you begin playing a script. If the tasks are numerous, a script keeps the computer busy without your devoted attention.

To write a script, you must first know what menu options must be selected to accomplish the task. The best way to do this is by performing the task and writing each keystroke and/or selected option on a sheet of paper. The series of instructions on the paper is the outline for your script.

After you outline your script, type S to select the Scripts option from the Main Menu. The Scripts submenu appears as in the following display.

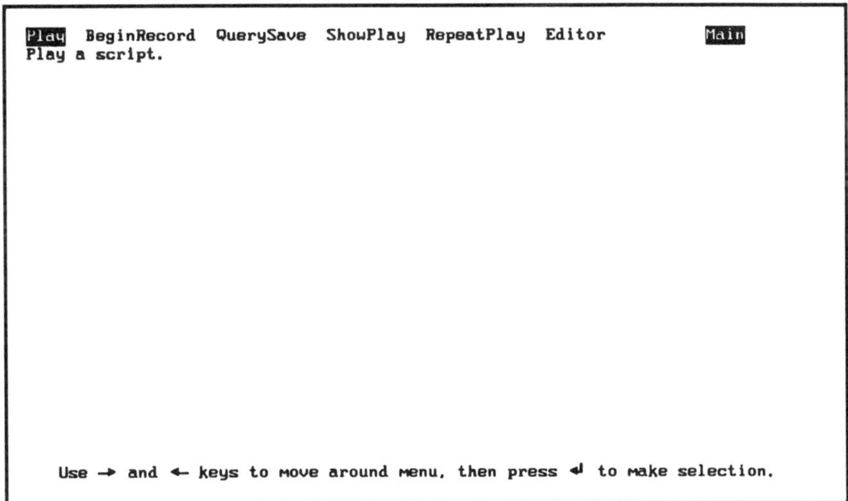

From this submenu, there are two options that let you write and save a script, BeginRecord or Editor. If you change your mind when this submenu appears, just press the Esc key to return to the Main Menu.

One way to write a script is by recording each menu option into a script file. Selecting the BeginRecord option on the Scripts submenu tells Paradox that you want to record the options as they are selected.

When the BeginRecord option is selected, Paradox asks for a script name. Type a name that helps you identify the tasks performed within the script and press the Enter key. The Main Menu returns to the screen, but do not be fooled. The "R" in the top right corner tells you that Paradox is ready to record each selected option.

Perform the keystrokes that you wrote on paper. When you are ready to stop the recording activity, press F10 (Menu) to access the submenu with the End-Record option. Select this option to tell Paradox to stop the recording activity, save the series of selected options on the disk, and name the file as you specified before recording began.

The second way to write and save a script with the Scripts submenu is by selecting the Editor option. Using the Paradox Editor is much like using a word processor to write a letter. There are special keys that tell the editor to insert lines, delete lines, move the cursor, etc. Proper spelling and syntax of each instruction are very important for the completed script to play successfully.

To write a new script or change an existing one (recorded or not), select the Editor option of the Scripts submenu. Paradox asks if you want to write a new script or edit (change) an existing script. Type W to select the Write option.

When Paradox asks for the name to be assigned to the new script, type a name that helps you identify the tasks performed within the script, and press Enter. If the name is found on the disk, you may replace the existing script, or try another name. Then, the workspace clears to provide a clean script area as in the following display.

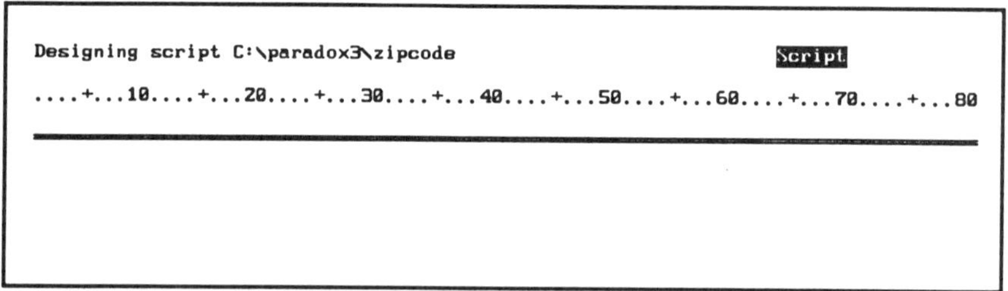

Type each instruction of your script so that Paradox knows what to do. As long as each instruction is spelled correctly, the case (uppercase, or lowercase) of the letters is not important. The available instructions for a script are menu options, PAL commands, PAL keywords, and PAL functions.

The menu options are the same ones seen on the menu line when running Paradox in the menu-driven mode. Each option must be spelled correctly and enclosed with braces ({ }).

If Paradox expects a table name, report number, etc., it must also be enclosed with braces and appear in the proper sequence among the menu options.

The PAL commands, keywords, and functions must be spelled correctly. Each PAL command has a special use. The keywords and functions must be combined with the proper command so that the syntax is correct.

For example, consider writing a script called ZipCode. It must read the Texas table, select report form number 1, send the report to the printer, and clear the workspace. When the report is complete, the computer beeps twice.

When ready to save the script on disk, press F10 (Menu). The menu along the top of your screen resembles the one in the following display.

```
Read  Go  Print  Help  DO-IT!  Cancel                          Script
Read contents of another script into this script starting at the cursor.
....+...10....+...20....+...30....+...40....+...50....+...60....+...70....+...80
{Report} {Output} {TEXAS} {1} {Printer}
BEEP
BEEP
```

Select the Read option when you decide to combine another script with the one on your screen. It is inserted at the point identified by your cursor.

Use the Go option to save the script on disk, leave the editor, and play the script. The Main Menu screen returns after the script is successful. Otherwise, Paradox gives you the choice of canceling (stop playing) or debugging (correcting) the script.

The Print option sends the script you see on your screen to your printer. Do this when you have successfully completed a script. Printed scripts are an important part of documenting your applications. If the script is deleted from the disk, use the printed script to recreate it.

Of course, the Help option presents the help screens for editing scripts. Remember that pressing F1 (Help) also provides the same help screens.

The DO-IT! option tells Paradox to save the script on disk and return a clean workspace. Pressing F2 (DO-IT!) accomplishes the same thing.

Use the Cancel option when you change your mind and do not like the changes you made since you last saved the script on disk. Paradox removes the script from your workspace without saving it on disk. The next time you select the Editor option for that script, Paradox presents the version last saved on disk.

When you write or change a script, you can test it immediately with the Go option. Remember that a script is not complete unless it is tested and played successfully. If an error exists within the script, you need to know before going on to other work.

If an error is encountered within the script, Paradox asks if you want to Cancel or Debug the script. Select the Cancel option to stop the test and return to the Main Menu screen. When the Debug option is selected, an error message and the instruction that caused the problem are presented at the bottom of the screen. An arrow at the bottom of the screen points to the instruction that caused the problem.

At this point, you have two choices. One choice is to press Ctrl-Q to stop the debugging activity, cancel the script test, and return to the Main Menu. The second choice is to change the script. Press Ctrl-E (Editor) to stop the debugging activity, cancel the script, and return to the Editor screen. Continue the change, test, and debug activity until the script plays successfully and the Main Menu returns to your screen automatically.

The Editor and Debug tools within Paradox let you write, test, and change scripts until you get the results you need. Use the Paradox menu-driven mode to do much of your development work. Then, use PAL commands to enhance the power and control you need for your applications.

When you are ready to quit your Paradox session, select the Exit option from the Main Menu screen. You are given the chance to change your mind before Paradox returns you to DOS.

THE SPECIAL KEYS

Of course, most of the keys on your computer keyboard are important, but some of them are special. These keys are used to tell Paradox what you want to do. Many of these key presses may be performed by a script instead of the user. Refer to Appendix B for valid special key words.

Alt (Alternate) Using this key with certain other keys, changes the effect of the other keys. For example, pressing F8 (Clear Image) alone erases the image where the cursor is positioned. With the Alt key held down, pressing F8 (Clear Image) erases *all* the images from the workspace.

Backspace Pressing this key while in your workspace deletes the character preceding the cursor. Pressing Ctrl-Backspace erases the contents of the field where the cursor is positioned.

Ctrl (Control) Using this key changes the effect of certain other keys. For example, pressing Home alone moves the cursor to the first line or record in your workspace. With the Ctrl key held down, pressing Home moves the cursor to the beginning of the current line or record.

Ctrl-Break (Control-Break) This is a combination of keys. Press the Ctrl key as if it were the Shift key of a typewriter. While holding it down, press the Break key. Paradox stops the current task and returns to your previous operation. For example, use this key combination when you want to stop printing a report.

Ctrl-D (Ditto) Press this key combination when you want the current field to contain the same value as the same field in the previous record.

Ctrl-E (Editor) When testing a script and an error is encountered, you have the option of canceling the test or debugging the script. If you select the Debug option, use this key combination when you are ready to stop the debugging activity and return to the script editor.

Ctrl-F (Field View) This key combination has the same effect as Alt-F5 (Field View). Use either key combination to tell Paradox that you want the ability to move the cursor across the value of a field that is not allocated enough space on the screen.

Ctrl-R (Rotate) When you want to move fields in your current table, use this key combination. Position the cursor to the field name you want to move. Then, press Ctrl-R (Rotate) to move the selected field to the end of the record.

Ctrl-V (Vertical Ruler Toggle) This key combination turns the vertical ruler line counter on and off. Use this toggle for report generators or script editors.

Ctrl-Y (Delete Line) When working with a script or report specifications, use this key combination to tell Paradox to delete the current line from the cursor to the end of the line.

Del (Delete) This key removes the character or record identified by the cursor position. For example, use the arrow (cursor) keys to move the cursor to the letter "u" of "ablue" in a memo. Press Del to erase the letter so the word is changed to "able." The current record is deleted when using this key in the Form or Table views.

Down Arrow This key is the same as the number 2 on your numeric keypad. If a 2 appears, instead of moving your cursor, press the Num Lock key to tell Paradox that you want to use the arrow (cursor) keys. This key moves the cursor down one record, field, or line.

End Pressing End moves the cursor to the last line of a memo or the last record of a table. In Field View, the End key moves the cursor to the last character of the current field. Press Ctrl-End to move the cursor to the last character of the current line or field.

Enter This key is used when the cursor is positioned on the option you want to select. It tells Paradox to perform that option. In this book, Enter and ↵ are the same key. Many computer keyboards label the key Return instead of Enter.

Esc (Escape) When you open a submenu but change your mind, pressing this key makes the submenu disappear. The Main Menu line is returned to the top of your screen without changing your work.

F1 (Help) Press F1 (Help) at any time to review the help screens. Paradox begins its help with the topic with which you are currently working.

F2 (DO-IT!) Press this key when you want Paradox to begin or end an operation. By pressing F2 (DO-IT!) when adding or editing records in a table, you tell Paradox to save the current table on disk. This has the same effect as selecting one of the DO-IT! options available on several of the submenus; however, this is the quickest way to tell Paradox to respond.

F3 (Up Image) Paradox lets you display several images of tables on your workspace at once. It's like stacking sheets of paper on top of each other. Each new table displayed is put on top of the stack. Press the F3 (Up Image) and F4 (Down Image) keys to move through the stack.

By pressing Alt-F3 (Instant Script Record), you turn on and off the Instant Script Record option. For example, press Alt-F3 (Instant Script Record) to turn on the capability. Each keystroke afterward is recorded in the Instant Script Record until Alt-F3 (Instant Script Record) is again pressed. The Instant Script is saved (replacing the old one) so that each time Alt-F4 (Instant Script Play) is pressed, the current instant script is performed.

F4 (Down Image) When you have several tables displayed on your workspace, press F4 (Down Image) to move the cursor down through a stack and F3 (Up Image) to move up the stack.

Press Alt-F4 (Instant Script Play) to play (perform) the current Instant Script of Paradox keystrokes which you saved by using Alt-F3 (Instant Script Record).

F5 (Example) Use F5 (Example) to query one or more tables. This key lets you establish a link between one or more tables by a common value. For example, if two tables contain customer number fields (with the same, or different field names), position the cursor in the customer number field of the first table, press F5 (Example) and type a number. Check the other fields in the file that you want to see in the query. Do the same for the second table. The result is the specified information for the customer from both tables.

When you press Alt-F5 (Field View), Paradox presents the currently selected field in a box. This is called the Field View. Use the arrow (cursor), Home, and End keys to scroll the field information within the box.

F6 (Check Mark) When creating query statements, press this key to select the fields you want to be displayed by the query. A check mark appears in the selected fields. Use this key as a toggle to turn the check mark on or off if you change your mind. A check marked field displays the information of all records except duplicates.

To list the duplicates too, press Alt-F6 (Check Plus) instead of F6 (Check Mark). A check mark and a plus sign appears in the selected field instead of just the check mark.

F7 (Form Toggle) When you first open a table on your workspace with the View option, several records are listed down the screen. Press F7 (Form Toggle) to switch between the original form and the form you created and assigned as the standard form for that table.

Using Alt-F7 (Instant Report) is similar to using F7 (Form Toggle). When you design reports, the one you identify as the standard report for the current table is printed when you press Alt-F7 (Instant Report).

F8 (Clear Image) Use this function key to remove the current image from your workspace. In other words, the sheet of paper on top of the stack is thrown away without saving it on disk.

Using Alt-F8 (Clear All) is similar to using F8 (Clear Image) except that the whole stack is removed from your workspace. It's a quick way to clean your desk.

F9 (Edit mode) Paradox prevents you from accidentally changing a table or form. You must select the Edit option from the Modify submenu or use this function key. When all changes are complete, save them on disk by pressing F2 (DO-IT!).

F10 (Menu) Pressing F10 (Menu) presents the menu that is applicable to the current option. Once this menu appears, select the option you need or press Esc to return the cursor to the workspace.

Home Pressing Home causes Paradox to move the cursor to the first line in your current workspace. Press Ctrl-Home to move the cursor to the beginning of the current line.

Ins (Insert) Press this key to tell Paradox you want to start or stop inserting characters within the current line of a report specification or memo. For example, use the arrow (cursor) keys to position the cursor on "l" of "probly," press Ins and type "ab." The word is changed to "probably." Press Ins again to turn off the insert mode. Each time you press Ins when working in Form or Table View, a new blank record is inserted in your open table.

Left Arrow This key is the same as the number 4 on your numeric keypad. If a 4 appears instead of moving your cursor, press Num Lock to tell Paradox that you want to use the arrow (cursor) keys. This key moves the cursor left one field, or character. Press Ctrl-Left Arrow to move left one screen when in Table view. When used in the script editor, this key combination moves the cursor left only one half of a screen.

Num Lock (Numeric Lock) Locate this key at the top of the numeric keypad. Some computers combine the arrow keys with numbers on the numeric keypad. For example, the same key is pressed for a 4 or a Right Arrow. This key lets you designate which one you want the key press to produce. Press this key to change the arrow keys to numbers. Press it again to change them from numbers to arrow keys again.

PgDn (Page Down) Press this key to tell Paradox to show you the next screen. This is like moving a frame down a page to see the next few lines of the text. Press Ctrl-PgDn to move the cursor to the same field of the next record.

PgUp (Page Up) Press this key to tell Paradox to show you the previous screen. This is like moving a frame up a page to see the previous few lines of the text. Press Ctrl-PgUp to move the cursor to the same field of the previous record.

Right Arrow This key is the same as the number 6 on your numeric keypad. If a 6 appears instead of moving your cursor, press Num Lock to tell Paradox that you want to use the arrow (cursor) keys. This key moves the cursor right one field, or character. Press Ctrl-Right Arrow to move right one screen when in Table View. When used in the script editor, this key combination moves the cursor right only one half of a screen.

Tab (Tab Right) Each time you press this key, the cursor moves a few spaces to the right. Use it like the Tab key on a typewriter to move the cursor quickly across the workspace. The Shift-Tab (Reverse Tab, or Tab Left) moves the cursor a few spaces to the left.

Up Arrow This key is the same as the number 8 on your numeric keypad. If an 8 appears instead of moving your cursor, press Num Lock to tell Paradox that you want to use the arrow (cursor) keys. This key moves the cursor up one record, field, or line.

As you are now aware, there are many options and special keys available. Just follow the recommended learning sequence and take small steps until you feel comfortable with Paradox scripts and PAL. Then, insert a new data disk and begin more serious tasks.

Good Luck!

Module 5

=

DESCRIPTION

This PAL command lets you create and change temporary fields called variables. When you create variables with the = command, or arrays with the ARRAY command, the computer keeps them in a scratchpad area of its memory. They are available only during the current Paradox session, or until you use the RELEASE command to remove them from memory.

You can also use this command to change (edit) the value of a variable, array element, or table field.

The proper syntax for the = command follows.

```
<Variable> = <expression>
<array element> = <expression>
<field specifier> = <expression>
```

Variables are similar to the fields in a table. The first character of the variable name must be a letter (A through Z). A variable name must not include spaces. The letters in the name may be uppercase, lowercase, or a combination of the cases. Choose meaningful names for your variables, but do not use commands, keywords, or other PAL reserved words.

The expression data type must be numeric, alphanumeric, or date. Create numeric variables by setting the value to a number. Create alphanumeric variables by enclosing the value with double quotation marks. Create date variables by setting the value to a date (e.g., 03/15/90).

For example, create one alphanumeric, four numeric, and one date variables in a script. Name them continue, counter1, counter2, rows, columns, and date1 as in the following script lines.

```
continue = "Yes"
counter1 = 0
counter2 = 0
rows = 0
columns = 0
date1 = 03/15/90
```

Later, change the values of the existing variables with the following script lines.

```
counter1 = 8
counter2 = counter2 + 2
rows = rows + 5
columns = (columns / 10) * 5
continue = "No"
```

Use arithmetic operators to change the value of numeric variables. When the data type is numeric, you can change the value by using the operators +, –, *, and /. The operators are addition, subtraction, multiplication, and division, respectively.

Use parentheses to tell the computer the order of operations. Paradox performs arithmetic operations according to the following sequence:

a) the inner-most sets of embedded parentheses are processed first, then the next set, working outward

b) multiplication and division, beginning from the left side of the expression

c) addition and subtraction, beginning from the left side of the expression.

All other changes must be specific values as shown for counter1, and continue in the preceding example. Counter1 is now equal to 8 instead of 0, and continue equals No instead of Yes. The other variables are changed according to the arithmetic operations.

There are times when you want to combine several variables, array elements, or fields to create a new variable. You can combine (concatenate) alphanumeric values *only*. Use the + to tell Paradox that you want concatenation performed as in the following example:

```
name = "David Lawson"
city = "Dallas"
state = "Tx"
line1 = name + ",   "+ city + ",  " + state
```

Include a numeric data type as part of a concatenated value by using the STRVAL function. This function temporarily makes the numeric value look like it is alphanumeric. Remember that the variable, array element, or field is not changed. To perform such a combination, use the STRVAL function and the + as follows.

```
num = 5
name = "The value of num is currently "+STRVAL(num)
? name
num = 10
? name
```

You can also use the = command to change the value of a field in a table. The new value must be the same data type as the field. Otherwise a script error occurs when you play the script. In that case, change the data type by including or removing quotation marks and play the script again.

APPLICATIONS

Sometimes you need fields that hold information temporarily. It's like making notes on a sheet of paper, and then throwing it away when your work is finished. These fields are called variables and are created and changed when you use the = command.

For example, you want your PAL application to ask the user to type a person's name and press Enter. Program your script to create a variable that holds the name in memory while the table is searched. When the user presses Enter, the script uses the variable to locate the requested table record. When the task is completed, use the RELEASE command to remove the variable from the scratchpad.

Also use this command to change the value of array elements and table fields. A value of an array element is changed just like that of a variable. However, to change the value of a table field, your script must make the field editable.

TYPICAL OPERATION

This example shows you how to use the = command. If you already have Paradox running, save your files on disk and remove them from your workspace.

Each step tells you to type the first letter of the selected option. Remember that options may be selected by using the arrow keys to position the cursor on the menu option and pressing Enter.

1. Begin a Paradox session so that you have the Main Menu on your monitor.
2. Type **S** to select the Scripts option. Then type **E** to access the Paradox Editor.
3. Type **W** to select the Write option.
4. Paradox asks for the name of the script. Type **Test2** and press **Enter**. An empty script screen appears.
5. Type **rows = 2** and press **Enter**.
6. Continue typing the script so that your screen resembles the following display. Since the script is short, the SLEEP command is included so that the results of the script stay on the screen for 10000 milliseconds.

```
Designing script C:\paradox3\test2                                    Script Ins
....+...10....+...20....+...30....+...40....+...50....+...60....+...70....+...80
rows = 2
border = "________________________________________________________________"
@rows,5
?? rows
?? "  "
?? border
rows = rows + 10
@ rows,5
?? STRVAL(rows)+"     "+border
SLEEP 10000
```

7. Press **F10** (Menu) to access the Editor's submenu.
8. Type **G** to select the Go option. Paradox saves the script on disk and then plays the script. Your screen resembles the following display.

```
                                                        Main
  2 ______________________________________________


  12 ______________________________________________
```

Notice that the result of the first ?? command is the same as the result of the last ?? command. Since the STRVAL( ) function is used to make the numeric variable (rows) look like an alphanumeric variable, it may be included in the concatenated PAL line with alphanumeric variables.

9. When the Main Menu screen reappears, type **S** to select the Scripts submenu. Then, type **P** to select the Play option of the Scripts submenu. When Paradox asks for the name of the script, type **Test2** and press **Enter**. The script is played again.
10. When the Main Menu returns to your screen, type **E** to select the Exit option. When the Exit submenu appears on your screen, type **Y** to tell Paradox that you want to end this Paradox session. The screen clears and the DOS system A> prompt appears. This Paradox session is complete.
11. Turn to Module 10 to continue the recommended learning sequence.

Module 6
@, ?, ??

DESCRIPTION

There are many times that you need the application to communicate with the person using it.

The @ command lets you position the cursor to a row and column of the screen or printer. There are 25 rows (0 through 24) down, and 80 columns (0 through 79) across a screen. The number of rows and columns on a page depends on the size of the paper. The syntax for this command follows.

```
@ <row number>,<column number>
```

Replace <row number> and <column number> with numbers that are valid for the screen or page. For example, to move the cursor to the top left corner of your screen, use the command @ 0,0 (read "at row 0, column 0") in your script. Remember that if you use numbers that exceed the screen capabilities, a script error occurs. Just edit the script so that the @ command uses row and column numbers that are valid. Then, play the script again. Once the cursor is where you want it, use the ? and ?? commands in your script to communicate with the user.

The ? and ?? commands send the information that follows to the screen or printer. The information goes to the screen unless you use the PRINTER ON command within the script prior to the ? or ?? command. The proper syntax for the ? and ?? commands follows.

```
? <expressions>
?? <expressions>
```

The only difference between the two commands is where the expressions begin. The ? command displays the expressions on the next row beginning in the column where the cursor is positioned in the current row. The ?? command displays the expressions beginning at the current cursor position. In other words, the ? command causes the cursor or printer to advance one line, the ?? does not.

An expression is a specific value which is enclosed with double quotation marks. The quotes are not part of the value; they only identify the start and finish of the value.

Replace <expressions> with one or more values. Separate each value by a comma.

The value within the quotes appears on the workspace with the cursor positioned immediately after the last character or blank space included within the quotes. For example, enclose a remark or question with double quotation marks as follows.

```
? "       Printing the ZipCode report - Please Wait..."
? "How many labels do you want to print? "
```

An expression may also be a value that the computer holds in a variable, or array element, or a field of a table. Variables and arrays are temporarily kept in the computer's memory, as when you use a scratchpad. (Refer to Module 5 to review variables and arrays.)

APPLICATIONS

Use the @, ?, or ?? commands in the scripts of your application when you need to send a value or message to the screen or printer. For example, tell the user to wait while the computer collects information from the Department table.

Use the @ command to position the cursor on the screen. Then, use ? and ?? commands to display values and/or messages to the user.

Remember that Paradox automatically sends the output to the screen unless the PRINTER ON command has been used within the script prior to the @, ?, and ?? command. Use the PRINTER OFF command when you want to make sure that the output is sent to the screen.

TYPICAL OPERATION

This example shows you how to use the @, ?, and ?? PAL commands. If you already have Paradox running, make sure you save your files on disk. Then, remove them from your workspace.

In this example, you type the first letter of an option. Remember that you can also use the arrow (cursor) keys to position the cursor on the menu option and then press Enter to select it.

1. Begin a Paradox session so that you have the Main Menu on your monitor as in the following display.

```
View  Ask  Report  Create  Modify  Image  Forms  Tools  Scripts  Help  Exit
View a table.
```

2. Type **S** to select the Scripts option. The Scripts submenu appears on your screen.
3. Type **E** to access the Paradox Editor. Your screen resembles the following display.

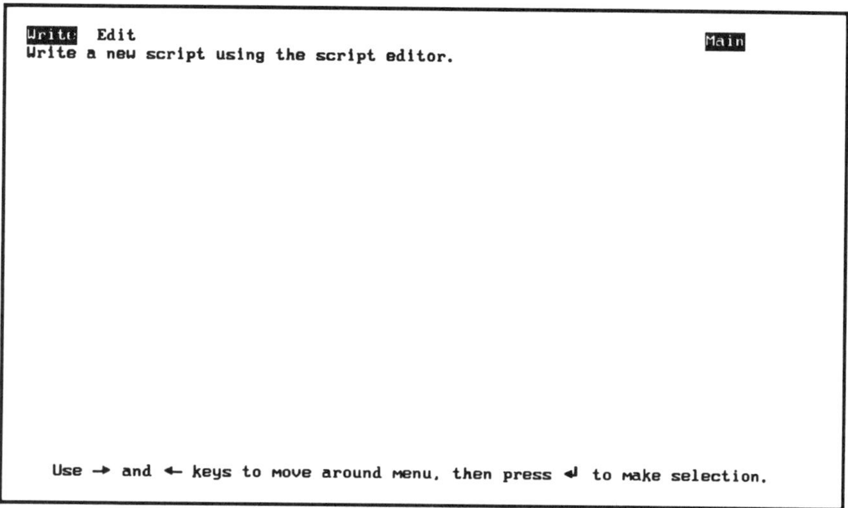

4. Type **W** to select the Write option.
5. Paradox asks for the name of the script. Type **Test1** and press **Enter**. An empty script screen appears. It resembles the following display.

```
Designing script C:\paradox3\test1                                    Script
....+...10....+...20....+...30....+...40....+...50....+...60....+...70....+...80
```

6. Type **? "This is easy! "** and press **Enter**.
7. Type **? "This is fun! "** and press **Enter**.
8. Press **F10** (Menu) to access the Editor's submenu as shown in the following display. Since the script is short, watch it carefully when you select the next option from this submenu.

```
Read  Go  Print  Help  DO-IT!  Cancel                                Script Ins
Read contents of another script into this script starting at the cursor.
....+...10....+...20....+...30....+...40....+...50....+...60....+...70....+...80
? "This is easy!"
? "This is fun!"
```

9. Type **G** to select the Go option. First, Paradox saves the script on disk. Then, it is played and the Main Menu screen returns.

10. Type **S** to select the Scripts option. Then, type **E** to access the Editor submenu. When asked if you want to Write or Edit, type **E** to edit an existing script. Again, type **Test1** when asked for the name of the script and press **Enter**. The script is available on your screen.

11. Press **Ins** so that "Ins" appears in the top right corner of your screen. Use Up Arrow, Down Arrow, Left Arrow, Right Arrow, Del, and Enter to move the cursor and make changes so that your script is like the following display.

```
Changing script C:\paradox3\test1                                    Script Ins

....+...10....+...20....+...30....+...40....+...50....+...60....+...70....+...80
? "This is easy!", "This is the second step."
?
?
?
?
? "This is fun!"
?
?
?
?
```

12. Press **F10** (Menu) and type **G** to select the Go option.

13. Type **SEE** (Script,Editor,Edit), then type **Test1** and change the script so that it is like the following display.

```
Changing script C:\paradox3\test1                                    Script Ins

....+...10....+...20....+...30....+...40....+...50....+...60....+...70....+...80
?? "This is easy!", "This is the second step."
??
??
??
??
?? "This is fun!"
??
??
??
??
```

14. Press **F10** (Menu) and type **G** to select the Go option. This time your script presents a very different screen. Since the ? commands were changed to ??, line advancement was not done.

15. Now, edit the Test1 script so that it is like the following display.

```
Changing script C:\paradox3\test1                                    Script Ins

....+...10....+...20....+...30....+...40....+...50....+...60....+...70....+...80
@10,,10
?? "This is easy!            ", "This is the second step."
@20,55
?? "This is fun!"
```

16. Press **F10** (Menu) and select the Go option. Paradox presents two options — Cancel and Debug. The message at the bottom of the screen says that there is a script error. Type **D** to select the Debug option. The line of your script that caused the error appears on the bottom line of your screen as follows.

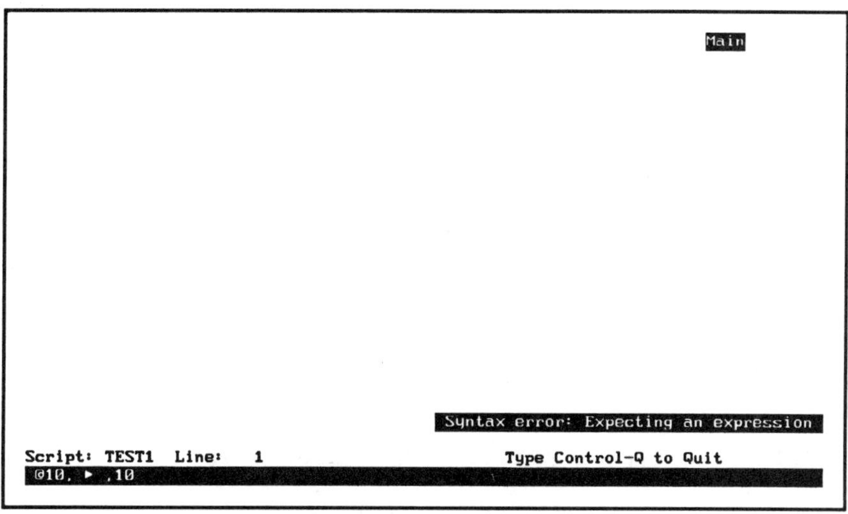

17. Press **Ctrl-E** to return to the Editor screen. The first line of your script has two commas instead of one. Use the arrow keys to position the cursor on one of the commas and press **Del**.

18. Play the script again by pressing **F10** (Menu) and typing **G** to select the Go option.

19. When the Main Menu returns to your screen, type **E** to select the Exit option. When the Exit submenu appears on your screen, type **Y** to tell Paradox that you want to end this Paradox session. The screen clears and the DOS system prompt appears. This Paradox session is complete.

20. Turn to Module 5 to continue the recommended learning sequence.

Module 7
ACCEPT

DESCRIPTION

The ACCEPT command reads information from the keyboard and stores the data to the variable specified in the command line. With this command, your scripts control the data entry environment, perform error handling if invalid data is attempted, and limit the format and size of the data accepted.

This command has several PAL functions which may be included to restrict the information entered. Use one or more of the functions that are enclosed with the << and >> symbols as follows.

```
ACCEPT <data type> <<PICTURE <picture>>> TO <variable>
                    <<MIN <minimum value>>>
                    <<MAX <maximum value>>>
                    <<LOOKUP <lookup table>>>
                    <<DEFAULT <default value>>>
                    <<REQUIRED>>
```

<data type> Include a data type in the command line to tell Paradox that the information must be numeric, short number, date, dollar, or alphanumeric (N, S, D, $, A, respectively). With the data type, specify the length of the variable (except for Date data types).

The data type and length create the variable and restrict the information accepted from the keyboard. For example, if the data type is "A13," the variable is Alphanumeric for thirteen positions. A data type of "D" establishes the variable so that only a valid date is acceptable. The data type and length validate and limit the information accepted from the keyboard.

PICTURE <picture> A picture is like a model or pattern. The symbols that you specify in this clause set the form for the variable. Enclose the symbols with quotation marks. For example, PICTURE "(###)###-####" tells Paradox that numbers must be typed where the # symbols appear. As the user types the information, the parentheses and dash appear automatically.

There are several symbols available for creating the picture you need. Each one sets different criterion for the information the user can type. Use the following symbols to create the picture that your application needs.

#	accepts only a number
?	accepts only a letter (upper- or lowercase) or space
@	accepts any character
&	accepts a letter and converts it to uppercase
!	accepts any character and converts letters to uppercase
;	supplies the next character literally
*	identifies the number for repeating a symbol or group of characters
[ ]	encloses an optional format
{ }	encloses a group of characters or choices
,	separates the choices that are enclosed with braces

The # requires that the user type one number (0-9) each time this symbol appears in the picture. The ? requires that the user type a letter (a-z, A-Z) or a space. The @ allows any character that is available on the keyboard.

Since the computer recognizes the case of letters, you may need to control the case of the user's input. The & accepts only letters or a space and converts lowercase letters to uppercase ones. The ! accepts any character that is available on the keyboard and converts all lowercase letters to uppercase.

The ; tells Paradox to supply the next character to the user. Use it when you need to include one of the picture symbols as part of the pattern. For example, "##;[&&&;]" lets the user type two numbers and three letters, and Paradox automatically encloses the letters with brackets.

To repeat a symbol several times, use * to tell Paradox that the following number specifies the repetition count for the following symbol. For example, PICTURE "&*12#" is the same as PICTURE "&############."

Use brackets [ ] to enclose an optional part of the picture. For example, the picture for a phone number is "[(###)]###-####." If the user types a left parenthesis, Paradox expects the next three keystrokes to be numbers for the area code. The right parenthesis is provided automatically.

If the user types a number first, Paradox skips the area code part of the picture.

If you want the user to repeat a group of characters, enclose them with braces. For example,

PICTURE "#*3{PARADOX}-&&&&&"

is the same as

PICTURE "#PARADOXPARADOXPARADOX-&&&&&."

This picture clause requires that the user type a number first. The next three keystrokes must be "P" so PARADOX appears three times. The dash is provided automatically and the last four keystrokes must be letters. If a number is not provided after the *, Paradox accepts as many keystrokes as the user types. Use "##*#" instead of "*##" because the # symbols in the second picture is never reached. A picture like "*##" does not limit the size of the number.

There may be times when you want to provide choices for the user. To indicate the choices, enclose the choices with braces ({ }) and separate them with commas. For example, if only three area codes are valid input, use the PICTURE clause to restrict them. Include PICTURE ";({214,512,817};)###-####" as part of the ACCEPT command to accept only the area codes specified in the picture. When the user types the first number of the area code, Paradox automatically fills in the rest.

This may be a problem when the valid area codes are 214, 224, and 234. The solution is to include the last two digits within the braces. For example, PICTURE ";(2{14,24,26};)###-####" handles the problem as soon as the second number is typed.

MIN <minimum value> Use the MIN clause to set the lowest acceptable limit for the variable. For example, if a date prior to 01/12/87 is unacceptable, include the MIN "01/12/87" clause with the ACCEPT command. When MIN "150" is included in the ACCEPT command, Paradox accepts only numbers 150 or higher from the user.

MAX <maximum value> This clause lets you set an upper limit for the variable. Include the MIN and MAX clauses in the ACCEPT command to establish an acceptable range.

LOOKUP <lookup table> Use the LOOKUP clause to compare the value typed by the user to those in the table specified by <lookup table>. If the value typed exists within the table, Paradox accepts it. If not, the computer beeps to get the user's attention and a message is displayed on the workspace. For example, if you want your script to validate the zip code, create a table (e.g., Zips) which contains the acceptable ones. Then, include LOOKUP "ZIPS" in the ACCEPT command.

DEFAULT <default value> This clause provides a value to be automatically supplied for the user and positions the cursor on the first character of the value. The user either presses Enter to accept the value, or types a new one. This clause is helpful when the value to be typed occurs frequently. For example, if the city is usually Dallas, include DEFAULT "Dallas" in the ACCEPT command.

REQUIRED A data entry script may ask the user for many pieces of information. Use the REQUIRED clause when the information is not optional. It tells Paradox that a value must be typed by the user or the script is not to continue.

Use any one, or a combination, of the clauses in the ACCEPT command to achieve the desired results. For example, the command line ACCEPT "N" MIN "100" MAX "199" REQUIRED TO HOLD tells Paradox that a number between 100 and 199 (inclusive) must be typed by the user and stored as the variable called HOLD.

APPLICATIONS

Many scripts require information from the user, even a simple yes or no answer. For example, your script is ready to perform a special report and you need to know that the printer is ready to print. Just display a message on the workspace to the user to turn on the printer, position the paper properly, and press Enter when ready.

Remember to position the cursor on the workspace with the @ command and use ?, or ?? to display the messages or instructions to the user. Then, use the @ command again to position the cursor on the screen for the input. (By including the ACCEPT command in the script, an answer from the operator is required before the report begins printing.)

A data entry screen normally requires several ACCEPT commands in the script. The first decision you must make for the data entry is where to place the descriptions and their input areas.

First, look at a document that provides the information to the operator. Rather than make the operator locate the information in the document (first piece of data is at the top, the second is at the bottom, and the third is in the middle, etc.), set up your input screen so it follows the order of the input document.

By doing this, you save time during the input process and greatly reduce the number of errors because the operator concentrates on typing instead of finding data. The order of the fields on the screen is not important for proper execution of the script.

The ACCEPT command retrieves the information that is typed on the keyboard. Each ACCEPT command requires a response from the user — even if the response is just pressing the Enter key.

Include the special clauses with this command to validate the data as it is being typed. By including such restrictions, you decrease the chance of errors that create problems for your application.

TYPICAL OPERATION

This example shows you how to use the ACCEPT command. If you already have Paradox running, make sure that you save your files on disk. Then, remove them from your workspace.

1. Type **S** to select the Scripts submenu option, then type **E** (Editor).
2. Type **W** to select the Write option.
3. When asked for the name of the script, type **Prtrdy** and press **Enter**.
4. Paradox presents an empty script on your workspace. Type the script so that your screen resembles the following display.

```
Designing script C:\paradox3\prtrdy                          Script

....+...10....+...20....+...30....+...40....+...50....+...60....+...70....+...80
clear
rows = 12
columns = 10
@ rows,columns
?? "Make sure that the printer is turned on, and the paper is positioned."
rows = 21
columns = 4
@ rows,columns
?? "Do you want to continue (Yes/No)? "
accept "A1" picture "{Y,N}" required to tprint
```

5. Press **F10** (Scripts Menu) and select the Go option by typing **G**. Paradox clears the script from your workspace and draws the results of the script's play. Your screen resembles the following display.

```
          Make sure that the printer is turned on, and the paper is positioned.




    Do you want to continue (Yes/No)?
```

6. Type **S**. The computer beeps at you because only "Y," and "N" are acceptable answers. The script does not continue until a valid answer is typed.

7. Type **N** and press **Enter** to satisfy the script's requirements. Paradox finishes playing the script and returns the Main Menu to your screen.

8. Write another script called Entry so that it resembles the following display.

```
Designing script C:\paradox3\entry                           Script Ins

....+...10....+...20....+...30....+...40....+...50....+...60....+...70....+...80
clear
rows = 3
columns = 10
@ rows,columns
?? "Name:"
@ rows,columns + 20
accept "A20" picture "*!" required to tname
rows = rows + 2
@ rows,columns
?? "Phone:"
@ rows,columns + 20
accept "A13" picture "[(###)]###-####" to tphone
rows = rows + 2
@ rows,columns
?? "Amount:"
@ rows,columns + 20
accept "N" picture "[#][#]{:,###}:.##" min 0 max 9999999.99 default 0.00 to
   tamount
```

9. Press **F10** (Scripts Menu) and select the Go option by typing **G**. Paradox clears the script from your workspace and draws the results of the script's play. Your screen resembles the following display.

```
Name:
```

10. Type **Abby Longsten** and press **Enter**.

11. Type **(2143333333** and press **Enter**. Notice that Paradox automatically provided the right parenthesis and the dash. Your screen resembles the following display.

```
Name:                ABBY LONGSTEN

Phone:               (214)333-3333

Amount:              0
```

12. Press **Backspace** to remove the zero. Type **1,000** and press **Enter**. Paradox displays a message that the field is not complete since the PICTURE clause expects two decimal places to be included in the number.

13. Type **10** so your screen resembles the following display. When ready to continue, press **Enter**.

```
Name:                ABBY LONGSTEN

Phone:               (214)333-3333

Amount:              1,000.10
```

NOTE

A reminder that the diamond (◆) will help you find the changed lines easier, but will not indicate lines that have been deleted. Check your script carefully.

14. Change the PICTURE clause in the last line of the Entry script so that your screen resembles the one in the following display.

```
Changing script C:\paradox3\entry                                Script Ins

....+...10....+...20....+...30....+...40....+...50....+...60....+...70....+...80
clear
rows = 3
columns = 10
@ rows,columns
?? "Name:"
@ rows,columns + 20
accept "A20" picture "*!" required to tname
rows = rows + 2
@ rows,columns
?? "Phone:"
@ rows,columns + 20
accept "A13" picture "[(###)]###-####" to tphone
rows = rows + 2
@ rows,columns
?? "Amount:"
@ rows,columns + 20
accept "N" picture "[#][#]{;,###}[;.##]" min 0 max 9999999.99 default 0.00 to  ◆
   tamount                                                                     ◆
```

15. Play the script again and type the same data for the name and phone fields from the previous steps. Type **1,000** and press **Enter** for the amount. This time, the script accepts the integer.

16. Turn to Module 91 and continue the recommended learning sequence.

Module 8
ADD

DESCRIPTION

This command lets you send records from one table to another table. It is a quick way to move data to other tables without retyping the records. The format for the ADD command follows.

```
ADD <source table> <destination table>
```

Replace <source table> and <destination table> with the names of two tables that exist on the data disk. A source and a destination table name must be specified in this command line. Also, the structures of both tables must be the same except for key field identifiers. Otherwise, a script error occurs when Paradox encounters the ADD command.

The <source table> contains the records to be added to the <destination table>. If the tables are keyed, Paradox looks for duplicate records during the add operation. When the same key exists in a record in both tables, Paradox replaces the record in the destination table with the record from the source table. Otherwise, the record is copied from the source table to the destination table.

If the destination table is not keyed, Paradox adds the records from the source table to the destination table. Duplicate records occur in the destination table when it already contains a record that is also in the source table. The ADD command does not do record replacement for non-keyed tables even though the source table is keyed.

After the ADD operation is complete, the <source table> records exist in both tables. Remove the records from <source table> with the EMPTY command to avoid repeating the operation. This is especially important when using non-keyed tables.

This command in a script is the abbreviated form of several menu options that are available through the Paradox menu-driven system. By including the following command line in the script instead of the ADD "Addrecs" "Mailtx" command line, you achieve the same results.

```
Menu {Tools} {More} {Add} {Addrecs} {Mailtx}
```

The updated destination table remains on the workspace after Paradox performs the ADD command. Include the ClearAll special keycode in the script to clear the table from the screen.

APPLICATIONS

This command is helpful when there are several people entering data on floppy disks. At the end of the day, each table on the floppy disks is added to the main table (master) by using the ADD command. This is called *batch processing*.

For example, three people enter data for the Mail List application. Write a separate application for these people so that they type records into a keyed table called Addrecs. At the end of the day, use each floppy disk to update the Mailtx table.

Since both tables are keyed, duplicate records are avoided in the Mailtx table. Records in the Addrecs table that have key field values that match those in the Mailtx table cause Paradox to replace the Mailtx record with the Addrecs record.

TYPICAL OPERATION

This example shows you how to use the ADD command.

1. Type **C** to select the Create option from the Main Menu. When asked for the name of the new table, type **Addrecs** and press **Enter**. An empty structure form appears on the screen.
2. Press **F10** (Menu) and select the Borrow option by typing **B**. When asked for the name of the table structure to borrow, type **Mailtx** and press **Enter**.
3. Press **F2** (DO-IT!) to save the new table structure. The Main Menu returns to the screen.
4. Select the Modify/DataEntry menu options. When asked for the name of the table, type **Addrecs** and press **Enter**. An empty table form appears on your screen.
5. Press **F7** (Forms Toggle) to change to Forms View. Type the record that appears in the following display.

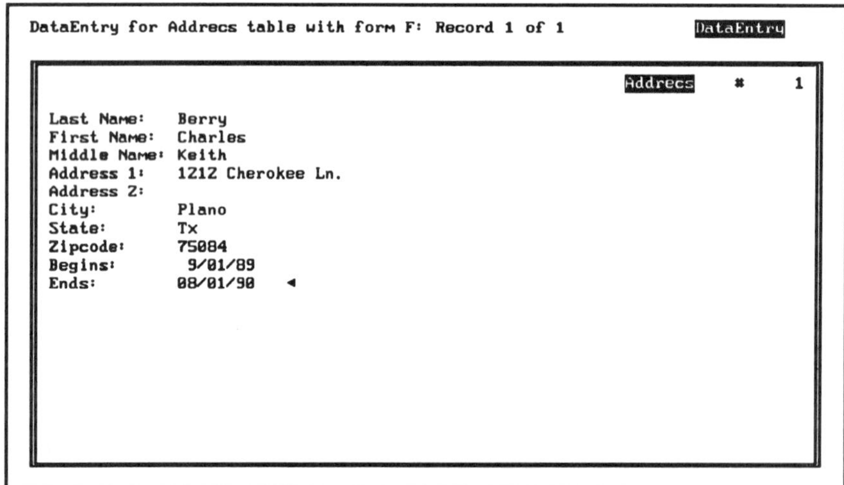

6. Type a second record into the table so that it matches the one in the following display.

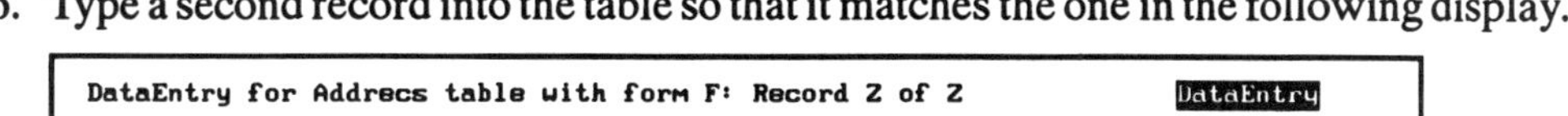

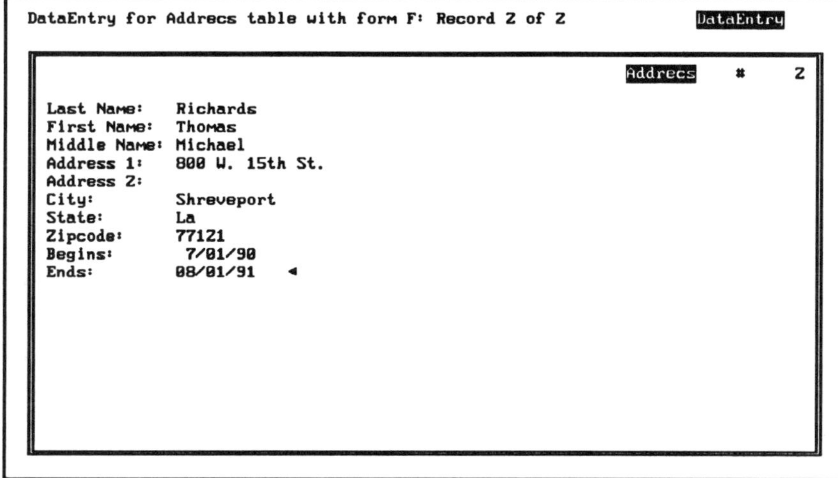

```
DataEntry for Addrecs table with form F: Record 2 of 2              DataEntry

                                                         Addrecs   #    2

Last Name:    Richards
First Name:   Thomas
Middle Name:  Michael
Address 1:    800 W. 15th St.
Address 2:
City:         Shreveport
State:        La
Zipcode:      77121
Begins:        7/01/90
Ends:         08/01/91   ◄
```

7. Press **F2** (DO-IT!) to save the table. Paradox displays it in Table View.
8. Press **F8** (Clear Image) to remove the table from the workspace.
9. Edit the Mainmenu script so that it includes an Update option as shown in the following display.

NOTE

Remember that the dots indicate a portion of the script that has not changed. Do not change those lines.

```
Changing script C:\paradox3\mainmenu                                 Script Ins
....+...10....+...20....+...30....+...40....+...50....+...60....+...70....+...80
while (true)
  clear
  showmenu
    "View" : "Find and review customer information.",
    "Maintenance" : "Maintains table data.",
    "Report" : "Print the columnar report.",
    "Labels" : "Print mailing labels.",
    "Update" : "Batch update master table from a floppy disk.",               ◆
    "Configure" : "Change application configuration.",
    "Weekcalc" : "Count the number of weeks between two dates."
  default "View" to mchoice
  switch
  case mchoice = "View" :
    play "Custview"
    .
    .
    .
   @ 10,10
   ?? "Printing Labels - Please Wait..."
   report "Mailtx" "1"
   play "prtnorm"
 case mchoice = "Update" :                                                   ◆
   add "Addrecs" "Mailtx"                                                    ◆
   clearall                                                                  ◆
 case mchoice = "Configure" :
```

10. Press **F10** (Scripts Menu) and select the Go option. When the application menu appears, select the Update option by typing **U**.
11. When the application menu returns to the screen, type **V** to select the View option. Press **Enter** twice to list all records in the table. Your screen lists four records as in the following display.

12. Press **Esc** to end the application.
13. Type **V** to select the View option from the Main Menu line. When asked for the name of the table, type **Mailtx** and press **Enter**.
14. Review the table until you are convinced that it was updated properly from the Addrecs table.
15. Press **F8** (Clear Image) to remove the table from the workspace.
16. View the Addrecs table to verify that the records used to update Mailtx remained in the table. Clear the screen.
17. Turn to Module 94 to continue the recommended learning sequence.

Module 9
ARRAY

DESCRIPTION

An array is a variable area that is divided into several pieces. Use it to hold a sequence of data temporarily. For example, use an array to hold and/or manipulate an entire record. The format for this command follows.

```
ARRAY <array name> [<dimension>]
```

Replace <array name> with a variable name that describes its contents. If the array is to be used often, keep the name short. When any part of the array is used in the script, <array name> is required for that reference.

The brackets ([ ]) around <dimension> are required. Replace <dimension> with a numeric value from 1 to 15,000. Provide a specific number or use a variable to supply the number within the brackets. The array is broken into the specified number of pieces called *elements*.

For example, ARRAY SUBLEN[36] establishes an array called SUBLEN (an abbreviation for SUBscription LENgth) that is broken into 36 elements. The array is able to hold 36 pieces of information as though each element is a separate variable.

Refer to an element by using the array name and a number that specifies the element within the array. This number is called a *subscript*. It must be enclosed with brackets and not exceed the number of array elements set by <dimension> in the ARRAY command. For example, SUBLEN[10] specifies the tenth element in the array. The subscript is 10.

Assign a value of any data type to any of the 36 elements in the array. Just because one element is set to a numeric value does not mean that all elements must contain the same data type. Like any variable, an array element is supplied a value by using the = command.

The following command lines establish and use an array called SUBLEN. Its array elements are used to count the number of three, six, twelve, eighteen, and twenty-four month subscriptions. Then the results are printed.

```
array sublen[36]
x = 1
while x <= 36
  sublen[x] = 0
  x = x + 1
endwhile
```

```
view "Mailtx"
scan
  y = year([Ends]) - year([Begins])
  x = y * 12
  x = x + month([Ends]) - month([Begins])
  sublen[x] = sublen[x] + 1
endscan
x = 1
lncnt = 1
while x <= 36
  if sublen[x] <> 0
    then
    @ lncnt,05
    ?? strval(x)+" months = "+strval(sublen[x])
    lncnt = lncnt + 1
  endif
  x = x + 1
endwhile
```

When an array is established, the elements contain whatever is in the computer memory area at that time. Therefore, each element in the array must be supplied a value.

Each time a value is assigned to an element, the previous value is lost. Like variables, arrays retain their contents until the array is re-declared, the RELEASE command is encountered for that array, or the Paradox session is ended.

To declare an array that is used specifically within a procedure, include the PRIVATE clause in the PROC command. This allows you to use the same name for the second array without re-declaring the first array.

APPLICATIONS

Use the ARRAY command to declare a set of variables (elements). A relationship among the elements is not necessary. However, the array must be declared before its elements are assigned values.

For example, declare an array to accumulate total dollars for an aged summary of accounts receivable. The first element is for debt that is less than 30 days, the second element is for 31 to 60 days, etc.

As well as using arrays for free-form information, they are also used to create or manipulate table records. Use the COPYTOARRAY command to store the current record from the table to an array. Change any of the values in the array, if necessary. Then use the COPYFROMARRAY command to transfer the array to a table. The ARRAYSIZE( ) function is used to determine the dimensions of the array.

TYPICAL OPERATION

This example shows you how to use the ARRAY command.

1. Edit the Mainmenu script to include the Summary option as shown in the following display. The dots indicate command lines that are omitted in the display. Do not change those lines in your script. The diamonds (◆) will help you locate changed lines faster.

```
Changing script C:\paradox3\mainmenu                                   Script Ins
....+...10....+...20....+...30....+...40....+...50....+...60....+...70....+...80
while (true)
  clear
  showmenu
    "View" : "Find and review customer information.",
    "Maintenance" : "Maintains table data.",
    "Report" : "Print the columnar report.",
    "Labels" : "Print mailing labels.",
    "Update" : "Batch update master table from a floppy disk.",
    "Summary" : "Provide statistics on subscription preferences.",             ◆
    "Configure" : "Change application configuration.",
    "Weekcalc" : "Count the number of weeks between two dates."
  default "View" to mchoice
.
.
.
      empty "Addrecs"
    endif
    clearall
 case mchoice = "Summary" :                                                  ◆
    clear                                                                    ◆
    @ 10,10                                                                  ◆
    ?? "Collecting statistics for subscriptions - Please Wait..."            ◆
    array sublen[36]                                                         ◆
    x = 1                                                                    ◆
    while x <= 36                                                            ◆
      sublen[x] = 0                                                          ◆
      x = x + 1                                                              ◆
    endwhile                                                                 ◆
    view "Mailtx"                                                            ◆
    tot = 0                                                                  ◆
    scan                                                                     ◆
      y = year([Ends]) - year([Begins])                                      ◆
      x = y * 12                                                             ◆
      x = x + month([Ends]) - month([Begins])                                ◆
      sublen[x] = sublen[x] + 1                                              ◆
      tot = tot + 1                                                          ◆
    endscan                                                                  ◆
    clear                                                                    ◆
    x = 1                                                                    ◆
    lncnt = 1                                                                ◆
    while x <= 36                                                            ◆
      if sublen[x] <> 0                                                      ◆
        then                                                                 ◆
        @ lncnt,05                                                           ◆
        ?? strval(x)+" months = "+strval(sublen[x])                          ◆
        @ lncnt,50                                                           ◆
        ?? strval(int((sublen[x]/tot) * 100)) + " %"                         ◆
        lncnt = lncnt + 1                                                    ◆
      endif                                                                  ◆
      x = x + 1                                                              ◆
    endwhile                                                                 ◆
    sleep 3500                                                               ◆
    clearall                                                                 ◆
 case mchoice = "Configure" :
```

2. Press **F10** (Scripts Menu) and select the Go option.
3. When the application menu appears on the screen, type **S** to select the Summary option. After the numbers are collected, your screen resembles the following display.

```
11 months = 1                              33 %
13 months = 1                              33 %
24 months = 1                              33 %
```

4. Press **Esc** when the application menu returns to the screen.
5. View the Mailtx table and verify that the Summary option performed the calculations correctly.
6. Press **F8** (Clear Image) to remove the table from the workspace.
7. Turn to Module 19 to continue the recommended learning sequence.

Module 10
BEEP

DESCRIPTION

When you want to get the user's attention, include the BEEP command in your script. This command causes the computer to make a low-pitched sound.

For example, when the script has completed its work, several beeps from the computer alert the user. The script in the following display causes the computer to beep five times after all tasks are complete.

```
Changing script C:\paradox3\test2                                    Script Ins

....+...10....+...20....+...30....+...40....+...50....+...60....+...70....+...80
rows = 2
border = "____________________________________________________________"
@rows,5
?? rows
?? "  "
?? border
rows = rows + 10
@ rows,5
?? STRVAL(rows)+"     "+border
SLEEP 10000
BEEP BEEP
BEEP BEEP
BEEP
```

Include one or more BEEP commands per line of your script, or use the WHILE command to control the number of beeps that are performed.

APPLICATIONS

Many scripts keep the computer busy with little or no user intervention. After the user initiates a script, the computer performs each task as instructed. If the script processes a large volume of data, the user can perform other important tasks while the computer operates. By programming the computer to beep when the script play is complete, the user can keep the computer busy.

The BEEP command is also used if an error occurs while the script is playing. For example, display a message on the screen and make the computer beep for attention. Also consider using the beep to warn that a document is ready to be removed from the printer.

TYPICAL OPERATION

This example shows you how to use the BEEP command. If you already have Paradox running, make sure that you save your files on disk. Then, remove them from your workspace.

Each step tells you to type the first letter of the selected option. Remember that options may be selected by using the arrow keys to position the cursor on the menu option and then pressing Enter.

1. Begin a Paradox session so that you have the Main Menu on your monitor.
2. From the Main Menu, type **S** to select the Scripts option.
3. Type **E** to access the Paradox Editor, then type **E** to select the Edit option.
4. Paradox asks for the name of the script. Type **Test2** and press **Enter**. The script is now available on your screen.
5. Press **Down Arrow** to move the cursor to the end of the script.
6. Type **BEEP BEEP BEEP BEEP BEEP** and press **Enter**. Your screen resembles the following display.

```
Changing script C:\paradox3\test2                                Script Ins

....+...10....+...20....+...30....+...40....+...50....+...60....+...70....+...80
rows = 2
border = "____________________________________________________________"
@rows,5
?? rows
?? "  "
?? border
rows = rows + 10
@ rows,5
?? STRVAL(rows)+"     "+border
SLEEP 10000
BEEP BEEP BEEP BEEP BEEP                                                       ◆
```

7. Press **F10** (Menu) to access the Editor's submenu and type **G** to select the Go option. Paradox saves the script on disk and then plays the script. When the BEEP command is encountered, the computer makes a low-pitched noise.
8. When the Main Menu screen reappears, type **S** to select the Scripts submenu. Then, type **P** to select the Play option of the Scripts submenu. When Paradox asks for the name of the script, type **Test2** and press **Enter**. The script is played again.
9. When the Main Menu returns to your screen, type **E** to select the Exit option. When the Exit submenu appears on your screen, type **Y** to tell Paradox that you want to end this Paradox session. The screen clears and the DOS system A> prompt appears. This Paradox session is complete.
10. Turn to Module 13 to continue the recommended learning sequence.

Module 11
CANCELEDIT

DESCRIPTION

When the edit mode is used to change the data in a table, Paradox duplicates the existing data to a temporary table. Any changes the user makes to the data during the edit session are actually made to the temporary table.

While using the menu-driven system, selecting the DO-IT! option tells Paradox to replace the old table with the temporary table. If you decide to leave the original table intact (not saving changes), cancel the edit session by selecting the Cancel option.

The same decisions are available through a script. When the DO_IT! special keycode is encountered, Paradox saves the table that includes the changes.

However, when the CANCELEDIT command is encountered during script play, Paradox does not save any of the changes made during the edit session. Then the table is made available to the user in view mode. This is a one-word command as follows.

```
CANCELEDIT
```

This command is an abbreviated form that combines three menu-driven options. It is equivalent to the following recorded script option line.

```
Menu {Cancel} {Yes}
```

Use the CANCELEDIT command or the menu option sequence in a script so that the edit session is ended without saving any of the changes made to the data. The results of each line are exactly the same.

Consider the following command lines. They are from a script that looks through the table for a specific record.

```
edit fileans
formkey {Image} {PickForm} {F}
while (true)
  End
  PgDn
  wait field message "Type the customer name, then press F2
    to begin the search..."
    until "F2"
  lastname = [Last Name]
```

```
firstname = [First Name]
canceledit
if isblank(lastname) and isblank(firstname)
  then
  quitloop
endif
locate lastname, firstname
```

First, the script presents a new, blank record in the edit mode. After the user types the first and last names, the script stores the values in variables and ends the edit session when the CANCELEDIT command is encountered. The new record is not saved on disk.

Remember that the Del special keycode removes the record from the table without ending the edit mode. On the other hand, the CANCELEDIT command ends the edit mode and does not save any changes made during that edit session. The original table is made available to the user for viewing.

The script then uses the LOCATE command and the variables to find the desired record. If the record is found in the table, it is presented to the user. The view mode does not allow changes to the record.

APPLICATIONS

Include the CANCELEDIT command in scripts that invoke the edit mode and allow data changes that are not to be saved on disk. When this command is encountered in the script, Paradox ends the edit session and makes the table available for viewing only.

By using the CANCELEDIT command, you protect the data in the original table. The user is not allowed to make changes to the record presented on the screen even when the F9 (EditKey) key is pressed.

TYPICAL OPERATION

This illustration shows you how to use the CANCELEDIT option of the Tools second (More) submenu.

1. Edit the Custmnt script. Notice that the Del special keycode is included in the script. This line removes the record that was added by the user but leaves the table available for data changes.

2. Press **F10** (Scripts Menu) and type **C** to select the Cancel option. When asked if you want to end the Editor and not save any changes, type **Y**.

3. Play the Mainmenu script.

4. Select the Maintenance option. Type **DLS1** and press **Enter** for the ID. When asked for the name of the table, type **Mailtx** and press **Enter**. The screen clears and presents a blank record.
5. Type **Appleby** for the Last Name and press **Enter**. Type **Shirley** for the First Name field. Press **F2** to begin the search. When the record is found, Paradox presents it on the screen. The cursor is positioned on the Begins field.
6. Press **Ctrl-Backspace** to remove the existing date.
7. Type **07/01/89** and press **Enter** for the Begins field. The cursor moves to the Ends field.
8. Press **Ctrl-Backspace**. Then type **07/01/90**. Press **F2**. The application menu returns to the screen.
9. Press **Esc** to end the application.
10. Use the Scripts Editor again to change the Custmnt script. Remove the Del special keycode line from the script and insert the CANCELEDIT command line so that it matches the script lines in the following display. Only the portion of the script that changes is shown.

```
Changing script C:\paradox3\custmnt                                      Script Ins

....+...10....+...20....+...30....+...40....+...50....+...60....+...70....+...80
;custmnt - customer maintenance script
clear
@ 10,10
?? "Enter the name of the table "
accept "a8" picture "&*&" to fileans
if not isblank(fileans)
  then
  if isfile(fileans+".db")
    then
    edit fileans
    formkey {Image} {PickForm} {F}
    while (true)
    end
    PgDn
    wait record message "Type customer name, then press F2 to begin search..." ◆
      until "F2"
    lastname = [Last Name]
    firstname = [First Name]
    canceledit                                                                 ◆
    del
    if isblank(lastname) and isblank(firstname)
      then
```

11. Save the changed script by pressing **F10** (Scripts Menu) and typing **D**.
12. Play the Mainmenu script and use the Mailtx table.
13. When asked for the Last Name, type **Appleby** and press **Enter**. Type **Shirley** for the First Name field. Then press **F2** to begin the search.

14. When the record is found, it is presented on the screen. The cursor appears in the Begins field. Press **Ctrl-Backspace**. The computer beeps and the message disappears.
15. Press **Left Arrow** to move the cursor to the left. Notice that the cursor moves up to the Zipcode field. Paradox does not allow changes.
16. Press **F2** to return to the application menu and press **Esc** to end the application. The Main Menu returns to your screen.
17. Turn to Module 64 to continue the recommended learning sequence.

Module 12
CANVAS

DESCRIPTION

The CANVAS command is used to turn on and off all display activity to the PAL canvas.

```
CANVAS <ON/off>
```

If CANVAS is turned OFF, you do not see anything that is written to the canvas. This capability allows you to build screens in the background and "pop" the results on the screen for the user. The default setting is ON so that all screen changes are seen at the same time.

NOTE: This command is available in version 3.0 and higher.

APPLICATIONS

The CANVAS command is useful in giving your PAL programs a polished, professional appearance. Turn the canvas off while you are changing or updating the canvas under script control. When ready to display the screen, issue the CANVAS ON command.

TYPICAL OPERATION

This example shows you how to use the CANVAS command.

1. Type **SEE** to use the Paradox script editor. When asked for the name of the script type **PRINTBOX** and press **Enter**.
2. Change the script so it matches the following command lines.

```
Changing script C:\paradox3\printbox                              Script Ins

....+...10....+...20....+...30....+...40....+...50....+...60....+...70....+...80
@ 03, 25 ?? "Aging Report"                                                      ◆
sleep 1000                                                                      ◆
@ 05, 25 ?? "by Department"                                                     ◆
sleep 1000                                                                      ◆
PAINTCANVAS BORDER REVERSE 10,10,15,60
@ 12, 24 ?? "Printing - Please Wait..."
sleep 3000
```

3. Press **F10** to access the menu. Type **G** to select the Go option. The script is saved and run. Notice that each line is displayed one at a time.

4. Change the script again to insert the CANVAS commands so the script matches the following command lines.

```
Changing script C:\paradox3\printbox                              Script  Ins

....+...10....+...20....+...30....+...40....+...50....+...60....+...70....+...80
canvas off                                                                     ◆
@ 03, 25 ?? "Aging Report"
sleep 1000
@ 05, 25 ?? "by Department"
sleep 1000
PAINTCANVAS BORDER REVERSE 10,10,15,60
@ 12, 24 ?? "Printing - Please Wait..."
canvas on                                                                      ◆
sleep 3000
```

5. Press **F10** (Menu) and select the Go option to run the changed script. This time the screen stays blank until all lines appear on the screen at the same time.

6. Turn to Module 34 to continue the recommended learning sequence.

Module 13
CLEAR

DESCRIPTION

This command is like using a big eraser on a sheet of paper. Use the CLEAR command when you want to erase all or part of the workspace.

There are three ways to use this command. Each version affects the screen differently.

```
CLEAR
CLEAR EOL
CLEAR EOS
```

When you want to remove everything from the screen, use the CLEAR command. Include the EOL option with the CLEAR command if you want to erase everything from the cursor position to the end of the line. Using EOS option specifies to erase the lines from the cursor position to the end of the screen.

APPLICATIONS

The Paradox workspace lets your application and the user communicate. However, it does not take long for the screen to get cluttered from all the communication. Include the CLEAR command in your scripts to erase part or all of the screen.

The CLEAR command is not applicable to images (forms). Use the CLEARIMAGE or CLEARALL special key commands to remove images from the workspace.

TYPICAL OPERATION

This illustration shows you how to use the CLEAR command.

1. Type **SEE** to select the Scripts, Editor, and Edit option.
2. Paradox asks for the name of the script. Type **Test2** and press **Enter**. The script is now available on your screen.
3. Press **Down Arrow** until the cursor is positioned on the SLEEP command. Press **Ins** so that "Ins" appears in the top right corner of your screen, and press **Enter** to insert a blank line in your script.

4. Press **Up Arrow** to move the cursor to the blank line and type **@ rows,30** and press **Enter**. On the next blank line type **CLEAR EOL** so that your screen resembles the following display.

NOTE

The diamonds (◆) shown in the following display are to help you locate changed lines. Some of the scripts in this book are very long, and the diamonds will make changes much easier. This will not tell you if a line has been deleted, so be sure to check very carefully the portion of the screen that is changed.

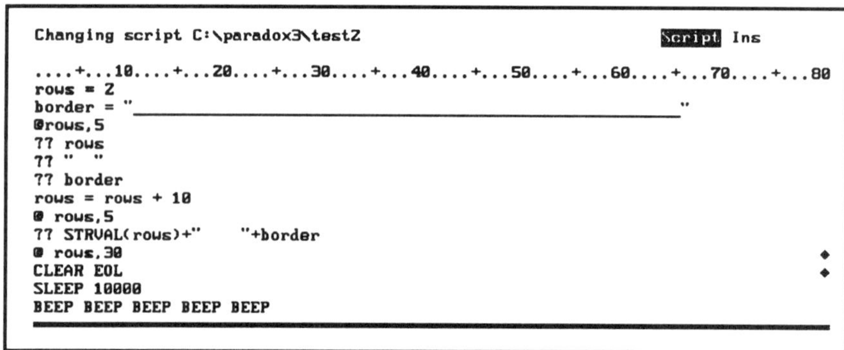

```
Changing script C:\paradox3\test2                                    Script Ins
....+...10....+...20....+...30....+...40....+...50....+...60....+...70....+...80
rows = 2
border = "______________________________________________________"
@rows,5
?? rows
?? "  "
?? border
rows = rows + 10
@ rows,5
?? STRVAL(rows)+"    "+border
@ rows,30                                                                    ◆
CLEAR EOL                                                                    ◆
SLEEP 10000
BEEP BEEP BEEP BEEP BEEP
```

5. Press **F10** (Menu) to access the Editor's submenu and type **G** to select the Go option. Paradox saves the script on disk and then plays the script.

Notice that the second line is drawn and then shortened. The lines you added to your script positioned the cursor on the line after it was drawn and erased the rest. Your screen resembles the following display before the Main Menu returns.

6. Type **SEE** to edit Test2 again and change the CLEAR EOL to CLEAR, as in the following display.

```
Changing script C:\paradox3\test2                                   Script

....+...10....+...20....+...30....+...40....+...50....+...60....+...70....+...80
rows = 2
border = "_______________________________________________________"
@rows,5
?? rows
?? "  "
?? border
rows = rows + 10
@ rows,5
?? STRVAL(rows)+"       "+border
@ rows,30
CLEAR                                                                   ◆
SLEEP 10000
BEEP BEEP BEEP BEEP BEEP
```

7. Press **F10** (Menu) to access the Script menu and select the Go option. When the script is played this time, the lines are drawn and then erased immediately. Instead of erasing a part of the screen, the script has erased everything. The cursor is positioned on the screen while the SLEEP command is executed.

8. Type **E** to select the Exit option and end the Paradox session. Otherwise, turn to Module 23 to continue the recommended learning sequence.

Module 14
COEDIT

DESCRIPTION

A local area network allows more than one user to access the same table at the same time. The VIEW command always allows several users to look at the same table. However, the EDIT command limits table changes to one user at a time. Use the COEDIT command instead of the EDIT command so changes are allowed from several users at the same time.

COEDIT has several features that make it superior to EDIT even in single user applications. Some of these are:

COEDIT	*EDIT*
Changes to a table occur immediately	Batch update of records
Automatic Prevent Full Lock	Automatic Full Lock
Automatic locking of records	None
Automatic update of indexes.	None
Support for key violations	None
None	Incremental UNDO of changes to records

The format of the COEDIT command follows.

```
COEDIT <table name>
```

Replace <table name> with the name of the file that contains the records to be changed. Unless provided in a variable, enclose <table name> with quotation marks. For example, COEDIT "Mailtx" tells Paradox to make the table called Mailtx available for your changes but allow others to make changes too.

The COEDIT command in a script is an abbreviated form of several menu options. By including the following command line in the script instead of the COEDIT command line, you achieve the same results.

```
Menu {Modify} {Coedit} {Mailtx}
```

When a COEDIT command is issued, an Automatic Prevent Full Lock is placed on the table. If the table is currently locked, Paradox will continue to try to place the Prevent Full Lock for the duration of the Set Retry Period. (See the SETRETRYPERIOD command.) If it cannot be obtained in the specified time, the script ends with an error.

NOTE: The COEDIT command was added to Paradox 2.0 and above.

APPLICATIONS

Use the coedit mode to allow several users to change the same table at the same time. If a user or script uses the edit mode for a table instead of the coedit mode, all other users are limited to using the view mode until the table is released from the edit mode.

Write your scripts to check the lock status of a table before accessing a table. When it is available, issue a LOCK PFL command line to prevent others from locking the table. When all changes are completed, issue an UNLOCK PFL command line before returning to the menu screen.

TYPICAL OPERATION

This illustration shows you how to use the COEDIT command in a script.

1. Type **SEW** to use the Script Editor. When asked for the name of the script, type **MultCust** and press **Enter**.
2. When the script is available on your screen, type it so it matches the one in the following display.

```
Designing script C:\paradox3\multcust                                Script

....+...10....+...20....+...30....+...40....+...50....+...60....+...70....+...80
; multcust - network customer maintenance script
clear
@ 10,10
?? "Enter the name of the table "
accept "A8" picture "&*&" to fileans
if not isblank(fileans)
  then
  if isfile(fileans+".db")
    then
    coedit fileans
    PickForm "F"
  else
    beep beep beep beep
    message "Table "+fileans+".db is not on the current data disk."
    sleep 2000
  endif
endif
; end multcust
```

3. Press **F2** to save the script.
4. Play the MultCust script.
5. When asked for the name of the table, type **Mailtx** and press **Enter**. Your screen resembles the following display.

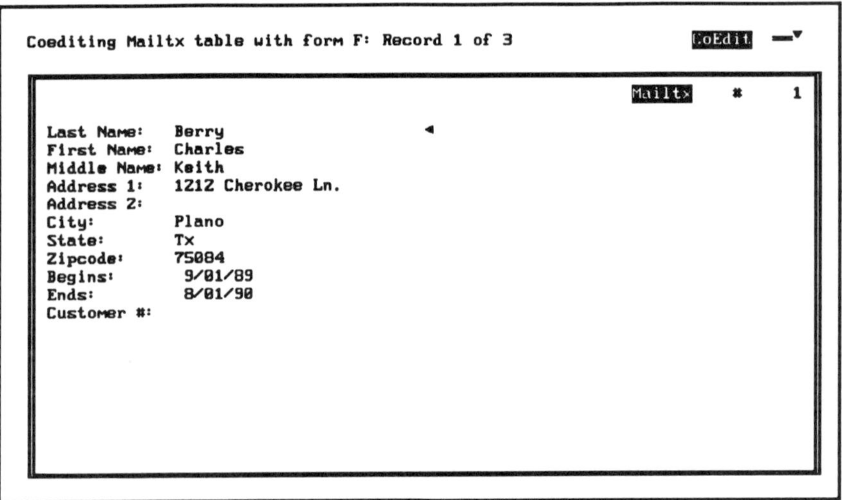

6. If you are using a local area network, run the script on two workstations for the same table. You cannot change the same record on both machines at the same time. When the second workstation moves to the record selected by the first workstation, a message is displayed to tell you that the record is locked by the first workstation user.
7. Press **F2** (DO-IT!) to end the coedit mode.
8. Press **F8** (Clear Image) to remove the table from the workspace.
9. Turn to Module 37 to continue the recommended learning sequence.

Module 15
COPY

DESCRIPTION

The indices, forms, and reports that you create, save, and test are part of the family for a specific table. If you need to create another table that is similar to the first, do not start from scratch. Use the COPY command to make a duplicate of the original table and its family. Then, customize it and its family so that it matches your requirements.

When this command is performed, the table and its family are saved on disk under a new table name. The format for this command follows.

```
COPY <existing table> <new table>
```

Replace <existing table> with the name of a Paradox data file that is currently available on disk. For example, Mailtx is a table that exists on disk. Unless provided in a variable, enclose <existing table> with quotation marks.

When the COPY command is performed successfully, a duplicate table is saved on disk and assigned the <new table> name. Replace <new table> with a table name that does not exist on the current disk. Otherwise, the existing table and its family are replaced by the new table and its family. Unless provided in a variable, enclose <new table> with quotation marks.

The COPY command is an abbreviated form of several menu options that are available through the Paradox menu-driven system. By including the following command line in the script instead of the COPY "Mailtx" "Mailok" command line, you achieve the same results.

```
Menu {Tools} {Copy} {Mailtx} {Mailok}
```

When the new table is created, remember that it contains the data of the original table. Use the EMPTY command to remove all records from the table created by the COPY command.

APPLICATIONS

Use the COPY command to make a duplicate of a table's structure, data, indices, forms, and reports. This command lets you make a new set of data available to the application without repeating the creation process or affecting the existing data.

For example, separate customer tables for each state are required for the Mail List application. Create and test the application with the Texas table. Then use the COPY command to create the tables for Oklahoma, Alabama, and Louisiana.

After the COPY command is performed, empty the new table structure and enter the proper data. Then verify that the reports and forms are applicable to the new data. When the table and its family are ready, test all the application options that need to access the new data.

TYPICAL OPERATION

This illustration shows you how to use the COPY command.

1. Edit the Utility script. Change it so that it includes a Newfile option as shown in the following display.

```
Changing script C:\paradox3\utility                                  Script Ins

....+...10....+...20....+...30....+...40....+...50....+...60....+...70....+...80
; utility.sc - allows various tasks for Mail List application
while(true)
  clear
  showmenu
    "Zipcodes" : "Replace new zipcode for all customers with old zipcode.",
    "Newfile" : "Create a new Mail List customer file.",                      ◆
    "Passfile" : "Restricted - Access Password file."
  default "Zipcodes" to mutility
  switch
.
.
.
      endif
    case mutility = "Newfile" :                                               ◆
      clear                                                                   ◆
      @ 10,10                                                                 ◆
      ?? "Enter the name for the new customer file (e.g. MAILTX) "            ◆
      accept "A8" picture "&*&" to mfile                                      ◆
      if isfile(mfile+".db")                                                  ◆
        then                                                                  ◆
        @ 21,05                                                               ◆
        ?? "That name already exits - This option is aborted..."              ◆
        sleep 3000                                                            ◆
      else                                                                    ◆
        @ 21,05                                                               ◆
        ?? "Creating new file - Please Wait..."                               ◆
        copy "Mailtx" mfile                                                   ◆
        empty mfile                                                           ◆
      endif                                                                   ◆
      release vars mfile                                                      ◆
    case mutility = "Passfile" :
      play "idcheck"
      if retval and passes[x+1] = "9"
        then
```

2. Press **F10** (Scripts Menu) and select the DO-IT! option.
3. Play the Mainmenu script and select the Utilities option.
4. Type **N** to select the Newfile option.

5. When asked for the new filename, type **Mailok** and press **Enter**. The message at the bottom of the workspace tells you that the new file is being created.
6. Press **Esc** twice to return to the Main Menu. Use the View option to list all existing tables.
7. Play the Mainmenu scipt and select the Newfile option again. Type **Mailok** and press **Enter** to see that the script aborts the operation if the tablë name already exists on the disk.
8. Press **Esc** twice to return to the Main Menu screen.
9. Type **TIF** to select the Tools/Info/Family menu options. Then type **Mailok** and press **Enter** to see the list of family members for the Mailok table. It resembles the following display.

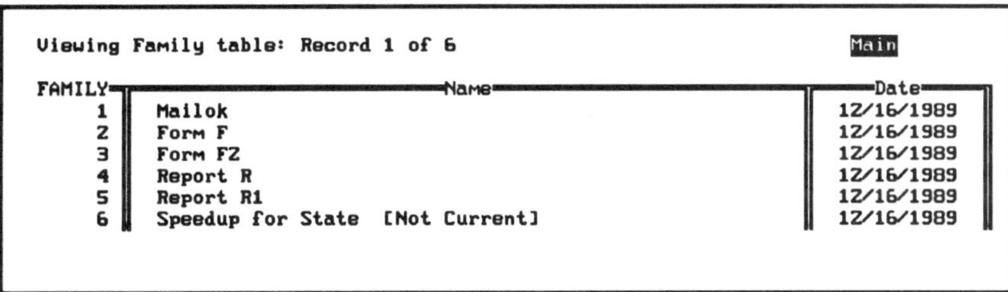

10. Press **F8** (Clear Image) to clear the workspace and return to the Main Menu screen.
11. Type **MD** to select the Modify/DataEntry options. Then type **Mailok** and press **Enter**. Press **F7** (Forms Toggle) and type the record that appears in the following display.

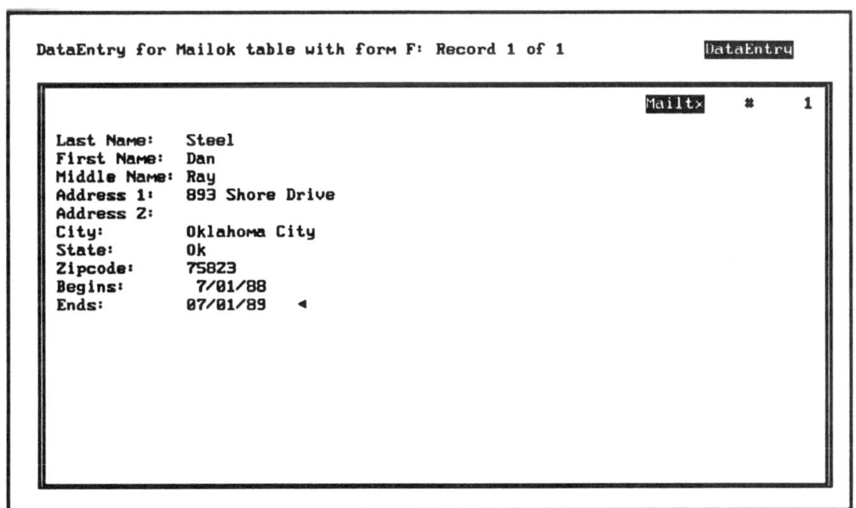

12. Press **F2** (DO-IT!) and **F8** (Clear Image) to return to the Main Menu screen.

13. Edit the Mainmenu script. Change it so that the Report and Labels options ask for the name of the file to be processed.

```
Changing script C:\paradox3\mainmenu                                    Script Ins

....+...10....+...20....+...30....+...40....+...50....+...60....+...70....+...80
  case mchoice = "Report" :
    clear                                                                    ◆
    @ 10,10                                                                  ◆
    ?? "Enter the name of the file (e.g. Mailtx) "                           ◆
    accept "A8" picture "&*&" to mfile                                       ◆
    if isfile(mfile+".db")                                                   ◆
      then                                                                   ◆
      clear                                                                  ◆
      @ 10,10                                                                ◆
      ?? "Printing the columnar report - Please Wait..."                     ◆
      report mfile "R"                                                       ◆
    endif                                                                    ◆
    release vars mfile                                                       ◆
  case mchoice = "Labels" :
    clear                                                                    ◆
    @ 10,10                                                                  ◆
    ?? "Enter the name of the file (e.g. Mailtx) "                           ◆
    accept "A8" picture "&*&" to mfile                                       ◆
    if isfile(mfile+".db")                                                   ◆
      then                                                                   ◆
    play "prtcond"
    .
    .
    .
    @ 10,10
    ?? "Printing Labels - Please Wait..."
    report mfile "1"                                                         ◆
    play "prtnorm"
  endif                                                                      ◆
  release vars mfile, ans                                                    ◆
  case mchoice = "Update" :
```

14. Now change it so that the Update option asks for the name of the file to be processed.

```
Changing script C:\paradox3\mainmenu                                    Script Ins

....+...10....+...20....+...30....+...40....+...50....+...60....+...70....+...80
  case mchoice = "Update" :
    clear                                                                    ◆
    @ 10,10                                                                  ◆
    ?? "Enter the name of the file (e.g. Mailtx) "                           ◆
    accept "A8" picture "&*&" to mfile                                       ◆
    if isfile(mfile+".db")                                                   ◆
      then                                                                   ◆
      clear
      @ 10,10
      ?? "Deleting customers - Please Wait..."
      subtract "Delrecs" mfile                                               ◆
      empty "Delrecs"
    endif
    if isfile("Addrecs.db")
      then
      clear
      @ 10,10
      ?? "Adding customers - Please Wait..."
      add "Addrecs" mfile                                                    ◆
      empty "Addrecs"
    endif
    clearall
    release vars mfile                                                       ◆
  case mchoice = "Summary" :
```

15. Change it again so that the Summary option asks for the name of the file to be processed. The dots indicate lines of the script that are omitted from the display. Do not change those lines in your script.

```
Changing script C:\paradox3\mainmenu                                  Script Ins

....+...10....+...20....+...30....+...40....+...50....+...60....+...70....+...80
  case mchoice = "Summary" :
    clear                                                                       ◆
    @ 10,10                                                                     ◆
    ?? "Enter the name of the file (e.g. Mailtx) "                              ◆
    accept "A8" picture "&*&" to mfile                                          ◆
    if isfile(mfile+".db")                                                      ◆
      then                                                                      ◆
      clear
      @ 10,10
    ?? "Collecting statistics for subscriptions - Please Wait..."
    array sublen[36]
    x = 1
    while x <= 36
      sublen[x] = 0
      x = x + 1
    endwhile
    view mfile                                                                  ◆
    tot = 0
    .
    .
    .
    sleep 3500
    clearall
  endif
  release vars mfile,lncnt,tot,sublen                                           ◆
  case mchoice = "Configure" :                                                  ◆
    @ 10,10
```

16. Press **F10** (Scripts Menu) and select the DO-IT! option.

17. Edit the Custmnt script. Change the EDIT command to the VIEW command. Then, insert the EDITKEY special key command and a CLEARALL command line as shown in the following display.

```
Changing script C:\paradox3\custmnt                                   Script Ins

....+...10....+...20....+...30....+...40....+...50....+...60....+...70....+...80
;custmnt - customer maintenance script
clear
@ 10,10
?? "Enter the name of the table "
accept "a8" picture "&*&" to fileans
if not isblank(fileans)
  then
  if isfile(fileans+".db")
    then
    view fileans                                                                ◆
    formkey {Image} {PickForm} {F}
    while (true)
      editkey                                                                   ◆
    end
    PgDn
    wait record message "Type customer name, then press F2 to begin search..."
      until "F2"
    lastname = [Last Name]
    firstname = [First Name]
    canceledit
    del
    if isblank(lastname) and isblank(firstname)
      then
      clearall                                                                  ◆
      quitloop
```

18. Continue to edit the Custmnt script as shown in the following display.

```
Changing script C:\paradox3\custmnt                                  Script Ins

....+...10....+...20....+...30....+...40....+...50....+...60....+...70....+...80
      then
      message "Record does not exist in table "+fileans+".db..."
      sleep 2000
    else
      while not atlast()
        moveto [Begins]
        pickform 1                                                            ◆
    wait record message "Press F2 for the menu, PgDn to continue searching..."
        until "F2", "PgDn"
      if retval = "PgDn"
        then
        if atlast()                                                           ◆
          then                                                                ◆
          beep beep beep beep                                                 ◆
          message "No other records were found in the table..."               ◆
          sleep 2000                                                          ◆
          release vars fileans,lastname,firstname                             ◆
          clearall                                                            ◆
          return                                                              ◆
        endif                                                                 ◆
        PgDn
        locate next lastname, firstname
```

19. Now insert the housekeeping commands as shown in the following display.

```
Changing script C:\paradox3\custmnt                                  Script Ins

....+...10....+...20....+...30....+...40....+...50....+...60....+...70....+...80
          sleep 2000
          quitloop                                                            ◆
        endif
      else
        release vars fileans,lastname,firstname                               ◆
        clearall                                                              ◆
        return                                                                ◆
      endif
    endwhile
    quitloop
  endif
endwhile
    do_it!
    clearimage
  else
    beep beep beep beep
    message "Table "+fileans+".db is not on the current data disk."
    sleep 2000
  endif
endif
clearall                                                                      ◆
release vars fileans,lastname,firstname                                       ◆
```

20. Press **F10** (Scripts Menu) and select the DO-IT! option.

21. Change the first section of the Custview script so that it matches the one in the following display.

```
Changing script C:\paradox3\custview                              Script Ins

....+...10....+...20....+...30....+...40....+...50....+...60....+...70....+...80
; custview - view customer data
clear                                                                          ◆
@ 10,10                                                                        ◆
?? "Enter the name of the file (e.g. Mailtx) "                                 ◆
accept "A8" picture "&*&" to mfile                                             ◆
if not isfile(mfile+".db")                                                     ◆
  then                                                                         ◆
  release vars mfile                                                           ◆
  return                                                                       ◆
endif                                                                          ◆
index mfile on "State"                                                         ◆
index "Sales" on "State"
view mfile                                                                     ◆
if isfile(mfile+".f2")                                                         ◆
  then
  PickForm "2"
else
  PickForm "f"
endif
while (true)
  clear
  @ 21,05
```

22. Continue changing the Custview script by inserting RELEASE command lines as shown in the following display. The dots indicate lines of the script that are omitted in the display. Do not change those lines in your script.

```
Changing script C:\paradox3\custview                              Script Ins

....+...10....+...20....+...30....+...40....+...50....+...60....+...70....+...80
      clearall
      release vars mfile,lastname,firstname,lncnt,ans                         ◆
      return
    endif
   .
   .
   .
        if retval = "Esc"
          then
          clearimage
          release vars mfile,lastname,firstname,lncnt,ans                      ◆
          return
        else
        .
        .
        .
endwhile
clearimage
release vars mfile,lastname,firstname,lncnt,ans                                ◆
; end custview
```

23. Press **F10** (Scripts Menu) and select the DO-IT! option.

24. Play the Mainmenu script and test each option in the application. When you are satisfied that the scripts are running properly, press **Esc** to end the application and return to the Main Menu screen.

25. Turn to Module 18 to continue the recommended learning sequence.

Module 16
COPYFORM

DESCRIPTION

Each script, form, or report that you design for an application increases the size of your library. When you need something similar to an existing part of an application, it is easier and quicker to copy and modify than to redo the work.

Instead of designing a form for a table that matches another form and table, just use the COPYFORM command. The proper syntax for this command follows.

```
COPYFORM <tablename1> <formname1> <tablename2> <formname2>
```

Replace <tablename1> with the name of an existing Paradox table that has the form you want to copy.

Specify the table's form number by replacing <formname1> with "F" or a number 1 through 14. It is unnecessary to enclose the number of a form within quotation marks. Paradox converts it to a string automatically.

Replace <tablename2> with the name of an existing Paradox table that needs a copy of the form from the <tablename1> table. The receiving table may be the same or another Paradox table. If copying a form between two tables, the structure of the receiving table must be the same as the sending table.

Specify "F" or a number 1 through 14 in <formname2> of the COPYFORM command. It is unnecessary to enclose the number of a form within quotation marks. Paradox converts it to a string automatically. If a form already exists for <formname2>, Paradox replaces the old one with the copied form without asking for confirmation.

The COPYFORM command is an abbreviated form of several menu options that are available through the Paradox menu-driven system. By including the following command line in the script instead of the COPYFORM "Mailtx" 2 "Mailok" 2 command line, you achieve the same results.

```
Menu {Tools} {Copy} {Form} {DifferentTable}
```

NOTE: This command is available in version 3.0 and higher.

APPLICATIONS

Designing new forms and reports has always been a time-consuming task. Now, the ability to have multi-record and multi-table forms has increased the design time.

For example, you are keeping a customer table for each state. If you need a new form, it must be made available for each existing customer table. Just use the COPYFORM command in a script to copy the new form to each of the customer tables.

The COPYFORM command gives you a head start. When possible, copy a form that is similar to the one you need. Copy the existing form from the same or another Paradox table. When the form is copied, change the new version to meet your needs.

TYPICAL OPERATION

This example shows you how to use the COPYFORM command.

1. Type **SEE** to use the Paradox editor. When asked for the name of the script, type **FORMS** and press **Enter**.
2. Change the script so it matches the following command lines.

```
Changing script C:\paradox3\forms                                    Script

....+...10....+...20....+...30....+...40....+...50....+...60....+...70....+...80
; FORMS.SC - COPIES ALL TEXAS FORMS & REPORTS TO ALL CUSTOMER TABLES

CLEAR
@ 10,10 ?? "Copying all customer forms & reports - Please Wait..."
COPYFORM "MAILTX" 2 "MAILOK" 2
COPYREPORT "MAILTX" 1 "MAILOK" 1
; END FORMS.SC
```

3. Press **F10** (Menu) and type **G** to select the Go option. The screen clears and the copy message is displayed while form 2 is copied from the Mailtx table to the Mailok table. Though those form numbers are already used, Paradox does not ask if you want to Cancel or Replace the forms.
4. Make a small change to one of the Mailtx forms. Then, run the FORMS script again. When the script ends, verify that the Mailok form is the same as the changed Mailtx form.
5. Turn to Module 63 to continue the recommended learning sequence.

Module 17
COPYFROMARRAY

DESCRIPTION

One COPYFROMARRAY command sends all values from an existing set of variables in an array to the current table record. The array is usually created by the COPYTO ARRAY command. Otherwise, it must have a similar form when created by the ARRAY command. The format for the COPYFROMARRAY command follows.

```
COPYFROMARRAY <array>
```

Replace <array> with the name assigned to the set of variables (array) that exists in memory. A script error occurs if the specified array is not available in the computer memory.

Each element (variable) in the array is copied to the current record until Paradox encounters the end of the array or end of the record. Remember that the first element contains the table name.

The array elements are copied consecutively. Paradox uses the table structure to establish field order for the record. The second element is copied to the first field of the record, the third element to the second field, etc., until Paradox encounters the end of the array or record.

The table that is to receive the array values must be in edit mode before this command is encountered. Do this in one of two ways. Use the EDIT command in the script to access the table so that the edit mode is established immediately. Otherwise, if the VIEW command is used to access the table, include the EDITKEY special keycode to tell Paradox that you want to change the current record.

Before the COPYFROMARRAY command is encountered, position the cursor on the proper record. Otherwise, the values in the fields of the current record are replaced by the values in the array. After this command is performed, the array is still available unless the array is redeclared, the RELEASE command is encountered, or you end the Paradox session.

APPLICATIONS

Use this command when you want to replace the values in the current record with those in the specified array. Remember that this one command copies all elements in the array to the record's fields. This lets the script make changes to the table without user activity.

For example, the zipcode for Plano, Texas is changed from 75084 to 75088. Since the task of changing the zipcode field is repetitive, write a script to do the work. Scan the file for the old zipcode, copy the record to an array, change the zipcode element, and copy the array to the record. Repeat this process until the script encounters the end of the table.

TYPICAL OPERATION

This example shows you how to use the COPYFROMARRAY command.

1. View the Mailtx table to see that Charles Berry's zipcode is 75084. Then press **F8** (Clear Image) to remove the table from the workspace.
2. Edit the Mainmenu script. Change the Weekcalc option to a Utilities option as shown in the following display. The dots represent lines that are omitted from the display. Do not change those lines.

```
Changing script C:\paradox3\mainmenu                                    Script Ins

....+...10....+...20....+...30....+...40....+...50....+...60....+...70....+...80
view "Mailfile"
copytoarray passes
clearall
while (true)
  clear
  showmenu
    "View" : "Find and review customer information.",
    "Maintenance" : "Maintains table data.",
    "Report" : "Print the columnar report.",
    "Labels" : "Print mailing labels.",
    "Update" : "Batch update master table from a floppy disk.",
    "Summary" : "Provide statistics on subscription preferences.",
    "Configure" : "Change application configuration.",
    "Utilities" : "Perform various tasks for the Mail List application."       ◆
  default "View" to mchoice
  switch
  case mchoice = "View" :
.
.
.
  case mchoice = "Configure" :
    @ 10,10
    ?? "Configure..."
    sleep 2000
  case mchoice = "Utilities" :                                                  ◆
    play "Utility"                                                              ◆
  case mchoice = "Esc" :
    quit
```

3. Press **F10** (Scripts Menu) and select the DO-IT! option.
4. When the Main Menu returns to the screen, write a new script called Utility so that it matches the following script.

```
Designing script C:\paradox3\utility                                Script

....+...10....+...20....+...30....+...40....+...50....+...60....+...70....+...80
; utility.sc - allows various tasks for Mail List application
while(true)
  clear
  showmenu
    "Zipcodes" : "Replace new zipcode for all customers with old zipcode.",
    "Passfile" : "Restricted - Access Password file."
  default "Zipcodes" to mutility
  switch
    case mutility = "Zipcodes" :
      clear
      @ 10,10
      ?? "Enter old zipcode "
      accept "A5" picture "#####" to mold
      @ 12,10
      ?? "Enter new zipcode "
      accept "A5" picture "#####" to mnew
      @ 21,05
      ?? "Do you want to continue (Y/N)? "
      accept "A1" picture "&" to mans
      if mans = "Y"
        then
        clear
        @ 10,10
        ?? "Replacing zipcodes - Please Wait..."
        view "Mailtx"
        scan for [zipcode] = mold
          copytoarray zips
          zips["Zipcode"] = mnew
          editkey
          copyfromarray zips
        endscan
        do_it!
        clearall
      endif
    case mutility = "Passfile" :
      play "idcheck"
      if retval and passes[x+1] = "9"
        then
        edit "Mailfile"
        formkey
        wait table message "Press F2 to return to the menu..." until "F2"
        do_it!
        clearall
      else
        message "You have typed an invalid ID code..."
        sleep 2000
        clearall
      endif
    case mutility = "Esc" :
      return
    otherwise :
      clear
      @ 10,10
      ?? "The requested option is not available from this menu..."
      sleep 2000
  endswitch
endwhile
; end utility.sc
```

5. Press **F10** (Scripts Menu) and select the DO-IT! option.
6. Play the Mainmenu script.
7. Press **Left Arrow** to position the cursor on the Utilities option and press **Enter**.
8. Select the Zipcodes option by typing **Z**. When asked for the old zipcode, type **75084** and press **Enter**. Then type **75088** for the new zipcode and press **Enter**.

9. You are asked if you want to continue this operation. Verify that the zipcodes are correct. If so, type **Y** and press **Enter**. Otherwise, type **N** and press **Enter** to return to the menu. Then select the Zipcode option and try again until you enter the proper zipcodes.
10. While the script plays, a message is displayed on the screen. When the submenu returns, press **Esc** twice so that the Main Menu line appears on your screen.
11. View the Mailtx table and verify that the zipcode for Charles Berry is 75088. If so, the script was successful. Then press **F8** (Clear Image) to remove the table from the workspace and return to the Main Menu.
12. Turn to Module 86 to continue the recommended learning sequence.

Module 18
COPYREPORT

DESCRIPTION

Each time you develop an application, you increase the size of your library of scripts, forms, and reports. When you need something similar to an existing part of an application, it is easier and quicker to copy and modify than to redo the work.

Instead of designing a report for a table that matches another report and table, just use the COPYREPORT command. The proper syntax for this command follows.

```
COPYREPORT <tablename1> <reportname1> <tablename2> <reportname2>
```

Replace <tablename1> with the name of an existing Paradox table that has the report you want to copy.

Specify the table's report number by replacing <reportname1> with "F" or a number 1 through 14. It is unnecessary to enclose the number of a report within quotation marks. Paradox converts it to a string automatically.

Replace <tablename2> with the name of an existing Paradox table that needs a copy of the report from the <tablename1> table. The receiving table may be the same, or a another Paradox table. If copying a report between two tables, the structure of the receiving table must be the same as the sending table.

Specify "F" or a number 1 through 14 in <reportname2> of the COPYREPORT command. It is unnecessary to enclose the number of a report within quotation marks. Paradox converts it to a string automatically. If a report already exists for <reportname2>, Paradox replaces the old one with the copied report without asking for confirmation.

The COPYREPORT command is an abbreviated report of several menu options that are available through the Paradox menu-driven system. By including the following command line in the script instead of the COPYREPORT "Mailtx" 2 "Mailok" 2 command line, you achieve the same results.

```
Menu {Tools} {Copy} {Report} {DifferentTable}
```

NOTE: This command is available in version 3.0 and higher.

APPLICATIONS

Designing new forms and reports has always been a time-consuming task. Now, the ability to have multi-record and multi-table reports has increased the design time.

For example, you are keeping a customer table for each state. If you need a new report, it must be made available for each existing customer table. Just use the COPYREPORT command in a script to copy the new report to each of the customer tables.

The COPYREPORT command gives you a head start. When possible, copy a report that is similar to the one you need. Copy the existing report from the same or another Paradox table. When the report is copied, change the new version to meet your needs.

TYPICAL OPERATION

This example shows you how to use the COPYREPORT commands.

1. Type **SEW** to use the Paradox editor. When asked for the name of the script, type **FORMS** and press **Enter**.
2. Type the following command lines in the script area.

```
Designing script C:\paradox3\forms                                    Script
....+...10....+...20....+...30....+...40....+...50....+...60....+...70....+...80
; forms.sc - copies all Texas forms & reports to all customer tables
clear
@ 10,15 ?? "Copying all customer reports - Please Wait..."
copyreport "Mailtx" 2 "Mailok" 2
; end forms.sc
```

3. Press **F10** (Menu) and type **G** to select the Go option. The screen clears and the copy message is displayed while report 2 is copied from the Mailtx table to the Mailok table. Though that report number is already used, Paradox does not ask if you want to Cancel or Replace the report.
4. Make a small change to the Mailtx report. Then, run the FORMS script again. When the script ends, verify that the Mailok report is the same as the changed Mailtx report.
5. Turn to Module 16 to continue the recommended learning sequence.

Module 19
COPYTOARRAY

DESCRIPTION

The COPYTOARRAY command declares an array and copies the field values from the current table record into the array elements. A complete record is saved in computer memory with one command. The format for this command follows.

```
COPYTOARRAY <array>
```

Replace <array> with a name you want assigned to the area of computer memory where the record is to be held. Make the array name meaningful so that other programmers understand the purpose of the array.

This command creates the array with an element for each field in the table structure plus one additional element. The table name is placed in the first element of the array. Then the first field of the table is placed in the second element, second field in the third element, etc. The order of field placement is dictated by the table structure.

When referencing an element, do not use numeric or variable subscripts. Use field names enclosed with brackets and quotation marks. For example, CUSTFILE["BEGINS"] provides the element that contains the beginning subscription date.

Always use the VIEW command to access the table. The mode must be for viewing only. Using the EDIT command to access the table causes a script error.

After making the table available to the script, position the cursor on the record you want to store in memory. Then use the COPYTOARRAY command. The record in the table is not affected unless an element in the array is changed and the COPYFROMARRAY command is performed by the script.

APPLICATIONS

Use the COPYTOARRAY command when you want to hold a table record in the computer memory. This is helpful when the table contains information that is needed while playing a script.

For example, create a table that contains passwords that restrict access to certain table information or application functions. Record 1 supplies passwords that limit the information displayed on the screen. Other records in the table provide passwords that allow more information.

Use tables to store any type of information for the application. Keep the last number used to print an invoice, P/O, or stock number.

By using a table to hold this type of information, your scripts are more flexible. They refer to the array elements instead of having the values included in the application scripts. Therefore, changes are made to one table instead of several scripts.

This method of designing an application is limited only by your imagination. However, the extra time required during the design phase is small when it eliminates script changes to maintain the application.

TYPICAL OPERATION

This example shows you how to use the COPYTOARRAY command.

1. Type **C** to Create a table. Type **Mailfile** for the table name and press **Enter**.
2. When the table structure form appears, type the field information so that the one on your screen matches the one in the following display.

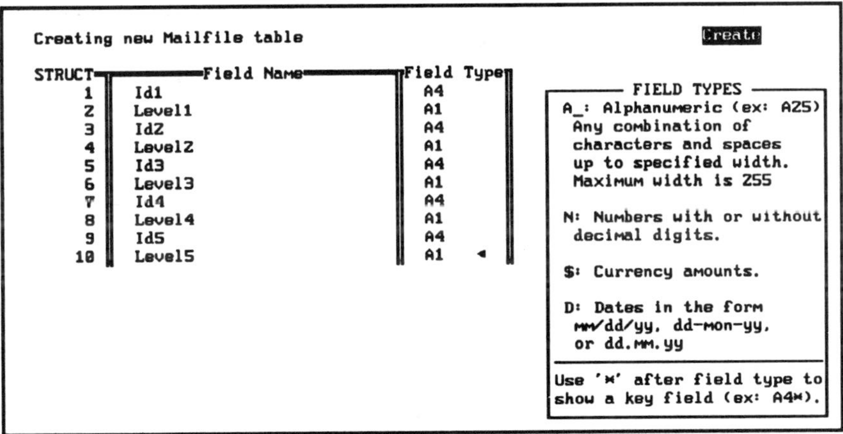

3. Press **F2** (DO-IT!) to save the new structure on disk.
4. When the Main Menu returns, type **MD** (Modify/DataEntry). Type **Mailfile** for the table name and press **Enter**.
5. Type the record so that the table on your screen matches the one in the following display.

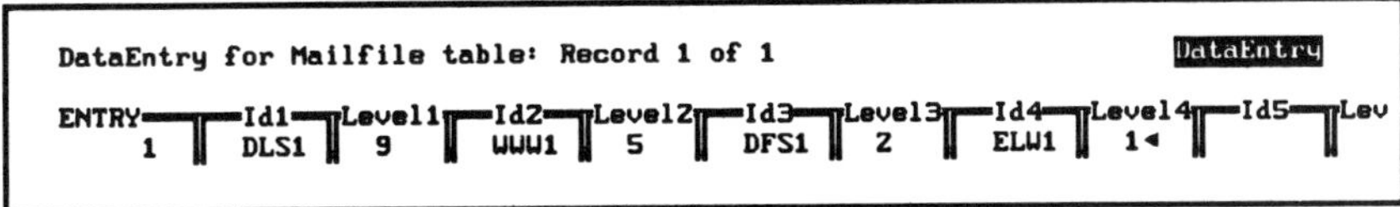

6. Press **F2** (DO-IT!) to save the new records on disk. Then press **F8** (Clear Image) to remove the table from the workspace.
7. Edit the Mainmenu script. Change it so that the first few command lines match the following display.

```
Changing script C:\paradox3\mainmenu                                   Script Ins

....+...10....+...20....+...30....+...40....+...50....+...60....+...70....+...80
view "Mailfile"
copytoarray passes
clearall
while (true)
  clear
  showmenu
    "View" : "Find and review customer information.",
    "Maintenance" : "Maintains table data.",
    "Report" : "Print the columnar report.",
    "Labels" : "Print mailing labels.",
    "Update" : "Batch update master table from a floppy disk.",
    "Summary" : "Provide statistics on subscription preferences.",
    "Configure" : "Change application configuration.",
    "Weekcalc" : "Count the number of weeks between two dates."
  default "View" to mchoice
  switch
  case mchoice = "View" :
    play "Custview"
  case mchoice = "Maintenance" :
    play "idcheck"
    if retval
      then
```

8. Press **F10** (Scripts Menu) and select the DO-IT! option. The Main Menu returns to the screen.
9. Edit the Idcheck script. Change it so that it verifies the identification code against the ones saved in the array as shown in the following display.

```
Changing script C:\paradox3\idcheck                                    Script Ins

....+...10....+...20....+...30....+...40....+...50....+...60....+...70....+...80
; idcheck - checks for valid identification codes
clear
@ 10,10
?? "Enter your identification code "
accept "A4" picture "&&&#" to idcode
x = 2
while x < 12
  if idcode <> passes[x]
    then
      x = x + 2
  else
    quitloop
  endif
endwhile
if x < 12
  then
  print file "c:log" "Customer table was last changed by ",idcode," on ",
    today()," at ",time()
  clearall
  return True
else
  message "You have typed an invalid ID code..."
  sleep 2000
  clearall
  return False
endif
; end idcheck
```

10. Press **F10** (Scripts Menu) and select the DO-IT! option. From the Main Menu screen, play the Mainmenu script.
11. From the application menu, type **M** to select the Maintenance option.
12. Type **FFF1** and press **Enter**. A message appears in the lower right corner that tells you that the ID code is invalid.
13. When the application menu returns to the screen, type **M**.
14. This time, type **WWW1** and press **Enter**. You are asked for the name of the table. Type **Mailtx** and press **Enter**.
15. A blank record form appears on the workspace. Press **F2** as instructed at the bottom of the screen. The application menu returns to the screen. Press **Esc** to end the application.
16. Turn to Module 17 to continue the recommended learning sequence.

Module 20
CREATE

DESCRIPTION

Paradox is a software package that organizes, maintains, and reports information. The information (data) is kept in a table on a disk. The table must be described so that Paradox knows the name, type, and length of each field (piece of information). The description is called a *table structure.*

Usually, table structures are established with the Create option that appears on the Main Menu screen. However, you may also create table structures by including the CREATE command in Paradox scripts.

There are two forms of the CREATE command available for scripts. Replace the "-n" with a number greater than zero.

```
CREATE <new table> LIKE <existing table>
CREATE <new table> <fieldname-1>:<fieldtype- 1>,...,<fieldname-n>:
   <fieldtype-n>
```

Replace <new table> with the name to be assigned to the file (table). Unless provided in a variable, enclose the name with quotation marks. If the table name already exists, Paradox immediately deletes the existing table and its family (forms, reports, etc.) from the working disk. Then the new table structure is created and saved.

Use the LIKE <existing table> phrase to copy the structure of a table that is already available on the disk. Replace <existing table> with the table name enclosed with quotation marks unless it is provided by a variable. Paradox makes a copy of the existing table structure and assigns it the name specified by <new table>.

Instead of borrowing an existing table structure, the second form of the command lets you specify each field for the structure. Replace <fieldname-1> through <fieldname-n> with names that are to be used when referring to one piece of information (field).

The field names you specify are used as column headings for your new table. Valid field names may be up to 25 characters long and cannot begin with a blank character. All alphabetic characters can be used except the left bracket ([ ), right bracket ( ]), and the combination of the dash and greater-than symbols (– >). Select meaningful names for your fields so that you know what each field contains and enclose it with quotation marks.

Identify the type and length of the data to be held in the field by replacing <fieldtype-1> through <fieldtype-n> with an acceptable data type character and length. Paradox supports "A" for Alphanumeric (1-255 characters), "D" for Date, "N" for Numeric, "S" for Short number, and "$" for Currency field types. Each field type must be separated from its field name by including a colon in the command line. Also, enclose the field type with quotation marks. For example, PHONE: "A13" identifies a field called "PHONE" as an alphanumeric field which holds thirteen characters.

Paradox also allows you to specify certain fields in your table structure as *key fields*. They keep your data in sorted order. Also, key fields prevent entry of duplicate records and make data retrieval considerably faster. For example, the data type "A5*" tells Paradox that the field is Alphanumeric, five characters long, and to be used for sequencing the records.

One drawback to using key fields is the restriction on duplicate keys. For example, it would not be very practical to use a last name field as a key field, since you would not be able to enter information for two people with the same last name.

Paradox supports Multi-field keys to bypass this type of problem. In a Multi-field keyed table, you are allowed duplicates for part of the key but not the whole key. For example, when you specify a last name field and first name field as a Multi-Field key, "Charles Johnson" and "Linda Johnson" are not considered duplicate keys.

When describing the table structure in the CREATE command, provide the field name, a colon, and the field type for each field. The field descriptions are separated with commas. For example, the following CREATE command describes a structure with seven fields.

```
create "mailout" "last":"a20*","first":"a15*","address 1":"a25",
  "address 2":"a20","city":"a15","state":"a2","zipcode":"a9",
  "begins":"d","ends":"d"
```

Since asterisks are included with the first two field types, the records in the table must be kept in order. Paradox sorts the records in last name, first name order so that "Smith, John" appears before "Smith, Sue."

APPLICATIONS

Since Paradox helps you handle information entered into tables, this option must be used before any data is saved. To establish a new table for your data, use the Create option of the Main Menu line or include a CREATE command line in your script.

If you specify key fields when the table is created, Paradox automatically keeps all table data in that order and does not allow records with duplicate keys. This is helpful when a social security number is used as a key field.

When a new table structure is the same as an existing structure, copy the structure of the existing table by including the LIKE clause in the CREATE command. Then make any changes needed and save the resulting structure.

TYPICAL OPERATION

This example shows you how to use the CREATE command.

1. Select the Create option by typing **C**. Paradox asks you to type the name for your new table.
2. Type **Mailout** and press **Enter**. The Create structure appears.

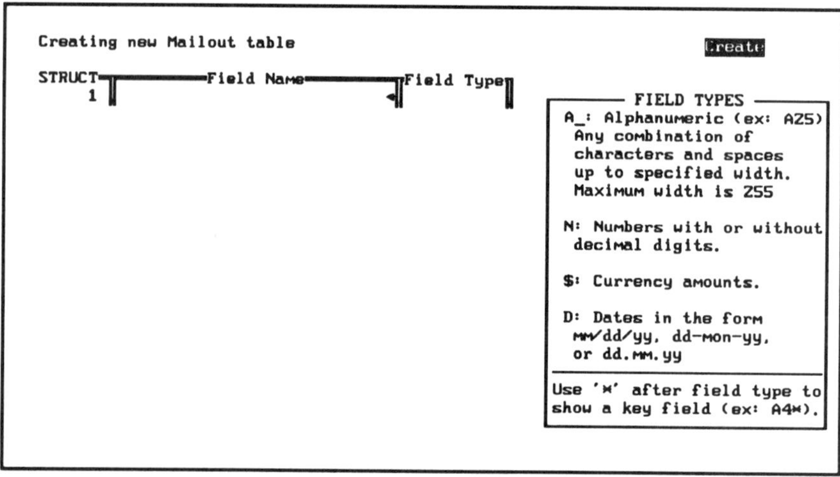

3. Type **Last Name** and press **Enter**. The cursor moves to the right for the field type.
4. Type **A25*** and press **Enter**. This tells Paradox that the field allows 25 characters of alphanumeric information. The asterisk specifies the field as a key. This tells Paradox that you want the data sorted and kept in last name sequence.
5. The cursor is positioned on line 2. This is for the second field. Type **First Name** and press **Enter**.
6. Type **A15*** and press **Enter**. This First Name field is 15 characters of alphanumeric information.
7. Continue the structure until your screen resembles the following display.

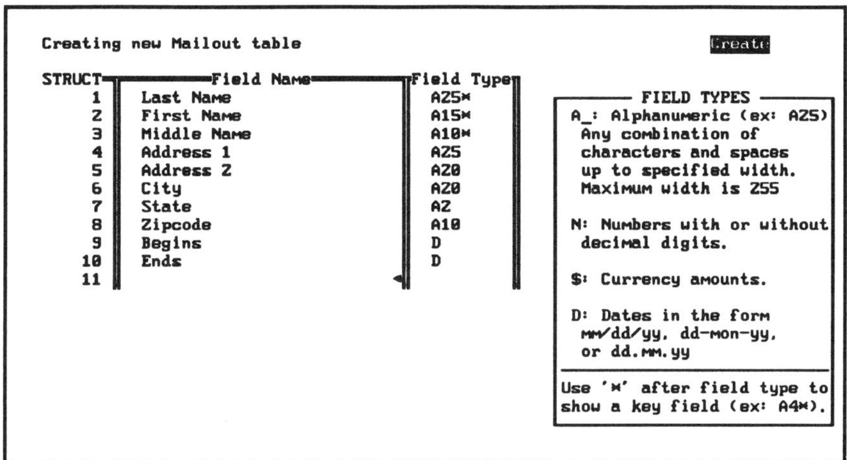

```
Creating new Mailout table                                        Create

STRUCT  Field Name          Field Type
  1     Last Name           A25*
  2     First Name          A15*
  3     Middle Name         A10*
  4     Address 1           A25
  5     Address 2           A20
  6     City                A20
  7     State               A2
  8     Zipcode             A10
  9     Begins              D
 10     Ends                D
 11

                 FIELD TYPES
A_: Alphanumeric (ex: A25)
  Any combination of
  characters and spaces
  up to specified width.
  Maximum width is 255

N: Numbers with or without
  decimal digits.

$: Currency amounts.

D: Dates in the form
  mm/dd/yy, dd-mon-yy,
  or dd.mm.yy

Use '*' after field type to
show a key field (ex: A4*).
```

8. Press **F2** (DO-IT!) to create the table and save it on disk. Paradox returns the Main Menu screen.
9. Type **SEW** (Script, Edit, Write) to write a new script. When asked for the name of the script, type **Createit** and press **Enter**.
10. Type the script in the following display.

```
Designing script C:\paradox3\createit                             Script

....+...10....+...20....+...30....+...40....+...50....+...60....+...70....+...80
clear
@ 10,10
?? "Enter the name for the table "
accept "a8" picture "&*&" to fileans
if not isblank(fileans) and not isfile(fileans+".db")
  then
  create fileans "Last Name":"A25*", "First Name":"A15*",
    "Middle Name":"A10*", "Address 1":"A25", "Address 2":"A20",
    "City":"A20", "State":"A2", "Zipcode":"A10", "Begins":"D", "Ends":"D"
endif
```

11. Press **F10** (Scripts Menu) and select the Go option by typing **G**. The screen clears and you are asked for the name of the table. Type **Mailtx** and press **Enter**. The screen clears, and the Main Menu screen returns to the monitor.
12. Type **T** to select the Tools option. Select the Info option by typing **I**.
13. Type **S** to select the Structure option. When asked for the name of the table, type **Mailtx** and press **Enter**. The table structure on your screen resembles the one in the following display.

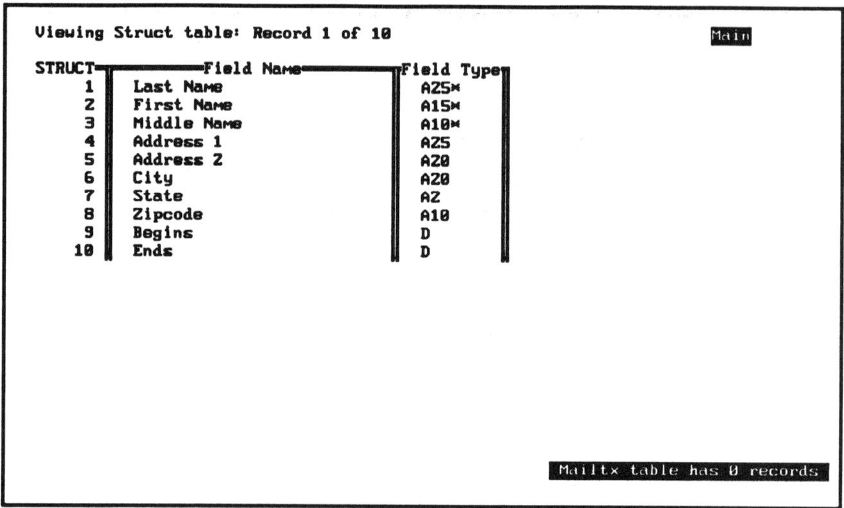

14. Now the table structure is ready for data. Press **F8** (Clear Image) to remove the table structure.

15. Turn to Module 27 to continue the recommended learning sequence.

Module 21
CREATELIB

DESCRIPTION

This command creates a Paradox library on disk that is used to store unreadable copies of procedures. A library is similar to a DOS subdirectory. Consider keeping a library for each application's procedures so that they are not mixed with others. A maximum of 50 procedures are allowed in each library.

Like a subdirectory, a library must be established before storing procedures. Use the following command format.

```
CREATELIB <library name>
```

Replace <library name> with a chosen filename that does not exceed eight characters. The first must be a letter. Unless provided in a variable, the name must be enclosed with quotation marks. The .lib extension identifies the file as a library. For example, the CREATE "Maillist" command line establishes a file on the disk called Maillist.lib.

Each procedure in the library is like a compiled program to the menu-driven system as well as the DOS. When using a procedure library, include a READLIB command in the application. It reads the specified procedures into memory. Then the application is able to play them.

Keep the readable procedure scripts on a floppy disk in a dry, safe place. When changing a procedure, edit the readable form on the floppy disk. Then use the WRITELIB command to compile the edited procedure before it replaces the existing library procedure.

If you want a list of the procedures stored in a specific library, use the INFOLIB command. When this command is encountered, Paradox creates a temporary table of procedure names and file sizes. Then the table is presented on the workspace for your review. It is deleted when you press the F8 (Clear Image) key.

Since CREATELIB, WRITELIB, and INFOLIB are commands, you must write one script that creates the library and others that maintain and list them. Consider keeping these scripts on the floppy disks with the readable procedures.

Do not accidentally play the CREATELIB script because Paradox deletes the old library and all of its procedures before replacing it with an empty library. Otherwise, a WRITELIB script that includes all procedures for that library must be available on disk.

APPLICATIONS

Security and speed must be considered when the application is ready for the users. A person who knows how to use the Paradox menu-driven system is able to access any unprotected table, script, procedure, form, or report.

A procedure library provides security for the procedures as well as providing speed for the application. Since the procedures are in a compiled form, they are smaller. Less disk space, memory space, and processing time are required for the procedure.

Before delivering the application to the user, consider changing several of the application's scripts to procedures. As you change and test each procedure, use the new file size to determine the amount of available memory. Include the READLIB and RELEASE PROCS commands in the remaining scripts to move procedures in and out of the computer memory.

For example, change the Idcheck and Utility scripts into procedures. Write a script that includes the CREATELIB command to create a procedure library called Maillist. Then write a script that includes a WRITELIB command that puts the new procedures in the library and the INFOLIB command to report the names and sizes of the unreadable procedures. Change the Mainmenu script to include at least one READLIB command that stores the procedures in memory before they are needed. When everything is in place, test, test, test!

TYPICAL OPERATION

This example shows you how to use the CREATELIB command.

1. Select the Tools/Info/Inventory/Files menu options. When asked for the pattern, type ***.lib** and press **Enter** to tell Paradox that you want only procedure libraries included in the list. The list resembles the one in the following display.

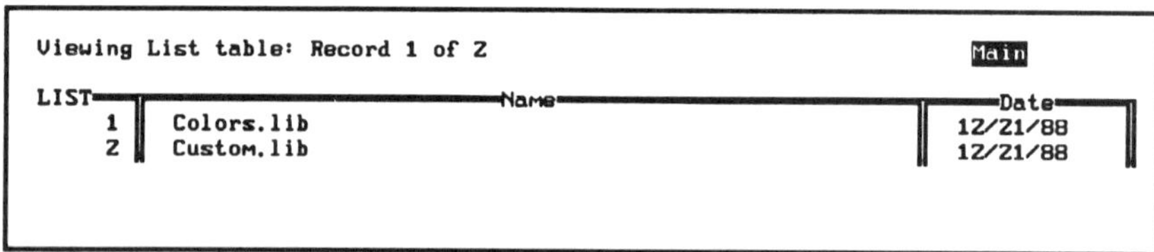

2. Press **F8** (Clear Image) to remove the list from the workspace.
3. Write a new script called Crealibs. Type the new script that follows.

```
Designing script C:\paradox3\crealibs                        Script

....+...10....+...20....+...30....+...40....+...50....+...60....+...70....+...80
; crealibs - creates a procedure library
clear
@ 10,10
?? "Enter the name for the procedure library (e.g. Maillist) "
accept "A8" picture "&*&" to mlib
```

```
  if isfile(mlib+".lib")
    then
    beep beep beep beep
    @ 21,05
    ?? "That name already exists! Do you want to continue anyway (Y/N)? "
    accept "A1" picture "&" to mans
    if mans <> "Y"
      then
      release vars mlib, mans
      quit
    endif
  endif
  @ 20,05
  clear eos
  @ 21,05
  ?? "Creating the new procedure library - Please Wait..."
  createlib mlib
; end crealibs.sc
```

4. Press **F10** (Scripts Menu) and select the Go option.
5. When asked for the name of the library, type **Maillist** and press **Enter**. A message tells you that the library is being created successfully.
6. When the Main Menu returns, play the script again. Type **Maillist** for the name and press **Enter**. A message tells you that the name already exists. Also, you are asked if you want to continue the operation.
7. Type **N** and press **Enter**. The Main Menu screen returns to the monitor.
8. Play the script for the Maillist library again. This time, continue the operation. The procedure library is recreated. If procedures existed in that library, it's empty now.
9. When the Main Menu returns, type **TlIF**. When asked for the pattern, type ***.lib** and press **Enter** to list all existing procedure library files. The list includes the Maillist library as in the following display.

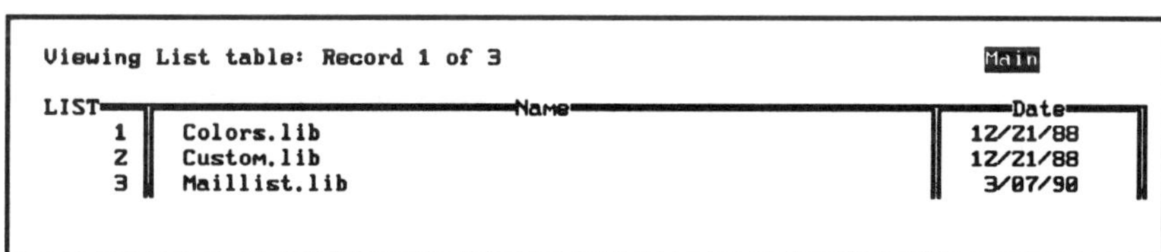

Viewing List table: Record 1 of 3 — Main

LIST	Name	Date
1	Colors.lib	12/21/88
2	Custom.lib	12/21/88
3	Maillist.lib	3/07/90

10. Press **F8** (Clear Image) to remove the list from the workspace. The library is ready for procedures.
11. Turn to Module 103 to continue the recommended learning sequence.

Module 22
CURSOR

DESCRIPTION

Use the CURSOR command to change the shape of the cursor on the PAL workspace. In Paradox, there are actually two different cursors. When you are using the Paradox menu system, the Paradox workspace cursor is active. When a PAL script is running, the PAL workspace cursor is active.

The CURSOR command has no effect on the Paradox workspace cursor. The syntax of the CURSOR command is:

```
CURSOR <BAR/BOX/NORMAL/OFF>
```

The available cursor shapes are:

BAR	-	A thicker bar shaped cursor
BOX	-	A reverse-video box cursor
NORMAL	-	Makes the cursor visible
OFF	-	Hides the cursor from view

NOTE: The CURSOR command was added to Paradox 2.0 and above.

APPLICATIONS

The CURSOR command allows you to change the shape of the cursor and customize your screen appearance. There are times that you do not want a cursor to appear on your screen. For example, a cursor would be distracting to the user when your program does not allow input.

TYPICAL OPERATION

This illustration shows you how to use the CURSOR command.

1. Type **SEW** to use the Script Editor. When asked for the name of the script, type **Curdemo** and press **Enter**.
2. Type the following PAL command lines.

```
Designing script C:\paradox3\curdemo                                 Script

....+...10....+...20....+...30....+...40....+...50....+...60....+...70....+...80
; curdemo.sc - Cursor Changing Demo
@ 01,01
cursor normal
? "Notice - A normal cursor is visible - PRESS THE ENTER KEY"
accept "A1" to X
clear
@ 01,01
cursor off
? "Notice - No cursor is present       - PRESS THE ENTER KEY"
accept "A1" to X
clear
@ 01,01
cursor bar
? "Notice - Now the CURSOR is a bar    - PRESS THE ENTER KEY"
accept "A1" to X
clear
@ 01,01
cursor box
? "Notice - Now the CURSOR is a box    - PRESS THE ENTER KEY"
accept "A1" to X
clear
@ 01,01
cursor normal
? "Notice - the CURSOR is now normal   - PRESS THE ENTER KEY"
accept "A1" to X
clear
; end curdemo
```

3. Press **F10** (Scripts Menu) and select the Go option. Watch the cursor shape change as the script plays.
4. Turn to Module 84 to continue the recommended learning sequence.

Module 23
DEBUG

DESCRIPTION

When you write a script, you must play it successfully before considering it complete. If you encounter an error while the script is being played, change the script and play it again. The process of changing and testing a script is called *debugging*.

Paradox provides a debugging capability that helps you identify errors in a script. The two types of errors that may occur are syntax errors and run errors.

Syntax errors occur when a command is not used properly. For example, if the BEEP command is misspelled, a syntax error occurs.

Run errors occur when something like a script, form, or table is not found on the disk. Many run errors can be corrected temporarily to finish playing the script. Then, the script must be edited so that the line that caused the error is corrected for the next time the script is played.

If an error is encountered while a script is being played, Paradox makes the Debugger available automaticallyand you are asked if you want to Cancel or Debug the script being played.

If you select the Cancel option, the script stops and the Main Menu returns to your workspace. Select the Cancel option when you need to do other work. Debug the script later when you have more time.

If you want to resolve the problem, select the Debug option. The Paradox Debugger shows you the line that caused the error as well as a message that helps identify the problem.

The arrow at the bottom of the screen points to the instruction that caused the problem. The error message in the lower right corner of the screen says that a report form numbered 1 does not exist and, therefore, cannot be printed.

At this point, you have two choices. One choice is to press Ctrl-Q to stop the debugging activity, cancel the script test, and return to the Main Menu.

The second choice is to change the script. Press Ctrl-E to stop the debugging activity, end the script play, and return to the Editor screen. Continue the change, test, and debug activity until the script plays successfully and the Main Menu returns to your screen automatically.

There are times when you want to initiate the Debugger yourself. For example, when the results of a script are not what you expect, initiate the Debugger and check the effect of each line as it is executed. There are three ways to initiate the Debugger.

Instead of playing a script, press Alt-F10 (Scripts Menu) to access the Play, BeginRecord, Debug, Value, and MiniScript options. Select the Debug option, type the name of the script to be debugged, and press the Enter key. The first line of the script is displayed at the bottom of the screen. Press Alt-F10 (Debugger Menu) and select the Debug option you want.

If you suspect that the problem exists in the last few lines of the script, choose another method of initiating the Debugger.

While a script is being played, press Ctrl-Break to access the Debug option. Paradox asks if you want to Cancel or Debug the script's play. This choice is presented the same as when an error is encountered. It is difficult, however, to press Ctrl-Break at just the right time.

If you suspect a certain area to be causing the problem, insert a DEBUG command in the script to review each line that follows. The Debugger is active for the first statement after the DEBUG command.

The command line is displayed on your screen as if it were an error, but no error message appears. The Debugger just displays the line to be performed.

Now you must decide what you want the Debugger to do. Press Alt-F10 (Debugger Menu) so that the menu line appears on your screen. The following paragraphs describe the options on the Debugger Menu.

Value Select this option when you want to know the current value of any existing variable, array element, or expression (e.g., rows + 3). When Paradox asks for the name of the variable or expression to be displayed, type a maximum of 50 characters per expression and press Enter. The value appears on the workspace where error messages are displayed.

Step This option tells Paradox to perform the current line and continue to the next one. Use this option to play the script one line at a time. This is helpful when the results of the script are not what you expect. Use the Debugger to step through the part that you suspect is causing the problem. Use the Value option of the Debugger Menu to check the values of variables as they are changed by the script.

Press Ctrl-S (Step) while a script is running to do the same thing as selecting this option from the Debugger Menu.

Next Use this option when you want to continue to the next line of the script without performing the current line. This is helpful when the current line caused a run error. Just remember to change that line of the script so that the error does not occur the next time it is played.

Press Ctrl-N (Next) to do the same thing as selecting this option from the Debugger Menu.

Go Select the Go option when you are ready to continue the script without using the Step or Next options. Paradox plays the rest of the script beginning with the current line. Pressing Ctrl-G (Go) is the same as selecting this option from the Debugger Menu.

MiniScript This option lets you write a very small script and play it before continuing the current script's play. This is often helpful when a run error occurs while playing a script. For example, suppose the original script stops with a run error because a variable is not currently available. Write and play a miniscript to establish the variable that is needed by the original script. Then, continue playing the original script by selecting the Go option or pressing Ctrl-G (Go).

Where Select the Where? option from the Debugger Menu to see the nesting of scripts, procedures, and debugging levels. A series of frames (like boxes within boxes) are drawn on your workspace to show which part of the script is currently operating. Press Ctrl-W (Where?) to do the same thing as selecting the Where option from the Debugger Menu.

Quit Use the Quit option when you are ready to stop playing the script. The Debugger is exited and values which have been assigned to variables and arrays are retained.

Press Ctrl-Q (Quit) to do the same thing as selecting the Quit option from the Debugger Menu.

Pop This option lets you tell Paradox that you want to return to the previous line of the script before performing the current line. This is helpful when an error occurs after using the Value or MiniScript option of the Debugger Menu. By returning to the previous line, you have another chance to perform it.

Press Ctrl-P (Pop) to do the same thing as selecting the Pop option from the Debugger Menu.

Editor Select this option when you want to edit the current script. The Debugger is exited, script play is canceled, and the script is presented on your workspace for changes.

Press Ctrl-E (Edit) to do the same thing as selecting the Editor option from the Debugger Menu.

Remember that the Debugger presents only the lines which are to be performed. For example, if a procedure is encountered within the script, the lines within the procedure are skipped automatically unless the procedure is being performed. Otherwise, only the procedure heading is displayed.

When the script plays successfully, and the results are what you expect, be sure to delete the DEBUG command from the script. If it remains, the Debugger is initiated the next time the script is played. This may cause a problem if the script is played by someone who is not familiar with PAL.

APPLICATIONS

Use this command when you want to initiate the Debugger within a script. When the DEBUG command is encountered, the Debugger presents the next line at the bottom of your workspace. This gives you a chance to follow the effect of each command line performed.

For example, if a calculation is not providing the results that you expect, use the Debugger to verify each line. When the problem is corrected and the script plays successfully, delete the DEBUG command line from the script and save it again.

TYPICAL OPERATION

In this example you use the DEBUG command with the Test2 script.

1. Begin at the Main Menu and press **Alt-F10** to access the Script Menu.
2. Type **D** to select Debug. Paradox asks for the name of the script to be debugged.
3. Type **Test2** and press **Enter**. The Debugger presents the first line of the script at the bottom of the screen for your review. No error message appears on the workspace because the line's syntax is correct. The Main Menu line appears at the top of the screen.

4. Press **Ctrl-S** to step to the next command line in the script.
5. Press **Alt-F10** (Debugger Menu) and select the Value option by typing **V**.
6. When Paradox asks for the expression, type **rows** and press **Enter**. The value of rows (2) is presented on the workspace as shown in the following display.

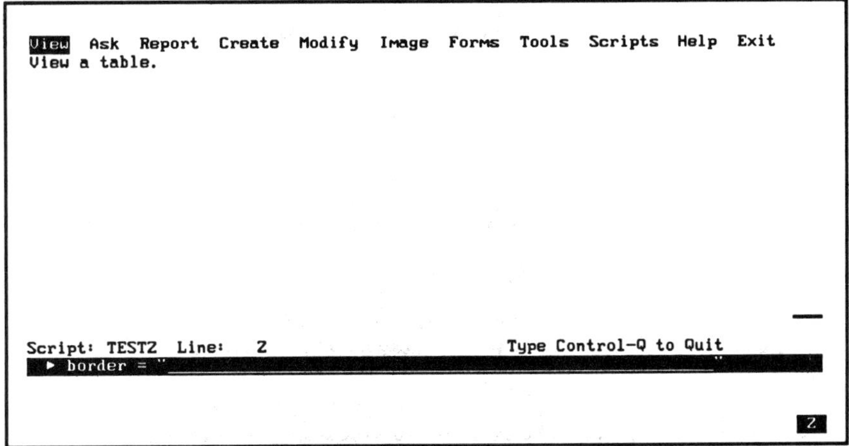

7. Type **Ctrl-S** to perform the current command line and step to the next line.
8. Press **Ctrl-N** four times to pass the next four command lines without performing them. The "rows = rows + 10" command line appears at the bottom of the screen.
9. Press **Alt-F10** (Debugger Menu) and select the Go option by typing **G**. The Debugger is released and the remaining lines of the script are played. When the script is completed, the Main Menu screen appears on your workspace.
10. Use the Scripts submenu to change the Test2 script. Insert the DEBUG command and delete the CLEAR command from the script so that it resembles the one in the following display.

```
Changing script C:\paradox3\test2                                    Script Ins
....+...10....+...20....+...30....+...40....+...50....+...60....+...70....+...80
rows = 2
border = "________________________________________________________"
@rows,5
?? rows
?? "  "
?? border
DEBUG
rows = rows + 10
@ rows,5
?? STRVAL(rows)+"     "+border
@ rows,30
SLEEP 10000
BEEP BEEP BEEP BEEP BEEP
```

11. Press **F10** (Menu) and select the Go option. The first line is drawn on your workspace and the Debugger presents the next line of the script at the bottom of the screen.

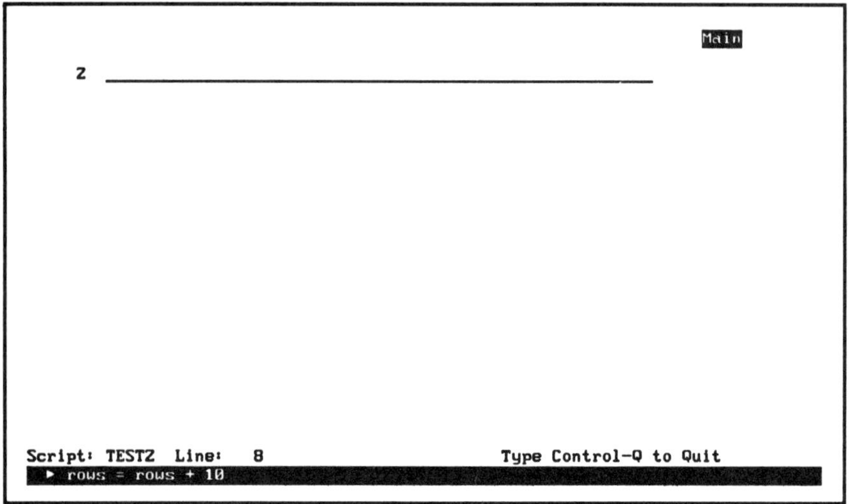

12. Press **Alt-F10** (Debugger Menu) and select the Where? option by typing **W**. A box appears for each nested procedure. Your screen resembles the following display.

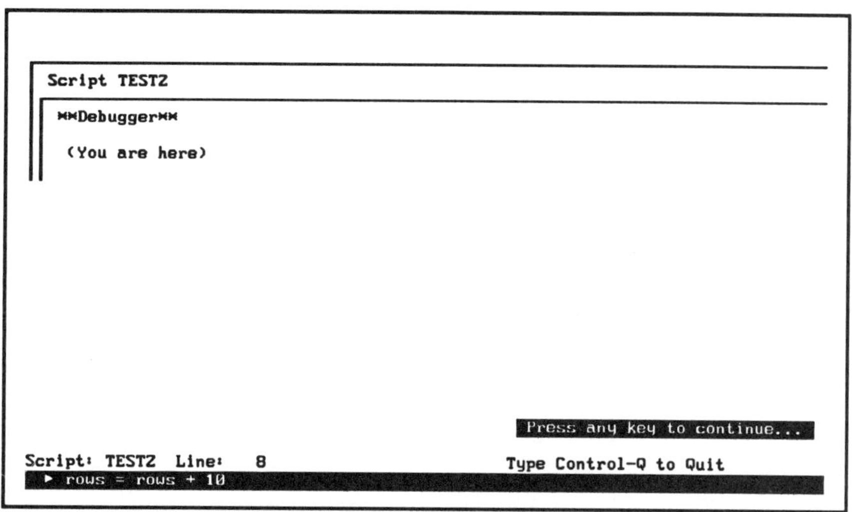

13. Press **Ctrl-S** (Step) to perform the current command line and present the next line until the BEEP command appears at the bottom of the screen.
14. Press **Ctrl-N** (Next) to skip each BEEP command. Since it is the last line of the script, the Main Menu appears immediately after this keystroke.
15. Use the Scripts submenu to edit Test2 by deleting the DEBUG command from the script. Press **F10** (Menu) and type **G** to play the script again.
16. Turn to Module 7 to continue the recommended learning sequence.

Module 24
DELETE

DESCRIPTION

When a table has served its purpose so that it is obsolete, use the DELETE command to remove the table and its family (indices, forms, reports) from the disk. This command format is:

```
DELETE <table name>
```

Replace <table name> with the name of a file with the .db extension that is available on the current disk. Unless provided in a variable, enclose <table name> with quotation marks. When this command is performed, Paradox removes the specified table and its family. A script error occurs if <table name> is not available when this command is encountered.

The DELETE command is an abbreviated form of several menu options that are available through the Paradox menu-driven system. By including the following command line in the script instead of the DELETE "Mailtx" command line, you achieve the same results.

```
Menu {Tools} {Delete} {Table} {Mailla} {Ok}
```

Remember that when the DELETE command is performed, the table and its family are removed from the disk immediately. The user is not asked for confirmation as in the menu-driven system. Write the script so that the user has a chance to abort the operation before the script performs the DELETE command.

APPLICATIONS

Use the DELETE command in your applications when a table needs to be removed from the disk. This helps keep the disk free of old, unused files.

For example, the user creates a table for Louisiana. Data is never entered into the table. Instead of the table and its family holding disk space, provide an option that lets the user perform deletion as part of the disk maintenance tasks.

Use the DELETE command to remove files from the disk instead of the DEL command available through DOS. Paradox deletes the table as well as all files (indices, forms, and reports) that are related to it from the disk. When you use DOS to do the same thing, you must be careful of an accidental deletion.

TYPICAL OPERATION

This example shows you how to use the DELETE command.

1. Type **V** (View), then type **Mailla** and press **Enter** to view the Mailla table. An empty Table View appears on your screen. The table and its family are holding disk space that is not being used.
2. Press **F8** (Clear Image) to remove the table from the screen.
3. Edit the Utility script. Insert the Delete option between the Newfile and Rename options as shown in the following display.

```
Changing script C:\paradox3\utility                              Script Ins

....+...10....+...20....+...30....+...40....+...50....+...60....+...70....+...80
; utility.sc - allows various tasks for Mail List application
while(true)
  clear
  showmenu
    "Zipcodes" : "Replace new zipcode for all customers with old zipcode.",
    "Newfile" : "Create a new Mail List customer file.",
    "Delete" : "Delete a Mail List customer file from disk.",              ◆
    "Rename" : "Renames an existing customer file.",
    "Passfile" : "Restricted - Access Password file."
    .
    .
    .
        ?? "Creating new file - Please Wait..."
        copy "Mailtx" mfile
        empty mfile
      endif
      release vars mfile
      clearall
    case mutility = "Delete" :                                              ◆
      clear                                                                 ◆
      @ 10,05                                                               ◆
      ?? "Enter the name of the customer file (e.g. Mailtx) "               ◆
      accept "A8" picture "&*&" to mfile                                    ◆
      if not isfile(mfile+".db")                                            ◆
        then                                                                ◆
        @ 21,05                                                             ◆
        ?? "That name does not exist - This option is aborted..."           ◆
        sleep 3000                                                          ◆
      else                                                                  ◆
        @ 21,05                                                             ◆
        ?? "Do you want to continue (Y/N)? "                                ◆
        accept "A1" picture "&" to ans                                      ◆
        if ans = "Y"                                                        ◆
          then                                                              ◆
          @ 21,05                                                           ◆
          clear eol                                                         ◆
          @ 21,05                                                           ◆
          ?? "Deleting file - Please Wait..."                               ◆
          delete mfile                                                      ◆
        else                                                                ◆
          @ 21,05                                                           ◆
          clear eol                                                         ◆
          @ 21,05                                                           ◆
          ?? "This operation is aborted..."                                 ◆
          sleep 3000                                                        ◆
        endif                                                               ◆
      endif                                                                 ◆
      release vars mfile,ans                                                ◆
    case mutility = "Rename" :
```

4. Press **F10** (Scripts Menu) and select the DO-IT! option.

5. Play the Mainmenu script.
6. Type **U** (Utilities), then type **D** (Delete).
7. Type **Maila** and press **Enter**. A message tells you that the customer file does not exist on the disk.
8. When the submenu returns, select the Delete option again. This time, type **Mailla** and press **Enter**. When asked if you want to continue, type **N** and press **Enter**. A message tells you that the operation is aborted.
9. When the submenu returns, select the Delete option again. This time, type **Mailla** and press **Enter**. When asked if you want to continue, type **Y** and press **Enter**. A message tells you that the file is removed from the disk. Return to the Main Menu.
10. Type **V** and press **Enter** to see a list of available tables. Use the arrow keys to move the list into view. Notice that the Mailla table is not included in the list. Redisplay the Main Menu.
11. Turn to Module 33 to continue the recommended learning sequence.

Module 25
DOS, DOSBIG

DESCRIPTION

This command makes a DOS prompt available without ending the Paradox session. When the DOS command is performed, all Paradox work is suspended temporarily. When ready to return to the Paradox workspace, type the word EXIT at the DOS A> prompt.

This command is an abbreviated form of several menu options that are available through the Paradox menu-driven system. By including the following command line in the script instead of the DOS command line, you achieve the same results.

```
Menu {Tools} {More} {ToDOS}
```

Do not load RAM resident programs when using the DOS command. For example, the PRINT and MODE commands cause problems for the current Paradox session.

The DOSBIG command is equivalent to the DOS command. However, the maximum amount of memory is allocated for the command or program. To provide the maximum memory, Paradox saves the current state before providing the DOS prompt to the user. This saving activity causes the DOSBIG command to be a little slower than the DOS command.

APPLICATIONS

While testing an application, use the SETKEY command and assign the DOS command to a specific key. If you need to access the DOS system, press the key. While in the DOS, run programs, commands, etc. that help you with the debugging process. When ready to return to the Paradox session, type the EXIT command at the system prompt and press Enter.

TYPICAL OPERATION

This example shows you how to use the DOS command.

1. Write the script called Doshelp so that it matches the one in the following display.

```
Designing script C:\paradox3\doshelp                                Script
....+...10....+...20....+...30....+...40....+...50....+...60....+...70....+...80
setkey "F5" DOS
```

2. Press **F10** (Scripts Menu) and select the Go option.
3. Press **F5** to run the DOS command. Your screen resembles the following display.

```
WARNING! Do not delete or edit Paradox objects, or load RAM-resident programs.
To return to Paradox, type exit.

The IBM Personal Computer DOS
Version 3.30 (C)Copyright International Business Machines Corp 1981, 1987
             (C)Copyright Microsoft Corp 1981, 1986

C:\PARADOX3>
```

4. From the system prompt, type **DIR** and press **Enter**. A full directory list scrolls past your screen. When it stops, your screen looks like Paradox is no longer available.
5. From the prompt, type **exit** and press **Enter**.
6. When the Main Menu returns to your screen, type **E** to select the Exit option and end the Paradox session.
7. Turn to Module 47 to continue the learning sequence.

Module 26
ECHO

DESCRIPTION

When a script plays, the screen does not change until the script changes it. For example, when the script performs the VIEW command, the table is not displayed on the screen. If it does appear, then the script encountered a WAIT command or it told Paradox to echo the effect of each command.

If you want to start or stop the display of each screen while the script plays, include the ECHO command in a script. There are three choices for this command.

```
ECHO FAST
ECHO SLOW
ECHO OFF
```

When you turn on the echoing activity, specify FAST or SLOW to tell Paradox the speed to play the script. To turn it off, use the ECHO OFF command. When the Paradox session begins, the echoing activity is turned off.

APPLICATIONS

Use the ECHO command in a script so that you or the user is able to watch the computer play the scripts. It is sometimes helpful when debugging a script since it is easier to follow the tasks as the script performs them.

TYPICAL OPERATION

This example shows you how to use the ECHO command.

1. Edit the Mainmenu script. Insert the ECHO SLOW command as one of the first few lines in the script as shown in the following display.

```
Changing script C:\paradox3\mainmenu                              Script Ins

....+...10....+...20....+...30....+...40....+...50....+...60....+...70....+...80
readlib "Maillist" Idcheck
echo slow
while (true)
  clear
  showmenu
    "View" : "Find and review customer information.",
    "Maintenance" : "Maintains table data.",
    "Report" : "Print the columnar report.",
    "Labels" : "Print mailing labels.",
    "Update" : "Batch update master table from a floppy disk.",
    "Summary" : "Provide statistics on subscription preferences.",
    "Configure" : "Change application configuration.",
    "Utilities" : "Perform various tasks for the Mail List application."
  default "View" to mchoice
  switch
  case mchoice = "View" :
    play "Custview"
  case mchoice = "Maintenance" :
    x = Idcheck()
    if x > "0" and x < "10"
      then
      play "Custmnt"
```

2. Press **F10** (Scripts Menu) and select the Go option.
3. Type **V** to select the View option.
4. When asked for the name of a customer file, type **Mailtx** and press **Enter**. Watch the screen display each operation as instructed by the scripts.
5. Press **Enter** twice so that a list of customers is displayed on the screen. Watch the screen display each task.
6. Press **Esc** to end the application.
7. Edit the Mainmenu script again. Change the ECHO SLOW command to an ECHO FAST command. Save and play the script.
8. Select the View option from the application menu and list all the Mailtx customers on the screen. This time the screens flash faster than during the previous run. However, it is still easy to follow the tasks.
9. When the menu returns, press **Esc** to end the application.
10. Change the Mainmenu script again. Insert the ECHO OFF command in the View option so that it matches the one in the following display.

```
Changing script C:\paradox3\mainmenu                                   Script Ins

....+...10....+...20....+...30....+...40....+...50....+...60....+...70....+...80
readlib "Maillist" Idcheck
echo fast
while (true)
  clear
  showmenu
    "View" : "Find and review customer information.",
    "Maintenance" : "Maintains table data.",
    "Report" : "Print the columnar report.",
    "Labels" : "Print mailing labels.",
    "Update" : "Batch update master table from a floppy disk.",
    "Summary" : "Provide statistics on subscription preferences.",
    "Configure" : "Change application configuration.",
    "Utilities" : "Perform various tasks for the Mail List application."
  default "View" to mchoice
  switch
  case mchoice = "View" :
    play "Custview"
    echo off
  case mchoice = "Maintenance" :
    x = Idcheck()
    if x > "0" and x < "10"
      then
```

11. Save and play the script. Select the View option for the Mailtx table. The operations are echoed to the screen.
12. Return to the application menu and select the View option for the Mailtx table. Since the ECHO OFF command turned off the echoing activity after the previous selection, the tasks are not displayed during this run.
13. Return to the application menu and press **Esc** to end it.
14. Edit the Mainmenu script again. Delete the two ECHO commands by positioning the cursor on the line and pressing **Ctrl-Y**.
15. Save the script with the DO-IT! command of the Scripts Menu.
16. Turn to Module 57 to continue the recommended learning sequence.

Module 27
EDIT

DESCRIPTION

As time passes, the information you have gathered will change. When the information is stored in a Paradox table, you want to update those records.

Use the EDIT command to tell Paradox that you want to change, delete, or add records to a specified table. The format of this command follows.

```
EDIT <table name>
```

Replace <table name> with the name of the file that contains the records to be changed. Unless provided in a variable, enclose <table name> with quotation marks. For example, EDIT "Mailtx" tells Paradox to make the table called Mailtx available for changes.

The EDIT command in a script is an abbreviated form of several menu options. By including the following command line in the script instead of the EDIT command line, you achieve the same results.

```
Menu {Modify} {Edit} {Mailtx}
```

When the EDIT command line is encountered, Paradox automatically provides the data in Table View. This form presents several records down the screen. However, only a few fields are visible across the screen. The following display shows a sample of the Table View form for Mailtx.

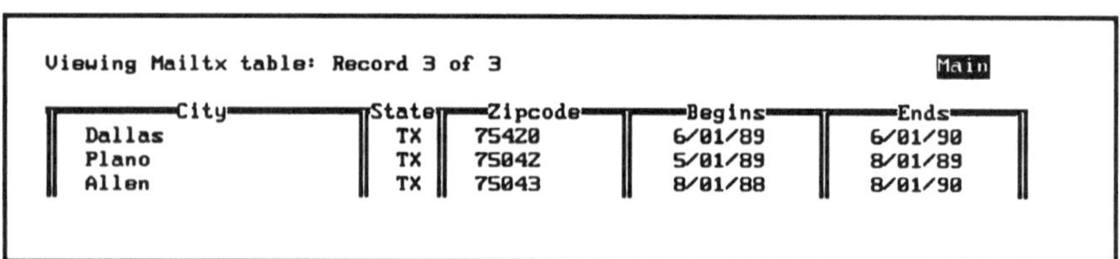

Viewing Mailtx table: Record 3 of 3 Main

City	State	Zipcode	Begins	Ends
Dallas	TX	75420	6/01/89	6/01/90
Plano	TX	75042	5/01/89	8/01/89
Allen	TX	75043	8/01/88	8/01/90

When the Table View is displayed on the screen, the cursor is positioned on the first record. To move the cursor to other records while in Table View, just press Up Arrow or Down Arrow. Other fields are made available by pressing Left Arrow or Right Arrow.

Paradox also provides a Forms View that presents only one record per screen. The fields are listed down the screen as in the following display.

```
Viewing Mailtx table with form F: Record 1 of 3                    Main

                                                         Mailtx   *   1

 Last Name:    Appleby
 First Name:   Shirley
 Middle Name:  Lynn
 Address 1:    2411 Abrams Rd
 Address 2:    # 111
 City:         Dallas
 State:        TX
 Zipcode:      75420
 Begins:        6/01/89
 Ends:          6/01/90
```

Press Up Arrow or Down Arrow to move the cursor from one field to another. If there are more than 20 fields, pressing Down Arrow moves the cursor to the second screen of fields.

If neither of the forms provided by Paradox is sufficient, design and save your own forms. These are called *custom forms*. Design these forms by using the Forms option on the Main Menu screen of the Paradox menu-driven system.

Custom forms provide several advantages. For example, the user sees only the fields you include in the form. Fields may be arranged on the screen so that they correspond to the input document. Include patterns (pictures) as often as possible to decrease the typing required from the user. Also, provide helpful information (e.g., a legend of special key presses) on the screen so that the user may work without having to refer to the application's documentation.

When a form is created, it is saved on disk so that it is available when the table is used. A maximum of ten forms may exist for each table. Replace the two automatic Paradox forms, or make your forms available as part of the other eight forms allowed for the specified table.

Since the EDIT command automatically presents the data in Table View, the script must specify the desired form. The following command lines tell Paradox to display the first record of Mailtx in the Form View that is provided.

```
edit "mailtx"
formkey
{Image} {Pickform} {F}
```

When the user presses the PgUp or PgDn keys, the previous or next record (respectively) is displayed on the screen. Press the Home key to move the cursor to the first record in the table. The End key tells Paradox to move the cursor to the last record in the table.

When the table is available on the screen, press F7 (FormKey) to switch between Forms View and Table View. For example, use the Table View to move the cursor to the desired record. Then press F7 (FormKey) again to return to the Forms View. Make the necessary changes and repeat the process until the table is updated. Then press F2 (DO-IT!). The editing capability is stopped. Paradox presents the records for viewing only. To remove the table from the workspace, press F8 (ClearImage).

If the table contains a large number of records, do not force the user to look for the desired record. Write your application so that the user is asked for the key value of that record (e.g., "Smith"). Use the LOCATE command or the QUERY, ENDQUERY command combination to search the table. When the record is found, make it available to the user. Otherwise, present a blank record so that a new record may be added to the table.

You must use extra care when writing a script so that the user does not accidentally get into trouble. Include as many of the special keystrokes as possible. By writing applications that are easy to use, you save yourself, as well as the user, a lot of time and confusion.

APPLICATIONS

Use this command in a script so that the user may change the data in a table. When this command line is encountered in a script, Paradox lets you change, delete, or add records in the specified table.

If the script that includes the EDIT command is played by another script, the table is presented for edit after the controlling scripts are played. For example, if Mainmenu plays a script that includes the EDIT command, the table is available for edit only when the menu is exited by pressing the Esc key.

After the EDIT command line, use the WAIT command within a WHILE, ENDWHILE loop to control the edit mode. The WAIT command tells the script to allow changes to one field, one record, or all records in the table.

The LOCATE command is usually included in scripts that allow changes to the data in a table. The user must provide specific field values that are included in the desired record (e.g., "Smith, John"). This information is used by the LOCATE command to quickly find the record in the table. When found, the record is displayed on the screen for the user. Otherwise, the script must present an error message to the user or a blank record so that the user may add the record to the table.

When the EDIT command is encountered, the user is responsible for finding the desired records within the table. For the script to maintain control and help the user, include the WAIT and LOCATE commands in the scripts that allow changes to the table.

TYPICAL OPERATION

This illustration shows you how to use the EDIT command.

1. Type **SEE** to use the Script Editor. When asked for the name of the script, type **Custmnt** and press **Enter**.
2. When the script is available on your screen, press **Ctrl-Y** until all lines are deleted.
3. Type the script that appears in the following display.

```
Changing script C:\paradox3\custmnt                                 Script

....+...10....+...20....+...30....+...40....+...50....+...60....+...70....+...80
;custmnt - customer maintenance script
clear
@ 10,10
?? "Enter the name of the table "
accept "a8" picture "&*&" to fileans
if not isblank(fileans)
  then
  if isfile(fileans+".db")
    then
    edit fileans
  else
    beep beep beep beep
    message "Table "+fileans+".db is not on the current data disk."
    sleep 2000
  endif
endif
; end custmnt
```

4. Press **F10** (Scripts Menu) and select the Go option.
5. When asked for the name of the table, type **FKDL** and press **Enter**. The computer beeps and the message "Table FKDL.db is not on the current data disk" appears in the lower right corner of the screen.
6. Select Script Play, type **Custmnt**, and press **Enter**.
7. When asked for the name of the table, type **Mailtx** and press **Enter**. Your screen resembles the following display.

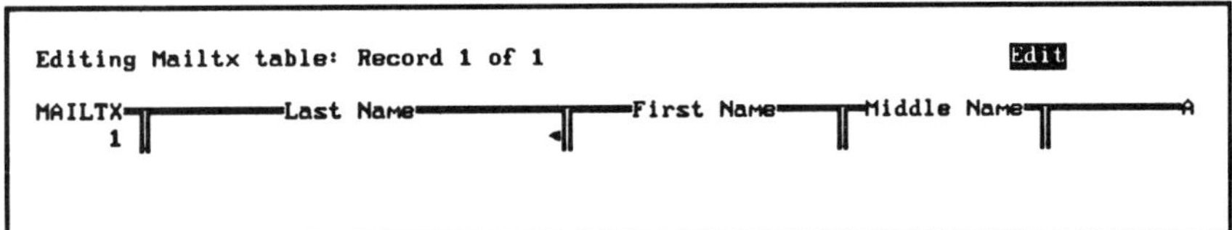

8. Type **Appleby** and press **Enter**. The cursor moves to the First Name field. Type **Shirley** and press **Enter**. The cursor moves to the Middle Name field.

9. Press **F2** (DO-IT!) to save the new record. A message appears in the lower right corner of the screen saying that the editing operation is ended. The table is available for viewing.

10. Press **F8** (Clear Image) to remove the table from the screen.

11. When the Main Menu returns, edit the script Custmnt.

12. The script currently displays the table in Table View so that all fields for one record are not available on the screen. Change the script so that records are presented in Forms View. Your script should match the one in the following display.

```
Changing script C:\paradox3\custmnt                                    Script Ins

....+...10....+...20....+...30....+...40....+...50....+...60....+...70....+...80
;custmnt - customer maintenance script
clear
@ 10,10
?? "Enter the name of the table "
accept "a8" picture "&*&" to fileans
if not isblank(fileans)
  then
  if isfile(fileans+".db")
    then
    edit fileans
    formkey {Image} {PickForm} {F}                                              ◆
  else
    beep beep beep beep
    message "Table "+fileans+".db is not on the current data disk."
    sleep 2000
  endif
endif
; end custmnt
```

13. Press **F10** (Scripts Menu) and select the Go option.

14. When asked for the name of the table, type **Mailtx** and press **Enter**. Your screen resembles the following display.

```
Editing Mailtx table with form F: Record 1 of 1                         Edit

                                                              Mailtx   *    1

 Last Name:    Appleby                    ◄
 First Name:   Shirley
 Middle Name:
 Address 1:
 Address 2:
 City:
 State:
 Zipcode:
 Begins:
 Ends:
```

15. Press **Enter** twice until the cursor is positioned on the Middle Name field. Type **Lynn** and press **Enter**. Continue typing the record until your screen matches the following display. Do not press Enter for the Ends field until your screen matches the display.

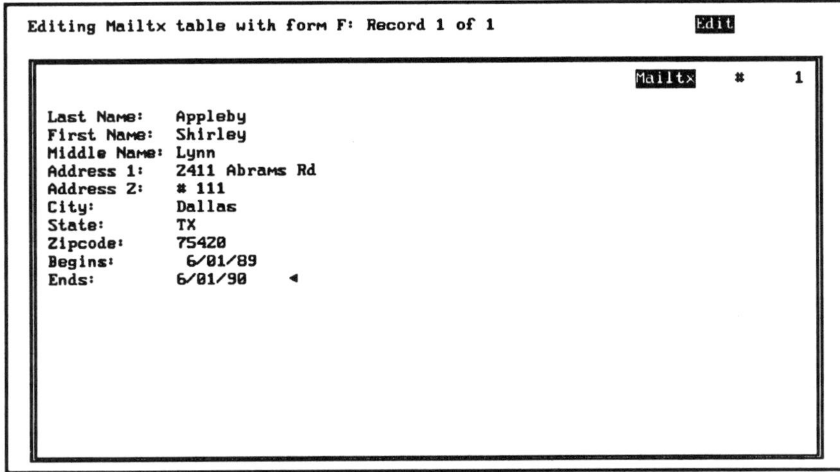

```
Editing Mailtx table with form F: Record 1 of 1                    Edit

                                                          Mailtx   #    1
Last Name:     Appleby
First Name:    Shirley
Middle Name:   Lynn
Address 1:     2411 Abrams Rd
Address 2:     # 111
City:          Dallas
State:         TX
Zipcode:       75420
Begins:         6/01/89
Ends:          6/01/90     ◄
```

16. When you press Enter after typing the Ends field, a second blank record is made available. Type the following record until your screen matches the display.

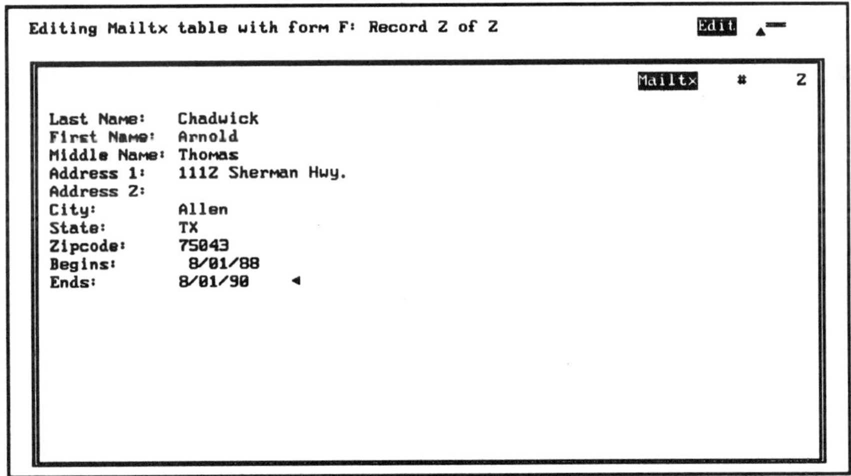

```
Editing Mailtx table with form F: Record 2 of 2                    Edit

                                                          Mailtx   #    2
Last Name:     Chadwick
First Name:    Arnold
Middle Name:   Thomas
Address 1:     1112 Sherman Hwy.
Address 2:
City:          Allen
State:         TX
Zipcode:       75043
Begins:         8/01/88
Ends:          8/01/90     ◄
```

17. Press **Enter** to move the cursor to record number 3. Press **F7** (FormKey) to return to Table View temporarily. Notice that the records are currently in alphabetical order. Press **F7** (FormKey) again to return to Forms View.

18. Type the third record so that your screen matches the display.

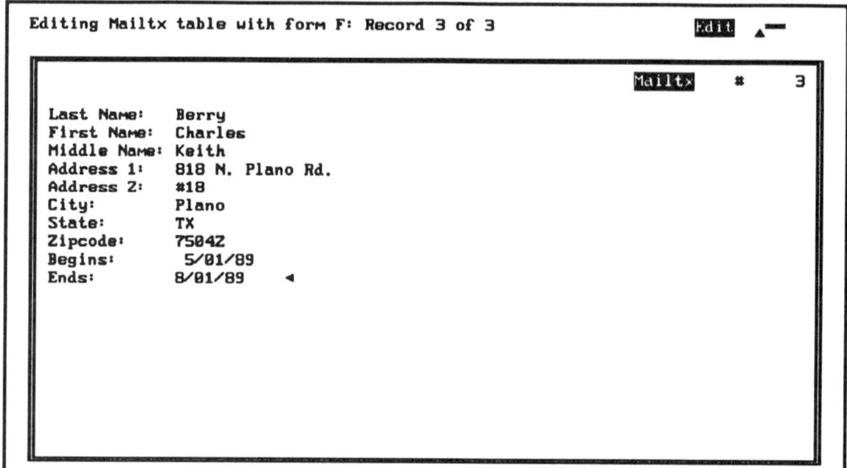
Editing Mailtx table with form F: Record 3 of 3 Edit

Mailtx # 3

Last Name: Berry
First Name: Charles
Middle Name: Keith
Address 1: 818 N. Plano Rd.
Address 2: #18
City: Plano
State: TX
Zipcode: 75042
Begins: 5/01/89
Ends: 8/01/89

19. Press **Enter** to move to record number 4. Press **F7** (FormKey) to see if the records are still in order. Your screen matches the following display.

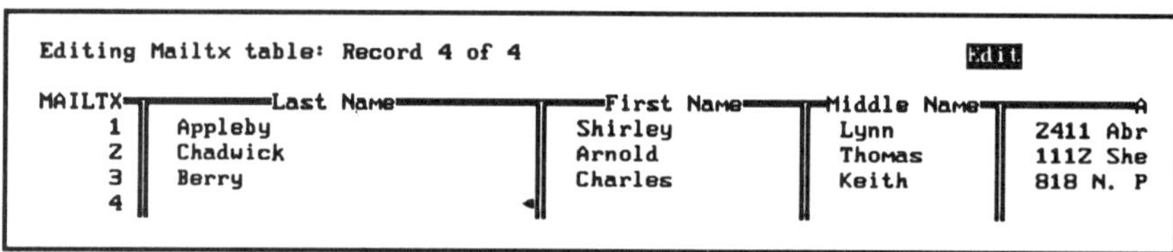
Editing Mailtx table: Record 4 of 4 Edit

MAILTX	Last Name	First Name	Middle Name	A
1	Appleby	Shirley	Lynn	2411 Abr
2	Chadwick	Arnold	Thomas	1112 She
3	Berry	Charles	Keith	818 N. P
4				

20. Press **F2** (DO-IT!). The table changes from editing mode to viewing mode. Notice that the records are now in proper sequence.
21. Press **F7** (FormKey) to return to Forms View.
22. Press **F8** (Clear Image) to remove the table from the workspace.
23. Play the Mainmenu script. The application menu is displayed at the top of the screen.
24. Press **Enter** to select the Maintenance option.
25. When asked for the ID code, type **DLS1** and press **Enter**.
26. When asked for the name of the table, type **Mailtx** and press **Enter**. The application menu returns to the screen.
27. Press **Esc** to exit the application. Notice that the table is finally presented for editing.
28. Press **F2** (DO-IT!) to change from the edit mode to the view mode.
29. Press **F8** (Clear Image) to remove the table from the workspace. Since the application menu is not available you know that the script is not currently in control.
30. Turn to Module 101 to continue the recommended learning sequence.

Module 28
EDITLOG

DESCRIPTION

The EDITLOG command is used to reverse changes, reindex the data, mark a position in a log, or make all changes to the current table permanent. The EDITLOG command uses the Paradox transaction log to control the table activity.

Use the EDITLOG command with any of the options in the following command syntax.

```
EDITLOG [MARK/REVERT/INDEX/PERMANENT]
```

Include the MARK option to identify a point in the transaction log as a stop or start point. Changes made to the table can be undone from the latest change to the previous marker.

The REVERT option reverses all changes recorded in the transaction log until it finds a marker. If several markers are set, you can undo the changes for each marker set. If no marker has been set, all changes to the table are reversed.

Use the INDEX option to rebuild the table's primary and secondary index files if the tables are indexed. It improves performance when using the QUERY, LOCATE, and ZOOM commands. The EDITLOG REVERT option still functions after the reindex operation.

Include the PERMANENT option to reindex the table and delete the transaction log that is used to reverse the changes made to the table. Please remember that you cannot reverse changes made to a table after using the EDITLOG PERMANENT command.

When several tables are on the workspace at the same time, there is a separate transaction log for each table. The EDITLOG command cannot be used with linked tables on multi-table forms. However, the interactive UNDO Ctrl-U feature reverses all changes made to linked tables.

NOTE: This command is available in version 3.0 and higher.

APPLICATIONS

Use the EDITLOG command to control all changes made to tables during transaction processing (invoicing, billing, etc.). The different options allow you to group changes together into transactions.

The EDITLOG command is a hybrid of the COEDIT and EDIT commands. The COEDIT command maintains your indexes but keeps no transaction log. The EDIT command keeps a log, but indexes are not maintained. EDITLOG has the best features of both commands.

Include the EDITLOG command in scripts that perform editing and data-entry processing. A run error occurs if you try to use the command elsewhere.

TYPICAL OPERATION

This example shows you how to use the EDITLOG commands.

1. Type **SEW** to use the Script Editor to write a new script. When asked for the name of the script, type **Custmnt1** and press **Enter**.
2. Type the script that appears in the following display.

```
Designing script C:\paradox3\custmnt1                              Script Ins

....+...10....+...20....+...30....+...40....+...50....+...60....+...70....+...80
; custmnt1.sc - customer maintenance screen
clear
@ 10,10
?? "Enter the name of the table "
accept "a8" picture "&*&" to fileans
if not isblank(fileans)
  then
  if isfile(fileans+".db")
    then
    edit fileans
    formkey {Image} {PickForm} {F}
    editlog mark
    while (true)
      wait table
        prompt "Press [F2] to save, [Alt-C] revert to mark, [Alt-M] to mark",
        "[Alt -I] to index (table must be indexed)"
          until -23, -46, -50, "F2"
      switch
        case retval = "F2" :                    ; F2 save and exit
          quitloop
        case retval = -23 :
          message "Reindexing table ...."        ; Alt-I Reindex
          editlog index
          editlog mark
        case retval = -50 :                     ; Alt-M Mark place in log
          message "Marking place in edit log."
          editlog mark
        case retval = -46 :                     ; Alt-C Revert back to mark
          message "Revering back to last mark."
          editlog revert
      endswitch
    endwhile
    do_it!
    clearall
  else
    beep beep beep beep
    message "Table "+fileans+".db is not on the current data disk."
    sleep 2000
  endif
endif
; end custmnt1.sc
```

3. Press **F10** (Scripts Menu) and select the Go option.

4. When asked for the name of the table, type **Mailtx** and press **Enter**. Your screen resembles the following display.

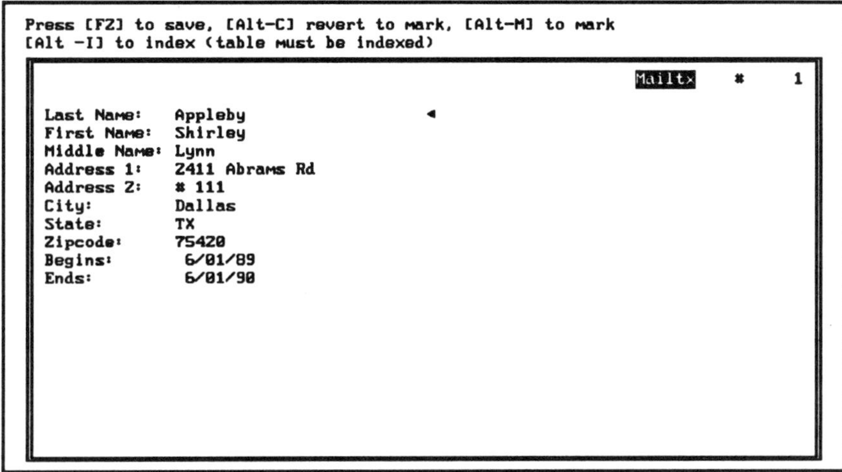

5. Change the Last Name field of the first record from Appleby to Peachtree. Press **Alt-M** to place a mark in the edit log.
6. Change the Last Name in the second record from Berry to Nutt.
7. Press **Alt-C** to reverse the changes in the second record from Nutt back to Berry. Notice that the change to the first record was not undone though the change to the second record returned to the original last name.
8. Press **F2** to make any changes to the table permanent.
9. Review the table to verify the changes. Then, change Peachtree back to Appleby and save the change.
10. Turn to Module 41 to continue the recommended learning sequence.

Module 29
EMPTY

DESCRIPTION

This command lets you remove all records from a table with one command. Using it leaves an empty table structure on the disk in seconds. The format for the EMPTY command follows.

```
EMPTY <table name>
```

Replace <table name> with the name of a data file (table) that exists on the disk. Unless provided in a variable, enclose it with quotation marks. A script error occurs if the table does not exist on the data disk.

This command is an abbreviated form of several menu options that are available through the Paradox menu-driven system. By including the following command line in the script instead of the EMPTY "Addrecs" command line, you achieve the same results.

```
Menu {Tools} {More} {Empty} {Addrecs} {Ok}
```

When this command line is encountered in a script, all records in the specified table are immediately deleted. The user is not given the chance to confirm or abort the operation as with the menu option command line.

APPLICATIONS

Use the EMPTY command when you have a table with records that are no longer needed for your application (i.e., delete records after they have been used to update the master file).

When writing the application, decide if you need to keep the data to update the master table. Use the records as an historical activity trail. Include the ADD or COPY commands in the script to save the records to another table before the EMPTY command is performed.

For example, send a copy of the Addrecs and Delrecs table records to history tables called Addhist and Delhistc. Remember, the ADD and COPY commands provide different results.

The ADD command tells Paradox to combine the records being sent with the existing records in the history table. For example, the destination table contains all records from the Addhist table as well as the Addrecs table.

Use the COPY command when you want to replace the current history table with the source table. All records that were kept in the destination table are gone. It is exactly like the source table.

Once the source records are saved in another table, remove all records from the Addrecs and Delrecs tables with the EMPTY command. This is a good technique to include in your scripts because it helps keep the master table from being updated by those records again. The empty table structures are available immediately for the next batch of table updates.

TYPICAL OPERATION

This example shows you how to use the EMPTY command.

1. View the Addrecs and Delrecs tables to verify that records exist in each table. Then clear the workspace so that the Main Menu line appears across the top of the screen.
2. Edit the Mainmenu script. Change the Update option of the script so that it matches the one in the following display.

```
Changing script C:\paradox3\mainmenu                                    Script Ins

....+...10....+...20....+...30....+...40....+...50....+...60....+...70....+...80
    report "Mailtx" "1"
    play "prtnorm"
  case mchoice = "Update" :
    if isfile("Delrecs.db")
      then
      clear
      @ 10,10
      ?? "Deleting customers - Please Wait..."
      subtract "Delrecs" "Mailtx"
      empty "Delrecs"                                                        ◆
    endif
    if isfile("Addrecs.db")
      then
      clear
      @ 10,10
      ?? "Adding customers - Please Wait..."
      add "Addrecs" "Mailtx"
      empty "Addrecs"                                                        ◆
    endif
    clearall
  case mchoice = "Configure" :
    @ 10,10
```

3. Press **F10** (Scripts Menu) and select the Go option. When the application menu appears across the top of the screen, type **U** to select the Update option.
4. Press **Esc** to exit the application and return to the Main Menu screen.
5. Type **V** to select the View option from the Main Menu line. When asked for the name of the table, type **Addrecs** and press **Enter**. The table is empty. Press **F8** (Clear Image) to remove the empty table form from the workspace.
6. View the Delrecs table. An empty table form appears on the workspace. Press **F8** (Clear Image) to clear the workspace.
7. Turn to Module 9 to continue the recommended learning sequence.

Module 30
EXECPROC

DESCRIPTION

Use the EXECPROC command to perform a procedure that does not require arguments. The proper command syntax follows:

```
EXECPROC <procname>
```

Substitute the name of a procedure for <procname>. Provide all or part of the procedure name through a variable. Remember, the procedure must not require arguments.

NOTE: EXECPROC is only valid in Paradox version 2.0 and above.

APPLICATIONS

The EXECPROC command is used like the EXECUTE command except it performs a procedure. Remember that the called procedure must not require arguments.

TYPICAL OPERATION

This illustration shows you how to use the EXECPROC command.

1. From the Main Menu, type **SEW** and write the Exectest script so that it matches the following PAL command lines.

```
Designing script C:\paradox3\exectest                              Script
....+...10....+...20....+...30....+...40....+...50....+...60....+...70....+...80
; exectest.sc - tests the execproc command
PROC OPT1()
  ? "Option 1 has been selected - Press the Enter key"
  ACCEPT "A1" TO X
ENDPROC

PROC OPT2()
  ? "Option 2 has been selected - Press the Enter key"
  ACCEPT "A1" TO X
ENDPROC

PROC OPT3()
  ? "Option 3 has been selected - Press the Enter key"
  ACCEPT "A1" TO X
ENDPROC

clear
? "Select a procedure by typing 1, 2, or 3:  "
ACCEPT "A1" picture "{1,2,3}" TO X
execproc "OPT" + X
; end exectest.sc
```

2. Press **F10** (Scripts Menu) and select the Go option. Remember, for this script you must select a number between 0 and 4. Notice how the procedure you selected is executed with the EXECPROC command.
3. Play the script several times and test 1, 2, 3, and 4. Notice that when you type four, the computer beeps since the number is not included in the picture clause of the last ACCEPT command line.
4. Turn to Module 86 to continue the recommended learning sequence.

Module 31
EXECUTE

DESCRIPTION

When you include this command in a script, you let the user perform a Paradox menu-driven option without being aware of it. Ask the user for specific information and then use the EXECUTE command to perform a menu option that requires the information provided by the user. The format for this command follows.

```
EXECUTE <script string>
```

Replace <script string> with the command you want Paradox to perform. If necessary, include variables in <script string> to provide the required information. Unless provided in a variable, enclose the command line with quotation marks.

For example, the following command lines let the user edit a selected field instead of one specified by the script.

```
showmenu
  "Address 1" : "",
  "Address 2" : "",
  "City" : "",
  "State" : "",
  "Zipcode" : "",
  "Quit" : ""
default "Address 1" to mchoice
if mchoice < > "Quit"
  then
  execute "moveto [" +mchoice+ "]"
  wait field message "Press F2=menu, Esc=quit..." until "F2", "Esc"
  do_it!
  if retval = "Esc"
    then
    quitloop
  endif
else
  do_it!
  clearall
  quit
endif
```

A list of field names appears in a menu at the top of the screen. The user selects the field for the cursor position. When the table is displayed, the cursor is positioned on the requested field.

APPLICATIONS

Use the EXECUTE to submit a command with variable information for execution. Paradox generates a temporary script (called Execute) that is performed as a result of the EXECUTE command.

TYPICAL OPERATION

This example shows you how to use the EXECUTE command.

1. Edit the Test2 script. Change it so that it matches the following script.

```
Changing script C:\paradox3\test2                              Script Ins

....+...10....+...20....+...30....+...40....+...50....+...60....+...70....+...80
while (true)                                                                   ◆
clear                                                                          ◆
edit "mailtx"
showmenu                                                                       ◆
  "Address 1" :"" ,                                                            ◆
  "Address 2" :"" ,                                                            ◆
  "City" :"",                                                                  ◆
  "State" :"" ,                                                                ◆
  "Zipcode" :"" ,                                                              ◆
  "Quit" : ""                                                                  ◆
default "Address 1" to mchoice                                                 ◆
if mchoice <> "Quit"                                                           ◆
  then                                                                         ◆
  execute "moveto [" +mchoice+ "]"                                             ◆
  wait field message "Press F2= menu, Esc=quit..." until "F2", "Esc"           ◆
  do_it!                                                                       ◆
  if retval = "Esc"                                                            ◆
    then                                                                       ◆
    quitloop                                                                   ◆
  endif                                                                        ◆
else                                                                           ◆
  do_it!                                                                       ◆
  clearall                                                                     ◆
  quit                                                                         ◆
endif                                                                          ◆
clearall                                                                       ◆
endwhile                                                                       ◆
release vars mchoice                                                           ◆
```

2. Select the Go option of the Scripts Menu.
3. The list of available fields appears in a menu across the top of the screen. Type **C** to select the City option. The table appears on the screen and the cursor is positioned in the City field of the first record.
4. Press **F2** to return to the menu.
5. Type **Z** to select the Zipcode field.
6. Press **F2** to return to the menu.
7. Type **Q** to select the Quit option.
8. Turn to Module 30 to continue the recommended learning sequence.

Module 32
EXIT

DESCRIPTION

The EXIT and the QUIT commands are similar since they both immediately stop the application's play. When the QUIT command is included in a script, control is given to the Paradox menu-driven system. The EXIT command ends the Paradox session and returns control to DOS.

This command combines three menu-driven options that may appear in a recorded script. It is equivalent to the following recorded script line.

```
Menu {Exit} {Yes}
```

Use the EXIT command or the menu command sequence in a script. The results are exactly the same.

The EXIT command is an abbreviated menu command that stops the application immediately, ends the Paradox session, and returns the user to the system prompt. Use this command instead of the QUIT command when the users of your application are not familiar with the Paradox menu-driven system.

APPLICATIONS

Most custom applications are written so that they are initiated at the system prompt (e.g., A>PARADOX WEEKCALC). By returning that prompt when the work is complete, the application limits the user's options.

Include the EXIT command in your Paradox applications when you want to return the user to the system prompt. This helps the user who is not familiar with the Paradox menu-driven system. It also helps protect your scripts, tables, and forms.

For example, an application's first script usually provides a menu of options on the screen. It allows one to use the application or quit to the system prompt.

When ready to quit, the user selects the option from the menu. As soon as the EXIT command in the script is encountered, Paradox ends the application and the Paradox session. The next thing the user sees on the screen is the system A> prompt. Your application is easy for the user to begin and end.

TYPICAL OPERATION

This example shows you how to use the EXIT command.

1. Edit the Weekcalc script.
2. Position the cursor on the first line of the script. Type **exit** and press **Ctrl-Y** to remove the rest of the previous QUIT command line. Your script resembles the one in the following display.

```
Changing script C:\paradox3\weekcalc                                    Script
....+...10....+...20....+...30....+...40....+...50....+...60....+...70....+...80
exit                                                                           ◆
clear
@ 8,0
text
                    This option counts the number of weeks
                    between two dates. The results are
                    displayed at the bottom of the screen.

                    Under the results line is an option. Type
                    0 (zero) to do another calculation.
                    Do this as often as necessary.

                    When ready to return to the previous menu,
                    type any number except zero.
endtext
sleep 5000
for tcontinue from 0 to 1
  clear
fromdate = today()
todate = today()
@ 10,10
?? "Enter the beginning date "
```

3. Press **F10** (Scripts Menu) and select the Go option. The next thing you see is the system prompt. When Paradox encountered the EXIT command in Weekcalc, all script play was cancelled and the session ended. The DOS prompt appears on your screen.
4. Type **Paradox3 Weekcalc** and press **Enter**. You know that the session is started since the disk is read and the cursor moves on your screen. As soon as Weekcalc is played, the session is ended.
5. Type **Paradox3** to begin another session.
6. Use the Editor to change Weekcalc. Delete the EXIT command line from the first line in the script. Then add an EXIT command to the last line of the script as in the following display.

```
Changing script C:\paradox3\weekcalc                                    Script
....+...10....+...20....+...30....+...40....+...50....+...60....+...70....+...80
.
.
.
endfor
@ 21,05
?? "There are "+strval(count)+" weeks between "
?? fromdate
?? "thru"
?? todate
@ 23,05
?? "Type 0 to do another calc, type any other number to quit "
accept "N" picture "#" to tcontinue
endfor
exit
```

7. Press **F10** (Scripts Menu) and select the Go option.
8. The script is played. When asked for the dates, provide two valid dates. Then, type **3** and press **Enter** to get out of the loop. As soon as the EXIT command is performed, Paradox ends the session. The system prompt appears on your screen.
9. Type **Paradox3 Weekcalc** and press **Enter**. Type two dates and let the script give you the results. Type **3** and press **Enter** to get out of the loop. The system prompt is the next thing you see on your screen.
10. Turn to Module 102 to continue the recommended learning sequence.

Module 33
FIRSTSHOW

DESCRIPTION

The FIRSTSHOW command is used to move the current image to the top of the workspace. The proper syntax for this command is:

```
FIRSTSHOW
```

NOTE: FIRSTSHOW is only valid in PARADOX 2.0 and above.

APPLICATIONS

In a PAL program, it is helpful to use the FIRSTSHOW command to move a desired screen image to the top of the workspace. If you place the image you want your user to view at the top of your workspace, it is easier for them to see and use.

TYPICAL OPERATION

This illustration shows you how to use the FIRSTSHOW command.

1. Type **SEW** to use the script editor. When asked for the name of the script, type **Fstshow** and press **Enter**.
2. Type the following PAL command lines.

```
Designing script C:\paradox3\fstshow                                Script

....+...10....+...20....+...30....+...40....+...50....+...60....+...70....+...80
; Fstshow.sc - Uses the FIRSTSHOW command
clear
view "Mailtx"
view "Mailok"
firstshow
wait table
  message "Press Esc to continue..."
  until "Esc"
moveto 1
firstshow
wait table
  message "Press Esc to continue..."
  until "Esc"
moveto 2
firstshow
wait table
  message "Press Esc to continue..."
  until "Esc"
clearall
; end fstshow.sc
```

3. Press **F10** (Scripts Menu) and select the Go option. Notice that the Mailok table view is at the top of the screen.
4. Press **Esc** to see both open tables on the screen.
5. Press **Esc** again to return to the Mailok table.
6. Press **Esc** to return to the Paradox Main Menu.
7. Turn to Module 49 to continue the recommended learning sequence.

Module 34
FOR, ENDFOR

DESCRIPTION

When a set of command lines within your script needs to be performed several times, enclose the set with a FOR, ENDFOR loop. It allows you to write a routine once and execute that piece of the script until a specified criteria is met. This process is called *looping*. Redundant code is therefore avoided and the script is easier to follow when changes are needed.

For example, you want the user to print a sample of a label and adjust the paper in the printer until the label is properly aligned. By performing the same commands until the user decides to quit, the application is flexible, short, and efficient. The format of this command combination follows.

```
FOR <variable> <<FROM <first> >>
               <<TO <last> >>
               <<STEP <step> >>
    <commands>
ENDFOR
```

The FOR command marks the beginning of the loop. The ENDFOR identifies the end of the loop. When you use the FOR command, there must be an ENDFOR command to match it. The two commands are always used as a pair.

The <variable> is the name of a variable whose value is checked each time the loop is processed. When the value meets the limit set by the TO clause, Paradox stops processing the loop and continues with the next line of the script following the ENDFOR command.

When the FROM clause is included, the variable is set to the value specified by <first> when the FOR command line is encountered. Once the looping process begins, this clause is no longer used.

Include the STEP clause to tell Paradox that each time the loop is processed, increase the variable by the value specified by <step>. When the variable is greater than the value specified by <last>, the looping activity is stopped and Paradox performs the line that follows the ENDFOR command. If the STEP clause is not included in the FOR command, Paradox increases the value of <variable> by 1.

The FROM, TO, and STEP clauses are optional. However, the TO clause is usually included to set the stopping point for the loop. Replace <first> and <last> with a date or a number as the limits for the FROM and TO clauses. Replace <step> with a positive or negative number; a date is not allowed.

Replace <commands> with one or more command lines that you want performed each time the loop is processed. For example, include the command lines that print a sample label and then asks the user if another sample is needed. The user's answer controls the looping process.

There are times when you need to include at least one FOR, ENDFOR command combination as part of <commands>. When a loop exists within another loop, it is called a *nested loop*. Use as many loops as you need but make sure that you use a different variable for each FOR command line.

If the QUITLOOP command is performed within a FOR, ENDFOR loop, the looping is stopped immediately. Paradox then performs the line following the ENDFOR command and finishes playing the rest of the script.

If the LOOP command is performed within a FOR, ENDFOR loop, all command lines between the LOOP and ENDFOR commands are not performed. The variable that controls the loop is evaluated to determine if the specified criteria is met. If not, the variable's value is increased (only when the STEP clause is included) and the looping continues. If the criteria is met, processing continues with the command line that follows the ENDFOR command.

To successfully include the QUITLOOP or LOOP commands in the FOR, ENDFOR loop, you must use the IF, ENDIF command combination. This lets you set criteria that must be met before the QUITLOOP or LOOP commands are performed; otherwise, they are skipped.

Be careful that the value of the variable is changed eventually. Since the loop continues being processed until the value of <variable> is greater than <last>, your application may get stuck within the loop.

If you suspect that this has happened, press the Ctrl-Break key combination to stop the script and access the Debugger. Before cancelling the script's play, use the Debugger to verify that the value of the variable is not being changed. Then edit the script and try again.

APPLICATIONS

Use the FOR, ENDFOR command combination to enclose command lines that need to be performed several times. For example, the command lines required to count the number of weeks between 04/14/89 and 06/01/89 follow.

```
tcount = 0
FOR tdate FROM 04/14/89 TO 06/01/89 STEP 7
  tcount = tcount + 1
ENDFOR
```

When the limits are included in the FOR command, they are *hardcoded*. This line in the script must be edited each time that the limits change. Instead, let the user or the table provide the limits as the values of variables or fields. For example, the user is asked for the beginning date and the ending date. The answers are stored to the variables called "fromdate" and "todate" as follows.

```
tcount = 0
FOR tdate FROM fromdate TO todate STEP 7
  tcount = tcount + 1
ENDFOR
```

Now it is possible for the limits to change at any time. This flexiblity is especially helpful because the script does not have to accommodate the change.

Always look for ways to make your scripts more efficient. The quality and speed of your application benefits the user as well as yourself. Use the FOR, ENDFOR command combination as often as possible to make your scripts short, effective, and easy to change.

TYPICAL OPERATION

This example shows you how to use the FOR, ENDFOR command combination.

1. Type **SEW** to write a new script.
2. When asked for the name of the script, type **Weekcalc** and press **Enter**.
3. Type the script so that your screen resembles the following display.

```
Designing script C:\paradox3\weekcalc                              Script

....+...10....+...20....+...30....+...40....+...50....+...60....+...70....+...80
fromdate = today()
todate = today()
@ 10,10
?? "Enter the beginning date "
accept "D" picture "##/##/##" to fromdate
@ 12,10
?? "Enter the ending date "
accept "D" picture "##/##/##" to todate
count = 0
for tdate from fromdate to todate step 7
  count = count + 1
endfor
@ 21,05
?? "There are "+strval(count)+" weeks between "
?? fromdate
?? "thru"
?? todate
sleep 2500
```

4. Press **F10** (Scripts Menu) and select the Go option by typing **G**.
5. When asked for the beginning date, type **040189** and press **Enter**.

6. Type **043089** for the ending date. Press **Enter**. Your screen resembles the following display.

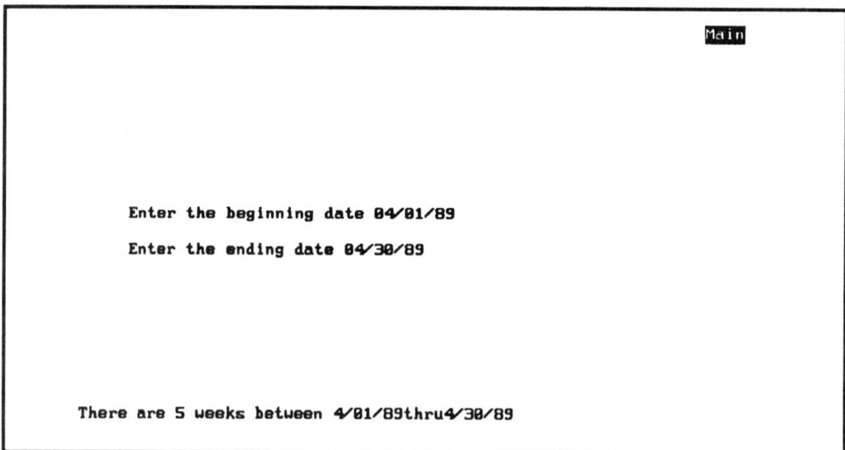

7. When the Main Menu returns to your screen, change Weekcalc so that it resembles the following display. You will add two lines to the top and three lines to the bottom.

```
Changing script C:\paradox3\weekcalc                                  Script Ins

....+...10....+...20....+...30....+...40....+...50....+...60....+...70....+...80
for tcontinue from 0 to 1                                                      ◆
  clear                                                                        ◆
fromdate = today()
todate = today()
@ 10,10
?? "Enter the beginning date "
accept "D" picture "##/##/##" to fromdate
@ 12,10
?? "Enter the ending date "
accept "D" picture "##/##/##" to todate
count = 0
for tdate from fromdate to todate step 7
  count = count + 1
endfor
@ 21,05
?? "There are "+strval(count)+" weeks between "
?? fromdate
?? "thru"
?? todate
@ 23,05                                                                        ◆
?? "Type 0 to do another calc, type any other number to quit "                 ◆
accept "N" picture "#" to tcontinue                                            ◆
endfor
sleep 2500
```

8. Press **F10** (Scripts Menu) and select the Go option by typing **G**.

9. Type **040189** and **043089** for the beginning and ending dates. Press **Enter** after each date. The bottom of your screen now asks if you want to do another calculation. This loop is controlled by you — not the script.

10. Type **0** and press **Enter**.
11. The screen clears and you are asked for the beginning date. Type some dates and continue this loop as long as you want.
12. When ready to quit, type a number other than zero.
13. Turn to Module 97 to continue the recommended learning sequence.

Module 35
FORMTABLES

DESCRIPTION

Provide as much error-checking in your applications as possible. For example, ensure that a table exists and is not locked, or a form exists before using it. Otherwise, the application user gets an error or warning message.

Prior to Paradox 3.0, a form or report involved only the table for which it was created. Now, a form or report can include information from other tables. Use the FORMTABLES command to identify the tables used in a multi-table form. The proper syntax for this command follows.

```
FORMTABLES <tablename> <formname> <arrayname>
```

Replace <tablename> with the name of the Paradox table to be examined. Before issuing the FORMTABLES command, verify that the table exists.

Specify the form number of the table by replacing <formname> with "F" or a number of 1 through 14. Before issuing the FORMTABLES command, use the ISMULTIFORM( ) function to determine if the specified form is a multi-table form.

Provide the name of the array to receive the other tables involved in the multi-table form in <arrayname>. If the array does not exist, Paradox creates it automatically. An array element is created for each table name included in the multi-table form.

NOTE: This command is available in version 3.0 and higher.

APPLICATIONS

The FORMTABLES command is valid only for multi-table forms. Before issuing the FORMTABLES command, verify that the table and its form exists. Then, use the ISMULTIFORM( ) function to determine if the form includes information from other tables.

When the FORMTABLES command is issued for a single-table form, the array is not created (or changed) and causes an error. If any of the tables, or the specified form does not exist, an error occurs. If any of the tables are locked by another user, a message is displayed on the screen. Your application must handle all these error situations for the user.

For example, if the table or form does not exist, display a message to the user and return to a menu. If the table is locked, ask the user to make the decision to try again, or return to the menu.

TYPICAL OPERATION

This example shows you how to use the FORMTABLES commands.

1. Type **FD** to design a form. When asked for the table name, type **Stocks** and press **Enter**. Assign the new form to 1 and type **Multi-record Form** for the form description.
2. Design a form that resembles the following single-record form. Include all fields in the Stocks table except Customer #.

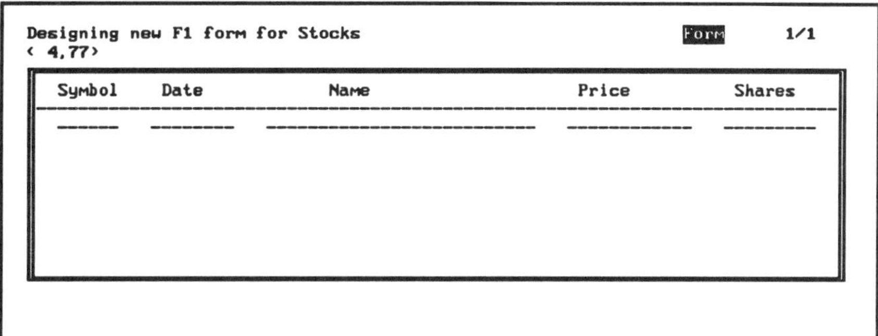

3. Press **F10** (Menu) and type **MRD** to select the Multi, Records, and Define options.
4. When asked to move to a corner of the region to define, move the cursor to the first position of the Symbol field and press **Enter**.
5. Use the arrow keys to move the cursor to the last position of the Shares field so the highlighted area covers all the fields. Press **Enter**.
6. Press **Down Arrow** until the row of fields is duplicated so they fill the box as shown in the following display. Press **Enter** to end the duplication activity.

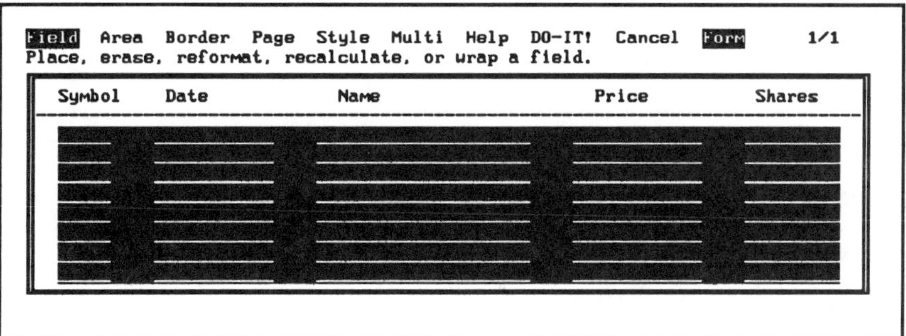

7. Press **F2** (DO-IT!) to save the multi-record form.
8. Type **FC** to select the Forms and Change options from the menu line. When asked for the name of the table, type **Mailtx** and press **Enter**. Select form 2 as the form to be changed and press **Enter** to accept the description.
9. If necessary, move the Subscription Dates line so it appears on line 8 instead of 14.
10. Move the cursor to line 10, column 1. Press **F10** (Menu).
11. Type **MTPL** to select the Multi, Tables, Place, and Linked options. When asked for the name of the table to link, type **Stocks** and press **Enter**.
12. Type **1** to select form 1. When asked for the field to match Customer # in the Stocks table, use the Left Arrow to position the highlight on Customer # and press **Enter**.
13. When the highlighted box appears, use the arrow keys to move it up and to the left so it is centered on the bottom portion of the screen. Press **Enter**.
14. Press **F2** (DO-IT!) to save the changed form.
15. Type **V** to select the View option. When asked for the name of the table, type **Mailtx** and press **Enter**.
16. Press **F10** (Menu) and select the Image, PickForm, 2 options.
17. When the form appears, press the **PgUp** and **PgDn** keys to move through the records. Your screen resembles the following display.

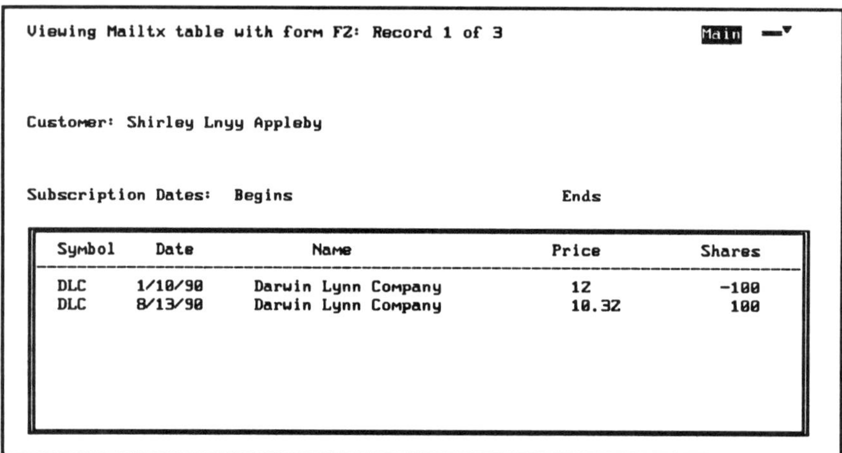

Viewing Mailtx table with form F2: Record 1 of 3 Main

Customer: Shirley Lnyy Appleby

Subscription Dates: Begins Ends

Symbol	Date	Name	Price	Shares
DLC	1/10/90	Darwin Lynn Company	12	-100
DLC	8/13/90	Darwin Lynn Company	10.32	100

18. Press **F8** (Clear) to remove the form from the workspace.
19. Type **SEW** to write a new script. When asked for the name of the script, type **TESTFORM** and press **Enter**.

20. Type the following command lines in the script area.

```
Designing script C:\paradox3\testform                              Script

....+...10....+...20....+...30....+...40....+...50....+...60....+...70....+...80
; testform.sc - lists all tables included in a form

if isfile("mailtx.db") then
  if isfile("mailtx.f2") then
    if ismultiform("mailtx",2) then
      formtables "mailtx" 2 tabname
        x = arraysize(tabname)
        y = 1
        clear
        @ 8,0 ?? "Mailtx form #2 includes the following tables:"
        ? " "
        while y <= x
          ? tabname[y]
          y = y + 1
        endwhile
      sleep 3000
    endif
  endif
endif
; end testform.sc
```

21. Press **F10** (Menu) and select the Go option. When the script runs, the screen is cleared and displays the following message.

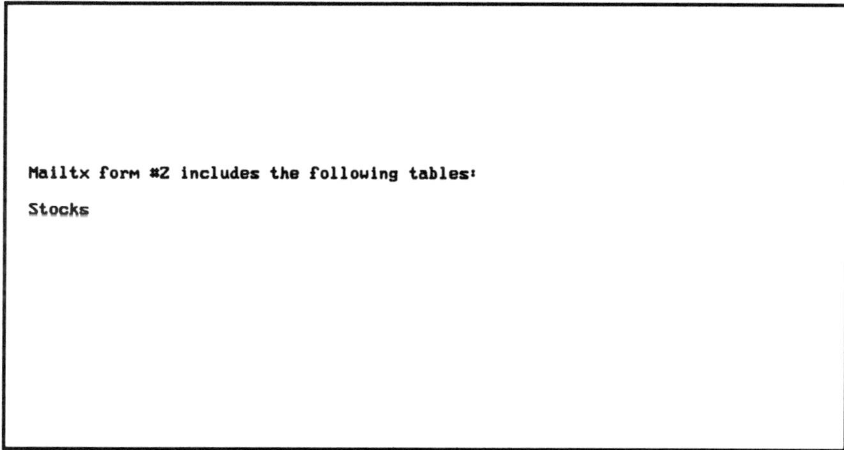

22. Turn to Module 77 to continue the recommended learning sequence.

Module 36
IF, ENDIF

DESCRIPTION

Scripts are usually written to perform repetitive tasks. The more decisions the script makes about data validity, which reports are to be printed, etc., the less operator intervention is required.

The script makes decisions by evaluating the value of a variable or field. This is called *conditional processing.*

The IF, ENDIF command combination lets you write a script so that it chooses the task to be performed. The format for the IF, ENDIF command combination follows.

```
IF <condition>
  THEN
   <commands-1>
ENDIF
```

The IF command marks the beginning and the ENDIF identifies the end of the conditional commands. When you use the IF command in a script, there must always be an ENDIF command to match it. The two commands are used as a pair.

Replace <condition> with a logical expression like those used in the WHILE, ENDWHILE command combination. It lets you specify criteria that must be met. If the condition specified in the IF command line is true, the command lines that follow it are performed.

Include THEN before the first command line of the task to be performed when <condition> is evaluated as true. It may be on a separate line or the same line as the first command line.

Replace <commands-1> with one or more command lines that you want performed when the condition is true. For this format of the IF, ENDIF command combination, when <condition> is evaluated as false, <commands-1> is skipped. Script play continues with the line that follows the ENDIF command line.

The IF, ENDIF command combination evaluates a condition and takes a specific action if the condition is true. It is also possible to perform a different action if the condition is false.

When you want the script to perform a task if <condition> is evaluated as false, include the ELSE phrase. The format of the IF, ENDIF command combination with the ELSE phrase follows.

```
IF <condition>
  THEN
   <commands-1>
ELSE
   <commands-2>
ENDIF
```

Include ELSE before the first command line of the task. It may be on a separate line or the same line as the first command line.

Replace <commands-2> with one or more command lines that you want performed when the condition is false. When this format is used, <commands-1> is performed when <condition> is true or <commands-2> when <condition> is false. Then script play continues with the line that follows the ENDIF command line.

There are times when you need to include at least one IF, ENDIF command combination as part of <commands-1> or <commands-2>. The following example nests four conditional statements.

```
if code1 = "1"
  then
  @ 21,05
  ?? "Department - "
  if dept = "1"
    then
    ?? "Accounting"
  else
    if dept = "2"
      then
      ?? "Warehouse"
    else
      if dept = "3"
        then
        ?? "Sales"
      endif
    endif
  endif
endif
```

If CODE1 does not equal 1, the conditional statements are skipped. Paradox plays the rest of the script beginning with the command line that follows the last ENDIF.

When CODE1 equals 1, "Department -" is displayed in the lower right corner of the screen. Then, a second field called DEPT is evaluated for 1, 2, or 3. If DEPT does not equal one of the three values, Paradox plays the rest of the script beginning with the line that follows the last ENDIF. Otherwise, "Accounting," "Warehouse," or "Sales," appears after "Department -" description.

The indention of each set of command lines within its IF, ENDIF command combination is not required by PAL. However, it makes the script easier to read and match the IF with its ENDIF command.

Paradox matches the IF and ENDIF commands from the innermost to the outermost matchup. By drawing vertical lines (on paper), it is easy to match the command combinations as in the following example.

```
if code1 = "1"
| then
| @ 21,05
| ?? "Department - "
| if dept = "1"
| | then
| | ?? "Accounting"
| else
| | if dept = "2"
| | | then
| | | ?? "Warehouse"
| | else
| | | if dept = "3"
| | | | then
| | | | ?? "Sales"
| | | endif
| | endif
| endif
endif
```

If an extra IF or ENDIF command is found in your script, the results are different from those you expect. The Debugger does not catch the mismatch as an error. You must carefully examine the results to make sure that they are correct. If you suspect a problem, initiate the Debugger before the IF command. Then step through the script line by line until you locate the problem.

APPLICATIONS

The IF, ENDIF command combination lets you specify when a special task must be performed. The evaluation of <condition> in the IF command line lets the script decide when to perform that task.

For example, use an IF, ENDIF command combination to choose a report form before sending the report to the printer. Use conditional commands anytime you want the computer to make a decision based on available information.

Scripts that include the LOOP, QUITLOOP, and EXIT commands usually depend on the evaluation of <condition>. If they are not controlled by the IF, ENDIF command combination, the script plays a very short time and the results are not the ones you expect.

Write your scripts so that the computer makes as many decisions as possible. The results are consistent decisions and faster processing time. While the computer does its work, the user is free to do other things.

TYPICAL OPERATION

This example shows you how to use the IF, ENDIF command combination.

1. Edit the Weekcalc script.
2. Insert the IF, ENDIF command combinations after the script asks for the beginning date as in the following display.

```
Changing script C:\paradox3\weekcalc                                    Script

....+...10....+...20....+...30....+...40....+...50....+...60....+...70....+...80
?? "Enter the beginning date "
accept "D" picture "##/##/##" to fromdate
if fromdate <> blankdate ()                                                      ◆
  then                                                                           ◆
  @ 12,10
  ?? "Enter the ending date "
  accept "D" picture "##/##/##" to todate
  if todate <> blankdate ()                                                      ◆
    then                                                                         ◆
    count = 0
    tdate = fromdate
    while tdate <= todate
      if todate - tdate >= 7                                                     ◆
        then                                                                     ◆
        count = count + 1
      endif                                                                      ◆
      tdate = tdate + 7
    endwhile
    @ 21,05
    ?? "There are "+strval(count)+" weeks between "
    ?? fromdate
    ?? "thru"
    ?? todate
  else                                                                           ◆
    beep beep beep                                                               ◆
    @ 21,05                                                                      ◆
    ?? "A valid ending date was not entered..."                                  ◆
  endif                                                                          ◆
endif                                                                            ◆
@ 23,05
?? "Do you want to do another (Y/N)? "
accept "A1" picture "&" to ans
endwhile
```

3. Press **F10** (Scripts Menu) and select the Go option.
4. When asked for a beginning date, press **Enter**. Since a beginning date was not typed, the script does not perform a calculation.
5. You are asked if you want to do another. Type **Y** and press **Enter**.

6. When asked for a beginning date, type **060189** and press **Enter**.
7. When asked for an ending date, press **Enter**. The computer beeps and a message is displayed in the lower left corner of your screen as follows.

```
        Enter the beginning date 06/01/89

        Enter the ending date




    A valid ending date was not entered...

    Do you want to do another (Y/N)?
```

8. Type **Y** and press **Enter**.
9. When testing the changes you make to a script, test all possiblities. The change might have affected a part of your script that was working correctly. Type **060189** as the beginning date and **061589** as the ending date. The old answer was 3 weeks; however, the new one is 2. Since there is only one day of the third week left over, it is not a full week. The third IF, ENDIF command combination controls the week counter.
10. Type **N** and press **Enter** when and if you want to do another.
11. Turn to Module 44 to continue the recommended learning sequence.

Module 37
IMAGERIGHTS

DESCRIPTION

The IMAGERIGHTS command is used to make changes to table access rights. Please note that the IMAGERIGHTS command changes your access rights but it does not give you more access rights than you currently have, nor does it override access rights controlled by an auxiliary password.

Use IMAGERIGHTS in programs that need to limit table access for users. The syntax of the IMAGERIGHTS command is:

```
IMAGERIGHTS << UPDATE/READONLY >>
```

The IMAGERIGHTS command used without its options clears any restrictions imposed by a previous use of the command. The UPDATE option restricts access to key fields. The READONLY option revokes a user's edit capability for the current image.

NOTE: The IMAGERIGHTS command was added to Paradox 2.0 and above.

APPLICATIONS

IMAGERIGHTS is useful in multi-user environments when you want to control edit capability of a table on a user-by-user basis. For instance, limit access to a project information table to READONLY instead of encrypting the table. Then, provide management with view capability of the project status information but not allow changes.

TYPICAL OPERATION

The following illustration shows you how to include the IMAGERIGHTS command in a script.

1. Type **SEW** to write a new script. When asked for the name of the script, type **Image1** and press **Enter**.
2. Type the following PAL command lines.

```
Designing script C:\paradox3\image1                                   Script

....+...10....+...20....+...30....+...40....+...50....+...60....+...70....+...80
; image1.sc - provides update capabilitites to certain users
edit "Mailtx"
imagerights readonly
clearall
```

3. Press **F10** and select Go option to play the script. Notice that the image of the Mailtx table appears in edit mode.
4. Try to change any of the information in the table. You are told that the field is not modifiable though the table is in edit mode.
5. Press **F2** to change to view mode.
6. Press **F9** to change back to edit mode. Try to make a change in the table. Again, they are not allowed though the edit mode appears to be in control.
7. Press **F2** to change to the view mode, and press **F8** (Clear Image) to remove the table from the screen.
8. Turn to Module 60 to continue the recommended learning sequence.

Module 38
INDEX

DESCRIPTION

The index in the back of a book tells you to go to a certain page to read about the desired subject. A Paradox index is a similar search method for specific information in the current table.

The table is like the textual part of the book. A Paradox table index consists of two separate files that provide key values and record locations.

The key values in the index are sequenced in ascending order so that the search is performed quickly. The data location associated with the key value points to a specific record in the table like the book index points to a specific page. The format for this command follows.

```
INDEX <table name> ON <field name>
```

Replace <table name> with the name of a table that has been saved on the current data disk. Unless provided in a variable, enclose it with quotation marks.

The ON <field name> clause specifies the name of a field in the table structure. Paradox uses that field to create (or recreate) the index. Unless provided in a variable, enclose <field name> with quotation marks.

If an index for <field name> exists when the INDEX command is encountered, Paradox scans it. If it's an up-to-date index, this command line is not performed. Otherwise, the index is recreated for <table name>.

The same scan is performed each time the index is used. If the table has been changed so that the index in not up-to-date, the index is recreated automatically.

Two files exist for each index. The root is the same as the table name. The extensions are assigned ".Xnn" and ".Ynn" where "nn" is a number associated with the field number.

For example, the State field in the Mailtx table structure is field number seven. Therefore, the command line INDEX "MAILTX" ON "STATE" creates two files called Mailtx.X07 and Mailtx.Y07. These two files are included as members of the table's family.

When performing a QUERY, ENDQUERY command combination or a LOCATE command, Paradox uses any index available that makes the operation run faster. Since existing indices are used automatically by Paradox, create an index for each non-key field that is used in a query or a LOCATE command line.

APPLICATIONS

Create an index when the keyed fields in the table structure do not provide the desired data sequence. Key fields specified in the table structure provide a primary index that is used automatically for the table. Each INDEX command creates (or updates) a secondary index that is used when searching a table on a non-key field.

A secondary index is not required by PAL or Paradox. Use them to speed the application or provide another sequence. For example, create an index for the Mailtx and Sales tables so that the records are available in state order. When the query in the View option of the application is performed, the indices are used to speed the processing time.

Do not use the INDEX command when the table that is to be indexed is available in the edit mode on the workspace. Remove it from the workspace, perform the INDEX command, and then put it back on the screen.

TYPICAL OPERATION

This example shows you how to use the INDEX command.

1. Type **TIIF** to select the Tools/Info/Inventory/Files menu options.
2. When asked for the DOS directory pattern, type **Mailtx.*** and press **Enter**. The family table appears in the following display.

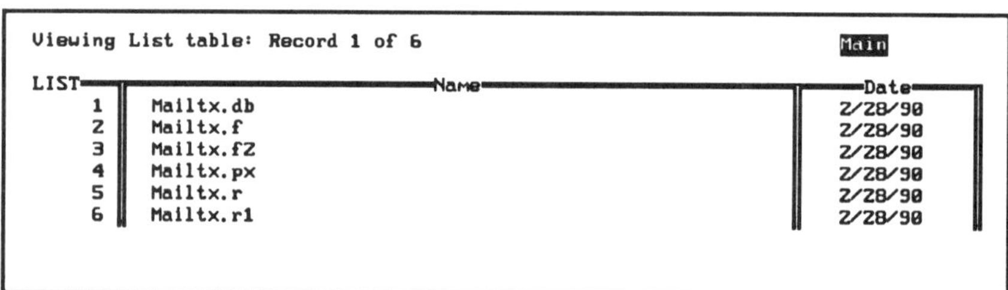

```
Viewing List table: Record 1 of 6                                Main

LIST  Name                                              Date
   1  Mailtx.db                                         2/28/90
   2  Mailtx.f                                          2/28/90
   3  Mailtx.f2                                         2/28/90
   4  Mailtx.px                                         2/28/90
   5  Mailtx.r                                          2/28/90
   6  Mailtx.r1                                         2/28/90
```

3. Press **F8** (Clear Image) to remove the family from the workspace.
4. Edit the Custview script. Insert the INDEX command lines as shown in the following display.

```
Changing script C:\paradox3\custview                              Script Ins

....+...10....+...20....+...30....+...40....+...50....+...60....+...70....+...80
; custview - view customer data
index "Mailtx" on "State"                                                      ◆
index "Sales" on "State"                                                       ◆
view "Mailtx"
if isfile("mailtx.f2")
  then
  PickForm "2"
else
  PickForm "f"
endif
while (true)
  clear
  @ 21,05
  ?? "For a list of customers, leave customer name blank..."
  @ 22,01
  ?? "(Type the first letter of last name for partial list with salespeople.)"
  @ 10,10
  ?? "Enter Last Name "
  accept "A30" to lastname
  if len(lastname) = 1
    then
    last = lastname
```

5. Press **F10** (Scripts Menu) and select the DO-IT! option.
6. When the Main Menu returns to the screen, play the Mainmenu script.
7. Type **V** to select the View option from the application menu. The light on the disk drives flicker while Paradox creates and saves the indices for the two tables.
8. When asked for the Last Name, type **B** and press **Enter**. Two customers are displayed on the screen. Since the indices are available on the disk, the next time this part of the View option is selected, the query performs its task faster.
9. When the Main Menu returns, press **Esc** to exit the application.
10. Select the Tools/Info/Inventory/Files menu options.
11. When asked for the DOS directory pattern, type **Mailtx.*** and press **Enter**. This time there are eight files. The Mailtx.X07 and Mailtx.Y07 files provide the index for the Mailtx table.

```
Viewing List table: Record 1 of 8                                    Main

LIST═╦═══════════════════════════Name══════════════════════════╦═══Date═══╗
   1 ║ Mailtx.db                                               ║ 2/28/90  ║
   2 ║ Mailtx.f                                                ║ 2/28/90  ║
   3 ║ Mailtx.f2                                               ║ 2/28/90  ║
   4 ║ Mailtx.px                                               ║ 2/28/90  ║
   5 ║ Mailtx.r                                                ║ 2/28/90  ║
   6 ║ Mailtx.r1                                               ║ 2/28/90  ║
   7 ║ Mailtx.x07                                              ║ 2/28/90  ║
   8 ║ Mailtx.y07                                              ║ 2/28/90  ║
```

12. Press **F8** (Clear Image) to remove the list from the workspace.
13. Check the inventory files for the Sales table to see that Sales.X01 and Sales.Y01 exist on the disk.

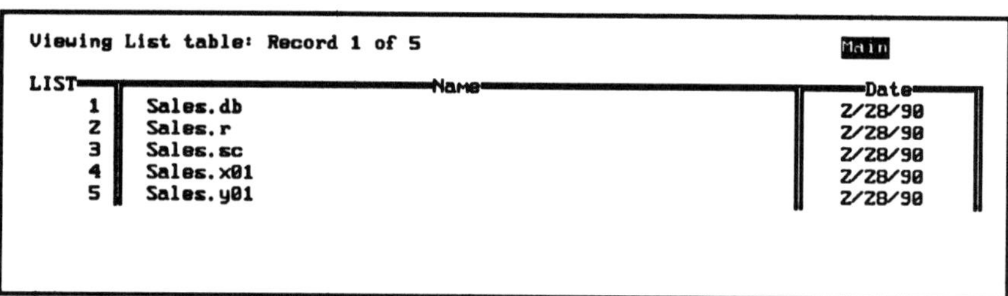

14. Press **F8** (Clear Image) to remove the list from the workspace.
15. Turn to Module 8 to continue the recommended learning sequence.

Module 39
INFOLIB

DESCRIPTION

If you want a list of the procedures stored in a specific library, use the INFOLIB command in a script. Paradox displays the list on the workspace. The format for this command follows.

```
INFOLIB <library name>
```

Replace <library name> with an existing procedure library filename that was created with the CREATELIB command. Unless provided in a variable, the name must be enclosed with quotation marks. The specified library file must exist on the disk before the script performs the INFOLIB command. Otherwise, the script encounters a script error.

APPLICATIONS

When this command is performed, Paradox creates a temporary table of procedure names and approximate file sizes (in bytes). Then the table is presented on the workspace for your review. The table is deleted when you press the F8 (Clear Image) key.

For example, procedures are stored together in a procedure library file. A DIR command from the DOS A> prompt or the Paradox FILESIZE( ) function tells you the size of the library.

Use the INFOLIB command to see the procedure file sizes. This helps you decide on a combination of procedures from the libraries to store in memory. Remember that the application stops immediately if the sum of procedure file sizes is too large for the available memory.

Remember that there is a little overhead involved when using a procedure library. You must consider your diskspace and the number of procedures that are to be stored in the library.

TYPICAL OPERATION

This example shows you how to use the INFOLIB command.

1. Edit the Maillist script. Insert the INFOLIB command as the last line of the script as shown in the following display.

```
Changing script C:\paradox3\maillist                                    Script Ins

....+...10....+...20....+...30....+...40....+...50....+...60....+...70....+...80
if x < 12
  then
  print file "c:log" "Customer table was last changed by ",idcode," on ",
    today()," at ",time()
  clearall
  return passes[x+1]
else
  message "You have typed an invalid ID code..."
  sleep 2000
  clearall
  return False
endif
endproc
; end idcheck
writelib "Maillist" Idcheck
@ 20,10
?? "Size of the Maillist procedure library = "
?? filesize("Maillist.lib")
sleep 2500
infolib "Maillist"                                                             ◆
; end maillist
```

2. Press **F10** (Scripts Menu) and select the Go option. As the script is played, notice that the library is almost 4100 bytes. However, the Idcheck procedure is only 1678 as displayed in the following list.

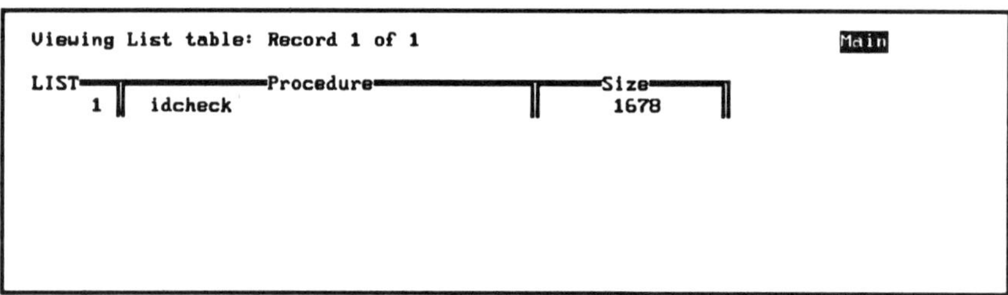

3. Press **F8** (Clear Image) to remove the table from the workspace.
4. Turn to Module 61 to continue the recommended learning sequence.

Module 40
KEYPRESS

DESCRIPTION

There are times when you want the application to make user-like choices. Use the KEYPRESS command to activate some of those selections in the following format.

```
KEYPRESS <keycode>
```

Replace <keycode> with a valid PAL keycode, menu choice, or ASCII number. Unless <keycode> is provided as a value of a variable or a number, enclose it with quotation marks.

APPLICATIONS

The KEYPRESS command is similar to the SELECT command. However, the SELECT command is restricted to valid menu options. Use the KEYPRESS command for all other selections performed by the application.

For example, you need to provide a selected screen of the F1 (Help) screens to the user. Include a KEYPRESS command to "press" the F1 (Help) key. Then include a SELECT command to specify each of the desired menu options. The user sees the end result of the script. All intermediate screens are not displayed on the screen.

Also, consider using the KEYPRESS command to provide a selection if there is no response from the user. For example, ask the user to type the letter "Q" to end an operation. If the Q is not received, have the script provide its own selection.

TYPICAL OPERATION

This example shows you how to use the KEYPRESS command.

1. Press **F1** (Help). The first help screen is displayed on your workspace.
2. Type **M** to select the MenuChoices option. The help screen changes to one that describes the menu options in the Main Menu line.
3. Type **V** to select the View option help screen. Then type **P** to select the Paradox option. The Main Menu screen returns to the workspace.
4. Edit the Test3 script. Change it so that it matches the one in the following display.

```
Changing script C:\paradox3\test3                                    Script

....+...10....+...20....+...30....+...40....+...50....+...60....+...70....+...80
keypress "F1"
keypress "M"
keypress "V"
```

5. Press **F10** (Scripts Menu) and type **G** to select the Go option. The View help screen is displayed immediately.
6. Type **P** to select the Paradox option.
7. When the Main Menu returns, change the Test3 script again so that it matches the following display.

```
Changing script C:\paradox3\test3                                    Script

....+...10....+...20....+...30....+...40....+...50....+...60....+...70....+...80
keypress "F1"
select "MenuChoices"
select "View"
```

8. Press **F10** (Scripts Menu) and select the Go option. The View help screen is displayed immediately. The script played the same as the first time. However, if more than one menu option began with "M," you would be asked to select the menu option yourself.
9. Type **P** to select the Paradox option.
10. Turn to Module 69 to continue the recommended learning sequence.

Module 41
LOCATE

DESCRIPTION

Most scripts are written to help the user work with the data in Paradox tables. Do not force the user to browse through all the records to find one. Write scripts that search the table by including the LOCATE command.

This command tells Paradox to search the table for a specific value in one or more fields. Substitute a number greater than one for the "-n" in the following command format.

```
LOCATE <<NEXT>> <field value-1>, ..., <field value-n>
```

Replace <field value-1> through <field value-n> with one or more values to be used in the search. For example, the command LOCATE "Smith" tells Paradox to search the table for a record which contains the value of "Smith."

The values may be provided by using variables in the command. For example, a variable is established called Lastname. It is set to the value of "Smith." The LOCATE Lastname command provides the same results as the LOCATE "Smith" command.

When more than one value is included in the list, separate them with commas. For example, LOCATE "Smith," "John" or LOCATE Lastname, Firstname tells Paradox to compare the record fields to the two values provided in the LOCATE command.

The word NEXT is optional in this command line. Without it, Paradox begins its search with the first record in the table. When NEXT is included in the command line, Paradox searches the rest of the file beginning with the current record. As soon as a record is found that contains the value(s), the LOCATE activity is complete.

The Paradox variable, Retval, is automatically set after the search is completed. If a record contains the value that the user provided, Retval is set to true. Otherwise, Retval is set to false.

The @,?,??, and ACCEPT commands are not used to ask the user for the values for the search. Instead, the table image (in Table View or Forms View) is required. Once you understand the process, writing the script is easy. The following command lines perform a search of the Mailtx table.

```
edit "Mailtx"                       ; edit mode for Mailtx
formkey {Image} {Pickform} {F}      ; selects Forms View
end                                 ; moves cursor to last record in table
PgDn                                ; moves cursor to next record (a new blank one)
```

```
wait table message "Type Last Name, then press F2 to begin search..."
  until "F2"
lastname = [Last Name]          ; saves the user values in a variable
del                             ; deletes the new record just added to table
locate lastname                 ; begins search from first record in table
if not (retval)                 ; if search is unsuccessful
  then
  message "Record does not exist in table "+fileans+".db..."
  sleep 2000
else                            ; if search is successful
wait record message "Press F2 when ready to return to the menu..."
    until "F2"                  ; present record to user for possible changes
endif
do_it!                          ; save changes and exit the edit mode
clearimage                      ; removes the table from the workspace
```

After the EDIT command line, use the End and PgDn keycodes (see Appendix B) to position the cursor on a new, blank record. The user types the required values in the appropriate fields. Then save the values in variables and delete the new record from the table. When the LOCATE command is encountered, Paradox begins the search of the table.

APPLICATIONS

Include the LOCATE command in scripts that need to find records for the user. The table is searched by the computer instead of the user. The desired record is found quickly.

If an index (see INDEX) is available for the table being searched, Paradox uses it automatically. Indices for tables often speed the search process.

TYPICAL OPERATION

This example shows you how to use the LOCATE command.

1. Edit the Custmnt script so that it matches the one in the following display.

```
Changing script C:\paradox3\custmnt                                  Script Ins

....+...10....+...20....+...30....+...40....+...50....+...60....+...70....+...80
    formkey {Image} {PickForm} {F}
    end                                                                         ◆
    PgDn                                                                        ◆
    wait table message "Type the Last Name, then press F2 to begin the search...
      until "F2"                                                                ◆
    lastname = [Last Name]                                                      ◆
    del                                                                         ◆
    locate lastname                                                             ◆
    if not (retval)                                                             ◆
      then                                                                      ◆
      message "Record does not exist in table "+fileans+".db..."                ◆
      sleep 2000                                                                ◆
    else                                                                        ◆
    wait record message "Press F2 when ready to return to the menu..."          ◆
      until "F2"                                                                ◆
    endif                                                                       ◆
    do_it!
    clearimage
  else
    beep beep beep beep
    message "Table "+fileans+".db is not on the current data disk."
    sleep 2000
```

2. Press **F10** (Scripts Menu) and select the DO-IT! option.
3. Play the script Mainmenu. Select the Maintenance option.
4. Type **DLS1** and press **Enter** when asked for the ID.
5. Type **Mailtx** and press **Enter** when asked for the name of the table. A blank record appears on the screen.
6. Type **Chadwick** and press **F2** as instructed by the message at the bottom of the screen. The Del command line in the script deletes record 4 from the table. The LOCATE command searches the table for the last name of "Chadwick." When found, the record is presented to the screen for changes. Your screen resembles the following display.

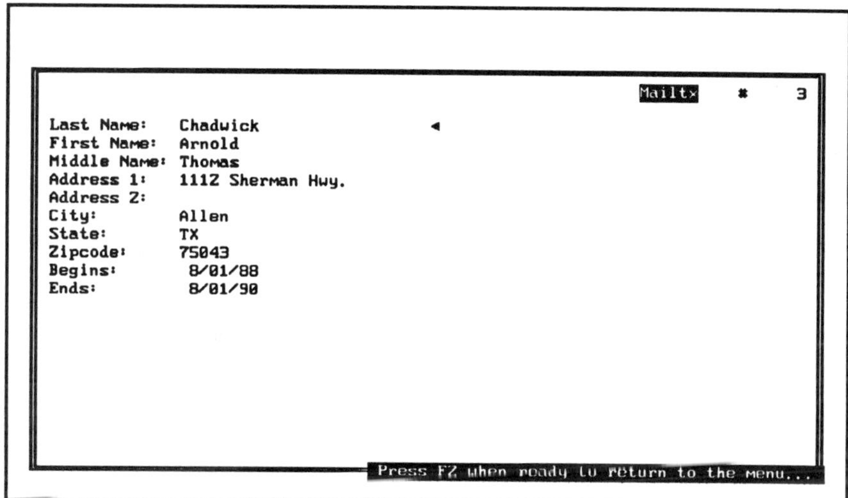

7. Press **Enter** until the cursor is positioned on the Zipcode field. Press **Ctrl-Backspace** to delete the zipcode. Then type **75045** and press **Enter**.
8. Press **F2** to return to the application menu.
9. Select the Maintenance option again by typing **M** and return to the Mailtx table.
10. When the blank record appears, type **Davis**. Then press **F2** to begin the search. The message at the bottom of the screen tells you that the record does not exist in the table. The application menu returns to the screen.
11. Select the Maintenance option again for Mailtx. When the blank record appears, type **Berry**. Then press **F2** to begin the search. When found, the record is displayed on the screen for changes.

12. Press **F2** to return to the application menu. Then press **Esc** for the Main Menu screen.
13. Change the Custmnt script again as shown in the following display.

```
Changing script C:\paradox3\custmnt                                   Script Ins

....+...10....+...20....+...30....+...40....+...50....+...60....+...70....+...80
    formkey {Image} {PickForm} {F}
    while (true)                                                            ◆
    end
    PgDn
    wait record message "Type customer name, then press F2 to begin search..." ◆
      until "F2"
    lastname = [Last Name]
    firstname = [First Name]                                                ◆
    del
    if isblank(lastname) and isblank(firstname)                             ◆
      then                                                                  ◆
      quitloop                                                              ◆
    endif                                                                   ◆
    locate lastname, firstname                                              ◆
    if not (retval)
      then
      message "Record does not exist in table "+fileans+".db..."
      sleep 2000
    else
      while not atlast()                                                    ◆
    wait record message "Press F2 for the menu, PgDn to continue searching..." ◆
        until "F2", "PgDn"
      if retval = "PgDn"
        then
        PgDn
        locate next lastname, firstname
        if not (retval)
          then
          beep beep beep beep
          message "No other records were found in the table..."             ◆
          sleep 2000                                                        ◆
        endif                                                               ◆
      else                                                                  ◆
        end                                                                 ◆
      endif                                                                 ◆
    endwhile                                                                ◆
    quitloop                                                                ◆
  endif                                                                     ◆
endwhile                                                                    ◆
    do_it!
    clearimage
  else
    beep beep beep beep
    message "Table "+fileans+".db is not on the current data disk."
    sleep 2000
  endif
endif
; end custmnt
```

14. Press **F10** (Scripts Menu) and select the DO-IT! option.
15. Play Mainmenu again and use the Mailtx table when you select the Maintenance option.
16. Type **Berry** in the Last Name field. Press **F2** to begin the search. Since the LOCATE command line specifies the lastname and the firstname fields, the record is not found in the table. The blank record returns to give you another chance.

17. Type **Berry** in the Last Name field and press **Enter**. Then type **Charles** in the First Name field. Press **F2** to begin the search. Notice the message at the bottom of the screen.
18. Press **PgDn** to continue searching the table for another record with the name of Charles Berry. The computer beeps and a message is displayed that tells you that another record for a last name of Berry was not found.
19. When the application menu returns to the screen, press **Esc**.
20. Turn to Module 46 to continue the recommended learning sequence.

Module 42
LOCK, UNLOCK

DESCRIPTION

Use the LOCK command in multi-user scripts to restrict access to at least one table. When you issue a LOCK command, you control access rights to an entire table for the duration of the LOCK command. The syntax of the LOCK and UNLOCK commands follow.

```
LOCK <locklist>
UNLOCK << <locklist>  ALL >>
```

Replace <locklist> with a list of tables to be locked and the lock types. The lock types are:

FL Full Lock - no other user may access the table while it is in effect.

WL Write Lock - no other user may write to the locked tables, but other users may read the table.

PWL Prevent Write Lock - no other user may issue a write lock command for the table(s).

PFL Prevent Full Lock - no other user may issue a full lock for the table(s).

When a lock command is encountered, Paradox attempts to lock the specified tables. If successful, the global variable RETVAL is set to TRUE. If Paradox cannot lock any or all of the specified tables, RETVAL is set to FALSE and none of them are locked.

Write your programs to query RETVAL to determine the outcome of the LOCK command. If the LOCK command cannot lock all specified tables, write the script so it returns to the menu or tries the lock again.

Always issue an UNLOCK command to remove each of your table locks. Paradox keeps track of who set the lock and requires the same user to unlock the table.

The UNLOCK command is ignored if the table is not locked. The system variable RETVAL is set to TRUE if the UNLOCK command is successful, or FALSE if it cannot be completed.

The ALL option on the UNLOCK command removes all locks placed by a user.

NOTE: The LOCK and UNLOCK commands were added to Paradox 2.0 and above and have no effect unless you installed Paradox in multi-user mode.

APPLICATIONS

Locking a table ensures the proper user access. For example, LOCK MAILTX WL sets a lock on the Mailtx table so that other users are allowed to view the table, not change it. Remember that this prevents them from getting their work done, so use the WL and FL options carefully and unlock the table as soon as possible.

If several users need access to the same table at the same time, use the LOCKRECORD command to establish a lock on a specific record. When the record is changed, issue the UNLOCKRECORD command to release it.

TYPICAL OPERATION

This example shows you how to use the LOCK and UNLOCK commands.

1. Type **SEE** to use the script editor. When asked for the name of the script, type **MultCust** and press **Enter.**
2. Change the program to match the following example.

```
Changing script C:\paradox3\multcust                                   Script Ins

....+...10....+...20....+...30....+...40....+...50....+...60....+...70....+...80
; multcust - network customer maintenance script
clear
@ 10,10
?? "Enter the name of the table "
accept "A8" picture "&*&" to fileans
if not isblank(fileans)
  then
  if isfile(fileans+".db")
    then
    while true                                                                 ◆
      lock fileans pfl                                                         ◆
      if retval then                                                           ◆
        quitloop                                                               ◆
      else                                                                     ◆
        message errormessage()+"...Esc stops next try"                         ◆
      endif                                                                    ◆
      sleep 2000                                                               ◆
      if charwaiting() then                                                    ◆
        x = getchar()                                                          ◆
        if not retval then                                                     ◆
          release vars fileans                                                 ◆
          return                                                               ◆
        endif                                                                  ◆
      endif                                                                    ◆
    endwhile                                                                   ◆
    coedit fileans
    PickForm "F"
  else
    beep beep beep beep
    message "Table "+fileans+".db is not on the current data disk."
    sleep 2000
  endif
endif
unlock fileans pfl                                                             ◆
; end multcust
```

3. Press **F10** and select the Go option to run the program.
4. If you have are running this script on a multi-user system, try to use the EDIT mode for the same table from another terminal. The PFL (Prevent Full Lock) set by the MultCust script created a Mailtx.lck file that does not allow the edit mode to lock the table.
5. Press **F2** to end the coedit mode. Then, press **F8** to clear the workspace.
6. Turn to Module 38 to continue the recommended learning sequence.

Module 43
LOCKRECORD, UNLOCKRECORD

DESCRIPTION

The LOCKRECORD command is used in multi-user applications to prevent other users from changing a record before you are finished with it. You can only lock a record if you have Paradox in Coedit mode.

The system variable RETVAL is set to TRUE if the command is successful and FALSE if unsuccessful. If the LOCKRECORD command is not successfully completed, use the ERRORCODE( ) function to determine the failure reason.

The syntax of the LOCKRECORD and UNLOCKRECORD commands follow.

```
LOCKRECORD
UNLOCKRECORD
```

When you wish to lock a record, follow these steps.

1. Move the cursor or record pointer to the record that must be changed.
2. Issue the LOCKRECORD command and verify that the lock is successful.
3. Change the record.
4. Unlock the record.

If you are adding a new record, the following occurs automatically:

1. The record is added to the table.
2. The record is locked.
3. The record is moved to its correct place (in key order) if the table is keyed.
4. It becomes the current record.

Your Paradox scripts control how records are added to a table. Query the value of the RETVAL system variable to determine whether the lock was successful in multi-user mode.

Use the UNLOCKRECORD command to unlock a record if you have locked it. Just Like the LOCKRECORD command, Paradox must be in Coedit mode before issuing the command.

If the UNLOCKRECORD command is issued on a record that is not locked, the system variable RETVAL is set to FALSE. If the record was successfully locked, RETVAL is set to TRUE. Use the ERRORCODE( ) function to determine the failure reason.

NOTE: The LOCKRECORD and UNLOCKRECORD commands were added to Paradox 2.0 and above and have no effect if issued on single-user systems.

APPLICATIONS

Use the LOCKRECORD and UNLOCKRECORD commands to control access to records in a table during multi-user access. This allows you to control the addition of new records and the modification of existing records.

TYPICAL OPERATION

This illustration shows you how to use the LOCKRECORD and UNLOCKRECORD commands in scripts that are played on network systems.

1. Type **SEE** to use the Paradox script editor. When asked for a filename, type **Custmnt** and press **Enter**.
2. Change the EDITKEY command line to COEDITKEY.
3. Insert the LOCKRECORD routine before the WAIT RECORD command and the UNLOCKRECORD command line after it. That portion of your script matches the following display.

```
Changing script C:\paradox3\custmnt                                 Script

....+...10....+...20....+...30....+...40....+...50....+...60....+...70....+...80
;custmnt - customer maintenance script
clear
@ 10,10
?? "Enter the name of the table "
accept "a8" picture "&*&" to fileans
if not isblank(fileans)
  then
  if isfile(fileans+".db")
    then
    view fileans
    formkey {Image} {PickForm} {F}
    while (true)
      coeditkey                                                                ◆
    end
    PgDn
    lockrecord                                                                 ◆
    wait record message "Type customer name, then press F2 to begin search..."
    unlockrecord                                                               ◆
      until "F2"
    lastname = [Last Name]
    firstname = [First Name]
    canceledit
```

4. Press **F2** to save the changed script.
5. Play the Mainmenu script on two workstations and select the customer maintenance option. Request the same customer on both workstations to see that one gets to change the record while the other has to wait.
6. Turn to Module 71 to continue the recommended learning sequence.

Module 44
LOOP

DESCRIPTION

The LOOP command tells Paradox to skip all command lines between the LOOP command and the next ENDWHILE or ENDSCAN command. The condition specified in the WHILE or SCAN command line is evaluated immediately after the LOOP is encountered.

If <condition> is true, the looping activity is continued. Otherwise, Paradox plays the rest of the script beginning with the line that follows the ENDWHILE or ENDSCAN command line.

For example, the computer is tied up unnecessarily when the user accidentally asks it to calculate the number of weeks between two dates that are several years apart. To help avoid this, insert a date range in the script to restrict the dates as follows. Remember that the dots indicate omitted command lines.

```
while ans = "Y"
    .
    .
    if fromdate < 01/01/89
      then
      beep beep beep
      @ 21,05
      ?? "The beginning date is earlier than 01/01/89..."
      sleep 3000
      loop
    endif
    .
    .
    if todate > 01/01/92
      then
      beep beep beep
      @ 21,05
      ?? "The ending date is later than 01/01/92..."
      sleep 3000
      loop
    endif
    .
    .
endwhile
```

As soon as the beginning date is typed, the script compares it to the earliest acceptable date. If the date typed is prior to the specified limit, the computer beeps and presents a message for three seconds.

When the LOOP command is encountered, Paradox returns to the WHILE command line of the current loop and evaluates "ans." Since the value of "ans" has not changed, the user is asked for another beginning date. The same method is provided for the ending date.

When writing a script, try to anticipate every possible situation. Each one happens eventually; however, you do not want problems when deadlines are short.

APPLICATIONS

This command is valid only when used within a WHILE, ENDWHILE or a SCAN, ENDSCAN command combination. It tells Paradox to return to the current WHILE or SCAN command line and evaluate its condition immediately.

The LOOP command is usually part of an IF, ENDIF command set since the LOOP command is to be performed only under certain circumstances. Use this command when the end of a table is encountered, a user types a wrong answer, or anytime you want to evaluate the condition again.

Most scripts may be written so that a LOOP command is avoided by using IF, ENDIF command combinations properly. However, the LOOP command is available if you need it or feel more comfortable by using it.

TYPICAL OPERATION

This example shows you how to use the LOOP command.

1. Edit the Weekcalc script.

2. Insert the IF, ENDIF command sets that limit the beginning and ending dates accepted by Weekcalc. Your script should resemble the one in the following display.

```
Changing script C:\paradox3\weekcalc                                    Script Ins

....+...10....+...20....+...30....+...40....+...50....+...60....+...70....+...80
?? "Enter the beginning date "
accept "D" picture "##/##/##" to fromdate
if fromdate <01/01/88                                                          ◆
  then                                                                         ◆
  beep beep beep                                                               ◆
  @ 21,05                                                                      ◆
  ?? "The beginning date is earlier than 01/01/88..."                          ◆
  sleep 3000                                                                   ◆
  loop                                                                         ◆
endif                                                                          ◆
if fromdate <> blankdate ()
 then
  @ 12,10
  ?? "Enter the ending date "
```

```
    accept "D" picture "##/##/##" to todate
    if todate > 01/01/92
      then
      beep beep beep
      @ 21,05
      ?? "The ending date is later than 01/01/92..."
      sleep 3000
      loop
    endif
    if todate <> blankdate ()
 .
 .
 .
```

3. Press **F10** (Scripts Menu) and select the Go option by typing **G**.
4. When asked for a beginning date, type **123187** and press **Enter.** Since the date is prior to 01/01/88, the computer beeps and a message appears in the lower left corner of the screen. When the LOOP command is encountered, the rest of the commands between the LOOP and the ENDWHILE commands are skipped. The looping process is begun again.
5. When asked for a beginning date, type **061589** and press Enter. When asked for an ending date, type **011592** and press **Enter**. The computer beeps and a message about the ending date appears in the lower left corner of the screen.
6. This time, type **060189** and **070190** as the beginning and ending dates, respectively. Your screen tells you:

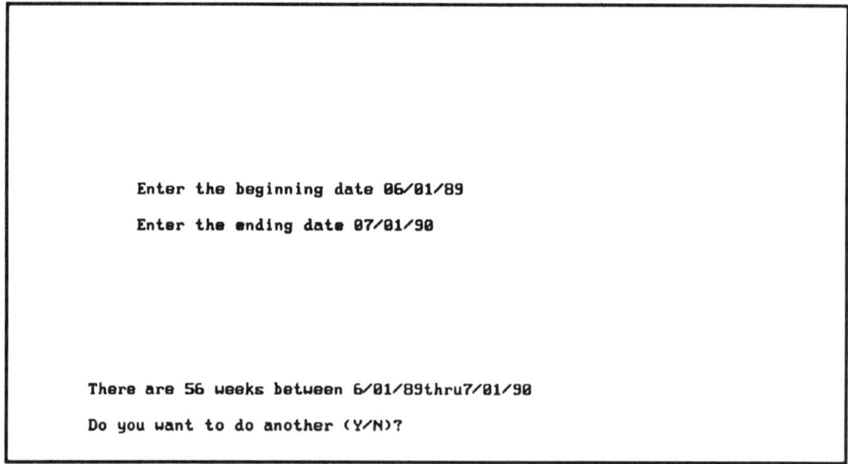

7. Type **Y** and press **Enter** to do another. This time, press **Enter** for the beginning date. The computer beeps, and the message tells you that the beginning date is prior to 01/01/89.
8. Press **Ctrl-Break** to stop the script. When asked if you want to Cancel or Debug, type **C** to cancel the script.

9. Change the new IF, ENDIF commands so that they match the following display.

```
Changing script C:\paradox3\weekcalc                                    Script

....+...10....+...20....+...30....+...40....+...50....+...60....+...70....+...80
?? "Enter the beginning date "
accept "D" picture "##/##/##" to fromdate
if fromdate <01/01/88 and fromdate <> blankdate ()                              ◆
  then
  beep beep beep
  @ 21,05
  ?? "The beginning date is earlier than 01/01/88..."
  sleep 3000
  loop
endif
if fromdate <> blankdate ()
 then
  @ 12,10
  ?? "Enter the ending date "
  accept "D" picture "##/##/##" to todate
  if todate > 01/01/92 and todate <> blankdate ()                               ◆
    then
    beep beep beep
    @ 21,05
    ?? "The ending date is later than 01/01/92..."
    sleep 3000
    loop
```

10. Press **F10** (Scripts Menu) and select the Go option.
11. Press **Enter** for the beginning date. You are asked if you want to do another. Type **Y** and press **Enter**.
12. When asked for a beginning date, type **060189** and press **Enter**.
13. Press **Enter** when asked for an ending date. The computer beeps and a message appears at the lower left corner of your screen. It tells you that a valid ending date was not entered.
14. Since tests were done before the last changes, they should be tested again. Enter dates to test the date range. When all possible situations are tested, type **N** and press **Enter** to return to the Main Menu screen.
15. Turn to Module 60 to continue the recommended learning sequence.

Module 45
MESSAGE

DESCRIPTION

The MESSAGE command lets you display messages in the same way as the Paradox Debugger. They are always displayed in the lower right corner of the screen. Also, the message is easy to see on the workspace since it is in reverse video on monochrome monitors or a contrasting color on color monitors. The format for the MESSAGE command follows.

```
MESSAGE <message-1>, <message- 2>, ..., <message-n>
```

Replace <message-1> through <message-n> with text enclosed with quotation marks, variables, fields, etc. so that when the parts are concatenated (linked), the desired message is presented to the user. Separate each part by a comma as in the following command line.

```
MESSAGE "There are ",count," weeks between ",fromdate," thru
",todate
```

PAL automatically makes any necessary conversions of data type, puts the pieces together, and displays the complete message to the user. If the MESSAGE line is already used, your message overlays as much of the line as necessary. As soon as a key is pressed, the message disappears and the line is returned to normal.

Since the message always appears in the same place on the screen, the user does not have to look for it. Also, the message is placed on top of the workspace (like a strip of paper on top of another). When you need all the space on the screen, the MESSAGE command is hard to beat.

APPLICATIONS

Use the MESSAGE command instead of the ? and ?? commands when you want to give the user a one-line message. Your messages conform automatically to a size, a location, and an appearance. The user knows where to look and what to expect.

For example, use the MESSAGE command to tell the user that the number typed is outside a specific range. The message appears on a line in the lower right corner of the screen. When the message is read, the user just presses a key. The message disappears as though it were never presented.

TYPICAL OPERATION

This illustration shows you how to use the MESSAGE command.

1. Edit the Weekcalc script.
2. Change the ?? command lines that present messages to the user so that they match the following display.

```
Changing script C:\paradox3\weekcalc                                    Script Ins

....+...10....+...20....+...30....+...40....+...50....+...60....+...70....+...80
if fromdate <01/01/88 and fromdate <> blankdate ()
  then
  beep beep beep
  message "The beginning date is earlier than 01/01/88..."                      ◆
  sleep 3000
  loop
endif
if fromdate <> blankdate ()
 then
  @ 12,10
  ?? "Enter the ending date "
  accept "D" picture "##/##/##" to todate
  if todate > 01/01/92 and todate <> blankdate ()
    then
    beep beep beep
    message "The ending date is later than 01/01/92..."                         ◆
    sleep 3000
    loop
  endif
  if todate <> blankdate ()
    then
    count = 0
        count = count + 1
      endif
      tdate = tdate + 7
      if tdate > todate
        then
        quitloop
      endif
    endwhile
    message "There are ",count," weeks between ",fromdate," thru ",todate       ◆
  else
    beep beep beep
    @ 21,05                                                                     ◆
    ?? "A valid ending date was not entered..."
  endif
endif
@ 23,05
?? "Do you want to do another (Y/N)? "
accept "A1" picture "&" to ans
endwhile
```

3. Press **F10** (Scripts Menu) and select the Go option by typing **G**.
4. Type **060189** and **061589** to test two valid dates. When asked if you want to do another, type **Y** and press **Enter**.
5. Type **010184** as the beginning date and press **Enter**. The computer beeps and the message tells you that the beginning date is outside the date range. The message disappears automatically when the LOOP command is encountered.

6. You are asked for a beginning date. Type **060189** and press **Enter**. Then type **010194** and press **Enter** for the ending date. The computer beeps and the message tells you that the ending date is outside the limit. The message disappears automatically when the LOOP command is encountered.
7. Press **Enter** and leave the beginning date blank. When asked if you want to do another, type **Y** and press **Enter**.
8. Type **060189** for the beginning date and press **Enter**. Then press **Enter** and leave the ending date blank. The computer beeps and the message tells you that the ending date is not valid.
9. All combinations of dates have been tested. When asked if you want to do another, type **N** and press **Enter**.
10. Turn to Module 93 to continue the recommended learning sequence.

Module 46
MOVETO

DESCRIPTION

When a record is presented to the user during the Edit mode, Paradox positions the cursor on the first field of the record automatically. The MOVETO command lets the script specify the cursor position. There are four forms for the MOVETO command.

```
MOVETO <field>
MOVETO RECORD <record number>
MOVETO <image number>
MOVETO <image string>
```

Replace <field> with the name of a field available in the table structure. When field names of a table are used in a script, they must be enclosed with brackets ([ ]).

If more than one image is currently available to the user, further identification is often needed to specify the field in a specific table. This is done by including the table name and an arrow with the brackets. For example, MOVETO[Mailtx -> Last Name] specifies the Last Name field in the table called Mailtx.

Use the RECORD <record number> format to move the cursor to a specific record within the table. To do this, you must know the number that is assigned to the desired record. The command line MOVETO RECORD 5 tells Paradox to position the cursor on the fifth record in the table.

For example, the following Table View shows three records for the Mailtx Table image. The numbers to the left of each Last Name field are the record numbers.

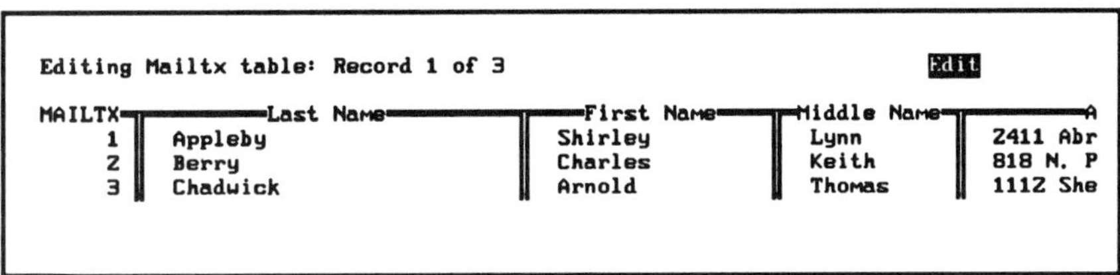

The current record is number 1 since the cursor is positioned on one of the fields of that record. When the table is kept in sequence, the record numbers usually change each time a new record is added to the table. They also change when records are deleted. Do not depend on a record retaining its original record number.

When multiple images are displayed on the screen, use the MOVETO command to position the cursor on a specific image. Replacing <image number> with the number 2 tells Paradox to move the cursor to the second table.

For example, two tables are displayed on the workspace. The cursor is positioned on the first table. When Paradox encounters a MOVETO 2 command line, the cursor is positioned on the second table.

The MOVETO <image string> form is similar to the MOVETO <image number>. However, replace <image string> with the name of the table and the image number for the cursor position. Unless provided in a variable, enclose <image string> with quotation marks. Also, the image number must be enclosed with parentheses.

For example, three table images appear on the workspace. Two of the images are for the same table. To position the cursor on the first image of the Mailtx table, use the MOVETO "Mailtx (1)" command line in your script.

APPLICATIONS

Paradox always positions the cursor in the first field of the first record. Include the MOVETO command in a script when you need to control the cursor position.

For example, the user of your application is responsible for changing the values in the fourth and fifth fields of the record. If Paradox positions the cursor on the first field automatically, the user must press the Enter key or one of the arrow keys until the proper field is available. By including the MOVETO command in the script, you position the cursor for the user.

TYPICAL OPERATION

This example shows you how to use the MOVETO command.

1. Play the Mainmenu script. The application menu appears across the top of the screen.
2. Type **M** to select the Maintenance option. Type **DLS1** and press **Enter** for the ID. When asked for the name of the table, type **Mailtx** and press **Enter**.
3. A blank record appears on the screen. Type **Berry** in the Last Name field and press **Enter**. The cursor moves to the First Name field.
4. Type **Charles** and press **F2** to begin the search of the table. When the record is found, it appears on the screen in Edit mode. The cursor is positioned in the First Name field as in the following display.

```
                                                        Mailt>    *    2

Last Name:    Berry
First Name:   Charles        ◄
Middle Name:  Keith
Address 1:    818 N. Plano Rd.
Address 2:    #18
City:         Plano
State:        TX
Zipcode:      75042
Begins:        5/01/89
Ends:          8/01/89



                  Press F2 for the menu, PgDn to continue searching...
```

5. Press **F2** to return to the application menu.
6. Press **Esc** to return to the Main Menu screen.
7. Type **SEE** and edit the Custmnt script.
8. Insert a MOVETO command line in front of the second WAIT command line so that it matches the script lines in the following display.

```
Changing script C:\paradox3\custmnt                          Script Ins
....+...10....+...20....+...30....+...40....+...50....+...60....+...70....+...80
      then
      message "Record does not exist in table "+fileans+".db..."
      sleep 2000
    else
      while not atlast()
        moveto [Begins]                                                    ◆
    wait record message "Press F2 for the menu, PgDn to continue searching..."
        until "F2", "PgDn"
      if retval = "PgDn"
        then
        PgDn
        locate next lastname, firstname
        if not (retval)
          then
          beep beep beep beep
          message "No other records were found in the table..."
          sleep 2000
        endif
      else
        end
      endif
    endwhile
```

9. Press **F10** (Scripts Menu) and select the DO-IT! option by typing **D**.
10. Type **SP** to play a script. When asked for the name of the script, type **Mainmenu** and press **Enter**. The application menu appears across the top of the screen.
11. Type **M** to select the Maintenance option. Type **DLS1** and press **Enter** for the ID. When asked for the name of the table, type **Mailtx** and press **Enter**.
12. A blank record appears on the screen. Type **Berry** in the Last Name field and press **Enter**. The cursor moves to the First Name field.
13. Type **Charles** and press **F2** to begin the search of the table. When the record is found, it appears on the screen in Edit mode. The cursor is positioned in the Begins field.
14. Press **Ctrl-Backspace** to delete the existing date. Then type **09/01/89** and press **Enter**.
15. Press **Ctrl-Backspace**. Type **08/01/90** in the Ends field.
16. Press **F2** to return to the application menu. Press **Esc** to end the application.
17. Turn to Module 11 to continue the recommended learning sequence.

Module 47
OPEN PRINTER, CLOSE PRINTER

DESCRIPTION

Use the OPEN PRINTER command to control a printer on a local area network. Printed output is preceded by a banner page and followed by a trailer page. If you use the PAL PRINT, ?, ??, and TEXT (PRINTER) commands in a program, the printer produces more header and trailer pages than output.

The OPEN PRINTER command suppresses all the extra header and trailer pages. The syntax of the OPEN PRINTER and CLOSE PRINTER commands are:

```
OPEN PRINTER

CLOSE PRINTER
```

OPEN PRINTER acts on the currently set printer device (normally LPT1). Remember, use the SETPRINTER command in a PAL program to change print devices.

The CLOSE PRINTER command is used to close a printer device that was opened with an OPEN PRINTER command.

NOTE: The OPEN PRINTER and CLOSE PRINTER commands were added to Paradox 2.0 and above.

APPLICATIONS

The OPEN PRINTER and CLOSE PRINTER commands are only used in local area network environments to prevent the production of extra header and trailer pages. For example, create a report with the OPEN PRINTER, PRINT, and CLOSE PRINTER technique when a table is too large to produce an answer table from a query.

When you issue the OPEN PRINTER command, remember to issue the CLOSE PRINTER command when printing is completed.

TYPICAL OPERATION

This example shows you how to use the OPEN PRINTER and CLOSE PRINTER commands in a PAL script.

1. Type **SEW** to write a script. When asked for a script name, type **ADHOC** and press **Enter**.
2. Type the following command lines in the new script file. The "\n" causes a line feed so the next record prints on a new line.

```
Designing script C:\paradox3\adhoc                                         Script

....+...10....+...20....+...30....+...40....+...50....+...60....+...70....+...80
; adhoc.sc - prints record information without a report form
open printer
view "mailtx"
scan
  print [first name] +" "+ [last name] +"\n"
endscan
clearimage
close printer
; end adhoc.sc
```

3. Press **F10** and select the Go option. The report prints each name in the Mailtx table.
4. Turn to Module 69 to continue the recommended learning sequence.

Module 48
PAINTCANVAS

DESCRIPTION

Draw the user's attention to specific areas of the screen by making it different from the rest of the screen. For example, draw a colored box, and display, or request information within the box. Use the PAINTCANVAS command to draw the box. The syntax for this command follows.

```
PAINTCANVAS <<BORDER>> <<FILL <string>>>
    <<BLINK/INTENSE/REVERSE/<ATTRIBUTE <number>>/BACKGROUND>>
    <row1>,<column1>,<row2>,<column2>
```

Include the BORDER option when you want to draw a box on the screen. The horizontal and vertical lines of the box are one character wide.

Use the FILL <string> clause to provide the character to replace the specified area. For example, FILL CHR(176) replaces the area with dots.

Specify the colors for the background and foreground of the area by replacing <number> in the ATTRIBUTE clause with the desired color code. For example, FILL CHR(176) ATTRIBUTE 20 provides red dots on a blue background (4=red foreground, and 16=blue background).

Foreground colors:

0	Black	8	Dark Grey
1	Blue	9	Light Blue
2	Green	10	Light Green
3	Cyan	11	Light Cyan
4	Red	12	Light Red
5	Magenta	13	Light Magenta
6	Brown	14	Yellow
7	Light Grey	15	White

Background colors:

0	Black	64	Red
16	Blue	80	Magenta
32	Green	96	Brown
48	Cyan	112	Light Grey

Style the area with the BLINK, INTENSE, and/or REVERSE options to cause it to blink on and off, display high intensity, or display reverse video.

Include the BACKGROUND option to leave the color and style of the area unchanged while changing the fill character. For example, leave the background the same as the rest of the screen and just put dots in the specified area.

Identify the rectangular area of the screen by specifying the top left corner, and lower right corner of the rectangle in the PAINTCANVAS command line. Replace <row1> and <row2> with a number 1 through 24 to specify the position down the screen. Replace <column1> and <column2> with 1 through 80 to specify the position across the screen.

For example, include the following command to draw a box that begins in row 10, column 10, and ends in row 15, column 60.

```
PAINTCANVAS BORDER FILL CHR(176) 10, 10, 15, 60
```

NOTE: This command is available in version 3.0 and higher.

APPLICATIONS

Use the PAINTCANVAS command to draw the user's attention to a specific area of the screen. For example, draw a red box to identify an error, or a blue box to ask for a date range.

TYPICAL OPERATION

This example shows you how to use the PAINTCANVAS command.

1. Type **S** to select the Script menu option, **W** to select the Write menu option. When asked for the name of the script, type **PRINTBOX** and press **Enter**.
2. Type the following commands in the script area.

```
Designing script C:\paradox3\printbox                                  Script

....+...10....+...20....+...30....+...40....+...50....+...60....+...70....+...80
PAINTCANVAS FILL CHR(176) ATTRIBUTE 20 10,10,15,60
@ 12, 24 ?? "Printing - Please Wait..."
sleep 3000
```

3. Press **F10** (Menu) to display the menu line.
4. Type **G** to select the Go option. Your screen resembles the following display.

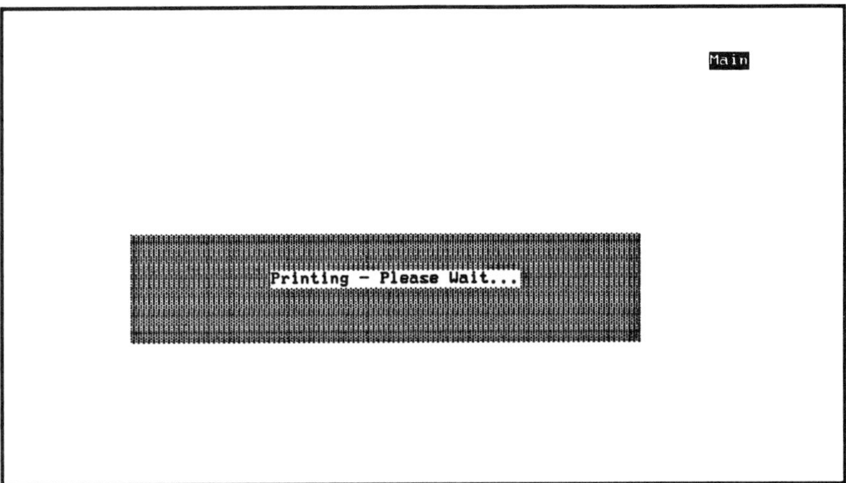

5. Type **SEE** to select the editor. Type **PRINTBOX** and press **Enter** to specify the script name. Change the PAINTCANVAS command so it matches the following.

```
Changing script C:\paradox3\printbox                                Script Ins

....+...10....+...20....+...30....+...40....+...50....+...60....+...70....+...80
canvas off
@ 03, 25 ?? "Aging Report"
sleep 1000
@ 05, 25 ?? "by Department"
sleep 1000
PAINTCANVAS BORDER FILL CHR(176) BACKGROUND 10,10,15,60                           ◆
@ 12, 24 ?? "Printing - Please Wait..."
canvas on
sleep 3000
```

6. Press **F10** to access the menu line. Type **G** to save and run the changed script. This time a dotted border is drawn around the message.
7. Change the PAINTCANVAS command again so it matches the following.

```
Changing script C:\paradox3\printbox                                Script

....+...10....+...20....+...30....+...40....+...50....+...60....+...70....+...80
canvas off
@ 03, 25 ?? "Aging Report"
sleep 1000
@ 05, 25 ?? "by Department"
sleep 1000
PAINTCANVAS BORDER REVERSE 10,10,15,60                                            ◆
@ 12, 24 ?? "Printing - Please Wait..."
canvas on
sleep 3000
```

8. Press **F10** and type **G**. A reverse video border is drawn around the message.
9. Turn to Module 12 to continue the recommended learning sequence.

Module 49
PASSWORD

DESCRIPTION

When a table is protected from unauthorized users, the script needs to include the PASSWORD command. It provides valid passwords for the protected tables that are accessed by the script. Use the following format for this command. Substitute "-n" with a number greater than 1.

```
PASSWORD <password-1>,...,<password-n>
```

Replace <password-1> through <password-n> with the passwords assigned to the tables that are referenced by the commands in the script. Unless provided in a variable, enclose the valid passwords with quotation marks.

When the proper password is provided, it is not required the next time that the script requests the table during the current session. Use the UNPASSWORD command to return the table to a protected status. Otherwise, they return to protected status upon ending the current session.

APPLICATIONS

Use the PASSWORD command before commands like the VIEW or EDIT command lines that access protected tables. Include a valid password for each protected table in the PASSWORD command line.

Remember that when a table's status is changed to unprotected, it remains that way for the rest of the Paradox session. Use the UNPASSWORD command to return a table's status to protected.

TYPICAL OPERATION

This example shows you how to use the PASSWORD command.

1. Play the Mainmenu script. Select the Utilities option. Then select the Passfile option. The application ends with a script error because the Mailfile table is requested by the Idcheck procedure. Since the table is protected, the script must provide the password.

2. Select the Cancel option by typing **C**. When asked for the password, press **Esc** twice to return to the Main Menu screen.

3. Edit the Maillist script. Insert the PASSWORD command line so that the first few lines of the Idcheck procedure match the one in the following display.

```
Changing script C:\paradox3\maillist                              Script Ins

....+...10....+...20....+...30....+...40....+...50....+...60....+...70....+...80
; maillist - prodedures for the Mail List application
clear
@ 05,10
?? "Size of the Maillist procedure library = "
?? filesize("Maillist.lib")
createlib "Maillist"
proc idcheck()
  private passes, idcode, x
password "LevelCodes"                                                          ◆
view "Mailfile"
copytoarray passes
clearall
clear
@ 10,10
?? "Enter your identification code "
accept "A4" picture "&&&#" to idcode
x = 2
while x < 12
  if idcode <> passes[x]
    then
    x = x + 2
  else
```

4. Press **F10** (Scripts Menu) and select the Go option. As the Maillist script is played, the changed Idcheck procedure is saved in the Maillist procedure library.

5. Press **F8** (Clear Image) to remove the procedure library list from the workspace.

6. Play the Mainmenu script again. Select the Utilitics option and then the Passfile option. This time you are asked for your identification code. Type **DLS1** and press **Enter**.

7. When the Mailfile table is displayed, press **F2** to return to the Utilities submenu.

8. Press **Esc** twice to end the application.

9. Type **V** to select the View option from the Main Menu line.

10. When asked for the name of the table, type **Mailfile** and press **Enter**. The table is displayed on the screen since its current status is unprotected.

11. Press **F8** (Clear Image) to remove the table from the workspace. Then exit Paradox.

12. Turn to Module 99 to continue the recommended learning sequence.

Module 50
PICKFORM

DESCRIPTION

Paradox provides a custom form automatically for each table structure that is created and saved. Forms (images) are used as patterns that tell Paradox the name and position of the fields to be presented on the screen to the user.

Each table is allowed ten different forms. The PICKFORM command lets the script specify which of the forms is to be used when presenting records to the user. The format for this command follows.

```
PICKFORM <form>
```

Replace <form> with the letter (F) or number (1 through 9) that is assigned to the form when it is designed and saved. The command line PICKFORM 1 tells Paradox to use the custom form that you assigned to the number 1. To select the automatic form, include PICKFORM F in the script.

When working with the Paradox menu-driven system, the form used to display a record is changed by selecting the Image option on the Main Menu line. When this option is selected, a submenu appears. It includes a PickForm option that lists the available forms for the selected table.

The PICKFORM command is an abbreviated form of the menu options. Include the PICKFORM command or the following command line in a script when selecting a custom form.

```
Menu {Image} {PickForm} {F}
```

The form identified by "F" is designed by Paradox when the table structure is created and saved. This form presents all fields down the screen as in the following display.

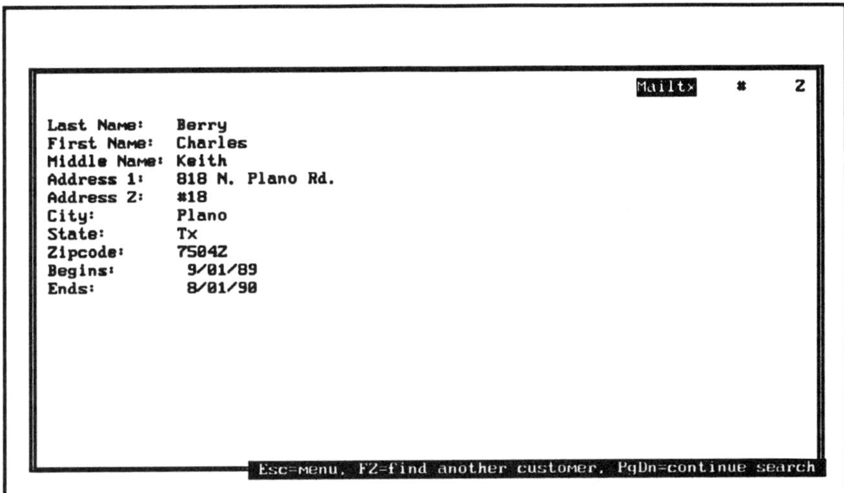

If this custom form is not sufficient, design and save your own forms. This is done by selecting the Forms option on the Main Menu screen. Design new forms or change the existing forms as needed.

When designing the form, consider the user who will work with it and include only the needed fields. For example, access to salary information is often limited to one or two users. Design one form that includes the salary field and another form that excludes it. By requiring different passwords from the users, the script is able to decide which of the two forms is to be specified in the PICKFORM command.

Use the DisplayOnly feature of custom form design for fields that must not be changed by the user. For example, access to key fields is often limited to certain users. One custom form only displays the key fields. Another form allows the user to change the values of those fields. Again, different passwords tell the script which form must be selected.

APPLICATIONS

Use the PICKFORM command in a script so that it selects the proper screen format to display a record for the user. If a form is not specified, Paradox presents the table in Table View. When the PICKFORM command is encountered, the record is presented to the user as specified by the form.

Do not use this command while the table is in edit mode. The PICKFORM command is valid when used with the VIEW command. A script error occurs if it is used with the EDIT command.

TYPICAL OPERATION

This example shows you how to use the PICKFORM command in a script.

1. Type **F** to select the Forms option. Then, select the Design option by typing **D**.
2. When asked for the name of the table, type **Mailtx** and press **Enter**.
3. The list of form identifiers appears across the screen. Press **Right Arrow** until the cursor is positioned on "2." Press **Enter**.
4. When asked for the form description, type **View Only** and press **Enter**. A blank screen similar to a new script screen appears on your workspace.
5. Design the form so that it matches the one in the following display.

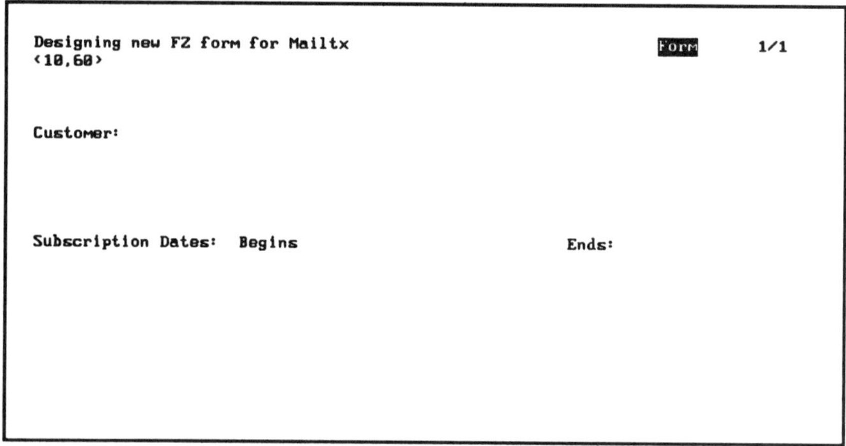

6. Use the arrow keys to position the cursor after the Customer description. Press **F10** (Forms Menu) and select the Field and Place options by typing **FP**.
7. Select the Calculated option by typing **C**. When asked for the expression, type **[First Name]+" " +[Middle Name]+" "+[Last Name]** and press **Enter**.
8. You are asked to position the cursor where you want the field to begin. Since it is already positioned, press **Enter**.
9. Press **Enter** again when asked to adjust the size of the field.
10. Move the cursor to the next line so that the cursor is under the first position of the name field. Press **F10** (Forms Menu) and select the Field and Place options.
11. Type **R** to select the regular option. A list of field names appear across the screen. Select the Address 1 field. Then position and adjust the size of the field on the screen. Put the Address 2 field on the next line.

12. Calculate the next line. When asked for the expression, type **[City]+", "+[State]+ " "+[Zipcode]** and press **Enter** three times.

13. Place the Beginning and Ending dates on the screen so that your screen resembles the one in the following display.

```
Designing new F2 form for Mailtx                              Form     1/1
<10,71>


Customer:  ______________________________________________________
           _________________________
           ____________________
           _____________________________________


Subscription Dates:  Begins __________              Ends __________
```

14. Press **F2** (DO-IT!) to save the form on disk. The Main Menu returns to the screen.

15. Edit the Custview script so that the PICKFORM command is used in the script instead of the FormKey command line.

```
Changing script C:\paradox3\custview                          Script Ins

....+...10....+...20....+...30....+...40....+...50....+...60....+...70....+...80
; custview - view customer data
view "Mailtx"
if isfile("mailtx.f2")                                                    ◆
  then                                                                    ◆
  Pickform "2"                                                            ◆
else                                                                      ◆
  Pickform "f"                                                            ◆
endif                                                                     ◆
while (true)
  clear
  @ 21,05
  ?? "To return to the menu, leave customer name blank..."
  @ 10,10
  ?? "Enter Last Name "
  accept "A30" to lastname
  @ 12,10
  ?? "Enter First Name "
  accept "A20" to firstname
  if lastname > "     " and firstname   > "     "
    then
    locate lastname, firstname
    if (retval)
```

16. Press **F10** (Scripts Menu) and select the DO-IT! option by typing **D**.

17. Play the Mainmenu script. Type **V** to select the View option. Type **Appleby** and press **Return**. Then type **Shirley** and press **Return**. Your screen resembles the following display.

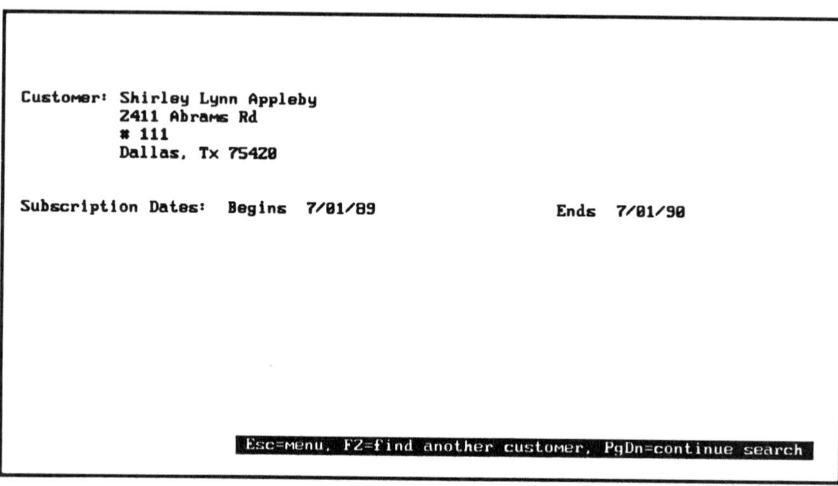
```
Customer: Shirley Lynn Appleby
          2411 Abrams Rd
          # 111
          Dallas, Tx 75420

Subscription Dates:  Begins  7/01/89                 Ends  7/01/90

                      Esc=menu, F2=find another customer, PgDn=continue search
```

18. Press **Esc** twice to exit the application.

19. Turn to Module 35 to continue the recommended learning sequence.

Module 51
PLAY

DESCRIPTION

When creating an application, write small scripts that perform certain tasks instead of including the same command lines in several scripts. This technique of writing modular scripts keeps them small and easy to edit. Instead of changing every script that performs the task, only one script requires your attention.

For example, a calculation must be performed by several scripts. Write a small one that includes the command lines needed to perform the calculation. Test the script thoroughly until it is producing the expected results.

When the calculation must be performed by a script in your application, use the PLAY command. The format of this command follows.

```
PLAY <script-name>
```

Replace <script-name> with the name of the script you want played. Unless provided in a variable, enclose <script-name> with quotation marks. The script that contains the PLAY command pauses while the other script is performed. When the second script's play is complete, the current script continues with the line that follows the PLAY command.

If <script-name> is not found on the disk, Paradox displays a script error on the screen. You must choose to cancel or debug the script.

Since a task-oriented script is played by several other scripts, the values are provided through variables, fields, and array elements. They must be available before Paradox encounters the PLAY command line. Otherwise, a run error occurs.

Any script may play one or more scripts but cannot play itself. When a script plays itself, a run error occurs.

Including the PLAY command in a script is similar to using the Play option of the Paradox menu-driven system. However, the application controls the scripts played so that the tasks are performed correctly.

APPLICATIONS

Use the PLAY command when you want one script to play another. For example, a script that displays a menu of options on the screen usually plays a different script for each option available. Instead of including all of the command lines necessary to perform each option, the script is written to play smaller, task-oriented scripts.

Even the script being played may include PLAY commands of its own. For example, script 1 plays script 2, and script 2 plays script 3.

As soon as the PLAY command in script 1 is encountered, Paradox begins script 2. When the PLAY command is encountered in script 2, Paradox begins script 3.

After Script 3 is played, Paradox returns to script 2 and plays the rest of the script. When script 2 is complete, Paradox plays the rest of script 1.

Each script is like a building block, one script supporting the next. Information is passed among the scripts through variables, fields, and array elements. An efficient, easy-to-use Paradox application is the result.

TYPICAL OPERATION

This example shows you how to use the PLAY command.

1. Type **S** to select the Scripts submenu. Select the Play option by typing **P**.
2. When asked for the name of the script, type **Mainmenu** and press **Enter**. The screen clears and your application menu is displayed across the top of the screen.
3. Type **L** to select the Labels option. The screen clears and "Labels. . ." appears on line ten. When your application menu reappears on the screen, press **Esc** to return to the Paradox Main Menu.
4. Open the Mainmenu script. Instead of displaying "Weekcalc. . ." on the screen when that option is selected, play the script called Weekcalc. Change your script so that it resembles the one in the following display.

```
Changing script C:\paradox3\mainmenu                        Script Ins

....+...10....+...20....+...30....+...40....+...50....+...60....+...70....+...80
    ?? "Maintenance..."
    sleep 2000
  case mchoice = "Labels" :
    @ 10,10
    ?? "Labels..."
    sleep 2000
  case mchoice = "Configure" :
    @ 10,10
    ?? "Configure..."
    sleep 2000
  case mchoice = "Weekcalc" :
    play "Weekcalc"
  case mchoice = "Esc" : quit
  otherwise :
    clear
    @ 10,10
    ?? "The requested option is not available from this menu..."
    sleep 2000
  endswitch
endwhile
```

5. Press **F10** (Scripts Menu) and select the Go option by typing **G**.
6. When the application menu appears, type **W** to select Weekcalc.
7. Test several date combinations to make sure that the script is playing correctly. When asked if you want to do another calculation, type **N** and press **Enter**.
8. Test the other three options to make sure that they were not affected by the script change. When the Maintenance, Labels, and Configure options are tested, press **Esc** to return to the Main Menu screen.
9. Change the script again. This time change the Maintenance option so that it plays a script called Custmnt.

```
Changing script C:\paradox3\mainmenu                                    Script Ins

....+...10....+...20....+...30....+...40....+...50....+...60....+...70....+...80
  default "Maintenance" to mchoice
  switch
  case mchoice = "Maintenance" :
    play "Custmnt"                                                             ◆
  case mchoice = "Labels" :
    @ 10,10
    ?? "Labels..."
    sleep 2000
  case mchoice = "Configure" :
    @ 10,10
    ?? "Configure..."
    sleep 2000
  case mchoice = "Weekcalc" :
    play "Weekcalc"
  case mchoice = "Esc" : quit
  otherwise :
    clear
    @ 10,10
    ?? "The requested option is not available from this menu..."
    sleep 2000
  endswitch
endwhile
```

10. Press **F10** (Scripts Menu) and select the Go option.
11. When the application menu appears on your screen, type **M** to select the Maintenance option. Since a script called "Custmnt" has not been written and saved on disk, a script error occurs.
12. Select the Cancel option by typing **C**.
13. Turn to Module 68 to continue the recommended learning sequence.

Module 52
PRINT

DESCRIPTION

This command combines the PRINTER command with the ?, ??, and TEXT commands. When it is encountered in a script, the printer is activated, the information is printed on the paper, and the printer is deactivated.

Instead of sending information to a printer, send it to a file on disk. This is helpful when you need an audit trail for table activity.

There are two forms of the PRINT command. Their formats follow.

```
PRINT <expression-1>,...,<expression-n>
PRINT FILE <file name> <expression-1>,...,<expression-n>
```

Replace <expression-1> through <expression-n> with at least one value that you want sent to the printer or disk. If more than one value is included in the command line, separate each one with a comma. Though the string expressions are expected in the PRINT command, any non-string value is automatically converted to a string value.

The values are linked (concatenated) as they appear in the command line. For example, PRINT "Customer table was last maintained by", "DLS1" sends "Customer table was last maintained by DLS1" to the printer since a space was not provided within the quotation marks.

Use the FILE <file name> clause when the values of <expression-1> through <expression-n> are to be saved in a file on disk. Replace <file name> with the name you want assigned to the resulting file. Do not separate <file name> from <expression-1> with a comma. Otherwise a syntax error occurs while playing the script.

Send any type of information to the printer or file. Replace <expression-1> through <expression-n> with string values enclosed with quotation marks, variables, Paradox functions (e.g., TIME( ), TODAY( ), etc.), or ASCII codes. Do not include ASCII code 255 to supply the NULL character in the PRINT command. It must be represented by "\0" (backslash, zero).

APPLICATIONS

Use the PRINT command in a script to send special information to the printer or a file on disk. Send information to the printer for the user. Send it to a file on disk as an audit trail for yourself.

For example, when a table is empty, its reports are not printed. To make sure that the user knows that the report was considered by the script, send a message to the printer that describes (on paper) the situation. Otherwise, the script is thought to have skipped the report.

If the printer is a dot matrix, use the PRINT command to send the proper codes so that it prints small or near letter-quality characters. If the printer is letter quality, but the ribbon is light, send the codes to tell the printer to double-strike each character. By setting the proper codes in the script, the user is relieved of that responsiblity.

Saving information in a file on disk is helpful for recording application activity. For example, use the PRINT FILE command to record the identification code, date, and time that a user performs the Maintenance option of the application.

If the file does not exist on the disk, Paradox creates it. Then the information is added to the end of the file.

Accumulate as much of the information as needed but remember that the file is limited to the remaining disk space. Establish a rule that the file is saved on a floppy disk. Change it each day, month, quarter, or within a specific time frame so that the available disk space is not exceeded.

TYPICAL OPERATION

This example shows you how to use the PRINT command.

1. Type **SEW** to write a new script. When asked for the name, type **Prtcond** and press **Enter**.

The script must set the dot matrix printer so that small letters are printed. Write the new script so that it matches the one in the following display. If your printer uses different codes, substitute the proper decimal number for the "15" that is used in this display.

```
Designing script C:\paradox3\prtcond                              Script

....+...10....+...20....+...30....+...40....+...50....+...60....+...70....+...80
;prtcond - set printer for condensed (small) IBM characters
print chr(15)
;end prtcond
```

2. Press **F10** (Scripts Menu) and select the DO-IT! option by typing **D**.

3. Write and save another script called Prtnorm so that it matches the script in the following display. If your printer uses different codes, substitute the proper decimal number for the "18" that is used in this display.

```
Designing script C:\paradox3\prtnorm                                  Script

....+...10....+...20....+...30....+...40....+...50....+...60....+...70....+...80
;prtnorm - set printer for normal IBM characters
print chr(18)
;end prtnorm
```

4. Press **F10** (Scripts Menu) and select the DO-IT! option.
5. Play the Mainmenu script. When the application menu appears, select the Labels option and print the labels. They are printed in normal sized letters. When the application menu returns to the screen, press **Esc** for the Main Menu screen.
6. Edit the Mainmenu script. Change the Label option by inserting the script line to play the Prtcond and Prtnorm scripts. The dots indicate lines not shown from the Mainmenu script. Do not change those lines.

```
Changing script C:\paradox3\mainmenu                                  Script Ins

....+...10....+...20....+...30....+...40....+...50....+...60....+...70....+...80
  case mchoice = "Labels" :
    play "prtcond"                                                          ◆
    ans = "Y"
    while ans = "Y"
      clear
      @ 10,10
      ?? "Print a sample label for alignment (Y/N)? "
      .
      .
      .
    endwhile
    clear
    @ 10,10
    ?? "Printing Labels - Please Wait..."
    report "Mailtx" "1"
    play "prtnorm"                                                          ◆
  case mchoice = "Configure" :
    @ 10,10
    ?? "Configure..."
```

7. Press **F10** (Scripts Menu) and select the DO-IT! option.
8. Play the Mainmenu script. Make sure that you turn on the printer. Select the Labels option from the application menu and print the labels. The characters printed on the labels are small (condensed).
9. When the application menu returns, print the columnar report by typing **R**. The report prints in normal letters since the Labels option played Prtnorm before returning to the application menu. When the application menu returns to the screen, press **Esc**. The Main Menu screen is displayed.

10. Type **SEE** to edit the Idcheck script. Insert the PRINT FILE script line as shown in the following display.

```
Changing script C:\paradox3\idcheck                                    Script Ins

....+...10....+...20....+...30....+...40....+...50....+...60....+...70....+...80....+...90....+
; idcheck - checks for valid identification codes
clear
@ 10,10
?? "Enter your identification code "
accept "A4" picture "&&&#" to idcode
if idcode = "DLS1" or idcode = "ELW1"
  then
  print file "c:log" "Customer table was last changed by ",idcode," on ",today()," at ",time()♦
  return True
else
  message "You have typed an invalid ID code..."
  sleep 2000
  return False
endif
; end idcheck
```

11. Press **F10** (Scripts Menu) and select the DO-IT! option. When the Main Menu returns to the screen, play Mainmenu again.

12. Select the Maintenance option from the application's menu. Type **DLS1** for the ID code and press **Enter**. When asked for the name of the table, type **Mailtx** and press **Enter**.

13. A blank record appears on the screen. Press **F2** to return to the application's menu. Then press **Esc** so that the Main Menu appears on your screen.

14. Select the Tools option by typing **T**. When the Tools submenu appears, select the More option by typing **M**. Type **T** to select the ToDOS option.

15. The screen changes so that the DOS prompt appears to the left of the cursor. Type **type log** and press **Enter**. The file called Log is listed on the screen. It matches the following display.

```
WARNING! Do not delete or edit Paradox objects, or load RAM-resident programs.
To return to Paradox, type exit.


The IBM Personal Computer DOS
Version 3.30 (C)Copyright International Business Machines Corp 1981, 1987
             (C)Copyright Microsoft Corp 1981, 1986

C:\PARADOX3>type log
Customer table was last changed by DLS1 on 2/28/90 at 14:55:58
C:\PARADOX3>
```

16. Type **Exit** to return to the Main Menu of the Paradox menu-driven system.
17. Play the application again. Use the Maintenance option with ELW1 as the ID code. Then exit the application and return to the ToDOS screen. List the file called Log to see that there are two messages saved in the file. This is a good technique for tracking the table maintenance.
18. When the system prompt appears on the ToDOS screen, type **Exit** and press **Enter**. The Main Menu returns to your screen.
19. Turn to Module 100 to continue the recommended learning sequence.

Module 53
PRINTER

DESCRIPTION

There are times when you want to print information on the printer before or after a report. Use the ?, ??, PRINT, or TEXT commands to supply that information. By including the PRINTER command in the script, you tell Paradox when to start and stop the printer. There are two options for this command.

```
PRINTER ON
PRINTER OFF
```

When the PRINTER ON command line is encountered, all output generated by the ?, ??, PRINT, and TEXT commands is sent to the printer. This activity continues until the PRINTER OFF command line is encountered.

For example, before the Mailtx columnar report is printed, send a report banner to the printer. The banner is printed on the page before the report as follows.

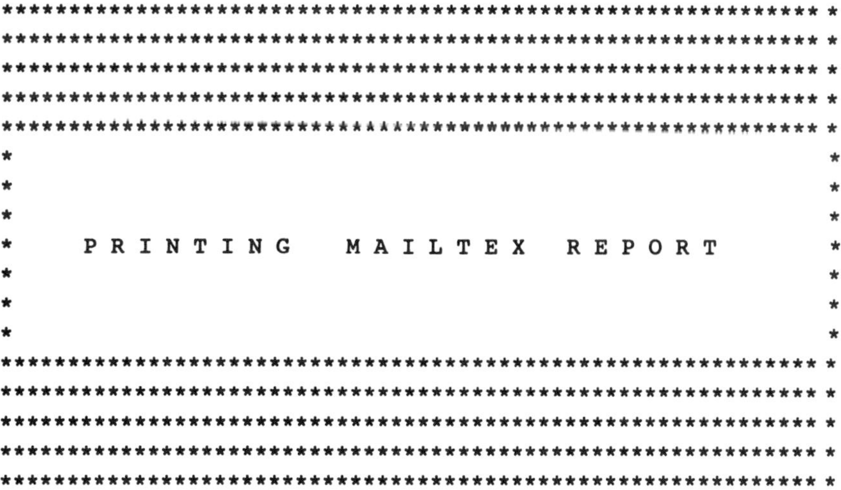

By including a banner page between several reports, the stack of paper is easier to divide since the banner page is different. The following command lines send a banner to the printer.

```
printer on
text
************************************************************** *
************************************************************** *
************************************************************** *
************************************************************** *
************************************************************** *
*                                                               *
*                                                               *
*                                                               *
*     P R I N T I N G     M A I L T E X     R E P O R T         *
*                                                               *
*                                                               *
*                                                               *
************************************************************** *
************************************************************** *
************************************************************** *
************************************************************** *
************************************************************** *
endtext
printer off
```

When printing table data on special forms, the paper needs to be aligned so that the information prints in the proper area. The job is easier when you print a sample form until the paper is correctly aligned in the printer.

Write the script so that the user is asked if another alignment attempt is needed. When the user says "Yes," a sample is printed. Otherwise, the table data is printed.

There are several ways to print sample forms. One way is to print a table that contains one or two records. This table is used only for paper alignment. Use the same report form for both tables.

Another way is to use ?, ??, PRINT, or TEXT commands within PRINTER ON and PRINTER OFF command lines. Fill several of the areas on the form so that the user knows that the paper is aligned properly. The following command lines print an alignment sample for labels each time the user answers "Yes."

```
ans = "Y"
while ans = "Y"
  clear
  @ 10,10
  ?? "Print a sample label for alignment {Y/N}? "
  accept "A1" picture "&" to ans
  if ans = "Y"
    then
    clear
    printer on
    @ 1,5
```

```
        text
          xxxxxxxxxxxxxxxxxxxxxxxxxxx
          xxxxxxxxxxxxxxxxxxxxxxxxxxx
          xxxxxxxxxxxxxxxxxxxxxxxxxxx
          xxxxxxxxxxxxxxxxxxxxxxxxxxx

        endtext
        printer off
      endif
    endwhile
```

Notice that the user is asked if another alignment attempt is needed. This is displayed only on the screen. When the user types Y, Paradox is told to activate the printer. The sample is printed. Then the printer is deactivated.

Remember that the commands PRINTER ON and PRINTER OFF only activate the echoing of information to the printer. They do not turn the electrical power on and off.

APPLICATIONS

Use the PRINTER command anytime you want information sent to the printer. For example, print a message for the user about why a report is not printed. By supplying a message instead of the report, the user is informed (on paper) that the report was considered by the script. Otherwise, the script is thought to have ignored or skipped the requested report.

The information must be provided through ?, ??, PRINT, or TEXT commands. When these command lines are encountered after a PRINTER ON command line, their information is sent to the printer as well as the screen. This echoing continues until the PRINTER OFF command line is encountered. If you turn it on, do not forget to turn it off.

TYPICAL OPERATION

This example shows you how to use the PRINTER command.

1. Use the Scripts Editor to call Mainmenu.
2. Change the Labels option in the script so that it matches the one in the following display.

```
Changing script C:\paradox3\mainmenu                                 Script Ins
....+...10....+...20....+...30....+...40....+...50....+...60....+...70....+...80
  case mchoice = "Report" :
    @ 10,10
    ?? "Printing the columnar report - Please Wait..."
    report "Mailtx" "R"
  case mchoice = "Labels" :
    ans = "Y"                                                                  ◆
    while ans = "Y"                                                            ◆
      clear                                                                    ◆
      @ 10,10                                                                  ◆
      ?? "Print a sample label for alignment (Y/N)? "                          ◆
      accept "A1" picture "&" to ans                                           ◆
      if ans = "Y"                                                             ◆
        then                                                                   ◆
        clear                                                                  ◆
        printer on                                                             ◆
        @ 1,5                                                                  ◆
        text                                                                   ◆
          xxxxxxxxxxxxxxxxxxxxxxxxxxxx                                         ◆
          xxxxxxxxxxxxxxxxxxxxxxxxxxxx                                         ◆
          xxxxxxxxxxxxxxxxxxxxxxxxxxxx                                         ◆
          xxxxxxxxxxxxxxxxxxxxxxxxxxxx                                         ◆
                                                                               ◆
        endtext                                                                ◆
        printer off                                                            ◆
      endif                                                                    ◆
    endwhile                                                                   ◆
    clear                                                                      ◆
    @ 10,10
    ?? "Printing Labels - Please Wait..."                                      ◆
    sleep 2000                                                                 ◆
  case mchoice = "Configure" :
    @ 10,10
    ?? "Configure..."
    sleep 2000
  case mchoice = "Weekcalc" :
    play "Weekcalc"
  case mchoice = "Esc" :
    quit
  otherwise :
    clear
    @ 10,10
    ?? "The requested option is not available from this menu..."
```

3. Press **F10** (Scripts Menu) and select the DO-IT! option.
4. Play the Mainmenu script. When the application menu appears on your screen, type **L** to select the Labels option.
5. Make sure that your printer is turned on. When asked if you want to print a sample label for alignment, type **Y** and press **Enter**. This lets you move the blank labels up or down until each sample prints in the same place for each new label. Print three sample labels then type **N** and press **Enter** to return to the menu. Your paper resembles the following.

```
XXXXXXXXXXXXXXXXXXXXX
XXXXXXXXXXXXXXXXXXXXX
XXXXXXXXXXXXXXXXXXXXX
XXXXXXXXXXXXXXXXXXXXX

XXXXXXXXXXXXXXXXXXXXX
XXXXXXXXXXXXXXXXXXXXX
XXXXXXXXXXXXXXXXXXXXX
```

XXXXXXXXXXXXXXXXXXXXX

XXXXXXXXXXXXXXXXXXXXX
XXXXXXXXXXXXXXXXXXXXX
XXXXXXXXXXXXXXXXXXXXX
XXXXXXXXXXXXXXXXXXXXX

6. When the application menu returns, press **Esc** for the Main Menu screen.
7. Return to the Main Menu and type **R** to select the Reports option. Type **D** to select the Design option of the Reports submenu. When asked for the name of the table to be used for this report form, type **Mailtx** and press **Enter.**
8. A list of possible identifiers appears across your screen. The current selection is the Mail List for Mailtx. Press **Right Arrow** to position the cursor on "1." Since this one is unused, press **Enter.**
9. When asked for a report description, type **Labels** and press **Enter.**
10. Type **F** to select the Free-form option when asked if the report is Tabular or Free-form. The following display appears on your screen.

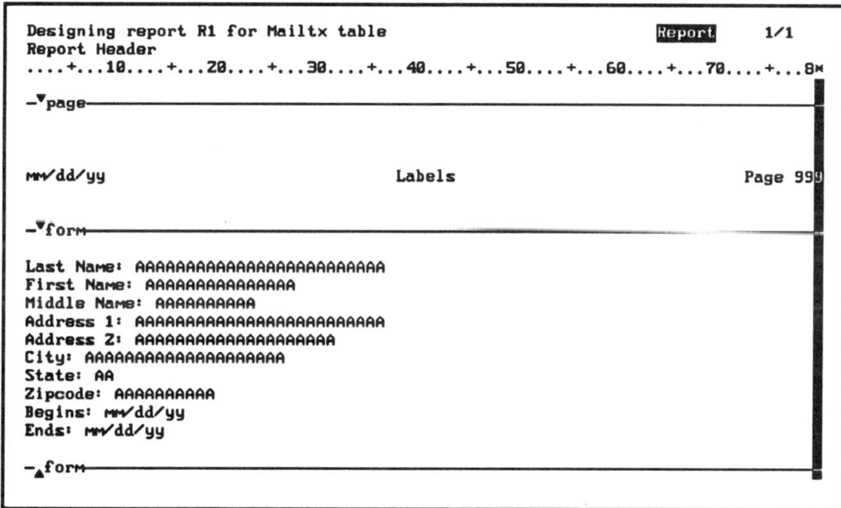

```
Designing report R1 for Mailtx table                          Report     1/1
Report Header
....+...10....+...20....+...30....+...40....+...50....+...60....+...70....+...80
-▼page-------------------------------------------------------------------------

MM/dd/yy                              Labels                            Page 999

-▼form-------------------------------------------------------------------------

Last Name: AAAAAAAAAAAAAAAAAAAAAAAAA
First Name: AAAAAAAAAAAAAAA
Middle Name: AAAAAAAAAA
Address 1: AAAAAAAAAAAAAAAAAAAAAAAAA
Address 2: AAAAAAAAAAAAAAAAAAAA
City: AAAAAAAAAAAAAAAAAAAA
State: AA
Zipcode: AAAAAAAAAA
Begins: MM/dd/yy
Ends: MM/dd/yy

-▲form-------------------------------------------------------------------------
```

11. Press **Ctrl-Y** to delete all blank lines and report heading from the report form. Press **Down Arrow** to position the cursor on the blank lines.
12. Use the arrow keys to position the cursor on the first character of "Last Name." Press **Del** until the field name is removed from the line and the field identifiers are in the first position of the line. Continue this activity for all field names in the report form so that your screen resembles the following display.

```
Designing report R1 for Mailtx table                          Report Ins 1/1
Form Band                                                               Ends
....+...10....+...20....+...30....+...40....+...50....+...60....+...70....+...8»

-▼page──────────────────────────────────────────────────────────────────────
-▼form──────────────────────────────────────────────────────────────────────
AAAAAAAAAAAAAAAAAAAAAAAAA
AAAAAAAAAAAAAAA
AAAAAAAAAA
AAAAAAAAAAAAAAAAAAAAAAAAA
AAAAAAAAAAAAAAAAAAAA
AAAAAAAAAAAAAAAAAAAA
AA
AAAAAAAAAA
mm/dd/yy
mm/dd/yy
-▲form──────────────────────────────────────────────────────────────────────
-▲page──────────────────────────────────────────────────────────────────────
```

13. Press **F10** (Report Menu) and select the Field option by typing **F**. When the Field submenu appears, select the Erase option by typing **E**.

14. You are asked to position the cursor on the field to be removed. Press **Up Arrow** until the cursor is positioned on the Last Name field. Press **Enter**. The line is now blank. Continue this activity to erase all fields from the report form. Each is replaced by a blank line.

15. Press **Up Arrow** until the cursor is positioned on the first blank line in the form band.

16. Press **F10** (Report Menu) and select the Field option by typing **F**. Select the Place option by typing **P**.

17. Since the complete name is to appear on the first line of the label, select the Calculated field option by typing **C**.

18. When asked for the field expression, type **[First Name]+" "+[Middle Name]+" "+[Last Name]** and press **Enter**. You are asked to position the cursor where the field is to begin. Press **Enter** since the cursor is already there.

19. When asked to adjust the field size, press **Left Arrow** twenty times to shorten the size of the print area. Then press **Enter**.

20. Use the arrow keys to move the cursor to the first position on the next blank line. Press **F10** (Report Menu) and select the Field option. Type **P** to select the Place option.

21. Type **R** to select the Regular option from the Place submenu. A list of the table's fields appears across the screen. Position the cursor on the Address 1 field name and press **Enter** three times to select the field, position it on the form, and resize it.

22. Do the same thing for the third blank line of the form band. This time place the Address 2 field.

23. The fourth line must be a Calculated field. When ready for the expression, type **[City]+", "+[State]+" "+[Zipcode]** and press **Enter** three times.

24. Delete blank lines until two remain within the form band so that your screen resembles the following display.

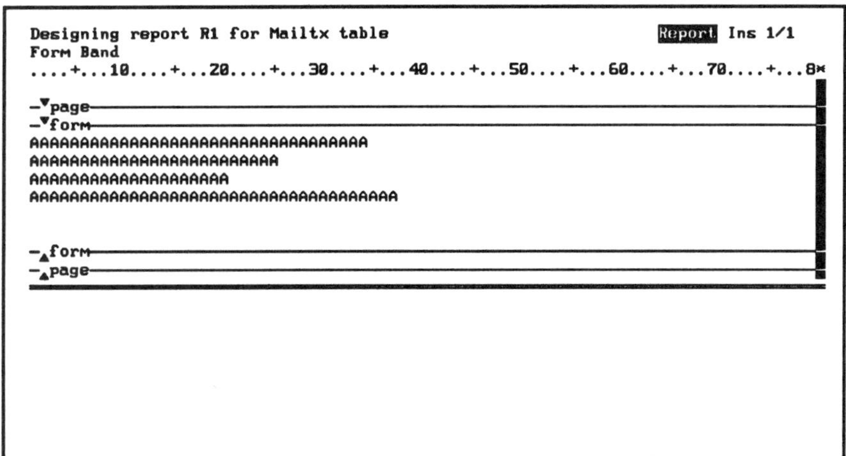

```
Designing report R1 for Mailtx table                        Report Ins 1/1
Form Band
....+...10....+...20....+...30....+...40....+...50....+...60....+...70....+...8
-▼page
-▼form
AAAAAAAAAAAAAAAAAAAAAAAAAAAAAAAAAA
AAAAAAAAAAAAAAAAAAAAAAAAA
AAAAAAAAAAAAAAAAAAAA
AAAAAAAAAAAAAAAAAAAAAAAAAAAAAAAAAAAAA

-▲form
-▲page
```

25. Press **F10** (Report Menu) and select the Settings option. Type **R** to select the RemoveBlanks option. When the submenu appears for Linesqueeze and Fieldsqueeze, type **L** to select the Linesqueeze option. When asked to confirm the selection, type **Y**.

26. When asked if the forms are Fixed or Variable length, type **F**.

27. Perform the same menu selections so that Fieldsqueeze is also selected. Notice the second line on your screen tells the position of the cursor and the form settings.

28. Press **F2** (DO-IT!) to save the new report form on disk. The Main Menu returns to your screen.

29. Change the Labels option of the Mainmenu script so that it matches the lines shown in the following display.

```
Changing script C:\paradox3\mainmenu                                    Script

....+...10....+...20....+...30....+...40....+...50....+...60....+...70....+...80
        printer on
        @ 1,5
        text
xxxxxxxxxxxxxxxxxxxxxxxxxxxx                                                   ◆
xxxxxxxxxxxxxxxxxxxxxxxxxxxx                                                   ◆
xxxxxxxxxxxxxxxxxxxxxxxxxxxx                                                   ◆
xxxxxxxxxxxxxxxxxxxxxxxxxxxx                                                   ◆

        endtext
        printer off
      endif
    endwhile
    clear
    @ 10,10
    ?? "Printing Labels - Please Wait..."
    report "Mailtx" "1"                                                        ◆
  case mchoice = "Configure" :
    @ 10,10
    ?? "Configure..."
    sleep 2000
  case mchoice = "Weekcalc" :
    play "Weekcalc"
```

30. Press **F10** (Scripts Menu) and select the DO-IT! option. The Main Menu returns to the screen.

31. Play the Mainmenu script. Select the Labels option from the application menu. Print two sample labels for alignment. Then type **N** so that the labels print from the table. The printout resembles the following.

```
XXXXXXXXXXXXXXXXXXXXX
XXXXXXXXXXXXXXXXXXXXX
XXXXXXXXXXXXXXXXXXXXX
XXXXXXXXXXXXXXXXXXXXX

Shirley Lynn Appleby
2411 Abrams Rd
# 111
Dallas, Tx 75240

Charles Keith Berry
818 N. Plano Rd.
#18
Plano, Tx 75042

Arnold Thomas Chadwick
1112 Sherman Hwy.
Allen, Tx
```

32. When the application menu returns, press **Esc**.

33. Turn to Module 52 to continue the recommended learning sequence.

Module 54
PRIVTABLES

DESCRIPTION

Use the PRIVTABLES command to create or copy tables into a user's private directory. In most multi-user environments, temporary tables are automatically stored in a user's private directory while all others are stored in the specified directory.

The PRIVTABLES command allows you to specify tables that are to be created in or copied to your private directory. When you request a home directory listing, PARADOX shows you the tables in your private directory.

NOTE: The PRIVTABLES command was added for Paradox 2.0 and higher. It causes an error in earlier versions.

APPLICATIONS

Issue the PRIVTABLES command to help reduce clutter in shared directories. The ability to store specified tables in a private directory also enhances the security of information.

For example, create an empty table structure and its associated report forms. If two users try to run the same report at the same time, one is locked out until the first report is complete and the table released.

Prevent this problem by declaring a temporary table name in a PRIVTABLES command line, and copy the empty table to the private directory. Once the copy is available in the home directory, the shared table is available for another user. Fill and report the private table at your convenience.

TYPICAL OPERATION

This illustration shows you how to use the PRIVTABLES command for creating a report on a network.

1. Type **SEW** to write a new script. When asked for the name, type **Rpt1** and press **Enter**.
2. Type the following command lines in the new script.

```
Designing script C:\paradox3\rpt1                                    Script

....+...10....+...20....+...30....+...40....+...50....+...60....+...70....+...80
; rpt1.sc - prints a report for a shared table
privtables "A1"
while true
  lock "Mailtx" pfl
  if retval then
    quitloop
  else
    message errormessage()+"...Esc stops next try"
  endif
  sleep 3500
  if charwaiting() then
    x = getchar()
    if not retval then
      release vars x
      return
    endif
    release vars x
  endif
endwhile
copy "Mailtx" "A1"
unlock "Mailtx" pfl
report "A1" 1
delete "A1"
; end rpt1.sc
```

3. Press **F10** and select the Go option. The report is printed.
4. Use two workstations to print the same report. Since the shared table is locked for a short time, it is not locked very long from the second user.
5. Turn to Module 70 to continue the recommended learning sequence.

Module 55
PROC, ENDPROC

DESCRIPTION

Instead of including the same set of command lines in several scripts of an application, save them in a script or a procedure. When a change is made to the command lines, it is immediately available to all scripts that use the command line.

A procedure is usually a small, specialized script that the application stores in the computer's memory. It is available immediately when the application needs to perform the task. Therefore, procedures speed the processing time.

Write a procedure as you do any script. However, use the following format so that Paradox knows that it is a procedure instead of a script.

```
PROC <name> (<parameters>)
     << PRIVATE <private variables> >>
  <commands>
ENDPROC
```

The PROC command marks the beginning of the procedure. The ENDPROC identifies the end of the procedure. When you use the PROC command, there must be an ENDPROC command to match it. The two commands are always used as a pair.

The procedure is identified by <name>. Supply a script-like name that describes the task performed by the procedure.

Though <parameters> is optional, the parentheses are required after <name>. For example, <name> is replaced by "SETUP." The procedure is always referenced as SETUP( ).

When <parameters> is included in the PROC command line, replace it with at least one variable name that is used within the procedure. Include only the variable names that require values from the script that is playing (calling) the procedure. When more than one variable replaces <parameters>, separate them with commas. These variables are called *private variables.*

The PRIVATE <private variables> clause is optional. Include it when you need to declare variables within the procedure. Replace <private variables> with all variable names used within the procedure that are not listed in <parameters>.

Procedures are restricted to using private variables. Before Paradox returns to the script that called the procedure, all private variables are released automatically.

Remember that it is possible to have a global variable and a private variable with the same name. For example, if variable MFILE is declared by a script, it is considered a global variable. Then a script calls a procedure that declares a private variable called MFILE. The procedure is allowed to use only private variables.

Replace <commands> with at least one command line. For example, include the command lines that ask the user for a valid identification code (password).

APPLICATIONS

It is easy to change a script into a procedure. Therefore, write all the scripts for the application and test it. Then decide which scripts are good procedure candidates.

For example, several scripts in the Mail List application require a valid password from the user. Therefore, a separate script called Idcheck is written and saved on disk. Since Idcheck is played by several scripts and is fairly small, consider changing it from a script to a procedure.

Use procedures to speed the processing time of a script. Once the procedure is stored in the computer's memory, it is available immediately. The disk is not read each time that the procedure is called by a script.

Be careful, however, that proper housekeeping is done so that the application always has plenty of memory available. Since procedures are actually scripts, they occupy more memory than variables. Use one of the RELEASE PROCS commands to remove the procedure from memory.

TYPICAL OPERATION

This example shows you how to use the PROC, ENDPROC command combination.

1. Type **TRS** (Tools/Rename/Script). When asked for the current name of the script, type **Idcheck** and press **Enter**. Type **Maillist** for the new name and press **Enter**.
2. Edit the Maillist script to change it from a script into a procedure that returns a True or False condition to the script that plays it.

```
Changing script C:\paradox3\maillist                                   Script Ins

....+...10....+...20....+...30....+...40....+...50....+...60....+...70....+...80
; idcheck - checks for valid identification codes
proc idcheck()                                                              ◆
  private passes, idcode, x                                                 ◆
view "Mailfile"                                                             ◆
copytoarray passes                                                          ◆
clearall                                                                    ◆
clear
@ 10,10
?? "Enter your identification code "
.
.
.
  clearall
  return passes[x+1]                                                        ◆
else
  message "You have typed an invalid ID code..."
  sleep 2000
  clearall
  return False
endif
endproc                                                                     ◆
; end idcheck
```

3. Press **F10** (Scripts Menu) and select the DO-IT! option.
4. Edit the Utility script. Change the Passfile option so that it plays the Idcheck procedure to validate the identification code as in the following display.

```
Changing script C:\paradox3\utility                                    Script Ins

....+...10....+...20....+...30....+...40....+...50....+...60....+...70....+...80
    case mutility = "Passfile" :
      x = idcheck()                                                         ◆
      if x = "9"                                                            ◆
        then
        edit "Mailfile"
        formkey
        wait table message "Press F2 to return to the menu..." until "F2"
        do_it!
        clearall
      else
        message "You have typed an invalid ID code..."
        sleep 2000
        clearall
      endif
      savevars all
      if isfile("Passes.sc")
        then
        Menu {Tools} {Rename} {Script} {Savevars} {Passes} {Replace}
      else
        Menu {Tools} {Rename} {Script} {Savevars} {Passes}
      endif
      release vars idcode, x                                                ◆
```

5. Save the script with the DO-IT! option of the Scripts Menu.
6. Edit the Mainmenu script so that it plays the Idcheck procedure.

```
Changing script C:\paradox3\mainmenu                              Script  Ins
....+...10....+...20....+...30....+...40....+...50....+...60....+...70....+...80
play "Maillist"                                                                ◆
while (true)
  clear
  showmenu
    "View" : "Find and review customer information.",
    "Maintenance" : "Maintains table data.",
    "Report" : "Print the columnar report.",
    "Labels" : "Print mailing labels.",
    "Update" : "Batch update master table from a floppy disk.",
    "Summary" : "Provide statistics on subscription preferences.",
    "Configure" : "Change application configuration.",
    "Utilities" : "Perform various tasks for the Mail List application."
  default "View" to mchoice
  switch
  case mchoice = "View" :
    play "Custview"
  case mchoice = "Maintenance" :
    x = Idcheck()
    if x > "0" and x < "10"                                                    ◆
      then                                                                     ◆
      play "Custmnt"
    endif
```

7. Save the changed script by pressing **F10** (Scripts Menu) and selecting the DO-IT! option. The Main Menu returns to your screen.
8. Play the Mainmenu script and select the Utilities option from the application menu.
9. Type **P** to select the Passfile option. Type **FFS1** and press **Enter** when asked for an ID code. A message appears telling you that the code is invalid for the option.
10. Select the Passfile option again. This time, type **DLS1** and press **Enter** for the ID code. The table is presented on the screen. Press **F2** as instructed to return to the menu. Press **Esc** to return to the application menu.
11. Since the Maintenance option is also password protected, test it twice for the ELW1 and DLS1 passwords. Then return to the Main Menu of the application.
12. Press **Esc** to end the application.
13. Use the Script Editor to see the variables saved in the Passes script. It resembles the following display.

```
Changing script C:\paradox3\passes                                Script
....+...10....+...20....+...30....+...40....+...50....+...60....+...70....+...80
; Variables Saved Using Savevars Command

x = "9"
mutility = "Passfile"
mchoice = "Utilities"
```

14. Press **F10** (Scripts Menu) and select the Cancel option. Type **Y** when asked to confirm the selection.
15. Turn to Module 21 to continue the recommended learning sequence.

Module 56
PROMPT

DESCRIPTION

Use the PROMPT command to customize the top two lines of the screen when a menu is not being displayed.

To use the PROMPT command, the ECHO NORMAL, FAST, or SLOW command must be in effect. The syntax of the PROMPT command is:

```
PROMPT << <prompt1>, <prompt2> >>
```

Replace <prompt1> and <prompt2> with information to be displayed at the top of the screen. Provide this information as text enclosed by quotation marks, or from variables.

Provide both prompt lines even if the second is blanks enclosed by quotes. Cancel the effect of the PROMPT command and allow Paradox to control the prompt area by placing the PROMPT command in your script on a line by itself.

NOTE: The PROMPT command is available in version 2.0 and higher.

APPLICATIONS

The PROMPT command allows you to customize the appearance of the screen through PAL scripts. It is particularly valuable when you want to inform the user of special conditions or keypresses.

TYPICAL OPERATION

This illustration shows you how to use the PROMPT command.

1. Make sure Paradox is in Main Menu mode. Type **SEW** (Scripts, Editor, Write) to use the Paradox script editor to create a new script.
2. When asked for the name of your new script, type **DEMOPRMP** and press **Enter**.
3. Type the following script.

```
Designing script C:\paradox3\demoprmp                                    Script

....+...10....+...20....+...30....+...40....+...50....+...60....+...70....+...80
; demoprmp.sc - demonstrates the prompt command
clear
Menu {Ask} {Mailtx} check
  moveto [state]          typein "Tx"
do_it!
clearall
view "Answer"
echo normal
prompt "This table contains information for TEXAS subscribers",
       "Press any key when ready to resume."
x = getchar()
clearall
; end demoprmp.sc
```

4. Press **F10** and select the Go option. Your screen resembles the following display.

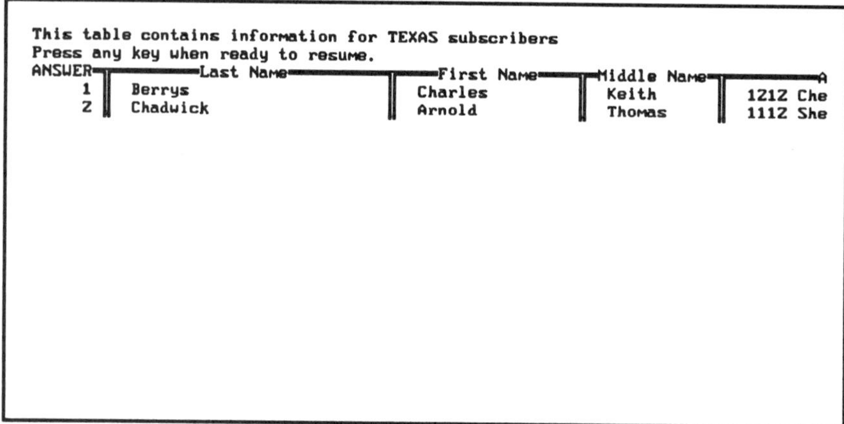

5. Press **Esc** to return to the Main Menu screen.
6. Turn to Module 60 to continue the recommended learning sequence.

Module 57
PROTECT

DESCRIPTION

This command lets you prevent unauthorized use of tables. When the PROTECT command is encountered in a script, Paradox encrypts and assigns a password to the table.

When you specify a password for a file, the person or script requesting it must provide the password assigned. Even using the menu-driven system requires the password to view a protected table. Use the following format for this command.

```
PROTECT <table> <password>
```

Replace <table> with the name of an existing Paradox table. Unless provided in a variable, enclose <table> with quotation marks. If the specified table does not exist on the disk when the PROTECT command is performed, the script encounters a script error.

The <password> is your choice of characters and spaces. It is assigned to <table> and required when the table is requested by the user. Unless provided in a variable, enclose <password> with quotation marks.

This command is an abbreviated form of several menu options that are available through the Paradox menu-driven system. By including the following command line in the script instead of the PROTECT "Mailtx" "DLS1" command line, you achieve the same results.

```
Menu {Tools} {More} {Protect} {Password} {Table} {Mailtx} {DLS1}
```

The string of menu options is required to assign passwords to other Paradox files. However, the PROTECT command is restricted to tables.

APPLICATIONS

Use the PROTECT command in a script to restrict access to tables that contain sensitive information. For example, the Mailfile table contains all valid passwords and access level codes. If it is left unprotected, anyone is able to find out and use or change the data. The Idcheck procedure loses its power to restrict access to certain options in the application.

Protect any table that contains information that is limited to selected users by assigning it a password. When more than one user is allowed access to the table, assign a password that is not included in the Mailfile table. For example, if DLS1 is the password for salary tables, the users that know it are allowed level 9 access to everything in the application.

TYPICAL OPERATION

This example shows you how to use the PROTECT command.

1. Type **V** to select the View option. For the table name, type **Mailfile** and press **Enter**. The table is displayed on the workspace.
2. Press **F8** (Clear Image) to remove the table from the screen.
3. Write a script called Setups that sets passwords for tables used in the application. Keep this script on the procedures floppy disk since it is used only for setting valid passwords. The user does not need it.

```
Designing script C:\paradox3\setups                                    Script

....+...10....+...20....+...30....+...40....+...50....+...60....+...70....+...80
; setups - establishes passwords for Mail List applications

protect "Mailfile" "LevelCodes"
ClearAll

; end setups.sc
```

4. Press **F10** (Scripts Menu) and select the Go option.
5. When the Main Menu screen returns, end the Paradox session, then begin another session.
6. Select the View option. Type **Mailfile** and press **Enter** for the table name. You are asked for a password.
7. Type **levelcodes** and press **Enter**. A message tells you that the password is invalid.
8. Type **LevelCodes** and press **Enter**. The table is displayed on the workspace.
9. Press **F8** (Clear Image) to remove the table from the workspace. Then exit Paradox.
10. Turn to Module 49 to continue the recommended learning sequence.

Module 58
QUERY, ENDQUERY

DESCRIPTION

There are times when you want specific data from one or more tables. Use the Ask option on the Main Menu during the Paradox menu-driven system to establish and perform a query. Then save it on disk with the QuerySave option of the Scripts menu.

When the query is available on disk, use the Script Editor to read it into the script that is to perform the task. When the query lines are inserted, the QUERY, and ENDQUERY commands are included. The format for this command combination follows.

```
QUERY
  <query>
ENDQUERY
```

The QUERY command marks the beginning and the ENDQUERY identifies the end of the query. When a QUERY command is used in a script, there must always be an ENDQUERY command line to match it. The two commands are used as a pair.

Replace <query> with the lines that provide the information needed to pull data from the table. Instead of typing each line to establish the query, it is easier to create and save it on disk by using the Paradox menu-driven system. Since the Paradox creates and tests the query lines, a script error is avoided.

The QUERY, ENDQUERY command combinations provide the query for the script. However, a DO-IT! special keycode must be encountered after the ENDQUERY command line. The QUERY, ENDQUERY command combination only supplies the query specifications. The DO-IT! special keyword tells Paradox to perform the query.

For example, the following query lines are included in a script. They display the First Name, Middle Name, and Last Name fields when a "B" is found in the first position of the Last Name field.

```
Query
  Mailtx  | Last Name   | First Name    | Middle Name     |
          | Check =B..  | Check         | Check           |
          |             |               |                 |
          |             |               |                 |

Endquery
do_it!
```

The special keywords CHECK and CHECKPLUS appear in the query lines instead of their symbols. When more than one table is used in the query, example elements are preceded by the underbar character (_).

Once the query lines are included in the script, make any necessary changes. For example, specify a variable name that contains the value that is used in the query. This lets the user provide the value for the table search as in the following command lines.

```
minit = "A"
clear
@ 10,10
?? "Enter the first letter of the last name "
accept "A1" picture "&" to minit
Query

   Mailtx   | First Name  | Middle Name  | Last Name      |
            | Check       | Check        | Check =~minit  |
            |             |              |                |
            |             |              |                |

Endquery
do_it!
```

Make sure that the script establishes the variable before including it in <query>. These variable names must be preceded with a tilde (~).

After the query is performed, the resulting information is saved in a temporary table called Answer. Since this table name is used each time a query is performed, use the RENAME command in the script to give the table another name and save it on disk. Then use the new table to display or print the information for the user. Remember that the new table must have its own forms, reports, and scripts (family) saved on disk.

APPLICATIONS

Use this command combination in scripts that must find and display information from at least one table. It is most helpful when information is required from more than one table since it uses the example element to match records from each table.

When only one table is involved, consider using the LOCATE command. Like the SCAN, ENDSCAN command combination, a query evaluates all records in the table. The time required to review 1000 records is longer than the time needed for 100 records.

TYPICAL OPERATION

This example shows you how to use the QUERY, ENDQUERY command combination.

1. Use the Create option to begin a new table called Sales so that it matches the structure in the following display.

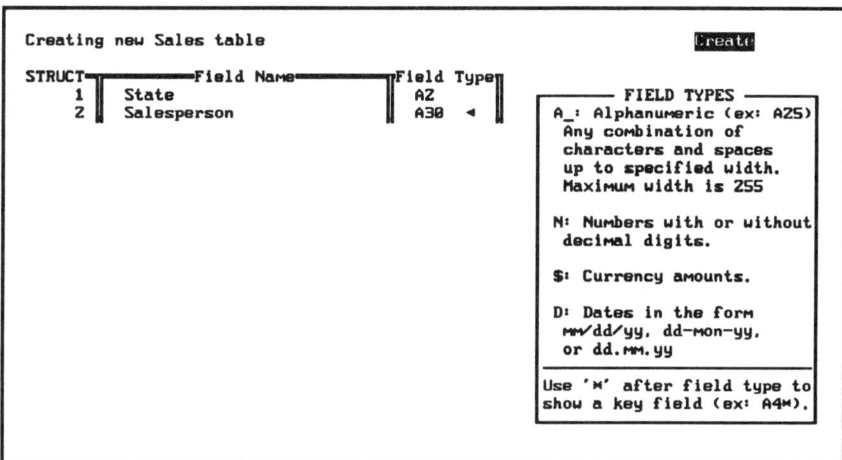

2. Press **F2** (DO-IT!) to save the new structure.
3. Type **MD** to enter data into the new Sales table. Type the records that appear in the following display.

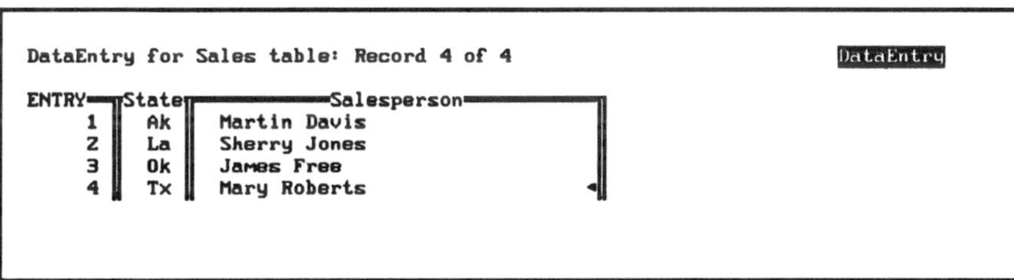

4. Press **F2** (DO-IT!) to save the table on disk. Then press **F8** (Clear Image) to remove the table from the workspace.
5. Type **A** to select the Ask option. Paradox asks for a table name. Type **Mailtx** and press **Enter**. A blank Query Form appears on your workspace as in the following display.

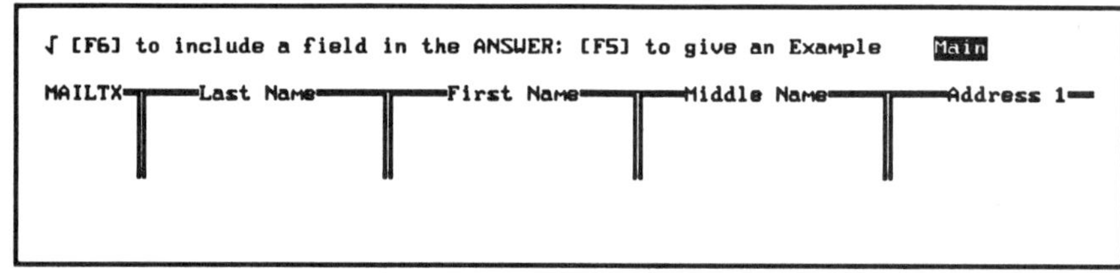

6. Since the cursor is positioned in the record number field, press **Right Arrow**. Now, it is in the Last Name field. Press **F6** (Check Mark) so that a check mark symbol appears in the field.
7. Now, type **=B..** and press **Enter**. The cursor moves to the First Name field.
8. Press **F6** (Check Mark) to select this field too. Then press **Enter**. The cursor moves to the Middle Name field.
9. Put a check mark in the Middle Name field. Press **Right Arrow** until the cursor is positioned in the State field, press **F6** then press **Right Arrow** until the cursor is positioned in the record number column of the query form as in the following display.

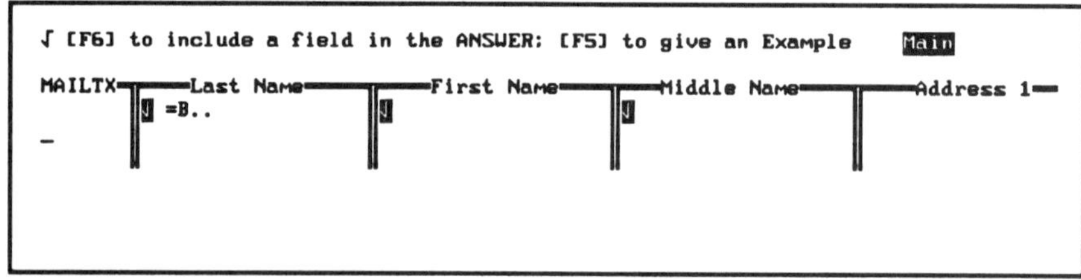

10. Finally, press **F2** (DO-IT!) so that Paradox begins the search for customers whose last names begin with B. Your screen resembles the following display.

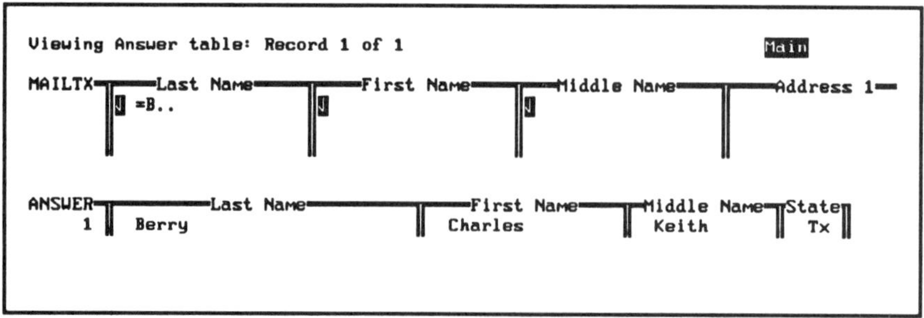

11. Notice that the cursor is positioned on the ANSWER table. Press **F8** (Clear Image) to remove it from your workspace and return the cursor to the Mailtx table.

12. Press **F10** (Menu) to access the Main Menu line. Type **A** and ask for the Sales table. A blank query form appears on the screen for the Sales table as in the following display.

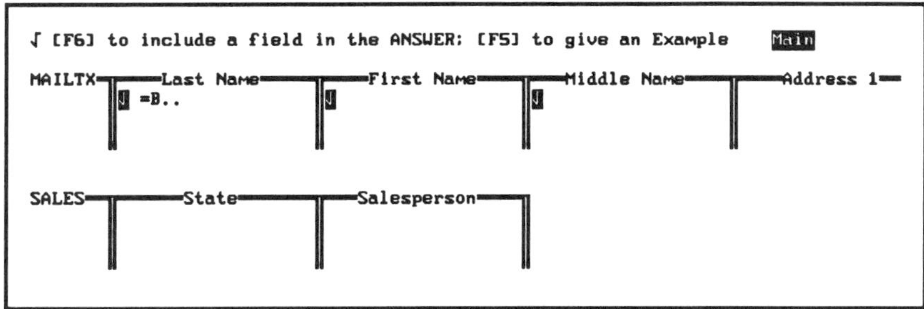

13. Press **Right Arrow** to move the cursor to the State field and press **F6** (Check Mark).
14. To establish the State field as the one to be matched between the Mailtx and Sales tables, press **F5** (Example), type **999**, then press **Enter**. The cursor moves to the Salesperson field. Press **F6** (Check Mark).
15. Press **F3** (Up Image) to move the cursor to the Mailtx query form. Then press **Enter** or **Right Arrow** until the cursor is positioned on the State field. Press **F6** to remove the checkmark.
16. To finish the link between the Mailtx and Sales tables, press **F5** (Example) and type **999**.
17. Press **F2** (DO-IT!). Your screen resembles the following display. Notice the Answer table at the bottom of the screen.

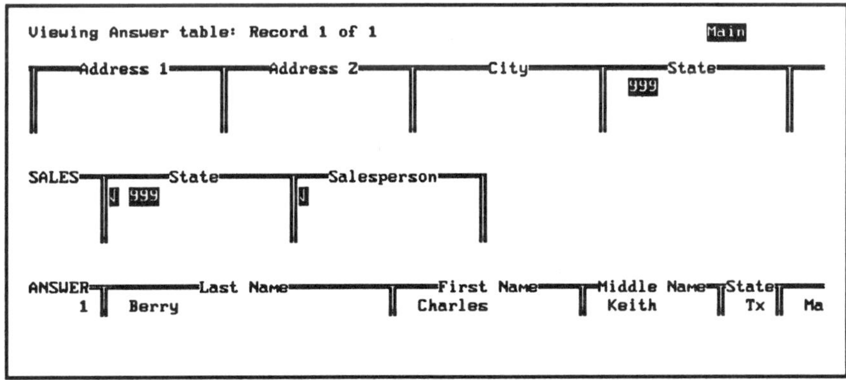

18. Since the cursor is positioned on the Answer table, press **F8** (Clear Image) to remove it from the workspace. Press **F10** (Menu).
19. Type **SQ** to select the QuerySave option of the Scripts submenu. When asked for a name, type **Lastname** and press **Enter**. The query is saved on disk.

20. Press **Alt-F8** (Clear All Images) to remove the query forms from the screen and return to the Main Menu.

21. Edit the Custview script. Change the script so that it lets the user type the first letter of the last name for a partial list of customers. Then position the cursor within the new IF, ENDIF command combination as shown in the following display.

```
Changing script C:\paradox3\custview                                    Script Ins

....+...10....+...20....+...30....+...40....+...50....+...60....+...70....+...80
  ?? "For a list of customers, leave customer name blank..."
  @ 22,01                                                                      ♦
  ?? "(Type the first letter of last name for partial list with salespeople.)" ♦
  @ 10,10
  ?? "Enter Last Name "
  accept "A30" to lastname
  if len(lastname) = 1                                                         ♦
    then                                                                       ♦
    last = lastname                                                            ♦
    : query goes here                                                          ♦
    do_it!                                                                     ♦
    if (isempty("Answer"))                                                     ♦
      then                                                                     ♦
      message lastname, " was not found in the table..."                       ♦
    else                                                                       ♦
      clear                                                                    ♦
      lncnt = 1                                                                ♦
      @ lncnt,10                                                               ♦
      ?? "Customer"                                                            ♦
      @ lncnt,60                                                               ♦
      ?? "Salesperson"                                                         ♦
      lncnt = lncnt + 2                                                        ♦
      ans = "Y"                                                                ♦
      while ans = "Y"                                                          ♦
        scan                                                                   ♦
          if lncnt > 20                                                        ♦
            then                                                               ♦
            @ 21,05                                                            ♦
            ?? "More (Y/N)? "                                                  ♦
            accept "A1" picture "&" to ans                                     ♦
            if ans = "Y"                                                       ♦
              then                                                             ♦
              clear                                                            ♦
              lncnt = 1                                                        ♦
              @ lncnt,10                                                       ♦
              ?? "Customer"                                                    ♦
              @ lncnt,60                                                       ♦
              ?? "Salesperson"                                                 ♦
              lncnt = lncnt + 2                                                ♦
            else                                                               ♦
              quitloop                                                         ♦
            endif                                                              ♦
          endif                                                                ♦
          @ lncnt,10                                                           ♦
          ?? [First Name]+" "+[Middle Name]+" "+[Last Name]                    ♦
          @ lncnt,60                                                           ♦
          ?? [Salesperson]                                                     ♦
          lncnt = lncnt + 1                                                    ♦
        endscan                                                                ♦
        @ 21,05                                                                ♦
        ?? "End of table..."                                                   ♦
        sleep 3000                                                             ♦
        ans = "N"                                                              ♦
      endwhile                                                                 ♦
      clearall                                                                 ♦
      return                                                                   ♦
    endif                                                                      ♦
    clearall                                                                   ♦
  endif                                                                        ♦
  @ 12,10
  ?? "Enter First Name "
  accept "A20" to firstname
  if lastname > "     " and firstname    > "     "
    then
    locate lastname, firstname
    if (retval)
```

22. Move the cursor to the "; query goes here" line and change it to blanks. Press **F10** (Script Menu) and select the Read option by typing **R**. When asked for the name of the script to be read into the current script, type **Lastname** and press **Enter**. The Query part of your script matches the one in the following display.

```
Changing script C:\paradox3\custview                               Script  Ins

....+...10....+...20....+...30....+...40....+...50....+...60....+...70....+...80
  if len(lastname) = 1
    then
    last = lastname

Query

 Mailtx | Last Name   | First Name | Middle Name | State |
        | Check =B..  | Check      | Check       | _999  |
        |             |            |             |       |
        |             |            |             |       |

 Mailtx |
        |
        |
        |

 Sales |   State      | Salesperson |
       | Check _999   | Check       |
       |              |             |
       |              |             |

Endquery
```

23. Change the "=B.." to "> ~last" in the query lines so that the query matches the one in the following display.

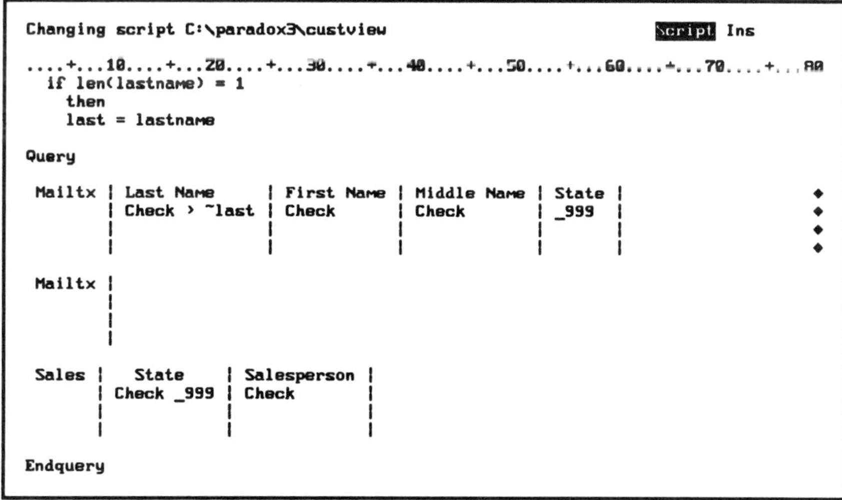

```
Changing script C:\paradox3\custview                               Script  Ins

....+...10....+...20....+...30....+...40....+...50....+...60....+...70....+...80
  if len(lastname) = 1
    then
    last = lastname

Query

 Mailtx | Last Name     | First Name | Middle Name | State |
        | Check > ~last | Check      | Check       | _999  |
        |               |            |             |       |
        |               |            |             |       |

 Mailtx |
        |
        |
        |

 Sales |   State      | Salesperson |
       | Check _999   | Check       |
       |              |             |
       |              |             |

Endquery
```

24. Press **F10** and select the DO-IT! option.

25. Play the Mainmenu script. Select the View option from the application menu.

26. Type **B** for the Last Name field and press **Enter**. The screen resembles the following display.

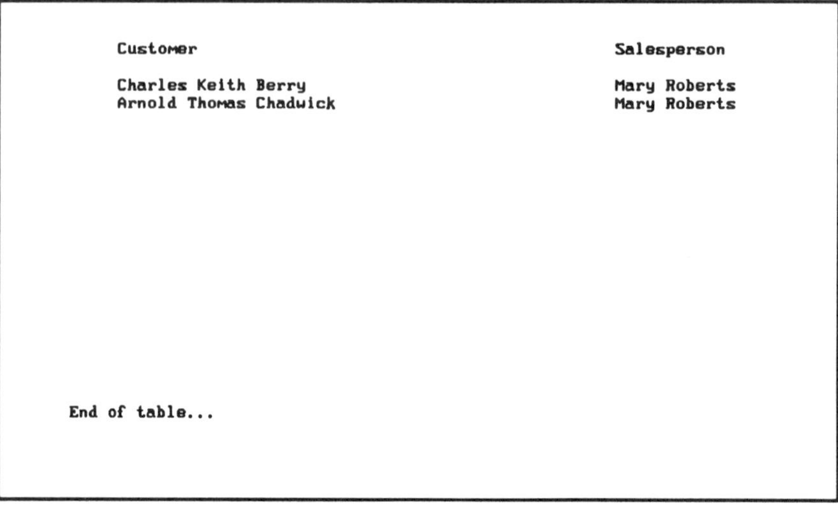

27. When the application menu returns, test the View option for a blank name to make sure that the script changes do not affect the expected result. Then test the View option for Charles Berry. Press **Esc** to exit the application.
28. Turn to Module 92 to continue the recommended learning sequence.

Module 59
QUIT

DESCRIPTION

Include an option in your application menu that lets the user get out of the application gracefully. The user may not remember to press Ctrl-Break or other special keystrokes.

To help the user end your application properly, you have two choices. Either write the script so that the user is returned to the Main Menu screen or to the DOS A> prompt.

Use the QUIT command when you want the application to give control to the Paradox menu- driven system. All script play is cancelled immediately, and the Main Menu appears on the screen.

When you decide to include this command in a script, the user needs to know how to work with the menu options that appear on the screen. If your application scripts, tables, etc. are protected by passwords, only approved changes are possible. The format for this command follows.

```
QUIT <message>
```

Replace <message> with a few words enclosed with quotation marks. When the QUIT command is performed, the message is always displayed in the lower right corner of your screen. For example, QUIT "Thank you for using MAILIT!" tells Paradox to stop the application, present the message, and make the Main Menu screen available.

If you prefer to end the Paradox session when the user quits your application, use the EXIT command to return control to DOS. This command stops script play and exits Paradox. The next thing the user sees is the system A> prompt. This is the best choice when the user does not know how to use the Paradox menu-driven options.

APPLICATIONS

Include this command in a script when you want to make the menu-driven Paradox system available to the user. When the QUIT command is encountered, Paradox cancels the application and presents the Main Menu. Make sure that the user is familiar with the menu-driven system before including this command in any script.

For example, all users of your application should be familiar with the option "Paradox" that appears on several submenus. When this option is selected, the current task is cancelled, and the user is returned to the Main Menu. If you provide a "Paradox" option within your application, the user is already familiar with the effect of selecting that option.

Even when the application is initiated by typing PARADOX MAILIT from the system A> prompt, the Paradox session is not ended when the QUIT command is encountered. Paradox stops the application and presents the Main Menu screen instead of the system A> prompt. To return to the system A> prompt, the user must select the Exit option from the Main Menu.

TYPICAL OPERATION

This example shows you how to use the QUIT command.

1. Edit the Weekcalc script.
2. Press **Up Arrow**, if necessary, until the cursor is positioned on the first line of the script. Press **Ins** until the word "Ins" appears in the top right corner of your screen. Press **Enter** to insert a blank line.
3. Press **Up Arrow** to move the cursor to the blank line. Type **quit "Weekcalc has been deactivated temporarily. . ."** so that your script resembles the one in the following display.

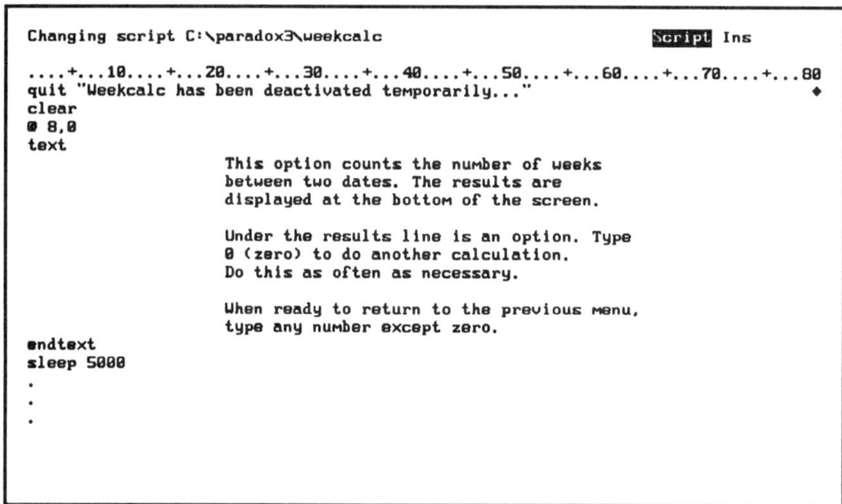

```
Changing script C:\paradox3\weekcalc                              Script Ins

....+...10....+...20....+...30....+...40....+...50....+...60....+...70....+...80
quit "Weekcalc has been deactivated temporarily..."                            ◆
clear
@ 8,0
text
                    This option counts the number of weeks
                    between two dates. The results are
                    displayed at the bottom of the screen.

                    Under the results line is an option. Type
                    0 (zero) to do another calculation.
                    Do this as often as necessary.

                    When ready to return to the previous menu,
                    type any number except zero.
endtext
sleep 5000
.
.
.
```

4. Press **F10** (Scripts Menu). Type **G** to select the Go option. You know the script was played since the message appears on your screen. However, you were not given the opportunity to use the script. The error message appears in the lower right corner of your screen.

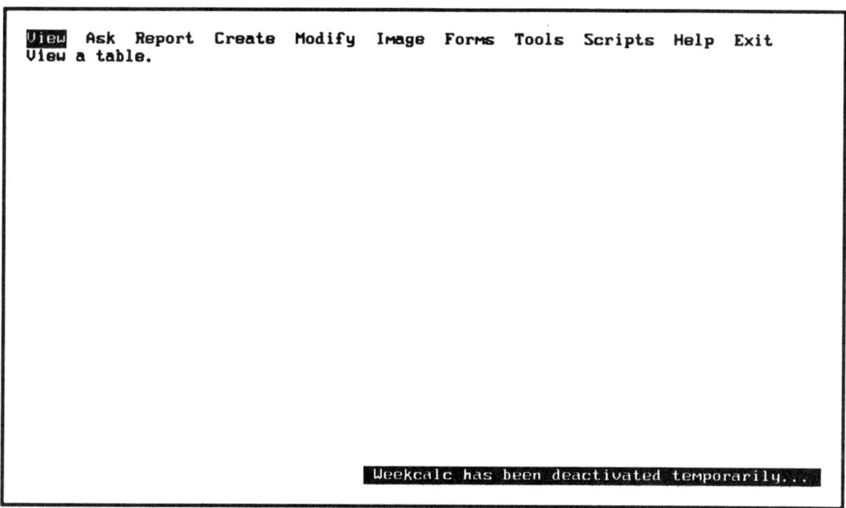

5. Type **E** to select the Exit option. When asked if you really want to end the Paradox session, type **Y**. The system prompt appears on your screen.
6. Type **PARADOX3 WEEKCALC** and press **Enter**. The script is played, but instead of returning to the system prompt, Paradox presents the Main Menu screen.
7. Turn to Module 32 to continue the recommended learning sequence.

Module 60
QUITLOOP

DESCRIPTION

When the QUITLOOP command is encountered, the looping activity of the nearest (current) WHILE, ENDWHILE or SCAN, ENDSCAN command combination is stopped. The command lines between the QUITLOOP command and the ENDWHILE or ENDSCAN commands are skipped. Paradox does not evaluate the condition specified by the current loop.

Since a loop is often nested within one or more other loops, remember that the QUITLOOP command applies only to the loop that performs it. For example, there are three nested loops in the following command lines. The dots represent omitted commands.

```
while (true)
  .
  while ans = "Y"
    .
    while not eot( )
      .
    endwhile
    if eot( )
      quitloop
    endif
    .
  endwhile
  if eot( )
    quitloop
  endif
  .
endwhile
```

Each loop processes data from a table. When the end of the table is encountered during the innermost loop, it is stopped automatically.

The next two outer loops need an IF EOT( ) command line to control the QUITLOOP command. As each IF command line is evaluated as true, the loop being processed is stopped. Processing continues with the line that follows the matching ENDWHILE command.

Consider replacing a LOOP with a QUITLOOP command in Weekcalc. Though the change is a minor one, it causes the script to play differently.

```
while ans = "Y"
       .
       if todate > 01/01/92 and todate <> blankdate( )
```

```
            then
            beep beep beep
            @ 21,05
            ?? "The ending date is later than 01/01/92..."
            sleep 3000
            quitloop
          endif
          .
    endwhile
```

When an ending date is typed, the script checks it for validity. If the date is later than 01/01/92, the computer beeps, a message is displayed in the lower left corner, and the Main Menu returns to the screen. Before the LOOP command was changed to QUITLOOP, the script asked for a new beginning date instead of returning the Main Menu screen.

As soon as the QUITLOOP command is encountered, the WHILE ANS = "Y" loop is stopped. Since the matching ENDWHILE command is the last command in the script, the Main Menu screen is displayed.

APPLICATIONS

The QUITLOOP command is valid only when used within a WHILE, ENDWHILE or SCAN, ENDSCAN command combination. Otherwise, since a loop is not active, the QUITLOOP causes an error.

This command is performed only under special circumstances. Therefore, it is usually controlled by an IF, ENDIF command combination so that it is performed only when the condition specified in the IF command is true.

Most scripts may be written so that a QUITLOOP command is avoided. When possible, write your scripts so that the condition controls the looping activity. Use the QUITLOOP command to handle the times when you need to force the loop to stop.

TYPICAL OPERATION

This example shows you how to use the QUITLOOP command.

1. Edit the Weekcalc script.
2. Insert the QUITLOOP command so that your script matches the one in the following.

```
Changing script C:\paradox3\weekcalc                              Script Ins

....+...10....+...20....+...30....+...40....+...50....+...60....+...70....+...80
clear
@ 8,0
text
                    This option counts the number of weeks
                    between two dates. The results are
                    displayed at the bottom of the screen.

                    Under the results line is an option. Type
                    0 (zero) to do another calculation.
```

```
                         Do this as often as necessary.

                         When ready to return to the previous menu,
                         type any number except zero.
endtext
sleep 5000
ans = "Y"
while ans = "Y"
quitloop                                                            ◆
clear
fromdate = today()
todate = today()
@ 10,10
```

3. Press **F10** (Scripts Menu) and type **G** to play the script. After the description is displayed, the Main Menu returns to your screen. The QUITLOOP was performed before a date could be entered.

4. Change the script again. Delete the QUITLOOP command that was inserted in step 2 by positioning the cursor on the line and pressing **Ctrl-Y**.

5. Insert the IF, ENDIF commands in the innermost loop as in the following display. Since the condition in the WHILE command line is always true, a QUITLOOP command *must* be included in the loop. It is performed when the condition in the IF command line is met.

```
      endif
      savevars all
      if isfile("Passes.sc")                                        ◆
        then                                                        ◆
        Menu {Tools} {Rename} {Script} {Savevars} {Passes} {Replace} ◆
      else                                                          ◆
        Menu {Tools} {Rename} {Script} {Savevars} {Passes}          ◆
      endif                                                         ◆
      release vars idcode                                           ◆
    case mutility = "Esc" :
      return
    otherwise :
      clear
      @ 10,10
      ?? "The requested option is not available from this menu..."
      sleep 2000
  endswitch
endwhile
; end utility.sc
```

6. Press **F10** (Scripts Menu) and type **G** to play the changed script.

7. When asked for a beginning date, type **060189** and press **Enter**. Type **061589** and press **Enter** for the ending date. Notice that the changes did not affect the results.

8. Since the script changes are performed only when two dates are accepted, other tests are not necessary. When asked if you want to do another, type **N** and press **Enter**.

9. Turn to Module 45 to continue the recommended learning sequence.

Module 61
READLIB

DESCRIPTION

This command reads at least one procedure from the disk into memory. It is available to the application immediately so that it decreases the processing time. Use the following format for this command.

```
READLIB <library name> <procname- 1>,...,<procname-n>
```

Use <library name> to supply the filename for the procedure library. Unless provided in a variable, enclose <library name> with quotation marks. The specified library must exist on the disk before the script performs the READLIB command. Otherwise, the script reports a script error.

Replace <procname-1> through <procname-n> with at least one procedure name that is available in memory. Include at least one name in this command line and separate each one with a comma. Do not use the parentheses with the procedure name. For example, procedure Idcheck( ) is listed without them in the READLIB "MAILLIST" IDCHECK command line.

When this command line is performed, the specified procedure is read from the procedure library and stored in memory. It remains there until a RELEASE PROCS command removes it or you end the Paradox session.

APPLICATIONS

Using this command is the only way to use the procedures that you have stored on disk in a procedure library file. Include the READLIB command to read the specified procedures into memory. Leave the most often played procedures in memory until the application is ended. Use the READLIB and RELEASE PROCS commands to move other procedures in and out of memory as needed.

For example, several scripts use the Idcheck procedure. Leave it in memory until the user ends the application. Store the Utility procedure in memory only when the Utilities option is selected. When the Esc key is pressed while the Utilities submenu is available, use a RELEASE PROCS "Utility" command to remove the procedure from memory.

TYPICAL OPERATION

This example shows you how to use the READLIB command.

1. To ensure that the Maillist script is not played by the Mainmenu script, rename it. Type **TRS** to select the Tools/Rename/Script menu options.
2. Type **Maillist** for the current script name and press **Enter**. Type **Maillis1** for the new name and press **Enter**.
3. Type **SEE** and press **Enter** to see a list of all existing scripts. Notice Maillist is not included in the list. Press **Esc** three times to redisplay the Main Menu.
4. Edit the Mainmenu script. Replace the PLAY "Maillist" command line with the READLIB command as shown in the following display.

```
Changing script C:\paradox3\mainmenu                                    Script

....+...10....+...20....+...30....+...40....+...50....+...60....+...70....+...80
readlib "Maillist" Idcheck                                                     ◆
while (true)
  clear
  showmenu
    "View" : "Find and review customer information.",
    "Maintenance" : "Maintains table data.",
    "Report" : "Print the columnar report.",
    "Labels" : "Print mailing labels.",
    "Update" : "Batch update master table from a floppy disk.",
    "Summary" : "Provide statistics on subscription preferences.",
    "Configure" : "Change application configuration.",
    "Utilities" : "Perform various tasks for the Mail List application."
  default "View" to mchoice
  switch
  case mchoice = "View" :
    play "Custview"
  case mchoice = "Maintenance" :
    x = Idcheck()
    if x > "0" and x < "10"
      then
      play "Custmnt"
    endif
```

5. Press **F10** (Scripts Menu) and select the Go option.
6. From the application menu, select the Utilities option. Then select the Passfile option.
7. Type **DLS1** for the password and press **Enter**. When the record is presented, press **F2** to return to the Utilities submenu.
8. Press **Esc** to return to the main application menu.
9. Test the Maintenance option. Use **ELW1** for the ID code. Use the Mailtx table. When the blank record appears, press **F2**.
10. Press **Esc** to end the application.
11. Turn to Module 84 to continue the recommended learning sequence.

Module 62
RELEASE

DESCRIPTION

When a script creates a variable, or array, it remains in memory until it is redeclared, the RELEASE command is encountered, or you end the Paradox session. As more and more memory is allocated to variables, arrays, scripts, and tables, the available computer memory is decreased. Running out of memory for your application is a problem you want to avoid.

Since redeclaring memory variables and arrays does not free any memory, reject that technique as a solution. Writing the application so that it ends the Paradox session is equally unacceptable. However, the RELEASE command removes variables and arrays so that computer memory is made available for allocation at a later time. The formats for this command follows. Substitute "-n" with a number greater than 1.

```
RELEASE VARS <var-1>,...,<var-n>
RELEASE VARS ALL
RELEASE PROCS <proc-1>,...,<proc-n>
RELEASE PROCS ALL
```

In the VARS <var-1>,. . .,<var-n> clause, replace <var-1> through <var-n> with the names of variables and/or arrays that are currently occupying memory. Include at least one variable name in this command line, and separate each variable with a comma. When this line is performed, the specified variables disappear. Procedures are not affected by this command. A script error occurs when a command line references a released variable.

The VARS ALL clause removes *all* existing variables and arrays from memory. Procedures are not affected by this command. Use this clause carefully because a script error occurs when a later command line references a variable or array that has been removed. For example, the mchoice variable keeps track of the option selected from the primary menu in the application. Do not release it until the user chooses to end the application.

When the application plays a script often, consider making that script into a procedure. A procedure is written like a script except that it includes a header line with the PROC command. Once the procedure is played, it remains in memory until the RELEASE command is encountered or you end the Paradox session.

If you use the PROCS <proc-1>,. . .,<proc-n> clause, replace <proc-1> through <proc-n> with the names of specific procedure names that are currently occupying memory. Include at least one procedure name in this command line and separate each procedure name with a comma. When this line is performed, the specified procedures are removed from memory. Variables are not affected by this command. A script error occurs when a command line references a released procedure name.

Use the RELEASE PROCS ALL command to release the memory currently occupied by existing procedures that have been played and saved in memory. The RELEASE PROCS ALL command line removes *all* procedures from memory. Do not use this command within a procedure.

APPLICATIONS

Use this command as a house-cleaning tool for your computer.

For example, a computer has a total of 640K of memory. When you begin a Paradox session, approximately 400K is used by DOS, Paradox, and other memory-resident programs. There is 240K available for running your Paradox application. When all memory is allocated, the application comes to a screeching halt.

Each script, form, and table used during the application is allocated some of the available memory. However, Paradox removes them automatically when the task is complete.

Each application is responsible for declaring and removing its variables, arrays, and procedures. Once declared, they remain in memory until the RELEASE command is encountered or the session is ended.

Include a RELEASE command in each script that declares a variable or an array. After they have served their purpose, do not keep them. If a script creates a variable or array that is used by another script, include the RELEASE command in the second script.

Include the RELEASE PROCS ALL and RELEASE VARS ALL command lines in the script that exits the application. These lines must be performed before the QUIT command line so that the next application begins with a clean slate.

Write your applications so that they keep as much computer memory available as possible. Remember that all software runs faster when there is plenty of memory and disk space.

TYPICAL OPERATION

This example shows you how to use the RELEASE command.

1. Edit the Utility script so that it includes two RELEASE commands as shown in the following display. The IF, ENDIF command sets replaces the Zipcodes and Passfile files if they exist. Otherwise, a new one is created.

```
Changing script C:\paradox3\utility                                 Script Ins
....+...10....+...20....+...30....+...40....+...50....+...60....+...70....+...80
          editkey
          copyfromarray zips
        endscan
        release vars mold,mnew,zips,mans                                       ◆
        do_it!
        if isfile("zipcodes.sc")                                               ◆
          then                                                                 ◆
    Menu {Tools} {Rename} {Script} {Savevars} {Zipcodes} {Replace}             ◆
        else                                                                   ◆
    Menu {Tools} {Rename} {Script} {Savevars} {Zipcodes}                       ◆
        endif                                                                  ◆
        clearall
      endif
    case mutility = "Passfile" :
      play "idcheck"
      .
      .
      .
      endif
      savevars all
      if isfile("Passes.sc")                                                   ◆
        then                                                                   ◆
        Menu {Tools} {Rename} {Script} {Savevars} {Passes} {Replace}           ◆
      else                                                                     ◆
        Menu {Tools} {Rename} {Script} {Savevars} {Passes}                     ◆
      endif                                                                    ◆
      release vars idcode                                                      ◆
    case mutility = "Esc" :
      return
    otherwise :
      clear
      @ 10,10
      ?? "The requested option is not available from this menu..."
      sleep 2000
  endswitch
endwhile
; end utility.sc
```

2. Press **F10** (Scripts Menu) and select the DO-IT! option.

3. Review the Zipcodes and Passes scripts with the Editor to see the list of variables saved by the SAVEVARS command lines. Press **F10** (Scripts Menu) and select the Cancel option to remove the script from the workspace.

4. Play the Mainmenu script.

5. Select the Utilities option and play the Zipcodes option. Type **75088** and **75084** for the old and new zipcodes. Type **Y** and press **Enter** when asked if you want to continue.

6. When the submenu returns, play the Passfile option. Type **DLS1** for the ID and press **Enter**. Press **F2** to return to the submenu.

7. Press **Esc** twice to return to the Main Menu screen.

8. Review the Zipcodes script. The same variables existed before it was rewritten by the application.

9. Review the Passes script to see that it contains fewer variables. It appears in the following display.

```
Changing script C:\paradox3\passes                                     Script

....+...10....+...20....+...30....+...40....+...50....+...60....+...70....+...80
; Variables Saved Using Savevars Command

ans = "N"
fileans = "MAILTX"
idcode = "DLS1"
Namscrpt = "Esc"
lncnt = 4
Array Descr[3]
Descr[1] = "View only Texas Customers"
Descr[2] = "View only Louisiana Customers"
Descr[3] = "View only California Customers"
Nametabl = "Esc"
Tablname = ""
Whattodo = "Delete"
Array passes[11]
passes[1] = "Mailfile"
passes[2] = "DLS1"
passes[3] = "9"
passes[4] = "WWW1"
passes[5] = "5"
passes[6] = "DFS1"
passes[7] = "2"
passes[8] = "ELW1"
passes[9] = "1"
passes[10] = ""
passes[11] = ""
mfile = "MailTx"
Array Choices[3]
Choices[1] = "Tx"
Choices[2] = "La"
Choices[3] = "Ca"
x = 2
lastname = ""
mutility = "Passfile"
mchoice = "Utilities"
firstname = ""
```

10. Press **F10** (Scripts Menu) and select the Cancel option to remove the script from the workspace.

11. Edit the Mainmenu script so that the Esc option includes RELEASE commands as shown in the following display.

```
Changing script C:\paradox3\mainmenu                                   Script Ins

....+...10....+...20....+...30....+...40....+...50....+...60....+...70....+...80
      x = x + 1
    endwhile
    sleep 3500
    clearall
  case mchoice = "Configure" :
    @ 10,10
    ?? "Configure..."
    sleep 2000
  case mchoice = "Utilities" :
    play "Utility"
  case mchoice = "Esc" :
    release procs all                                                         ◆
    release vars all                                                          ◆
    quit
  otherwise :
    clear
    @ 10,10
    ?? "The requested option is not available from this menu..."
    sleep 2000
  endswitch
endwhile
```

12. Press **F10** (Scripts Menu) and select the DO-IT! option. This change removes all variables, arrays, and procedures from memory before displaying the Main Menu screen. The next application played is not hampered by leftover memory allocations.
13. Turn to Module 15 to continue the recommended learning sequence.

Module 63
RENAME

DESCRIPTION

There are times when you need to change the name of an existing table. For example, the department number is changed from 210 to 211. One solution for the situation is to use the COPY command to save a duplicate copy of the old file (and its family) to the new name. Then use the DELETE command to remove the old file (and its family) from the disk.

Instead of a two step operation, use the RENAME command to accomplish the same thing. The format for this command follows.

```
RENAME <old table> <new table>
```

Replace <old table> with the name of the existing table that needs to be changed. This table must be available when the RENAME command is performed. Otherwise, a script error occurs when the table is not found on the disk. Unless provided in a variable, enclose <old table> with quotation marks.

Use <new table> to supply the new name for the existing file. The RENAME "DEPT210" "DEPT211" command line changes the name for the Dept210 table to Dept211. After the table is renamed, its data and family (indices, reports, forms) are accessed through the <new table> name. Unless provided in a variable, enclose <new table> with quotation marks.

The RENAME command is an abbreviated form of several menu options that are available through the Paradox menu-driven system. By including the following command line in the script instead of the RENAME "DEPT210" "DEPT211" command line, you achieve the same results.

```
Menu {Tools} {Rename} {Table} {Dept210} {Dept211}
```

Remember that if the <new table> name already exists on the disk when this command is performed, that table and its family are replaced immediately. All the data, indices, reports, and forms for that table are removed from the disk and replaced by the <old table> and its family. Before the RENAME command line is performed, use the ISFILE( ) function to check the disk for an existing <new table> name.

APPLICATIONS

Use the RENAME command when the current name of a table is misspelled or invalid so that the table name does not identify the data properly. Give the user the ability to rename a table and its family through an application option. Otherwise, when a table name needs to be changed, the user must know how to do it through the Paradox menu-driven system.

TYPICAL OPERATION

This illustration shows you how to use the RENAME command.

1. Edit the Utility script. Insert a Rename option between the Newfile and Passfile options as shown in the following display.

```
Changing script C:\paradox3\utility                                    Script Ins

....+...10....+...20....+...30....+...40....+...50....+...60....+...70....+...80
; utility.sc - allows various tasks for Mail List application
while(true)
  clear
  showmenu
    "Zipcodes" : "Replace new zipcode for all customers with old zipcode.",
    "Newfile" : "Create a new Mail List customer file.",
    "Rename" : "Renames an existing customer file.",                            ◆
    "Passfile" : "Restricted - Access Password file."
  default "Zipcodes" to mutility
  .
  .
  .
      release vars mfile
      clearall                                                                  ◆
    case mutility = "Rename" :                                                  ◆
      clear                                                                     ◆
      @ 10,05                                                                   ◆
      ?? "Enter the name for the existing customer file (e.g. MAILTX) "         ◆
      accept "A8" picture "&*&" to mfile1                                       ◆
      if not isfile(mfile1+".db")                                               ◆
        then                                                                    ◆
        @ 21,05                                                                 ◆
        ?? "That name does not exist - This option is aborted..."               ◆
        sleep 3000                                                              ◆
      else                                                                      ◆
        @ 12,05                                                                 ◆
        ?? "Enter the new name (e.g. MAILTX) "                                  ◆
        accept "A8" picture "&*&" to mfile2                                     ◆
        if isfile(mfile2+".db")                                                 ◆
          then                                                                  ◆
          @ 21,05                                                               ◆
          ?? "That name already exists - this option is aborted..."             ◆
          sleep 3000                                                            ◆
        else                                                                    ◆
          @ 21,05                                                               ◆
          ?? "Renaming the customer file - Please Wait..."                      ◆
          rename mfile1 mfile2                                                  ◆
        endif                                                                   ◆
      endif                                                                     ◆
      release vars mfile1,mfile2                                                ◆
    case mutility = "Passfile" :
```

2. Press **F10** (Scripts Menu) and select the DO-IT! option.
3. Play the Mainmenu script. Select the Utilities option from the application menu.

4. Type **N** to select the Newfile option. When asked for the new name, type **Miamla** and press **Enter**. Press **Esc** twice to return to the Main Menu and select the View option to see the list of tables, then press **Esc**.
5. Return to the Utilities submenu and type **R** to select the rename option.
6. Type **Mailla** and press **Enter** for the existing filename. You are told that the table does not exist on the disk.
7. When the submenu returns, select the Rename option again. This time, type **Miamla** and press **Enter**.
8. When you are asked for the new name, type **Mailla** and press **Enter**. A message appears on the screen to inform you of the renaming activity. Return to the Main Menu.
9. Type **V** to select the View option. Press **Enter** for a list of all existing tables. Notice that the Miamla table is not in the list but Mailla is included in the list.
10. Turn to Module 24 to continue the recommended learning sequence.

Module 64
REPORT

DESCRIPTION

When data is collected and saved on the computer, it is usually because there is a need to print it on paper. When the REPORT command line is encountered in a script, Paradox organizes the fields of the specified table according to the report form. Then the results are sent to the printer. The format for this command follows.

```
REPORT <table name> <report>
```

Replace <table name> with the name of a table that has been saved on the current data disk. Unless provided in a variable, enclose it with quotation marks.

Each table is allowed ten report formats that specify the fields and their positions on the report. The letter or number (R or 1 through 9) of an existing report form for <table name> replaces <report>. Unless using a variable for <report>, enclose the letter or number with quotation marks as in the following command line.

```
REPORT "Mailtx" "R"
```

The REPORT command in a script is an abbreviated form of several menu options. By including the following command line in the script instead of the REPORT command line, you achieve the same results.

```
Menu {Reports} {Output} {Mailtx} {R} {Printer}
```

Paradox provides a report form automatically when the table structure is created. It is similar to the Table View form that is also created automatically for the screen. This form is assigned the "R" as its identifier.

If the form that is created automatically by Paradox is not sufficient, design and save your own forms. These are called *custom report forms*. Design these report forms by using the Reports option on the Main Menu screen of the Paradox menu-driven system.

When a custom report form is created, it is saved on disk so that it is available to print the table. A maximum of ten report forms may exist for each table. Replace the automatic Paradox report form or make yours available as part of the other nine that are allowed for the table.

APPLICATIONS

Use the REPORT command to tell Paradox to send the data from a specific table to the printer. It also identifies the report form to be used so that the data is printed a certain way.

TYPICAL OPERATION

This example shows you how to use the REPORT command.

1. Edit the Mainmenu script.
2. Add a reporting option to the menu as shown in the following display.

```
Changing script C:\paradox3\mainmenu                                  Script

....+...10....+...20....+...30....+...40....+...50....+...60....+...70....+...80
while (true)
  clear
  showmenu
    "Maintenance" : "Maintains table data.",
    "Report" : "Print the columnar report.",                                ◆
    "Labels" : "Print mailing labels.",
    "Configure" : "Change application configuration.",
    "Weekcalc" : "Count the number of weeks between two dates."
  default "Maintenance" to mchoice
  switch
  case mchoice = "Maintenance" :
    play "idcheck"
    if retval
      then
      play "Custmnt"
    endif
  case mchoice = "Report" :                                                 ◆
    @ 10,10                                                                 ◆
    ?? "Printing the columnar report - Please Wait..."                      ◆
    report "Mailtx" "R"                                                     ◆
  case mchoice = "Labels" :
    @ 10,10
    ?? "Configure..."
    sleep 2000
  case mchoice = "Weekcalc" :
    play "Weekcalc"
  case mchoice = "Esc" :
    quit
  otherwise :
    clear
    @ 10,10
    ?? "The requested option is not available from this menu..."
    sleep 2000
  endswitch
endwhile
```

3. Press **F10** (Scripts Menu) and select the Go option by typing **G**. When the application menu appears at the top of your screen, make sure that your printer is turned on and the paper adjusted.
4. Type **R** to select the Report option. The first page of the report on your printer resembles the following sample.

```
 6/17/89              Standard report          Page  1

Last Name      First Name  Middle Name  Address 1
_____________  __________  ___________  ___________

Appleby        Shirley     Lynn         2411 Abrams Rd
Berry          Charles     Keith        818 N. Plano Rd.
Chadwick       Arnold      Thomas       1112 Sherman Hwy.
```

5. When the application menu returns, press **Esc** to end the application.
6. Since the report is spread across three pages, it needs some work! Type **R** to select the Report option from the Main Menu. Since the report form exists, it must be changed. Type **C** to select the Change option.
7. When asked for a table name, type **Mailtx** and press **Enter**. The existing report identifiers are displayed. Since there is only one, press **Enter** to select the "R" identifier.
8. The description is presented for possible changes. Press **Ctrl-Backspace** to remove the existing description. Since it is used for a title, type **Mail List for Mailtx** and press **Enter**. The report format appears on your screen. It resembles the one in the following display.

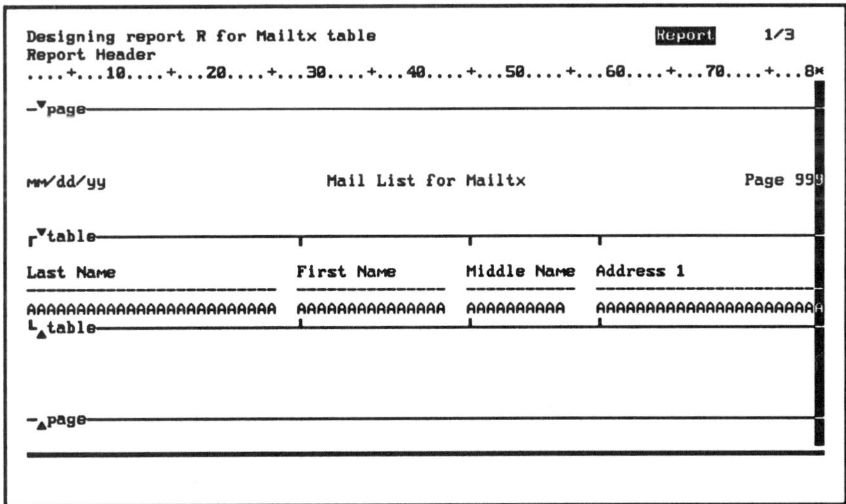

9. Press **Down Arrow** to move the cursor to the heading of the Last Name column. Press **Del** five times to remove "Last" from the column heading.
10. Press **Right Arrow** to the First Name column.

11. Press **F10** (Report Menu) and type **T** to select the TableBand option. Remove the column by typing **E** to select the Erase option. When asked to position the cursor on the column to be erased, use the arrows, if necessary, so that the cursor appears within the column area. Then press **Enter**. Do the same for the Middle Name field so that your report form matches the one in the following display.

```
Designing report R for Mailtx table                                  Report    1/3
Table Band
....+...10....+...20....+...30....+...40....+...50....+...60....+...70....+...8
-▼page-----------------------------------------------------------------------------

mm/dd/yy                     Mail List for Mailtx                          Page 999

r▼table----------------------------------------------------------------------------
Name                       Address 1                  Address 2             City
-------------------------  -------------------------  --------------------  ----
AAAAAAAAAAAAAAAAAAAAAAAAA  AAAAAAAAAAAAAAAAAAAAAAAAA  AAAAAAAAAAAAAAAAAAAA  AAAA
L▲table----------------------------------------------------------------------------


-▲page-----------------------------------------------------------------------------
```

12. Delete the Address 2, City, State, and Zipcode columns so that the report form resembles the one in the following display.

```
Designing report R for Mailtx table                                  Report    1/3
Table Band
....+...10....+...20....+...30....+...40....+...50....+...60....+...70....+...8
-▼page-----------------------------------------------------------------------------

mm/dd/yy                     Mail List for Mailtx                          Page 999

r▼table----------------------------------------------------------------------------
Name                       Address 1                  Begins    Ends
-------------------------  -------------------------  --------  --------
AAAAAAAAAAAAAAAAAAAAAAAAA  AAAAAAAAAAAAAAAAAAAAAAAAA  mm/dd/yy  mm/dd/yy
L▲table----------------------------------------------------------------------------


-▲page-----------------------------------------------------------------------------
```

13. Press **Left Arrow** to position the cursor on the last space in the Address 1 column. Press **F10** (Report Menu) and select the TableBand option.

14. The address column needs to be larger. Select the Resize option by typing **R**. When asked to position the cursor on the column to be changed, press **Enter**.

15. Press **Right Arrow** eight times and press **Enter**.

16. Press **Left Arrow** until the cursor is positioned on the Name field (identified by "A" letters).

17. Press **F10** (Report Menu) and select the Field option by typing **F**. Then select the Erase option to erase the field identifiers. Press **Enter**.

18. Press **F10** (Report Menu) and select the Field option. Type **P** to select the Place option. Then type **C** to select the Calculated option so that the last, first, and middle names may be combined in one field.

19. When asked for the expression, type **[Last Name]+", "+[First Name]+" "+[Middle Name]** and press **Enter**. Position the cursor on the first space in the name column and press **Enter**. You are asked to use the arrow keys to specify the number of characters the field is allowed. Press **Left Arrow** twice and press **Enter**.

20. The Address column also needs the fields combined. When asked for the expression, type **[Address 1]+" "+[Address 2]** and press **Enter**. Position the cursor on the first space in the Address column and press **Enter**. Shorten the maximum number of characters by pressing **Left Arrow** once. Then press **Enter**.

21. Press **Enter** to move the cursor to the table band. Press **Ins** until "Ins" appears in the upper right corner of the screen. Press **Enter** to insert a new line within the tableband.

22. Position the cursor in the first position of the Address 1 column on the new line.

23. Press **F10** (Report Menu) and select the Field option by typing **F**. Select the Place option by typing **P**. Then type **C** to select the Calculated option. When asked for the expression, type **[City]+", "+[State]+", "+[Zipcode]** and press **Enter**. If necessary, position the cursor on the first position of the new line in the address column and press **Enter**. When asked to adjust the length of the field, press **Left Arrow** once and press **Enter**.

24. Adjust the column headings so that your screen resembles the following display.

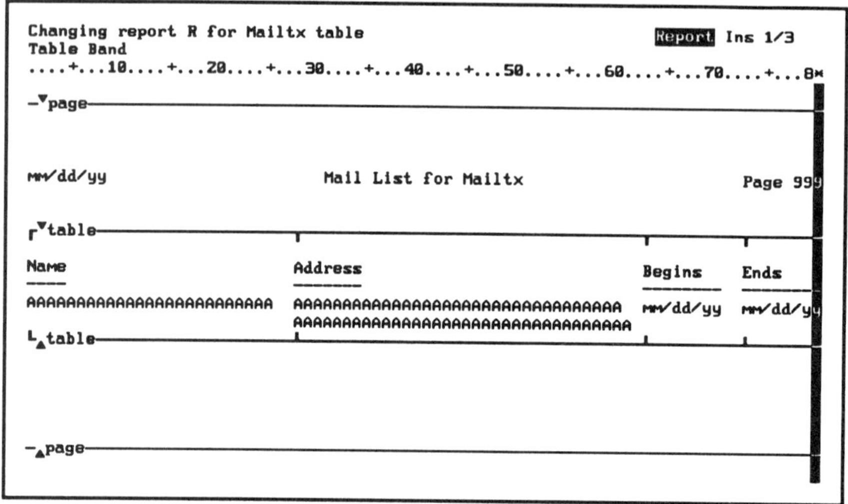

25. Press **F2** (DO-IT!) to save the changed report on disk. The Main Menu appears on your screen.
26. Type **SP** to play a script. Type **Mainmenu** and press **Enter**.
27. When the application menu appears on your screen, make sure that the printer is turned on. Then select the Report option by typing **R**. Your report is printed to resemble the one in the following display.

```
6/17/89                    Mail List for Mailtx                   Page  1

Name                       Address                     Begins    Ends
----                       -------                     ------    ----

Appleby, Shirley Lynn      2411 Abrams Rd & 111        7/01/89   7/01/90
                           Dallas, Tx, 75240
Berry, Charles Keith       818 N. Plano Rd.            9/01/89   8/01/90
                           Plano, Tx, 75042
Chadwick, Arnold Thomas    1112 Sherman Hwy.           8/01/88   8/01/90
                           Allen, Tx, 75045
```

28. When the application menu returns, press **Esc**.
29. Turn to Module 65 to continue the recommended learning sequence.

Module 65
REPORTTABLES

DESCRIPTION

Provide as much error-checking in your applications as possible. For example, ensure that a table exists and is not locked, or a report layout exists before using it. Otherwise, the application user gets an error or warning message and cannot continue the work.

Prior to Paradox 3.0, a form or report involved only the table for which it was created. Now, a form or report can include information from other tables. Use the REPORTTABLES command to identify the tables used in a multi-table report. The proper syntax for this command follows.

```
REPORTTABLES <tablename> <reportname> <arrayname>
```

Replace <tablename> with the name of the Paradox table to be examined. Before issuing the REPORTTABLES command, verify that the table exists.

Specify the report number of the table by replacing <reportname> with "F" or a number 1 through 14. Before issuing the REPORTTABLES command, use the ISMULTIREPORT( ) function to determine if the specified form is a multi-table report.

Provide the name of the array to receive the other tables involved in the multi-table report in <arrayname>. If the array does not exist, Paradox creates it automatically. An array element is created for each table name included in the multi-table form.

NOTE: This command is available in version 3.0 and higher.

APPLICATIONS

The REPORTTABLES command is valid only for multi-table reports. Before issuing the REPORTTABLES command, verify that the table and its report exist. Then, use the ISMULTIREPORT( ) function to determine if the form includes information from other tables.

When the REPORTTABLES command is issued for a single-table report, the array is not created (or changed) and an error occurs. If any of the tables or the specified report do not exist, an error occurs. If any of the tables are locked by another user, a message to identify the user is displayed on the screen. Your application must handle all these error situations for the user.

For example, if the table or report does not exist, display a message and return to a menu. If the table is locked, ask the user to make the decision to try again or return to the menu.

TYPICAL OPERATION

This example shows you how to use the REPORTTABLES commands.

1. Select the Modify option from the Main Menu, then select the Restructure option.
2. Change the Mailtx and Mailok table structures so they include the Customer # field as shown in the following display. Press **F2** to save the changed structure.

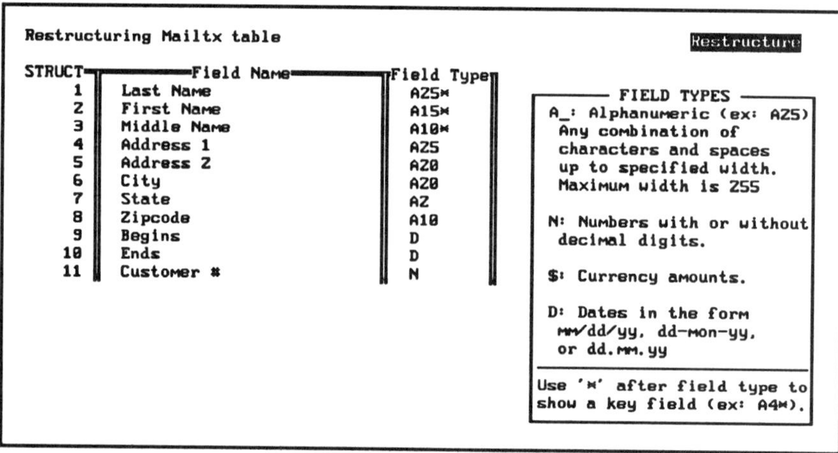

```
Restructuring Mailtx table                                  Restructure

STRUCT  Field Name              Field Type
  1     Last Name               A25*
  2     First Name              A15*
  3     Middle Name             A10*
  4     Address 1               A25
  5     Address 2               A20
  6     City                    A20
  7     State                   A2
  8     Zipcode                 A10
  9     Begins                  D
 10     Ends                    D
 11     Customer #              N

FIELD TYPES
A_: Alphanumeric (ex: A25)
 Any combination of
 characters and spaces
 up to specified width.
 Maximum width is 255

N: Numbers with or without
 decimal digits.

$: Currency amounts.

D: Dates in the form
 mm/dd/yy, dd-mon-yy,
 or dd.mm.yy

Use '*' after field type to
show a key field (ex: A4*).
```

3. Press **F9** and edit the Mailtx table to assign the following customer numbers. Then, press **F2** to save the changed table. Press **F8** to clear the workspace.

```
Last Name        Cust #
  Berry            1
  Chadwick         2
  Richards         3
```

4. Create and save a new table called Stocks with the following fields. Press **F8** to clear the workspace.

```
Customer #          N*
Stock Symbol        A5
Purchase Date       D
Name                A20
Price               N
Number of Shares    N
```

5. Edit the Stocks table and add the records listed in the following table. When all records are added, press **F2** to save the information on disk. Remove the table from the workspace by pressing **F8**.

Cust #	Symbol	Date	Name	Price	Shares
1	DLC	08/13/89	Darwin Lynn Company	10.32	100
3	CUP	05/18/89	Cinch-Up Inc.	5.50	100

6. Type **RD** to design a report layout. When asked for the table name, type **Mailtx** and press **Enter**. Assign the new report to 2 and type **Stock Transaction Report** for the report description. Then, type **F** to designate it as a free-form report

7. Design a report that resembles the following report layout.

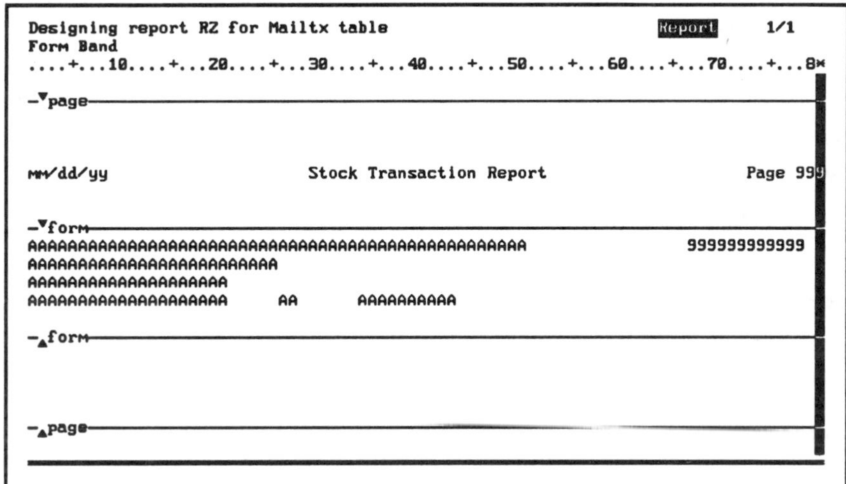

8. Press **F10** (Menu) and type **FLL** to select the Field, Lookup, and Link options. When asked for the table name, type **Stocks** and press **Enter**.

9. When asked for the Mailtx field to match Customer # in Stocks, select Customer #.

10. Change the report so it includes fields from the Stocks table. It resembles the following.

```
Designing report R2 for Mailtx table                           Report Ins 1/1
Form Band                                        [Stocks->Number of Shares]
....+...10....+...20....+...30....+...40....+...50....+...60....+...70....+...8
-▼page──────────────────────────────────────────────────────────────────────────


mm/dd/yy                    Stock Transaction Report                   Page 999

-▼form──────────────────────────────────────────────────────────────────────────
AAAAAAAAAAAAAAAAAAAAAAAAAAAAAAAAAAAAAAAAAAAAAAAAAA            999999999999
AAAAAAAAAAAAAAAAAAAAAAAAA
AAAAAAAAAAAAAAAAAAAA
AAAAAAAAAAAAAAAAAAAA     AA      AAAAAAAAAA

    Stock   Purchase
    Symbol   Date        Name                Price           # of Shares
    ------  --------  ------------------  ------------    ------------
    AAAAA   mm/dd/yy  AAAAAAAAAAAAAAAAAAAA 999999999999    999999999999
-▲form──────────────────────────────────────────────────────────────────────────
```

11. Press **F2** (DO-IT!) to save the report layout.
12. Type **RO** to select the Report and Output options. When asked for the name of the table, type **Mailtx** and press **Enter**.
13. Select the 2 and Printer options and print the report.
14. Type **SEW** to write a new script. When asked for the name of the script, type **TESTRPT** and press **Enter**.
15. Type the following command lines in the script area.

```
Designing script C:\paradox3\testrpt                              Script

....+...10....+...20....+...30....+...40....+...50....+...60....+...70....+...80
; testrpt.sc - lists all tables included in a report layout

if isfile("mailtx.db") then
  if isfile("mailtx.r2") then
    if ismultireport("mailtx",2) then
      reporttables "mailtx" 2 tabname
        x = arraysize(tabname)
        y = 1
        clear
        @ 0,0 ?? "Mailtx report #2 includes the following tables:"
        ? " "
        while y <= x
          ? tabname[y]
          y = y + 1
        endwhile
      sleep 3000
    endif
  endif
endif
; end testrpt.sc
```

16. Press **F10** (Menu) and select the Go option. When the script runs, the screen is cleared and displays the following message.

```
Mailtx report #2 includes the following tables:

Stocks
```

17. Turn to Module 53 to continue the recommended learning sequence.

Module 66
REQUIREDCHECK

DESCRIPTION

Include the REQUIREDCHECK command in scripts to override field validity checks that require non-blank values. The syntax of the REQUIREDCHECK command is:

```
REQUIREDCHECK < ON/OFF >
```

Turn the validity check on or off by issuing this command. The REQUIREDCHECK command is valid only to modify existing validity checks, not create new ones.

NOTE: This command is available in Paradox 2.0 and higher.

APPLICATIONS

There are situations when you need to override field validity checks. While a script is running, if you move the cursor to a required field, you cannot leave the field without entering a value. If the user does not know what to enter, give them a way out by turning off the REQUIREDCHECK and canceling the table change.

For example, the table on the screen has a field that is required and specifies a table lookup as the validity check. The user cannot leave the record without entering a value that is included in the lookup table. The REQUIREDCHECK command can be used to override the field validity and allow blanks in the field.

TYPICAL OPERATION

This illustration shows you how to use the REQUIREDCHECK command.

1. Type **ME** (Modify, Edit) to change a table. When asked for the table name, type **Mailtx** and press **Enter**.
2. Press **F10** and select the ValCheck option. Then, type **D** to select the Define option.
3. Move the cursor to the State field and press **Enter**.
4. Select the Required option and answer Yes to require non-blank values in the state field.

5. Repeat steps 2 and 3 but this time select the Picture option. When asked for the picture, type **Tx** and press **Enter**.
6. Press **F2** to end the Edit mode. Then, press **F8** to remove the image from the screen.
7. Type **SEW** to write a new script. When asked for the script name, type **DEMOREQD** and press **Enter**.
8. Type the following command lines in the script area.

```
Designing script C:\paradox3\demoreqd                                     Script

....+...10....+...20....+...30....+...40....+...50....+...60....+...70....+...80
; demoreqd.sc - demonstrates REQUIREDCHECK command
edit "Mailtx"
pickform "F"
wait table message "Press F2 to save, or Esc to abort changes..."
  until "F2", "Esc"
canceledit
clearall
; end demoreqd.sc
```

9. Press **F10** and select the Go option. Try to change the state to something other than Tx. Each time you press a key, the computer beeps. Change it back to Tx and press **Esc**.
10. Change the DEMOREQD script so it matches the following command lines.

```
Changing script C:\paradox3\demoreqd                                      Script Ins

....+...10....+...20....+...30....+...40....+...50....+...60....+...70....+...80
; demoreqd.sc - demonstrates REQUIREDCHECK command
edit "Mailtx"
pickform "F"
requiredcheck off                                                              ◆
wait table message "Press F2 to save, or Esc to abort changes..."
  until "F2", "Esc"
canceledit
requiredcheck on                                                               ◆
clearall
; end demoreqd.sc
```

11. Play the script again and try to change the State field. It does not allow any value other than Tx. Leave the field empty and press **Esc**. This time the blank state is allowed so the record is released. Since the CANCELEDIT command is included in the script, the record is not changed and the State field contains Tx.
12. Turn to Module 23 to continue the recommended learning sequence.

Module 67
RESET

DESCRIPTION

When you begin a Paradox session, you know that you are starting out with a clean slate. Your applications should always close open tables, release variables, and leave the slate clean before it ends so that the next Paradox application is not affected accidentally.

For example, a script is written to edit the Mailtx file. The next command line tells Paradox to play the Mail List application. Until the Edit mode is ended, Paradox is not allowed to perform the application. The result is a script error.

Since you never know what the Paradox workspace contains when your scripts are played, include the RESET command in the script that begins the application. When this command is encountered, Paradox returns to the Main mode and clears the workspace. All variables, arrays, and procedures remain in memory after Paradox performs the RESET command.

APPLICATIONS

When people begin writing scripts, there is a certain amount of experimentation involved in the learning process. Sometimes the scripts they write affect existing applications accidentally.

Use the RESET command in the first script of your application to ensure the Main mode status of the workspace. If the Edit mode is in control, your application ends with a script error.

TYPICAL OPERATION

This illustration shows you how to use the RESET command.

1. Edit the Test2 script. Change the script so that it matches the one in the following display.

```
Changing script C:\paradox3\test2                                    Script

....+...10....+...20....+...30....+...40....+...50....+...60....+...70....+...80
edit "Mailtx"
play "Mainmenu"
```

2. Press **F10** (Scripts Menu) and select the Go option. The application menu appears on the screen. Press **Esc**. Your screen resembles the following display.

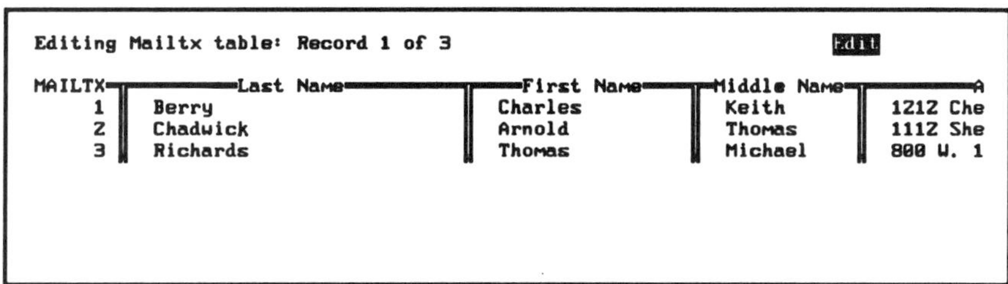

```
Editing Mailtx table: Record 1 of 3                                   Edit

MAILTX  Last Name                   First Name      Middle Name      A
     1  Berry                       Charles         Keith            1212 Che
     2  Chadwick                    Arnold          Thomas           1112 She
     3  Richards                    Thomas          Michael          800 W. 1
```

3. Press **F2** to cancel the Edit mode. Then press **F8** (Clear Image).
4. When the Main Menu returns, edit the Mainmenu script. Insert a RESET command as the first command line in the script.

```
Changing script C:\paradox3\mainmenu                              Script Ins

....+...10....+...20....+...30....+...40....+...50....+...60....+...70....+...80
reset                                                                          ◆
readlib "Maillist" Idcheck, editpass
while (true)
  clear
  showmenu
    "View" : "Find and review customer information.",
    "Maintenance" : "Maintains table data.",
    "Report" : "Print the columnar report.",
    "Labels" : "Print mailing labels.",
    "Update" : "Batch update master table from a floppy disk.",
    "Summary" : "Provide statistics on subscription preferences.",
    "Configure" : "Change application configuration.",
    "Utilities" : "Perform various tasks for the Mail List application."
  default "View" to mchoice
  switch
  case mchoice = "View" :
    play "Custview"
  case mchoice = "Maintenance" :
    x = Idcheck()
    if x > "0" and x < "10"
      then
      play "Custmnt"
```

5. Press **F10** (Scripts Menu) and select the DO-IT! option.
6. Play the Test2 script again. This time the application menu is displayed on the screen. When the RESET command was encountered, Paradox ended the Edit mode and closed the open table.
7. Press **Esc** to end the application.
8. Turn to Module 74 to continue the recommended learning sequence.

Module 68
RETURN

DESCRIPTION

This command is similar to the EXIT and QUIT commands because it tells Paradox to stop playing the current script or procedure. Then, Paradox resumes the play of the original script. The format for the RETURN command follows.

```
RETURN << <value> >>
```

The <value> phrase is optional. When used, it returns a value from the script or procedure that encountered the RETURN command. Replace <value> with a value (True, False, etc.) or an expression (variable, field, array element, etc.). Then, the value is used as needed by the script that performed the script or procedure.

For example, only certain people are allowed to maintain the data in the table. Identification codes are assigned to those people. The script in the following display asks for valid ID codes.

```
Designing script C:\paradox3\idcheck                                Script

....+...10....+...20....+...30....+...40....+...50....+...60....+...70....+...80
; idcheck - checks for valid identification codes
clear
@ 10,10
?? "Enter your identification code "
accept "A4" picture "&&&#" to idcode
if idcode = "DLS1" or idcode = "ELW1"
  then
  return True
else
  message "You have typed an invalid ID code..."
  sleep 2000
  return False
endif
; end idcheck
```

When this script is played by another script, Paradox asks for an identification code. When one is typed, Idcheck validates it. If the code typed equals DLS1, DFS1, or ELW1, the value returned to the original script is True. Otherwise, an error message is displayed, and the value returned is False.

For example, a valid ID code is required before allowing the user to access the table. The command lines that play Idcheck and evaluate the results follow.

```
case mchoice = "Maintenance" :
  play "Idcheck"
  if retval                    ; valid ID code
    then
    play "Custmnt"
  endif
```

When the user selects the Maintenance option, Idcheck is played. A True or False value is returned from Idcheck in a variable called "retval." This variable name is provided automatically by Paradox when a value is returned but <value> is not specified in the RETURN command line.

Paradox resumes play of the original script beginning with the line that follows the PLAY command. Remember that the screen is not cleared when the RETURN command is performed. The message that was displayed by Idcheck remains on the screen.

The script for table maintenance (Custmnt) is played only when a True value is returned from Idcheck. If the value is False, access to the table is not allowed and the user is returned to the application menu.

The semicolons identify comments. Include comment lines in your scripts to provide information to yourself or another programmer. This is called *documentation.*

As the number of scripts increases, the need for documentation is greater. A brief line or two in your scripts may jog your memory enough to make changes easier.

The RETURN command is also available for procedures (PROC, ENDPROC). When this command is encountered within a procedure, the procedure is exited but not the script that includes the procedure.

APPLICATIONS

Use the RETURN command in a script or procedure that is to be played. When the RETURN command is encountered, Paradox stops the play of the script or procedure.

A value is often passed to the original script through the RETURN command line. Then Paradox resumes the original script beginning with the line that follows the command line that caused the play.

TYPICAL OPERATION

This example shows you how to use the RETURN command.

1. Type **SEW** to write a new script. When asked for the name of the script, type **Idcheck** and press **Enter**.

2. The script asks the user for a valid ID code. Type the script that appears in the following display. The semicolon identifies comments about the script. The first comment line is the name of the script and the last identifies the end of the script.

```
Designing script C:\paradox3\idcheck                                    Script

....+...10....+...20....+...30....+...40....+...50....+...60....+...70....+...80
; idcheck - checks for valid identification codes
clear
@ 10,10
?? "Enter your identification code "
accept "A4" picture "&&&#" to idcode
if idcode = "DLS1" or idcode = "ELW1"
  then
  return True
else
  message "You have typed an invalid ID code..."
  sleep 2000
  return False
endif
; end idcheck
```

3. Press **F10** (Scripts Menu) and select the Go option.
4. When asked for an ID code, type **PLM1** and press **Enter**. Notice the message in the lower right corner of the screen that says

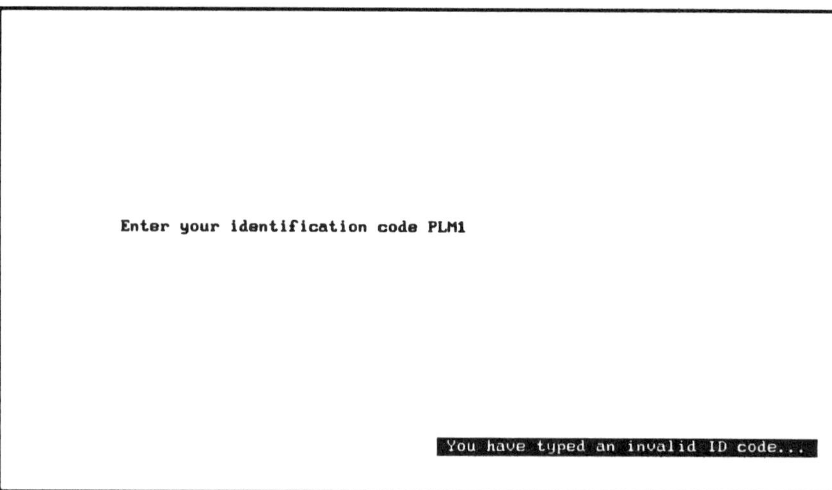

5. When the Main Menu screen returns, the word "False" appears in the lower right corner. It disappears as soon as you press a key.
6. Type **SP** to play a script. When asked for the name of the script, type **Idcheck** and press **Enter**.

7. This time, type **DLS1** and press **Enter**. The True message appears in the lower right corner of the screen.
8. Edit the Mainmenu script.
9. Change the script for the Maintenance option so that it includes the IF, ENDIF command set as shown in the following display.

```
Changing script C:\paradox3\mainmenu                               Script Ins

....+...10....+...20....+...30....+...40....+...50....+...60....+...70....+...80
while (true)
  clear
  showmenu
    "Maintenance" : "Maintains table data.",
    "Labels" : "Print mailing labels.",
    "Configure" : "Change application configuration.",
    "Weekcalc" : "Count the number of weeks between two dates."
  default "Maintenance" to mchoice
  switch
  case mchoice = "Maintenance" :
    play "idcheck"                                                            ◆
    if retval                                                                 ◆
      then                                                                    ◆
      play "Custmnt"                                                          ◆
    endif                                                                     ◆
  case mchoice = "Labels" :
    @ 10,10
    ?? "Labels..."
    sleep 2000
  case mchoice = "Configure" :
    @ 10,10
    ?? "Configure..."
```

10. Press **F10** (Scripts Menu) and select the Go option. When the application menu appears, type **M** to select the Maintenance option.
11. Type **PLM1** and press **Enter**. The message in the lower right corner tells you that the ID was invalid. Then the application menu returns to your screen. Press **Esc** to return to the Main Menu screen.
12. Write a new script called Custmnt and type the script that appears in the following display.

```
Designing script C:\paradox3\custmnt                               Script

....+...10....+...20....+...30....+...40....+...50....+...60....+...70....+...80
@ 22,40
?? "This option is not yet available..."
sleep 2000
```

13. Press **F10** (Scripts Menu) and select the Go option.

14. The message "This option is not yet available. . ." is displayed in the lower right corner of the screen. Then the Main Menu returns to the screen.
15. Type **SP** to play a script. When asked for the name of the script, type **Mainmenu** and press **Enter**.
16. Since the cursor is positioned on the Maintenance option, press **Enter** to select that option.
17. When asked for an ID, type **DLS1** and press **Enter**. The message "This option is not yet available. . ." appears in the lower right corner of the screen. Then the screen clears and the application menu appears across the top.
18. Select the Maintenance option again. Type **PLM1** and press **Enter**. You are told that the identification code is invalid. Then the application menu appears across the top of the screen.
19. Press **Esc** to stop the application script and return to the Main Menu screen.
20. Turn to Module 73 to continue the recommended learning sequence.

Module 69
RUN

DESCRIPTION

When writing an application, include several options for the user. By providing the user with menu options, you increase productivity, build confidence, and encourage independence.

Consider including a few options that perform the RUN command. It is formatted as follows.

```
RUN << SLEEP <milliseconds> >> <command line>
```

The SLEEP <milliseconds> clause is optional. It tells Paradox to wait the specified number of milliseconds after performing the RUN command so that the user is able to read the results of the command. It is similar to the SLEEP command.

Replace <command line> with any valid DOS command string. Unless the string is provided in a variable, enclose it with quotation marks. For example, RUN "DIR *.LIB" tells Paradox to list all procedure library files by using the DOS directory command. Include the SLEEP clause so that the user is able to read the results.

APPLICATIONS

Use the RUN command to provide the user with necessary DOS commands without ending the Paradox session. Though similar to the ToDOS option of the Tools/More submenu, the script is able to perform the operation without user input.

For example, provide a utility option that reports a list of Mail*.db files currently on the disk. This allows the user to check the disk for a table name before creating a new one or renaming an existing one.

TYPICAL OPERATION

This example shows you how to use the RUN command.

1. Edit the Utility script. Insert the List option so that the script matches the one in the following display. The dots indicate script lines that are omitted from the display. Do not change those lines.

```
Changing script C:\paradox3\utility                                      Script Ins
....+...10....+...20....+...30....+...40....+...50....+...60....+...70....+...80
; utility.sc - allows various tasks for Mail List application
while(true)
  clear
  showmenu
    "Zipcodes" : "Replace new zipcode for all customers with old zipcode.",
    "Newfile" : "Create a new Mail List customer file.",
    "Delete" : "Delete a Mail List customer file from disk.",
    "Rename" : "Renames an existing customer file.",
    "List" : "Lists the names of all customer files.",                    ◆
    "Passfile" : "Restricted - Access Password file."
  default "Zipcodes" to mutility
  .
  .
  .
        ?? "Renaming the customer file - Please Wait..."
        rename mfile1 mfile2
      endif
    endif
    release vars mfile1,mfile2
  case mutility = "List" :                                                ◆
    run sleep 5000 "dir *.db/w"                                           ◆
  case mutility = "Passfile" :
    x = idcheck()
    if x = "9"
      then
      editpass()
    else
      message "You have typed an invalid ID code..."
      sleep 2000
      clearall
    endif
    savevars all
    if isfile("Passes.sc")
      then
      Menu {Tools} {Rename} {Script} {Savevars} {Passes} {Replace}
    else
```

2. Press **F10** (Scripts Menu) and select the DO-IT! option.
3. When the Main Menu screen returns, type **SPMainmenu** and press **Enter**.
4. Select the Utilities option. Then select the List option from the Utilities submenu. The screen resembles the following display.

```
 Volume in drive C is AN ILLUSION
 Directory of  C:\PARADOX3

MAILOUT  DB     MAILTX   DB     STOCKS   DB     SALES    DB     ADDRECS  DB
DELRECS  DB     MAILOK   DB     STRUCT   DB     MAILFILE DB
        9 File(s)   6950912 bytes free
```

5. When the submenu returns, press **Esc** twice to end the application.
6. Turn to Module 25 to continue the recommended learning sequence.

Module 70
SAVEVARS

DESCRIPTION

Consider an application that assigns and prints invoices. The last invoice number assigned by the application must be available for its next run. Instead of creating a table for that one field, use the SAVEVARS command.

There are two forms for this command. Substitute a number greater than 1 for "-n."

```
SAVEVARS <var-1>,...,<var-n>
SAVEVARS ALL
```

Replace <var-1> through <var-n> with the names of existing variables and arrays. Include at least one name in this form of the command line and separate them with a comma.

When the SAVEVARS command is performed, the values of the specified variables and arrays are saved in a Paradox generated script on disk. This script contains command lines that declare and set variables and arrays as in the following display of the Savevars script.

```
Changing script C:\paradox3\savevars                                    Script Ins

....+...10....+...20....+...30....+...40....+...50....+...60....+...70....+...80
; Variables Saved Using Savevars Command

fileans = "Mailtx"
ans = "Y"
mchoice = "Esc"
```

Since the current values are saved on disk, use the RELEASE command to remove the unnecessary variables and arrays from memory. Later, when you are ready to restore the variables and arrays, play the Savevars script.

To save all memory variables, include the SAVEVARS ALL command line in the script. If the Paradox variable (Retval) exists, it is also included in the Savevars script.

If you need to save private variables or arrays, use the SAVEVARS command within the procedure that identifies them. Otherwise, if the same name exists for public variables or arrays, Paradox saves the public ones.

APPLICATIONS

Use this command to provide the most recent value for a variable and/or array to the application. Each time the SAVEVARS command is performed, variables are recorded in the Savevars script. When this script is played, the variables and arrays from the last SAVEVARS command are restored in the computer's memory.

For example, save the variables that provide consecutive invoice numbers to the accounts receivable application. Each time that the A/R application is begun, restore the last number used during the previous run. Each time that an invoice is printed, increase the memory variable and save it by using the SAVEVARS command.

By saving current values for your application often, you are better protected from power failures and other unforeseen situations. However, if you do encounter a problem, edit the Savevars script until it includes all the required values.

Remember, there is only one Savevars script. Each time the SAVEVARS command is encountered, the script is rewritten for the current variables and arrays. This is especially important when several applications that use the Savevars script are run in the same subdirectory.

However, it is easy to avoid this situation. Use the RENAME command (or its equivalent menu options) after the SAVEVARS command line. Be careful that you use a script name that has not been used for another script. Otherwise, it is replaced by the renamed Savevars script. Then restore the variables for a certain application by playing the renamed script instead of Savevars.

TYPICAL OPERATION

This illustration shows you how to use the SAVEVARS command.

1. Type **SEE** and edit the Utility script. Insert the SAVEVARS command lines so that your script matches the one in the following display. The dots indicate lines of the script that are omitted from the display. Do not change those lines in your script.

```
Changing script C:\paradox3\utility                                Script Ins

....+...10....+...20....+...30....+...40....+...50....+...60....+...70....+...80
        ?? "Replacing zipcodes - Please Wait..."
        view "Mailtx"
        savevars mold, mnew                                                   ◆
        scan for [zipcode] = mold
          copytoarray zips
          zips["Zipcode"] = mnew
          editkey
          copyfromarray zips
        endscan
        .
        .
        .
        clearall
      else
        message "You have typed an invalid ID code..."
        sleep 2000
        clearall
      endif
      savevars all                                                            ◆
    case mutility = "Esc" :
```

2. Press **F10** (Scripts Menu) and select the DO-IT! option.
3. When the Main Menu returns to the screen, type **SEE** and press **Enter** to see a list of all existing scripts. The Savevars file is not in the list.
4. Press **Esc** until the Main Menu screen is displayed on your monitor.
5. Play the Mainmenu script. Press **Left Arrow** to position the cursor on the Utilities option, then press **Enter**.
6. Type **Z** to select the Zipcodes option. For the old zipcode, type **75088** and press **Enter**. Then type **75084** for the new zipcode and press **Enter**. Type **Y** and press **Enter** to continue.
7. Press **Esc** until you exit the application.
8. Type **SEE** and **Savevars**. Press **Enter**. The script resembles the following display.

```
Changing script C:\paradox3\savevars                                    Script
....+...10....+...20....+...30....+...40....+...50....+...60....+...70....+...80
; Variables Saved Using Savevars Command

mold = "75088"
mnew = "75084"
```

9. Press **F10** (Scripts Menu) and select the DO-IT! option.
10. Play the Mainmenu script again and select the Utilities option. This time select the Passfile option and type **DLS1** for the ID. Then press **Enter**.
11. Press **F2** to return to the submenu. Then press **Esc** twice to return to the Main Menu.
12. Use the editor again to see that the Savevars script resembles the following display. Notice that it is different from the previous script.

```
Changing script C:\paradox3\savevars                                    Script
....+...10....+...20....+...30....+...40....+...50....+...60....+...70....+...80
; Variables Saved Using Savevars Command

fileans = "MAILTX"
idcode = "DLS1"
Namscrpt = "Esc"
Array Descr[3]
Descr[1] = "View only Texas Customers"
Descr[2] = "View only Louisiana Customers"
Descr[3] = "View only California Customers"
Nametabl = "Esc"
Tablname = ""
Whattodo = "Delete"
Array zips[12]
zips[1] = "Mailtx"
zips[2] = "Berry"
zips[3] = "Charles"
zips[4] = "Keith"
zips[5] = "1212 Cherokee Ln."
zips[6] = ""
zips[7] = "Plano"
zips[8] = "Tx"
zips[9] = "75084"
```

13. Press **F10** (Scripts Menu) and select the DO-IT! option.
14. Select the Tools/Delete/Script menu options. Type **Savevars** and press **Enter**. Type **O** to delete the script.
15. Change the Utility script again. Insert the menu option line after the SAVEVARS command lines as shown in the following display.

```
Changing script C:\paradox3\utility                                    Script Ins

....+...10....+...20....+...30....+...40....+...50....+...60....+...70....+...80
        endscan
        do_it!
    Menu {Tools} {Rename} {Script} {Savevars} {Zipcodes}                        ◆
        clearall
      endif
    case mutility = "Passfile" :
      play "idcheck"
      if retval and passes[x+1] = "9"
        then
        edit "Mailfile"
        formkey
        wait table message "Press F2 to return to the menu..." until "F2"
        do_it!
        clearall
      else
        message "You have typed an invalid ID code..."
        sleep 2000
        clearall
      endif
      savevars all
      Menu {Tools} {Rename} {Script} {Savevars} {Passes}                        ◆
    case mutility = "Esc" :
```

16. Press **F10** and select DO-IT! to save the changed script.
17. Play the Mainmenu script again. Run both of the options in the Utilities submenu. Then exit the application.
18. Use the Scripts Editor to review the Zipcodes and Passes scripts. Since the Savevars script was renamed each time it was created, it is not included in the list of scripts.
19. Turn to Module 62 to continue the recommended learning sequence.

Module 71
SCAN, ENDSCAN

DESCRIPTION

Write scripts that include loops when you need to perform repetitive command lines. Using the WHILE, ENDWHILE and the FOR, ENDFOR command combinations are two ways to establish a loop. Another is the SCAN, ENDSCAN command combination.

It tells Paradox to perform the loop for each record in the current table. If the table is empty, the loop is not performed.

When the loop begins, the first record in the table immediately becomes the current record. Each time a loop is performed, the next record in the table becomes the current record automatically. When the last record in the table is processed, Paradox stops the looping activity and plays the rest of the script. The format for this command combination follows.

```
SCAN <<FOR <condition> >>
  <commands>
ENDSCAN
```

The SCAN command marks the beginning and the ENDSCAN identifies the end of the loop. When a SCAN is used in a script, there must always be an ENDSCAN command line to match it. The two commands are used as a pair.

The FOR <condition> clause is optional. When included in the SCAN command line, replace <condition> with an expression that Paradox evaluates as true or false. Since it specifies criteria that must be met, it is used the same way as the expressions in the IF, ENDIF and the WHILE, ENDWHILE command combinations.

Replace <commands> with at least one command line that you want performed during the looping activity. This set of commands is performed once for every record in the table unless the FOR <condition> clause is included in the SCAN command line. The FOR <condition> clause restricts the set of commands to only those records that meet the criteria. When the looping activity is completed, the last record in the table is the current record.

For example, the following command lines tell Paradox to print the customers that have "Texas" in the State field. All others are skipped.

```
view "Mailtx"
lncnt = 99
printer on
```

```
scan for [State] = "Texas"
  if lncnt >55
    then
    lncnt = 5
    @ lncnt,35
    ?? "Texas Customers from Mailtx"
    lncnt = lncnt + 3
  endif
  @ lncnt,05
  ?? [First Name]+ " " +[Middle Name]+ " " +[Last Name]
  lncnt = lncnt + 1
endscan
printer off
```

If Paradox encounters the QUITLOOP command while processing the loop, the looping activity is stopped immediately. Paradox then performs the line that follows the ENDSCAN command line and finishes playing the rest of the script. Since this command interrupts the looping activity, Paradox does not move the cursor from the current record.

If the LOOP command is performed while processing <commands>, Paradox skips all script lines between the LOOP and ENDSCAN commands. Then the next record in the table becomes the current record and the loop is performed for that record.

Regardless of what record in the table is the current record when the SCAN command is encountered the first time, Paradox moves the cursor to the first record in the table before beginning the loop. The cursor is moved automatically to the next record in the table each time the loop is processed. Therefore, when the loop ends, the last record in the table is the current record.

If the QUITLOOP command is encountered before the loop ends normally, the cursor remains positioned on the current record. It is not moved to the last record in the table. Then Paradox plays the rest of the script.

APPLICATIONS

This command is valid only for tables in View mode. The table must be read by the VIEW command instead of the EDIT command.

Use the SCAN, ENDSCAN command combination in scripts that need to process each record in the current table. Restrict the processing to records that meet specific criteria by including the FOR <condition> clause in the SCAN command line. Though any expression is allowed, <condition> usually evaluates a field in the table structure.

For example, the command line SCAN FOR [State] = "Texas" tells Paradox to perform <commands> for records that have a "Texas" in the State field. All other records are skipped.

Before using the SCAN FOR, ENDSCAN command combination, review the fields included in <condition>. If the loop involves one section of consecutive records, scanning every record in the table is not an efficient programming method.

For example, the command line SCAN FOR SUBSTR([Last Name],1,1) = "B" tells Paradox to process <commands> for records that have a "B" in the first position of the Last Name field. Since the table is sorted in Last Name, First Name, and Middle Name order, it is unneccesary (and time-consuming) to scan every record in the table.

Instead, use the LOCATE command to find the first record that contains the specified value in the key field. Then a WHILE SUBSTR[Last Name],1,1) = "B" command line controls the loop. Including a SKIP command in <commands> moves the cursor to the next record. As long as the current record meets <condition> and it is not the last record in the table, continue processing the loop.

TYPICAL OPERATION

This example shows you how to use the SCAN command.

1. Edit the Custview script so that it includes the SCAN, ENDSCAN command set as shown in the following display.

```
Changing script C:\paradox3\custview                                Script

....+...10....+...20....+...30....+...40....+...50....+...60....+...70....+...80
; custview - view customer data
view "Mailtx"
if isfile("mailtx.f2")
  then
  Pickform "2"
else
  Pickform "f"
endif
while (true)
  clear
  @ 21,05
  ?? "For a list of customers, leave customer name blank..."                  ◆
  @ 10,10
  ?? "Enter Last Name "
  accept "A30" to lastname
  @ 12,10
  ?? "Enter First Name "
  accept "A20" to firstname
  if lastname > "     " and firstname   > "     "
    then
    locate lastname, firstname
    if (retval)
    .
    .
    .
      ?? "Requested Customer name not found in table..."
      sleep 2000
    endif
  else
    clear                                                                     ◆
    lncnt = 1                                                                 ◆
      ans = "Y"                                                               ◆
      while ans = "Y"                                                         ◆
        scan                                                                  ◆
          if lncnt > 20                                                       ◆
            then                                                              ◆
            @ 21,05                                                           ◆
```

```
             ?? "More (Y/N)? "
             accept "A1" picture "&" to ans
             if ans = "Y"
               then
               clear
             lncnt = 1
           else
             quitloop
           endif
         endif
         @ lncnt,10
         ?? [First Name]+" "+[Middle Name]+" "+[Last Name]
         lncnt = lncnt + 1
       endscan
       @ 21,05
       ?? "End of table..."
       sleep 3000
       ans = "N"
     endwhile
     quitloop
   endif
endwhile
clearimage
; end custview
```

2. Save the changed script by pressing **F10** (Script Menu) and typing **D** for DO-IT!.
3. Play the Mainmenu script.
4. When the application menu appears, type **V** to select the View option. Press **Enter** twice to leave the last and first name fields blank. Your screen resembles the following display.

```
          Shirley Lynn Appleby
          Charles Keith Berry
          Arnold Thomas Chadwick






     End of table...
```

5. If the table contains more than 20 records, the user is asked if another screen of records is to be displayed. If the answer is "Yes," this activity continues until the last record in the table is displayed. Otherwise the application menu returns to the screen. Press **Esc** to end the script and return to the Main Menu.
6. Turn to Module 58 to continue the recommended learning sequence.

Module 72
SELECT

DESCRIPTION

There are times when you need to use a menu option line in a script. However, if that line requires a value that is not provided, the script encounters a script error. Include a SELECT command after the menu option line to provide the missing information. Use the following format for this command.

```
SELECT <selection>
```

Replace <selection> with menu options or information that is not allowed in curly braces. For example, the following command lines let the user specify the table to be accessed by the menu option line.

```
menu {Tools} {Info} {Structure}
select mfile
```

The menu option line selects as many of the options as possible in the braces. When the SELECT command provides the table name, Paradox displays a table structure on the screen.

Remember that the variable must not be included on the menu option line. Otherwise, the script ends with a script error.

APPLICATIONS

Use the SELECT command in a script that needs to access the Paradox menus. It lets you select Paradox menu options as though the user is performing each selection. Also, the SELECT command lets you provide information from the user to the menu-driven system.

Write the script so that the user is asked for the information in English. Then, perform the command line of menu options. The next line in the script must be a SELECT command. It includes the variable that contains the value provided by the user.

TYPICAL OPERATION

This illustration shows you how to use the SELECT command.

1. Edit the Test1 script. Change it to match the one in the following display.

```
Changing script C:\paradox3\test1                                   Script

....+...10....+...20....+...30....+...40....+...50....+...60....+...70....+...80
clear
@ 10,10
?? "Enter the name of the table "
accept "A8" picture "&*&" to mfile
menu {Tools} {Info} {Structure} mfile
release vars mfile
```

2. Press **F10** (Scripts Menu) and select the Go option.
3. When asked for the name of the table, type **Mailtx** and press **Enter**. The script encounters a script error.
4. Type **C** to Cancel the script. Paradox asks for the name of the table. Press **Esc** three times to return to the Main Menu screen.
5. Edit the Test1 script again. Change it to include the SELECT command line as shown in the following display.

```
Changing script C:\paradox3\test1                                   Script Ins

....+...10....+...20....+...30....+...40....+...50....+...60....+...70....+...80
clear
@ 10,10
?? "Enter the name of the table "
accept "A8" picture "&*&" to mfile
menu {Tools} {Info} {Structure}                                                ◆
select mfile                                                                   ◆
release vars mfile
```

6. Press **F10** (Scripts Menu) and select the Go option.
7. Type **Mailtx** and press **Enter** when asked for a table name. The table structure is displayed on the workspace successfully.
8. Press **F8** (Clear Image).
9. Turn to Module 31 to continue the recommended learning sequence.

Module 73
SETDIR

DESCRIPTION

When a Paradox session begins, the drive and directory are preset to those selected when you installed Paradox. All scripts and tables are read from or written to the specified disk or directory while you work.

Though they are preset, you can change the working disk drive or working directory to meet your application needs. For example, the mailing list application is saved in the subdirectory called "MAILOUT." The inventory application is saved in the "INVENTRY" subdirectory. Write the menu script so that the proper subdirectory is available automatically when the option is selected by the user.

Include the SETDIR command in a script when you need to specify a different working drive identifier and/or a working subdirectory. The format for this command follows.

```
SETDIR <path>
```

To change the working disk drive, replace <path> with the drive identifier and a colon. If you also want a specific subdirectory, type two backslashes and the subdirectory name after the colon. Though DOS requires only one backslash, Paradox requires two. Enclose <path> with quotation marks.

For example, SETDIR "A:\\ap" tells Paradox that all work is to be read from and written to the "ap" subdirectory on drive A. This path remains set until changed by another SETDIR command or until the Paradox session is ended.

The same changes may be accomplished through Paradox's menu-driven system. Though several menu options are required, the result is the same as when using the SETDIR command. The following string of menu options may be included in a script instead of the SETDIR command line.

```
Menu {Tools} {More} {Directory} {A:\\ap\\} {OK}
```

This command line tells Paradox to begin at the Main Menu screen. Each word or phrase that is enclosed with braces specifies the Paradox menu selections.

For example, the Tools option is selected from the Main Menu line. The More option is selected from the Tools submenu. When the Directory option is selected, Paradox asks for the new working disk and/or directory. After it is provided, Paradox asks you to verify the answer or cancel it.

Though such a line is not a PAL command line, it is accepted and performed when the script is played. As long as the script line provides the options in proper order, spelling, and enclosed with braces, Paradox performs them as though the Paradox menus are in control.

Before the SETDIR command line is encountered, be sure to save anything you want to keep and close any open tables. The SETDIR command erases the screen and deletes all temporary tables from memory. Then the working disk and/or directory is set.

APPLICATIONS

Do not force the user to change the working disk or directory with the Paradox menu-driven system. Instead, include the SETDIR command in one of the application's scripts.

If the application requires a specific disk or directory, the script should change it before starting the application. Otherwise, present a menu of options so that only valid disks and directories are available to the user.

When possible, keep applications on separate disks or in separate directories. This technique helps you keep the disks organized. Therefore, it is easy for you and the computer to find a script or table.

TYPICAL OPERATION

This example shows you how to use the SETDIR command.

1. Insert a blank, formatted disk into drive B.
2. At the Main Menu, type **T** to select the Tools option.
3. Type **M** to select the More option from the Tools submenu.
4. Type **D** to select the Directory option. Paradox presents the current directory setting which resembles the one in the following display.

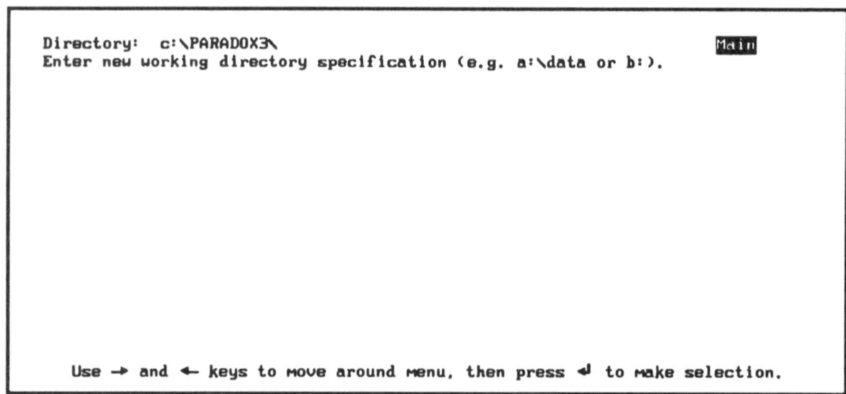

5. Press **Backspace** to remove the current setting. Then type **A:** and press **Enter**.
6. Paradox asks if you want to cancel or accept the setting. Type **C** to select the Cancel option. The directory is reset to drive C and presented to you again. Press **Enter**.
7. Type **O** to accept the current working directory. The Main Menu appears across the top of the screen. A message in the lower right corner tells you that the current directory is "C:\paradox3."
8. Open the Mainmenu script to be edited with the Script Editor.
9. Insert SETDIR commands in the script as shown in the following display. If you are using drive A, type **setdir "a:\\"** as the first SETDIR command line shown. The dots indicate command lines are omitted from the display. Do not change those lines.

```
Changing script C:\paradox3\mainmenu                                    Script
....+...10....+...20....+...30....+...40....+...50....+...60....+...70....+...80
setdir "c:\\paradox3"                                                          ◆
while (true)
  clear
  showmenu
.
.
.
  case mchoice = "Weekcalc" :
    play "Weekcalc"
  case mchoice = "Esc" :
    setdir "a:\\"                                                              ◆
    quit                                                                       ◆
  otherwise :
    clear
    @ 10,10
    ?? "The requested option is not available from this menu..."
    sleep 2000
  endswitch
endwhile
```

10. Press **F10** (Scripts Menu) and select the Go option. Drive A lights and the application menu appears across the top of your screen.
11. Press **Esc** to stop the application menu and return to the Main Menu screen.
12. Type **SP** to play a script. When asked for the name of the script, type **Mainmenu** and press **Enter**. This time, drive A lights as the disk is read. Then a message telling you that Mainmenu is not on the disk in drive A appears in the lower right corner of your screen.
13. Press **Esc** to return to the Scripts submenu.
14. Type **EE** to select the Paradox Editor. When asked for the script name, type **C:\PARADOX3\Mainmenu** (or the path your scripts are written to) and press **Enter**.

15. Position the cursor on the last SETDIR command line by pressing **Down Arrow**. It is the SETDIR command line that sets the working disk to drive A. Press **Ctrl-Y** to delete the line so that the end of your script matches the one in the following display.

```
Changing script C:\paradox3\mainmenu                                     Script

....+...10....+...20....+...30....+...40....+...50....+...60....+...70....+...80
    endif
  case mchoice = "Labels" :
    @ 10,10
    ?? "Labels..."
    sleep 2000
  case mchoice = "Configure" :
    @ 10,10
    ?? "Configure..."
    sleep 2000
  case mchoice = "Weekcalc" :
    play "Weekcalc"
  case mchoice = "Esc" :
    quit
  otherwise :
    clear
    @ 10,10
    ?? "The requested option is not available from this menu..."
    sleep 2000
  endswitch
endwhile
```

16. Press **F10** (Scripts Menu) and select the DO-IT! option by typing **D**. The Main Menu appears on the screen.
17. Type **SP** to play a script. When asked for the name, type **Mainmenu** and press **Enter**. Drive A lights and you are told that the script does not exist.
18. Press **Backspace** until the script name is removed from the input line.
19. Type **C:\PARADOX3\Mainmenu** and press **Enter**. The application menu appears across the top of the screen.
20. Press **Esc** to stop the application and return to the Main Menu screen.
21. Type **TMD** to verify that the working directory is set to drive C.
22. Press **Enter** to accept the current setting. When asked if the setting is OK, type **O**.
23. Edit the Mainmenu script and remove the SETDIR commands at the top of the file.
24. Turn to Module 20 to continue the recommended learning sequence.

Module 74
SETKEY

DESCRIPTION

If a user needs a little help with the Paradox menu-driven system, it is not necessary to write a dedicated application. By writing a small script that sets certain keys, the user is able to complete work successfully without much knowledge about Paradox.

There are two ways to use the SETKEY command. The formats for this command follow.

```
SETKEY <keycode> <commands>
SETKEY
```

Replace <keycode> with a keyboard symbol (/, –, 1, 2, A, B, etc.) or one of the function keys (F1, F2, F3, etc.). Unless provided in a variable, enclose <keycode> with quotation marks. It is temporarily assigned a new value.

Supply those values by replacing <commands> with at least one menu option or PAL command line. These commands are called *macros*. For example, the SETKEY "F1" MENU VIEW "MAILTX" command line changes the F1 (Help) key so that the Mailtx table is displayed on the workspace.

When the SETKEY <keycode> command is encountered without specifying <commands>, Paradox resets the key to its original value. For example, SETKEY "F1" returns the key to the Paradox Help macro.

APPLICATIONS

Use the SETKEY command to write a quick script that helps the user operate the Paradox menu-driven system. This type of script provides an immediate (temporary) solution for the user. When time permits, consider providing the user with a full application.

TYPICAL OPERATION

This example shows you how to use the SETKEY command.

1. Press **F1** (Help). The workspace is filled with help information and a menu at the top.
2. Type **P** to select the Paradox option and return to the Main Menu screen.
3. Write the Test3 script so that it matches the one in the following display.

```
Designing script C:\paradox3\test3                                   Script

....+...10....+...20....+...30....+...40....+...50....+...60....+...70....+...80
setkey "F1" Menu View "Mailtx"
setkey "F2" Menu View "Mailok"
setkey "Esc" play "test4"
```

4. Press **F10** (Scripts Menu) and select the DO-IT! option.
5. Write a new script called Test4 as shown in the following display.

```
Designing script C:\paradox3\test4                                   Script

....+...10....+...20....+...30....+...40....+...50....+...60....+...70....+...80
setkey "F1"
setkey "F2"
setkey "Esc"
```

6. Press **F10** (Scripts Menu) and select the DO-IT! option.
7. When the Main Menu screen returns, play the Test3 script. The Main Menu line returns after Paradox plays the script.
8. Press **F1**. Instead of the Help screen, Paradox presents the Mailtx table in View mode.
9. Press **F2**. The Mailok table is displayed on the workspace with the Mailtx table. Your screen resembles the following display.

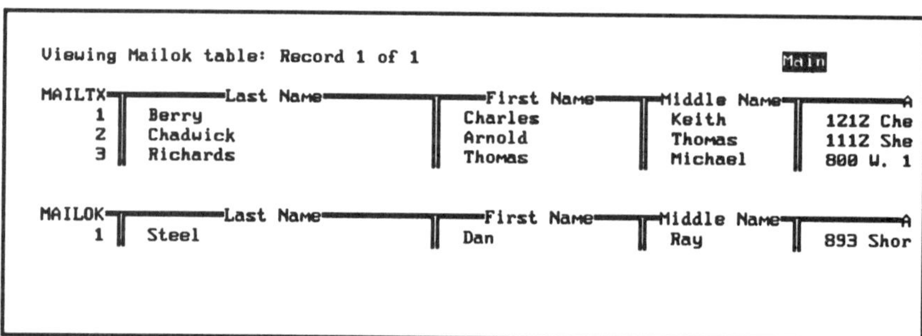

```
Viewing Mailok table: Record 1 of 1                                  Main

MAILTX    Last Name              First Name    Middle Name        A
    1  Berry                     Charles       Keith        1212 Che
    2  Chadwick                  Arnold        Thomas       1112 She
    3  Richards                  Thomas        Michael      800 W. 1

MAILOK    Last Name              First Name    Middle Name        A
    1  Steel                     Dan           Ray          893 Shor
```

10. Press **Alt-F8** (Clear All Images) to remove both tables from the workspace.
11. Press **Esc**. Press **F1** to see that the key is reset to display the Help screen. Then type **P** to select the Paradox option.
12. Turn to Module 72 to continue the recommended learning sequence.

Module 75
SETMARGIN

DESCRIPTION

When you used the ? or TEXT, ENDTEXT command set prior to version 3.0 to display information on the screen, centering had to be done by including enough spaces in the text displayed on the screen.

Use the SETMARGIN command to specify the number of spaces to indent the text on the screen. It is similar to setting the margin on a typewriter. The proper syntax for this command follows.

```
SETMARGIN <<number>>
SETMARGIN <<OFF>>
```

Replace <number> with an integer 1 through 79 to specify the desired indention. For example, SETMARGIN 30 tells Paradox that all lines between all following ? and TEXT, ENDTEXT commands begin in column 30 of the screen. The margin remains set until another SETMARGIN command is encountered or the Paradox session ends.

Use the OFF option to disengage the most recent SETMARGIN command. After this command is encountered, all following ? and TEXT, ENDTEXT results begin at the left edge of the screen.

NOTE: This command is available in version 3.0 and higher.

APPLICATIONS

Include the SETMARGIN command line in scripts that display information to the user. Instead of providing enough spaces within the text for indention, set the margin with the SETMARGIN command. The margin remains set until another SETMARGIN command is encountered or you end the session.

TYPICAL OPERATION

This example shows you how to use the SETMARGIN commands.

1. Type **SEW** to use the Script Editor. When asked for the name of the script, type **DEMOMARG** and press **Enter**.

2. Type the following command lines on the screen.

```
Designing script C:\paradox3\demomarg                              Script

....+...10....+...20....+...30....+...40....+...50....+...60....+...70....+...80
clear
@ 6,10
text
This option counts the number of weeks between two
dates. The results are displayed at the bottom of
the screen.

Under the results line is an option. Type 0 (zero)
to do another calculation. Do this as often as
necessary.

When ready to return to the previous menu, type any
number except zero.
endtext
sleep 5000
```

3. Press **F10** (Menu) and select the Go option by typing **G**. Your screen resembles the following display.

```
          This option counts the number of weeks between two
dates. The results are displayed at the bottom of
the screen.

Under the results line is an option. Type 0 (zero)
to do another calculation. Do this as often as
necessary.

When ready to return to the previous menu, type any
number except zero.
```

4. Change the DEMOMARG script by inserting the SETMARGIN command line as follows.

```
Changing script C:\paradox3\demomarg                               Script Ins

....+...10....+...20....+...30....+...40....+...50....+...60....+...70....+...80
clear
@ 6,10
setmargin 15                                                                   ◆
text
This option counts the number of weeks between two
dates. The results are displayed at the bottom of
the screen.

Under the results line is an option. Type 0 (zero)
to do another calculation. Do this as often as
necessary.

When ready to return to the previous menu, type any
number except zero.
endtext
sleep 5000
setmargin off                                                                  ◆
```

5. Insert a SETMARGIN OFF command line after the SLEEP command line. Otherwise, all following TEXT, ENDTEXT messages might be indented fifteen positions too.

6. Press **F10** (Menu) and type **G** to run the script again. This time the screen resembles the following display.

```
This option counts the number of weeks between two
dates. The results are displayed at the bottom of
the screen.

Under the results line is an option. Type 0 (zero)
to do another calculation. Do this as often as
necessary.

When ready to return to the previous menu, type any
number except zero.
```

7. Turn to Module 59 to continue the recommended learning sequence.

Module 76
SETMAXSIZE

DESCRIPTION

Use the SETMAXSIZE command to control the maximum size of a table for the current session. By default, the largest table size is 64 megabytes. The proper syntax for the SETMAXSIZE command follows.

```
SETMAXSIZE << 64/128/192/256 >>
```

When a number is entered other than 64, 128, 192, or 256, the number entered is rounded up to the nearest number in the list of valid numbers.

NOTE: The SETMAXSIZE command was added to Paradox 2.0. Issuing this command causes an error in previous versions of Paradox.

APPLICATIONS

Issue the SETMAXSIZE command to tell Paradox to allow tables larger than 64 megabytes. The SETMAXSIZE command must be used with caution since it changes the way PARADOX internally blocks records in a table. If you write to a table with SETMAXSIZE set to a different block size than the one used when it was created, you might damage the table.

Use this command only for maintaining tables larger than 64 megabytes in size. Also, consider this command for local area network environments to ensure that all users have the same SETMAXSIZE setting for the tables.

TYPICAL OPERATION

This illustration shows you how to use the SETMAXSIZE command.

1. Type **SEW** and change the Init script so it matches the following command lines.

```
Changing script C:\paradox3\init                                    Script
....+...10....+...20....+...30....+...40....+...50....+...60....+...70....+...80
; Init.sc - initializes each Paradox session
SETMAXSIZE 256
; end init.sc
```

2. Press **F10** and select the Go option. Each table used during the session after playing the Init script is blocked at 256K.
3. End the current session and return to DOS.
4. Turn to Module 54 to continue the recommended learning sequence.

Module 77
SETNEGCOLOR

DESCRIPTION

Use the SETNEGCOLOR command to control color settings for negative currency and numeric values in tables. This allows the user to quickly see the negative values on the screen. The SETNEGCOLOR command is available with the following options:

```
SETNEGCOLOR [CURRENCY/NUMERIC/BOTH] [ON/OFF]
```

Red is the default color used for negative values. Change it to another color by selecting the Video and SetColors options in the Custom Configuration Program.

Specify which data type of negative values are to appear in the specified color by including CURRENCY ($) or NUMERIC (N or S) in the SETNEGCOLOR command. The BOTH option specifies that all negative values are displayed in the selected color. The Paradox default is the BOTH option.

The ON and OFF options turn on and off the negative color for the data types as specified by the CURRENCY, NUMERIC, or BOTH options. The Paradox default is the ON option.

NOTE: This command is available in version 3.0.

APPLICATIONS

Use the SETNEGCOLOR command to attract the user's attention to fields with negative values. For example, a field that contains customer account balances. When a customer overpays the account, the credit amount displays in red.

TYPICAL OPERATION

This example shows you how to use the SETNEGCOLOR commands.

1. Type **MR** to select the Modify and Restructure options from the Main Menu. When asked for the name of the table, type **Stocks** and press **Enter**.
2. Change the table structure by adding asterisks (*) to the second and third fields as shown in the following display.

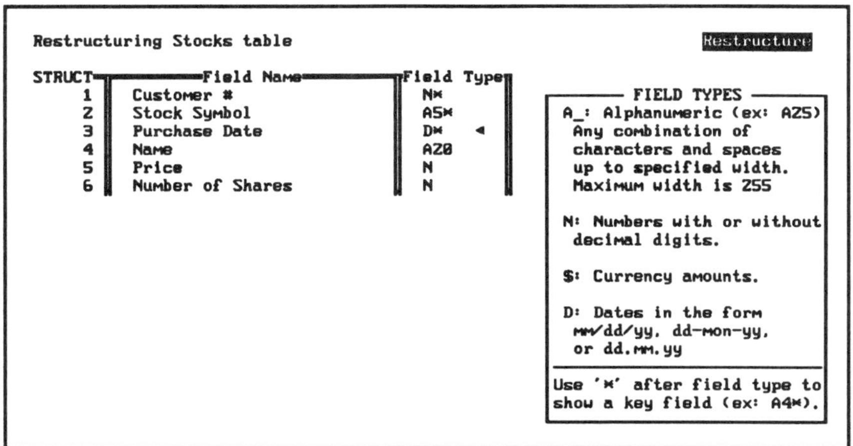

3. Press **F2** (DO-IT!) to save the changed structure on disk. Then, press **F8** (Clear Image) to remove the table from the workspace.
4. Type **SEW** to use the Script Editor. When asked for the name of the script, type **Testnegs** and press **Enter**.
5. Type the following script on the available screen.

```
Designing script C:\paradox3\testnegs                                    Script

....+...10....+...20....+...30....+...40....+...50....+...60....+...70....+...80
; testnegs.sc - tests SETNEGCOLOR command
edit "Mailtx"
pickform "2"
; end testnegs.sc
```

6. Press **F10** (Scripts Menu) and select the Go option.
7. When the edit screen for the Mailtx table appears, press **PgDn** if necessary to move to the Charles Keith Berry record.
8. Press **F4** (Down Image) to move the cursor to the Stocks table information.
9. Press **Down Arrow** until a new blank record appears.
10. Type the following information into the new record:

```
Stock Symbol :                 DLC
Purchase Date:            01/10/90
Name         : Darwin Lynn Company
Price        :                  12
Number of Shares:             -100
```

If you have a color monitor, the number of shares field turned red when you entered the negative number. If you have a monochrome monitor, the field is highlighted as shown in the following display.

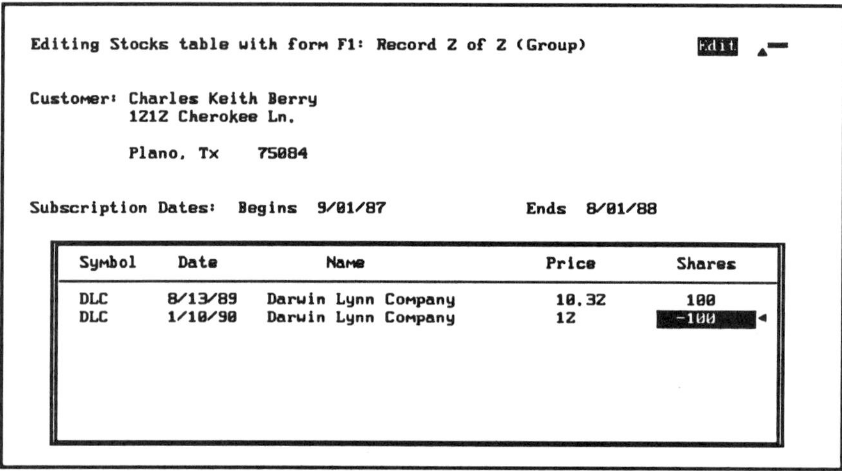

```
Editing Stocks table with form F1: Record 2 of 2 (Group)          Edit

Customer: Charles Keith Berry
          1212 Cherokee Ln.

          Plano, Tx    75084

Subscription Dates:  Begins  9/01/87            Ends  8/01/88

  Symbol    Date       Name                        Price      Shares
  DLC       8/13/89    Darwin Lynn Company         10.32       100
  DLC       1/10/90    Darwin Lynn Company         12         -100
```

11. Press **F2** (DO-IT!) to save the new record.
12. Press **F8** to clear the table from the workspace.
13. Change the Testnegs script so it matches the following command lines.

```
Changing script C:\paradox3\testnegs                              Script Ins

....+...10....+...20....+...30....+...40....+...50....+...60....+...70....+...80
; testnegs.sc - tests SETNEGCOLOR command
edit "Mailtx"
setnegcolor both off
pickform "2"
; end testnegs.sc
```

14. Press **F10** (Menu) and select the Go option.
15. Press **PgDn** to move to the Charles Keith Berry record and notice that the negative number is not highlighted.
16. Press **F2** (DO-IT!) to save the new record.
17. Press **F8** to clear the table from the workspace.
18. Turn to Module 81 to continue the recommended learning sequence.

Module 78
SETPRINTER

DESCRIPTION

Use the SETPRINTER command to change the port for your printer. The syntax for this command follows.

```
SETPRINTER << LPT1/LPT2/LPT3/COM1/COM2 >>
```

The LPT1 port is the default setting. Enclose the printer port option within double quotes.

NOTE: The SETPRINTER command is available in Paradox 2.0 and higher.

APPLICATIONS

Issue the SETPRINTER command to control the destination of printing for the REPORT, PRINT, and PRINTER commands. It also controls the destination of output for the OPEN PRINTER and CLOSE PRINTER commands.

TYPICAL OPERATION

This example shows you how to use the SETPRINTER command.

1. Type **SEE** and change the Init script so it matches the following command lines.

```
Changing script C:\paradox3\init                                    Script Ins

....+...10....+...20....+...30....+...40....+...50....+...60....+...70....+...80
; Init.sc - sets the output device for the current session
SETPRINTER "LPT1"
; end init.sc
```

2. Press **F10** and select the Go option. All printed output during the current session is directed to the LPT1 printer.
3. Turn to Module 48 to continue the recommended learning sequence.

Module 79
SETPRIVDIR

DESCRIPTION

When Paradox is used in a multi-user environment, your private directory is used to store any temporary tables you create and also any tables you specify in a PRIVTABLES command.

Use the SETPRIVDIR command to override your normal private directory setting for the current session. It will also overrides any PRIVDIR setting specified with the Custom Configuration command. The SETPRIVDIR command does not override the Paradox working directory.

The proper syntax for the SETPRIVDIR command follows.

```
SETPRIVDIR DOSPath
```

Replace DOSPath with the complete subdirectory path. If DOSPath is a quoted string, any backslashes appearing in it must be doubled.

NOTE: The SETPRIVDIR command was added to Paradox 2.0. It causes an error if used in previous versions.

APPLICATIONS

Issue the SETPRIVDIR command to override your normal PRIVDIR setting. This is useful when you know that you will not be needing tables created in your scripts after this Paradox session. After you finish the session, delete all files in your temporary private directory. This technique will assist you in keeping your normal private directory uncluttered.

TYPICAL OPERATION

This illustration shows you how to use the SETPRIVDIR command to save all Paradox files, tables, etc., to an existing subdirectory called \Paradox3\temp.

1. Type **SEE** and change the Init script to match the following command lines.

```
Changing script C:\paradox3\init                                    Script

....+...10....+...20....+...30....+...40....+...50....+...60....+...70....+...80
; Init.sc - sets the output device for the current session
SETPRIVDIR C:\\PARADOX3\\TEMP
; end init.sc
```

2. Press **F10** and select the Go option. All new tables created during the current session are kept the Paradox\Temp subdirectory on drive C.
3. Turn to Module 13 to continue the recommended learning sequence.

Module 80
SETQUERYORDER

DESCRIPTION

Prior to Paradox 3.0, a query produced an Answer table of the selected fields in the order of the queried table structure. Use the SETQUERYORDER command to establish the order for the Answer table to table structure or query image order. The proper syntax for this command follows.

```
SETQUERYORDER [TABLEORDER/IMAGEORDER]
```

Specify the TABLEORDER option when you want the Answer table fields to be in the same order as the structure of the queried table. Changing the order of the fields in the query by rotating the fields with Ctrl-R has no effect on the Answer table.

Use the IMAGEORDER option to return the Answer table fields in the same order as the query image on your screen. Use Ctrl-R to rotate fields to the end of the image until you achieve the desired order. Then, press the F2 (DO-IT!) key to create the Answer table.

NOTE: This command is available in version 3.0.

APPLICATIONS

Moving records from one table to another existing table is dependent on the proper table structure. The structure of the table with the records to be added must be the same as the structure of the receiving table.

If the existing table structures do not match, use Ctrl-R (Rotate) to create a query image that produces an Answer table with the necessary table structure. Save the query image to be used at a later time.

Issue the SETQUERYORDER IMAGEORDER command line in a script (or MiniScript) before performing query. The fields in the resulting Answer table are in the same order as the query image.

For example, the IMAGEORDER option is useful to graph the results of a query. Before you perform your query, set the desired field order in the image on your screen. This eliminates the need to move fields after performing the query.

When using multiple tables in a query image, the fields from the first image are used to create the first fields in the Answer table. Those fields are followed by the fields from the second table image, and so on. If the resulting Answer table needs to be rearranged, rename the table, rotate the fields, and create a new Answer table.

TYPICAL OPERATION

This example shows you how to use the SETQUERYORDER commands.

1. Select the Ask option from the Main Menu. When asked for the table name, type **Mailtx** and press **Enter**.
2. While the cursor is in the Mailtx column, press **F6** (Check) so all fields in the table are selected for the Answer table.
3. Press **Enter** to move the cursor to the Last Name field. Then, press **Ctrl-R** ten times to rotate all fields to the end of the image until Customer # is the first field, and the Last Name field is the second field.
4. Press **F2** (DO-IT!) to perform the query. If you installed Paradox so the QueryOrder defaults to ImageOrder, the Answer table has Customer # as the first field, and Last Name as the second field. Otherwise, Last Name is first, and Customer # is the last field of the Answer table since that is the structure of the Mailtx table.
5. Press **Alt-F8** (Clear All) to remove all images from the screen.
6. Select the Ask option from the Main Menu. When asked for the table name, type **Stocks** and press **Enter**.
7. With the cursor in the Stocks column, press **F6** (Check) to select all fields for the Answer table.
8. Move the cursor to the Customer # field, press **F5** (Example), and type **A**.
9. Press **F10** (Menu) and select the Ask option again. When asked for the table name, type **Mailtx** and press **Enter**.
10. Move to the Customer # column, press **F5** (Example), and type **A**.
11. Move to the Last Name field, and press **F6** (Check) to select the field for the Answer table. Do the same for the First Name and Middle Name columns.
12. Press **F10** (Menu). Select the Script and QuerySave options. When asked for the Query script name, type **Info1** and press **Enter**.
13. Press **F2** (DO-IT!) to perform the query. Use the arrow keys to review the resulting Answer table.
14. Press **Alt-F8** (Clear All) to remove all images from the workspace.

15. Type **SEW** to write a new script. When asked for the script name, type **Testimag** and press **Enter**.
16. Type the script so it matches the following command lines.

```
Changing script C:\paradox3\testimag                                   Script Ins

....+...10....+...20....+...30....+...40....+...50....+...60....+...70....+...80
; Testimag.sc - Tests SETQUERYORDER command
play "info1"
do_it!
clearall
rename "answer" "temp"
menu {ask} {temp} check
  moveto [stock symbol] rotate rotate rotate rotate rotate
setqueryorder tableorder
do_it!
; end Testimag.sc
```

17. Press **F10** (Menu) and select the Go option. The Info1 query is performed, the Answer table renamed to Temp, and the fields in its image rotated so the Customer # and Last Name fields are first and second. When the query of the Temp table is performed, your screen resembles the following display.

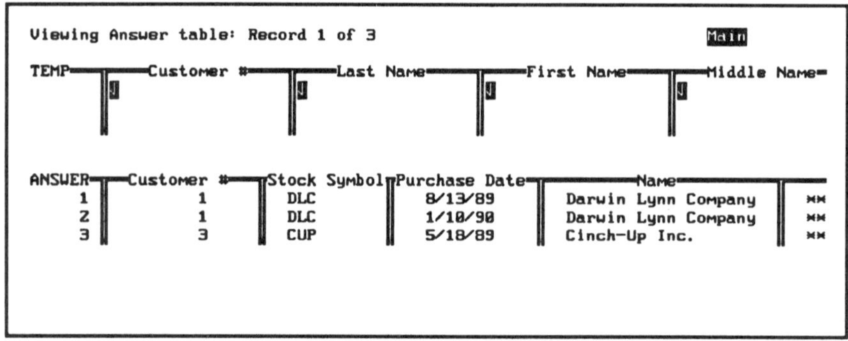

```
Viewing Answer table: Record 1 of 3                                  Main

TEMP     Customer #     Last Name     First Name     Middle Name
      √              √             √              √

ANSWER   Customer #   Stock Symbol   Purchase Date   Name
   1          1        DLC            8/13/89        Darwin Lynn Company    **
   2          1        DLC            1/10/90        Darwin Lynn Company    **
   3          3        CUP            5/18/89        Cinch-Up Inc.          **
```

18. Press **Alt-F8** (Clear All) to clear the workspace.
19. Change the SETQUERYORDER TABLEORDER line in the Testimag script to SETQUERYORDER IMAGEORDER and play the script again. This time, the fields in the Answer table are in the same order as the Temp table. Your screen resembles the following display.

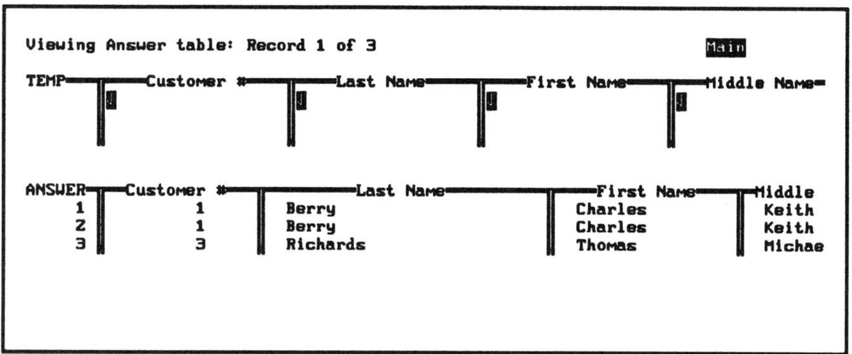

20. Press **Alt-F8** (Clear All) to clear the workspace.
21. Turn to Module 82 to continue the recommended learning sequence.

Module 81
SETRECORDPOSITION

DESCRIPTION

Writing scripts that help the user work with multi-table records would be a challenge without the SETRECORDPOSITION command. Use it to control the scrolling of records in the current multi-record form. The syntax for the SETRECORDPOSITION command follows.

```
SETRECORDPOSITION <number> <row>
```

Replace <number> with a number from 1 to the number of records minus 1. Provide the number as a constant, in a memory variable, or with the Recno( ) (current record) function. This value is the record number of a record in the secondary table. For example, specify the second record in the Stocks table.

Specify the line of the multi-record form by replacing <row> with a number from 0 to the number of rows on the form. This value is the row number of a record multi-record form. For example, specify the fifth row in the screen format of the Stocks table.

NOTE: This command is available in version 3.0.

APPLICATIONS

Use the SETRECORDPOSITION command to position the cursor on a specific record and row within the multi-table form. For example, automatically position the fifteenth Stock record for Charles Keith Berry on row 1 in the Stocks screen form. This saves time and effort for the user.

TYPICAL OPERATION

This illustration shows you how to use the SETRECORDPOSITION commands.

1. Type **SEE** to select the Script, Editor, and Edit menu options. When asked for the script name, type **Testnegs** and press **Enter**.
2. Change the script so it matches the following command lines.

```
Changing script C:\paradox3\testnegs                                    Script Ins

....+...10....+...20....+...30....+...40....+...50....+...60....+...70....+...80
; testnegs.sc - tests SETNEGCOLOR command
edit "Mailtx"
moveto [last name]
locate "Berry"
pickform "2"
downimage
end
setrecordposition recno() 1
; end testnegs.sc
```

3. Press **F10** (Menu) and select the Go option. The last record from the Stocks table for Charles Keith Berry is positioned on the top row of the multi-record area. Your screen resembles the following display.

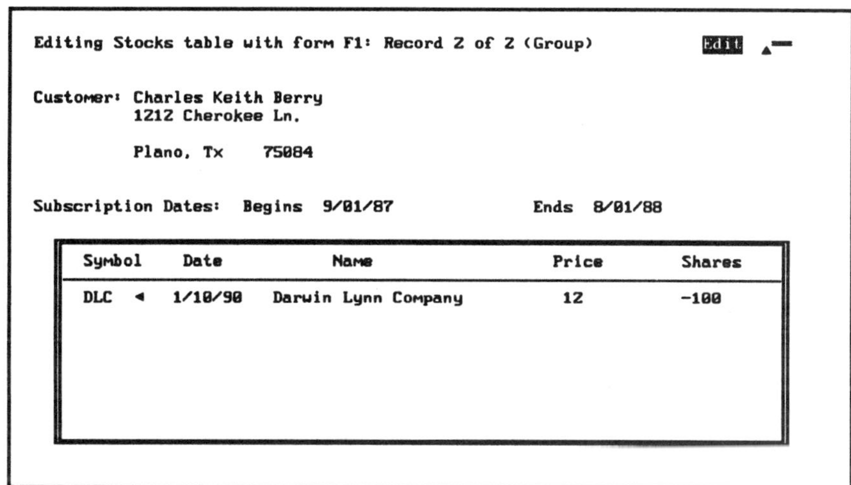

4. Move to the previous record by pressing **Up Arrow**.
5. Press **F2** (DO-IT!) to end the edit session.
6. Remove the form from the workspace by pressing **F8** (ClearImage).
7. Turn to Module 90 to continue the recommended learning sequence.

Module 82
SETRESTARTCOUNT

DESCRIPTION

When performing a query, report, or crosstab, Paradox tries to take a snapshot of the tables involved in the operation. When using Paradox on a network, the snapshot of a table must be restarted if the table is edited by someone else on the network before the snapshot is complete.

Use the SETRESTARTCOUNT command to set a limit for restarting a query, report, or crosstab on shared tables. The syntax for this command follows.

```
SETRESTARTCOUNT <number>
SETRESTARTCOUNT OFF
```

Replace <number> with a positive integer. This number tells Paradox the number of times to restart the query, report, or crosstab.

Specify the OFF option to tell Paradox to retry until successful. This is the Paradox default. If performing the operation through the menus instead of a script, press Ctrl-Break to stop the retry. Wait a little while, or coordinate with the person who is updating the table and find a time when a complete snapshot is possible.

If performing a query, report, or crosstab from a script, use the ERRORCODE( ) function to determine if the operation was successful before continuing script play. If the function returns a value of 36, the operation was not successful.

NOTE: The SETRESTARTCOUNT command was added for Paradox 3.0.

APPLICATIONS

When using shared tables on a network, issue a SETRESTARTCOUNT command in a script or MiniScript to set a limit on the number of snapshot restarts. Otherwise, Paradox keeps trying until successful, or the user (in interactive mode only) presses Ctrl-Break. If the snapshot is successful within the specified number of tries, control returns to the user or script.

TYPICAL OPERATION

This illustration shows you how to use the SETRESTARTCOUNT command. You must be using a network available to test the effects of this command.

1. Type **SEE** to select the Script, Editor, and Edit options. When asked for the name of the script, type **Testimag** and press **Enter**.
2. Change the script so it matches the following command lines.

```
Changing script C:\paradox3\testimag                                    Script Ins

....+...10....+...20....+...30....+...40....+...50....+...60....+...70....+...80
; Testimag.sc - Tests SETQUERYORDER command
play "info1"
setrestartcount 2
do_it!
clearall
if errorcode() = 0 then
  rename "answer" "temp"
  menu {ask} {temp} check
    moveto [stock symbol] rotate rotate rotate rotate rotate
  setqueryorder tableorder
  do_it!
else
  2 10,10 ?? "Query restarts were unsuccessful - try again later..."
endif
; end Testimag.sc
```

3. Log onto another terminal of the network. Select the Modify, CoEdit options and request the Mailtx table.
4. Play the Testimag script on the first terminal while making several quick changes to the Mailtx table on the second terminal. Since the script only tries two times to get a successful snapshot, the script may not be able to complete a snapshot of the table. However, since the Mailtx table is so small, you probably cannot make changes fast enough to stop the query.
5. Press **F8** (Clear) to remove the message from the screen.
6. Turn to Module 92 to continue the recommended learning sequence.

Module 83
SETRETRYPERIOD

DESCRIPTION

If your program cannot access a resource (table, record etc.) in a multi-user environment, Paradox can automatically keep trying to access it for the duration of the RETRYPERIOD.

Issue the SETRETRYPERIOD command to set or change the number of seconds of the RETRYPERIOD. The proper syntax follows.

```
SETRETRYPERIOD <number>
```

Replace <number> with a value from 0 to 30,000 seconds (roughly 8 hours and 20 minutes) with a default RETRYPERIOD of 0. If the RETRYPERIOD is 0, no retry is ever attempted.

If you need to reset the RETRYPERIOD, save the current RETRYPERIOD setting in a variable to be restored later. Determine the current RETRYPERIOD setting with the RETRYPERIOD( ) function.

Remember that the user cannot do anything until the RETRYPERIOD expires or the resource becomes available. In other words, the workstation is temporarily locked.

NOTE: SETRETRYPERIOD command was added to Paradox 2.0 and above.

APPLICATIONS

Use the SETRETRYPERIOD to control how long Paradox will wait for a resource to become available. The optimum setting for the retry period will vary depending on your environment. In batch environments, you might not mind waiting for resources to become available, while online users might not want to wait.

In most programs, set a relatively short retry period. When your program regains control, let the user know what is happening, and let them decide if they want to try again.

TYPICAL OPERATION

This illustration shows you how to use the SETRETRYPERIOD command.

1. Type **SEE** and change the Init script so it matches the following command lines.

```
Changing script C:\paradox3\init                                    Script

....+...10....+...20....+...30....+...40....+...50....+...60....+...70....+...80
; Init.sc - sets the output device for the current session
SETRETRYPERIOD 5
; end init.sc
```

2. Press **F10** and select the Go option. Each time a table is requested by the script during the current session, Paradox retries the request for five seconds or until the table is available.

3. Turn to Module 73 to continue the recommended learning sequence.

Module 84
SETSWAP

DESCRIPTION

Include SETSWAP command to force Paradox to swap procedures out of memory. In most situations, Paradox will automatically handle memory management and will start swapping procedures out when the MEMLEFT( ) function returns 0 (indicating no available memory). However, for performance reasons, adjust the SETSWAP level to always leave room for images and variables.

```
SETSWAP <number>
```

Replace <number> with a numeric value representing the number of bytes to leave available.

NOTE: The SETSWAP command is available in Paradox 2.0 and higher.

APPLICATIONS

The SETSWAP command is used to reserve a specified amount of memory for your scripts to use. Once the SETSWAP size is specified, Paradox will always maintain at least that much free memory.

TYPICAL OPERATION

This illustration shows you how to use the SETSWAP command.

1. Type **SEE** and change the Init script so it matches the following command lines.

```
Changing script C:\paradox3\init                                    Script Ins
....+...10....+...20....+...30....+...40....+...50....+...60....+...70....+...80
; Init.sc - sets the output device for the current session
SETRETRYPERIOD 5
SETSWAP 64
; end init.sc
```

2. Press **F10** and select the Go option. During this session, Paradox keeps 64K free for working.

3. Turn to Module 68 to continue the recommended learning sequence.

Module 85
SETUSERNAME

DESCRIPTION

Issue the SETUSERNAME command to specify the name of the current user. The syntax of the SETUSERNAME command is:

```
SETUSERNAME <name>
```

Replace <name> with any string value (maximum length 15 characters). Paradox uses this name to let other network users know who has locked a resource.

The SETUSERNAME overrides the network name and the USERNAME setting from the Custom configuration program.

NOTE: SETUSERNAME is available in Paradox 2.0 and higher.

APPLICATIONS

The SETUSERNAME command is used to let other users know who has a resource locked. Network names may have coded meanings (USER4, ACCT-DFS, etc.), so you should use SETUSERNAME to override network names with a more descriptive name.

TYPICAL OPERATION

This illustration shows you how to use the SETUSERNAME command.

1. Type **SEE** and change the Init script so it matches the following command lines.

```
Changing script C:\paradox3\init                                  Script Ins
....+...10....+...20....+...30....+...40....+...50....+...60....+...70....+...80
; Init.sc - sets the output device for the current session
SETRETRYPERIOD 5
SETSWAP 64
SETUSERNAME "Administrator"
; end init.sc
```

2. Press **F10** and select the Go option. During this session, your user name is set to Administrator.
3. Exit the current Paradox session.
4. Turn to Module 65 to continue the learning sequence.

Module 86
SHOWARRAY

DESCRIPTION

Issue the SHOWARRAY command to build a Paradox style menu from two arrays.

The syntax of the SHOWARRAY command is:

```
SHOWARRAY
  <Array1>
  <Array2>
[UNTIL KeyCodeList [KEYTO KeyVarName]]
[DEFAULT Choice]
TO VarName
```

Array1 consists of Choice Strings to display on the top line.

Array2 consists of prompt strings to display on the second line.

DEFAULT Choice is used to automatically highlight one of the choices when the menu is displayed.

VarName is used to store the user choice as a string.

SHOWARRAY is case sensitive and VarName is set so that the first character is capitalized. This removes any confusion over upper- and lowercase choices.

If the user presses Esc, the variable VarName is set to "Esc" and retval is set to False.

NOTE: The SHOWARRAY command is available in Paradox 2.0 and above.

APPLICATIONS

The SHOWARRAY command allows you to build menus during program execution. The SHOWARRAY command can even be used to build your menus from data contained in tables.

TYPICAL OPERATION

This illustration shows you how to use the SHOWARRAYS command.

1. Type **SEW** to write a new script. When asked for the script name, type **DEMARRAY** and press **Enter**. Type the script as shown in the following example.

```
Designing script C:\paradox3\demarray                          Script

....+...10....+...20....+...30....+...40....+...50....+...60....+...70....+...80
; demarray.sc - demos a menu created from an array
clear
Array Choices[3]
Array Descr[3]
Choices[1] = "Tx"
Choices[2] = "La"
Choices[3] = "Ca"
Descr[1] = "View only Texas Customers"
Descr[2] = "View only Louisiana Customers"
Descr[3] = "View only California Customers"
showarray
   Choices Descr
   default Choices[1]
TO x
mfile = "Mail"+x
edit mfile
wait table until "F2"
do_it!
clearall
; end demarray
```

2. Press **F10** and select the Go option. The three choices in the array are displayed at the top of the screen.
3. Type **T** to select the Texas option. The Mailtx table is available for changes.
4. Press **F2** to return to the Main Menu screen.
5. Turn to Module 75 to continue the recommended learning sequence.

Module 87
SHOWFILES

DESCRIPTION

Issue the SHOWFILES command to build a Paradox style menu from a directory file listing and allow a user to choose a file. The syntax of the SHOWFILES command is:

```
SHOWFILES << NOEXT <DOSPath> <Prompt> >>
  << UNTIL KeyCodeList << KEYTO KeyVarName >> >>
TO <varname>
```

Include the NOEXT clause to display the files without the three-character extension.

Replace <DOSPath> with a character string for the DOS pathname. Remember, if the DOSPath string contains backslash characters, you must double them. The DOSPath string often includes wildcard characters.

Prompt appears on the top line of the screen to inform the user.

Replace <varname> with the chosen variable for the selected filename.

The directory menu is displayed in the same format as a Paradox "directory prompt." Your user gets a "directory prompt" when the user presses Enter in response to a request to enter the name of a table or script.

If Esc is pressed, <varname> is set to ESC and RETVAL is set to FALSE. If no files are found in your directory path, <varname> is set to the string "NONE."

NOTE: The SHOWFILES command is available in Paradox version 2.0 and higher.

APPLICATIONS

Use the SHOWFILES command to build a menu from the filenames in a user specified directory. Your user can then select a file without worrying about misspelling its name.

TYPICAL OPERATION

This illustration shows you how to use the SHOWFILES command.

1. Type **SEW** to write a new script. When asked for the name of the script, type **DEMFILES** and press **Enter**.

2. Type the following command lines in the script.

```
Designing script C:\paradox3\demfiles                                Script

....+...10....+...20....+...30....+...40....+...50....+...60....+...70....+...80
; DEMFILES - DEMOS SHOWFILES COMMAND
CLEAR
SHOWMENU
    "DELETE" : "Delete a script",
    "EXIT" : "Leave this menu"
TO Whattodo
SWITCH
   CASE Whattodo = "DELETE" :
      @ 0,0 ?? "Script: "
      @ 1,0 ?? "Enter script to delete or press ENTER to see a list."
      @ 0,8 ACCEPT "A8" TO Namscrpt
      IF Namscrpt = ""
         THEN SHOWFILES NOEXT
         "C:\\PARADOX3\\*.SC"
         "Select a script to delete"
         TO Namscrpt
         IF Namscrpt <> "None" AND Namscrpt <> "Esc" THEN
            {Tools} {Delete} {Script} TYPEIN Namscrpt Enter {OK}
         ENDIF
      ENDIF
   CASE Whattodo = "EXIT" : QUIT
ENDSWITCH
; END DEMFILES
```

3. Press **F10** and select the Go option. When asked if you want to Delete or Exit, type **D** to select the Delete option.
4. Press **Enter** to see a list of files. Use the arrow keys to move across the filenames.
5. Press **Esc** to return to the Main Menu screen.
6. Turn to Module 77 to continue the recommended learning sequence.

Module 88
SHOWMENU

DESCRIPTION

The Paradox menu-driven system presents options across the top of the screen. One way to select an option is by using the arrows to position the cursor and pressing the Enter key. The other way is by typing the first letter of the selected option.

Use the SHOWMENU command to create the same kind of menus for your custom applications. The format for the SHOWMENU command follows. Substitute a number greater than zero for "-n."

```
SHOWMENU
  <choice-1> : <prompt-1>
      .            .
      .            .
      .            .
  <choice-n> : <prompt-n>
  <<DEFAULT <choice>>> TO <variable>
```

Replace <choice-1> through <choice-n> with the menu options that you want to display across the top of the screen. If you want the user to be able to select an option by typing the first letter, begin each option with a different one so that each option is unique.

For example, if two of the options are "Departments" and "Divisions," an option is not selected by typing D. The only way to select one of the options is by moving the cursor and pressing the Enter key. Enclose each option listed in the SHOWMENU command with quotation marks.

As the cursor is moved from option to option, a brief description is displayed on the line under the menu line. These descriptions are provided by <prompt-1> through <prompt-n>. Each description is enclosed with quotation marks.

The option and its description are typed on the same line in the script and are separated by a colon (:). End each of these lines, except the last one, with a comma so that Paradox knows that there is another option on the next line.

For example, a script line "Labels" : "Print mailing labels for all customers." presents an option called Labels on the top line of the screen. When the cursor is positioned on that option, the message "Print mailing labels for all customers." appears on the second line of the screen. If another option exists on the next line, a comma must end the "Labels" line.

Use the DEFAULT clause to position the cursor on one of the options automatically. As soon as the menu is displayed, the cursor highlights the option specified by <choice>. It must be one of the menu options that replaced <choice-1> through <choice-n> in the SHOWMENU command. Enclose the selected option with quotation marks. Though this clause is optional, it provides consistency for your user.

When an option is selected, it is saved in memory by the TO <variable> clause. The value of the variable is the same as <choice-1> through <choice-n>. Compare the value of the variable in an IF, ENDIF or SWITCH, ENDSWITCH command combination so that the script is able to decide what the user wants done.

For example, the following command lines display a menu across the top of the screen. There are three options in the menu.

```
showmenu
  "Maintenance" : "Maintain table data.",
  "Labels" : "Print mailing labels.",   "Configure" :
"Change application configuration."
default "Maintenance" to mchoice
if mchoice = "Maintenance"
  then
  .
  .
endif
if mchoice = "Labels"
  then
  .
  .
endif
if mchoice = "Configure"
  then
  .
  .
endif
```

The SHOWMENU command displays three menu options across the top line of the screen. As the cursor moves from one option to another, the description is displayed on the second line. When an option is selected, the choice is saved in the variable called menuchoice. Then it is evaluated by IF commands so that when the condition is true, processing continues.

When the user presses the Esc key, "Esc" is saved in <variable>. Be sure that you include an IF, ENDIF or SWITCH, ENDSWITCH command combination that lets the user out of the menu.

APPLICATIONS

A menu of options makes running an application easy. The available choices are presented to the user. When an option is selected, the script performs the required tasks.

Use the SHOWMENU command to present a menu of options across the screen. Each option is responsible for performing a certain task. For example, "Maintenance" lets the user access the table, "Labels" lets the user print labels, and "Configure" lets the user direct the application to a certain disk drive or directory.

In short, the script does as much work and decision-making as possible. The user's options are limited to those provided by the application.

TYPICAL OPERATION

This example shows you how to use the SHOWMENU command.

1. Type **SEW** (Scripts, Edit, Write) to write a new script. When asked for the name of the script, type **Mainmenu** and press **Enter**.
2. Type the script that appears in the following display.

```
Designing script C:\paradox3\mainmenu                                   Script

....+...10....+...20....+...30....+...40....+...50....+...60....+...70....+...80
while (true)
  clear
  showmenu
    "Maintenance" : "Maintains table data.",
    "Labels" : "Print mailing labels.",
    "Configure" : "Change application configuration.",
    "Weekcalc" : "Count the number of weeks between two dates."
  default "Maintenance" to mchoice
  if mchoice = "Maintenance"
    then
    @ 10,10
    ?? "Maintenance..."
    sleep 2000
  endif
  if mchoice = "Labels"
    then
    @ 10,10
    ?? "Labels..."
    sleep 2000
  endif
  if mchoice = "Configure"
    then
    @ 10,10
    ?? "Configure..."
    sleep 2000
  endif
  if mchoice = "Weekcalc"
    then
    @ 10,10
    ?? "Weekcalc..."
    sleep 2000
  endif
  if mchoice = "Esc"
    then
    quit
  endif
endwhile
```

3. Press **F10** (Scripts Menu) and select the Go option by typing **G**. Your screen resembles the following display.

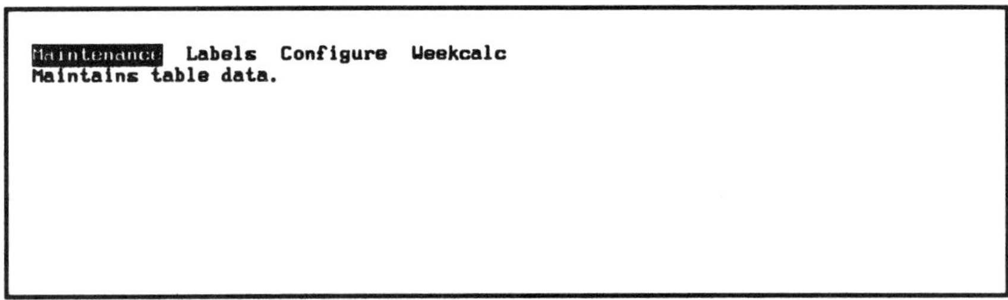

4. Press **Right Arrow** to review each menu option and its description. When the cursor passes the last option, it automatically loops to the Maintenance option.
5. Press **Left Arrow** to move the cursor to the left.
6. Position the cursor on the Labels option and press **Enter**. Your screen flashes:

   `Labels...`

7. When the menu returns, type **C** to select the Configure option. This time, "Configure. . ." appears on your screen. Select the other options until each one is tested. Though the menu options only display a word, you know that the menu is working properly.
8. Press **Esc** to return to the Main Menu screen.
9. Turn to Module 95 to continue the recommended learning sequence.

Module 89
SHOWTABLES

DESCRIPTION

Use the SHOWTABLES command to build a Paradox style menu from the table names found in a directory and allow a user to choose a file by positioning the bounce-bar. The syntax of the SHOWTABLES command follows.

```
SHOWTABLES <DOSpath> <prompt>
  << UNTIL <keycodelist> << KEYTO <keyvarname> >> >>
TO <varname>
```

Replace <DOSpath> with a character string that specifies the DOS pathname. If the <DOSpath> string contains backslash characters, you must double them. The string may also contain wildcard characters.

The <prompt> is displayed at the top of the screen to instruct the user.

Replace <varname> with a variable name to be used to store the selected table name.

The directory menu is displayed in the same format as a Paradox "directory prompt." Your user gets a "directory prompt" when he presses Enter in response to a request to specify the name of a table.

If Esc is pressed, <varname> is set to ESC and RETVAL is set to FALSE. If no tables are found in the specified directory, <varname> is set to the string "NONE."

NOTE: The SHOWTABLES command is available to Paradox version 2.0 and higher.

APPLICATIONS

Include the SHOWTABLES command to build a menu from the table names in a user specified directory. Your user can then select a table without worrying about misspelling its name.

TYPICAL OPERATION

This illustration shows you how to use the SHOWTABLES command.

1. Type **SEW** to write a new script. When asked for the name, type **DEMTABLE** and press **Enter**.

2. Type the following PAL command lines for the new script.

```
Designing script C:\paradox3\demtable                                  Script

....+...10....+...20....+...30....+...40....+...50....+...60....+...70....+...80
; DEMTABLE.SC - Demo showtables command
CLEAR
SHOWMENU
    "Delete" : "Delete a table and its family",
    "Exit" : "Leave this menu"
TO Whattodo
SWITCH
   CASE Whattodo = "Delete" :
      @ 0,0 ?? "Table?: "
      @ 1,0 ?? "Type table to delete or press ENTER to see a list."
      @ 0,8 ACCEPT "A8" TO Tablname
      IF Tablname = ""
         THEN SHOWFILES NOEXT
         "C:\\PARADOX3\\*.DB"
         "Select a table to delete"
         TO Nametabl
         IF Nametabl <> "None" AND Nametabl <> "Esc" then delete Nametabl endif
      ENDIF
   CASE Whattodo = "EXIT" : QUIT
ENDSWITCH
; end demtable.sc
```

3. Press **F10** and select the Go option.
4. Type **D** to select the Delete option.
5. When asked for a table name, press **Enter**. Use the arrow keys to move the bounce-bar across the table names.
6. Press **Esc** to return to the Main Menu screen.
7. Turn to Module 63 to continue the recommended learning sequence.

Module 90
SKIP

DESCRIPTION

The position of the cursor in any field of a record in the table identifies the current record. The information in the current record is available to the user or script. The cursor must be moved before the information in another record is made available for changes or evaluation.

When a table is displayed on the screen in Table View, press the Down Arrow to move the cursor to the next record. Each time the Up Arrow is pressed, the cursor moves up to the previous record.

Instead of using the Up and Down special keycodes in a script to move the cursor up and down the table, use the SKIP command. The format for this command follows.

```
SKIP << <n> >>
```

The <n> is an optional parameter. Use it to tell Paradox the number of records to move the pointer. If omitted, <n> is automatically replaced by a positive 1 so that the pointer is moved down to the next record.

When included in the SKIP command, <n> is replaced either with a positive or negative number. When the number is positive, Paradox moves the cursor down the specified number of records in the table. A negative number tells Paradox to move the cursor up that number of records in the table.

For example, the command line SKIP 3 in a script has the same effect as pressing Down Arrow three times while the table is presented on the screen in Table View. The command line SKIP -4 in a script is the same as pressing Up Arrow four times while the Table View is displayed on the screen.

Paradox does not allow the cursor to move past the first or last record in the table. If the first record is encountered during a SKIP command with a negative number, the cursor is positioned on the first record and the BOT( ) function is set to true. Use it to verify that the "beginning of table" condition exits before performing another SKIP command. For example, the BOT( ) function is evaluated in the following command lines before and after performing the SKIP -1 command.

```
while not bot( )
skip -1
if bot( )
```

```
    message "First record in the table has been encountered..."
    sleep 2000
  endif
  endwhile
```

If the last record is encountered during a SKIP command with a positive number, Paradox positions the cursor on the last record and sets the EOT( ) function to true. Performing other SKIP commands has no effect on cursor movement.

Anytime that a loop (WHILE, ENDWHILE) in the script moves the cursor, it must evaluate the BOT( ) or EOT( ) function for the true condition. Otherwise, the script is stuck in an endless loop that performs the same command lines on the same record.

If this happens, the script play must be stopped by pressing Ctrl-Break. Then change the script so that the looping activity is stopped when the beginning or end of the table is encountered.

Before playing the script again, think about the data in the table. Never use the real table unless you have a current backup copy of it on another disk. If the script made changes to the data, use the backup disk to replace the half-changed table before replaying the script.

As one of the menu options for every application, write a script that copies the table on floppydisk. Establish rules for yourself and/or the user to make a copy of the table regularly.

For example, if the table changes daily, copy the table on a floppy disk at the end of each day to another disk. Keep the last five disks so that there is always a week's backup.

APPLICATIONS

Use the SKIP command to move the cursor up or down a specified number of records. The effect is the same as pressing PgUp or PgDn while the table is on the screen in Forms View and Up Arrow or Down Arrow while in Table View.

This command is valid only when the table is presented on the screen in View mode. Also, skipping past the first or last record is not allowed.

For example, use the SKIP command in a script to let the user move the cursor quickly up or down the records in a table. When the user presses a certain key while viewing the table, ask how many records to skip and save the answer in a variable called "mskip." The command line SKIP mskip moves the cursor the specified number of records so that the current record is displayed to the user.

TYPICAL OPERATION

This example shows you how to use the SKIP command.

1. Edit the Custview script to include a Skip option as shown in the following display.

   NOTE

   The dots indicate that lines of the script are omitted in the display. Do not change those lines in your script.

```
Changing script C:\paradox3\custview                                   Script

....+...10....+...20....+...30....+...40....+...50....+...60....+...70....+...80
    locate lastname, firstname
    if (retval)
      then
      while (true)                                                                ◆
        wait record message "Esc=menu, F2=find another customer, PgDn=continue search, S=skip"◆
          until "Esc", "F2", "PgDn", "S"                                          ◆
        if retval = "Esc"
        .
        .
        .
           message "No other records were found in the table for that customer."
           sleep 2000
         endif
       else
         if retval = "S"                                            ◆
           then                                                     ◆
           @ 21,05                                                  ◆
           ?? "How many records (e.g., 6, -3)? "                    ◆
           accept "S" picture "{#*#,-#*#}" default 1 to mskip       ◆
           skip mskip                                               ◆
         else                                                       ◆
           quitloop                                                 ◆
         endif                                                      ◆
       endif
     endif
   endif
  endwhile
else
  @ 21,05
  beep beep beep beep
  ?? "Requested Customer name not found in table..."
  sleep 2000
```

2. Press **F10** (Script Menu) and select the DO-IT! option.
3. When the Main Menu appears on your screen, type **SP** to play a script. Type **Mainmenu** and press **Enter**.
4. Type **V** to select the View option.
5. Type **Berry** for the Last Name and press **Enter**. Type **Charles** for the First Name and press **Enter**. Your screen resembles the following display.

```
Customer: Charles Keith Berry
          818 N. Plano Rd.
          #18
          Plano, Tx 75042

Subscription Dates:  Begins  9/01/89                 Ends  8/01/90

           Esc=menu, F2=find another customer, PgDn=continue search, S=skip
```

6. Type **S** to skip records. You are asked "How many records?" Press **Backspace** to remove the number 1. Then type **5** and press **Enter**. The information for Arnold Thomas Chadwick appears on the screen.
7. Type **S** again. Press **Backspace**. Type **–3** and press **Enter**. The information for Shirley Lynn Appleby appears on the screen.
8. Type **S** and press **Enter** to accept the default number. The information for Charles Keith Berry appears on the screen.
9. Type **s**. The computer beeps each time a key is pressed other than Esc, F2, PgDn, or S. The problem occurs because the script only accepts an uppercase "S" in the WAIT command line.
10. Press **Esc** twice to exit the application.
11. Change the Custview script so that it accepts a lowercase letter for the Skip option too.

```
Changing script C:\paradox3\custview                                 Script

....+...10....+...20....+...30....+...40....+...50....+...60....+...70....+...80
        wait record message "Esc=menu, F2=find another customer, PgDn=continue s
          until "Esc", "F2", "PgDn", "S", "s"                                  ♦
        if retval = "Esc"
          then
          clearimage
          return
        else
          if retval = "F2"
            then
            quitloop
          else
            if retval = "PgDn"
              then
              PgDn
              locate next lastname, firstname
```

```
                if not (retval)
                  then
                  beep beep beep beep
                  message "No other records were found in the table for that custo
                  sleep 2000
                endif
              else
                if retval = "S" or retval = "s"                                    ◆
                  then
                  @ 21,05
                  ?? "How many records (e.g., 6, -3)? "
                  accept "S" picture "{*#*,-*#*}" default 1 to mskip
                  skip mskip
                else
                  quitloop
                endif
              endif
            endif
          endif
        endwhile
      else
        @ 21,05
        beep beep beep beep
        ?? "Requested Customer name not found in table..."
        sleep 2000
      endif
    else
      quitloop
    endif
```

12. Save the changed script. Then test the View option again to make sure that it accepts "s" and "S."

13. When all testing is completed, press **Esc** until the Main Menu screen returns to the workspace.

14. Turn to Module 71 to continue the recommended learning sequence.

Module 91
SLEEP

DESCRIPTION

This command lets you stop the play of the script for up to thirty seconds. When the SLEEP command is performed, Paradox begins counting until the specified number of milliseconds is reached. Then, the script continues as though the pause had not occurred. The format of the command follows.

```
SLEEP <milliseconds>
```

Replace <milliseconds> with an integer between 0 and 30,000. For example, the command line SLEEP 30000 tells Paradox to wait thirty seconds before performing the next line in the script.

Set the time for the pause to a realistic number. When the user is ready to work with your application, one or more thirty-second pauses are usually unacceptable. During your tests (and debugging) of a script that includes the SLEEP command, adjust the length of the pause until you find one that is reasonable.

APPLICATIONS

Use the SLEEP command when you want to display a message to the user. For example, many applications have a banner screen that briefly describes the application. The script is played too fast for the user to read the screen unless a SLEEP command line is encountered.

This command tells Paradox to wait for a specified length of time before continuing the play of the current script. Specify enough time for the user to be able to read the messages but do not overdo it. After a user has worked with your application a few times, a thirty-second wait is unnecessary.

TYPICAL OPERATION

This example shows you how to use the SLEEP command.

1. Type **SP** to select the Scripts Play option.

2. When asked for the name of the script, type **Test2** and press **Enter**. Since a SLEEP 10000 command exists in the script, the screen is available for a long time. Your screen resembles the following display.

```
   2  ______________________________________________



   12  ______________________________________________
```

3. When the Main Menu reappears on your screen, select the Scripts option again by typing **S**.
4. To change the script, type **E** to select the Editor.
5. Select the Edit option by typing **E**.
6. When asked for the name of the script, type **Test2** and press **Enter**. The following script appears on your screen.

```
Changing script C:\paradox3\test2                                     Script

....+...10....+...20....+...30....+...40....+...50....+...60....+...70....+...80
rows = 2
border = "______________________________________________"
@rows,5
?? rows
?? "  "
?? border
rows = rows + 10
@ rows,5
?? STRVAL(rows)+"    "+border
@ rows,30
SLEEP 10000
BEEP BEEP BEEP BEEP BEEP
```

7. Press **Down Arrow** until the cursor is positioned on the @ rows,30 command line and press **Ctrl-Y** three times to delete the last three lines of the script.

8. Press **F10** (Menu) to access the Editor's submenu and type **G** to select the Go option. The script is played but the Main Menu appears before you are able to read the screen.
9. Edit the script again. Type **SLEEP 5000** as the last line in the script.
10. Press **F10** (Menu) and select the Go option again. This time the screen is readable though the specified time is only five seconds.
11. When the Main Menu returns to your screen, type **E** to select the Exit option. When the Exit submenu appears on your screen, type **Y** to tell Paradox that you want to end this Paradox session. The screen clears and the DOS system A> prompt appears. This Paradox session is complete.
12. Turn to Module 48 to continue the recommended learning sequence.

Module 92
SORT

DESCRIPTION

It is much easier to locate a record in a large table if the data has been sorted. For example, when you use the phone book to find a name, it is easier to locate because all names (records) are in alphabetical order.

Paradox keeps the data in sequence automatically for a table when its structure specifies key fields. Otherwise, the records remain in the order that they were typed into the table.

When a different sequence is needed, use the SORT command. It copies all records from one table to another table in the order specified in the command line. The format for this command follows. Substitute a number greater than zero for "-n."

```
SORT <table name> << ON <field name-1> <<D>>, ..., <field
name-n> <<D>> >> << TO <target> >>
```

Replace <table name> with the name of a table that has been saved on the current data disk. Unless provided in a variable, enclose it with quotation marks.

The ON clause is optional. When included, replace <field name-1> through <field name-n> with the names of fields in the table structure. These fields are used for sorting the data. List them in decreasing order of significance in the SORT command. Enclose each field name with quotation marks.

When the ON clause is omitted, Paradox sorts the table as though the first field in the structure is <field name-1>, the second field is <field name-2>, and so on until each field is included in the sort activity. Include the ON clause in the SORT command to control the sort criteria.

After each field name, include an "A" or "D" to tell Paradox to sort the data in the field in ascending (low to high) or descending (high to low) order. If omitted, the data in that field is sorted in ascending order.

For example, the clause ON "Last Name" A, "First Name" A, "Middle Name" A sorts the record with the name "James Lee Smith" before the "Larry Thomas Smith" record. The clause ON "Last Name," "First Name," "Middle Name" accomplishes the same results.

The TO <target> clause specifies a destination table name. When included, the data in <table name> is copied in sorted order into the <target> table. If the destination table does not exist when the SORT command is encountered, Paradox creates a table structure that matches the <table name> structure. Then, it is filled with the sorted data.

If a table named the same as <target> exists on the disk, it and its family are deleted without asking the user for confirmation. Then the previous table is replaced by the table that is created by the SORT command line. Its family consists of the screen form and report form that Paradox creates and saves for new tables. Use the ISFILE( ) function in an IF, ENDIF command combination to check the disk for an existing <target> file before encountering the SORT command.

The SORT command does not need the TO <target> clause when the table structure does not have key fields specified. When omitted, the sorted data is returned to the original table name. The TO <target> clause must be included in the SORT command line when <table name> is keyed.

APPLICATIONS

Include the SORT command in scripts that need the table data in a special order. Sequence the records on one or more fields as needed.

For example, use the SORT command to sequence the customer table Mailtx by the Zipcode field so that the records are in ascending zipcode order. Since the Mailtx table structure includes key fields (last, first, and middle names), use the TO <target> clause. A new table must be created so that the Mailtx table remains in customer name order.

TYPICAL OPERATION

This illustration shows you how to use the SORT command.

1. Write the Sales script so that it matches the one in the following display.

```
Designing script C:\paradox3\sales                              Script

....+...10....+...20....+...30....+...40....+...50....+...60....+...70....+...80
; sales.sc - territory application
while (true)
  clear
  showmenu
    "Maintenance" : "Maintains table data.",
    "Report" : "Print territory report."
    default "Maintenance" to mchoice
    switch
      case mchoice = "Maintenance" :
        edit "Sales"
        wait table message "Press F2 to return to the menu..."
          until "F2"
        do_it!
        clearimage
      case mchoice = "Report" :
        report "Sales" "R"
      case mchoice = "Esc" :
        quitloop
    endswitch
endwhile
;end sales.sc
```

2. Press **F10** (Scripts Menu) and select the Go option.
3. When the application menu appears, type **R** to select the Report option. The printout resembles the following sample.

```
7/06/89                  Standard report            Page 1

State    Salesperson
_____    ______________

Ak       Martin Davis
La       Sherry Jones
Ok       James Free
Tx       Mary Roberts
```

4. When the application menu returns to the screen, press **Esc** to exit the application.
5. Edit the the Sales script by inserting the SORT command. Since the table is not keyed, the Sales table is the source and the destination for the data. Make the script match the one in the following display.

```
Changing script C:\paradox3\sales                              Script Ins

....+...10....+...20....+...30....+...40....+...50....+...60....+...70....+...80
    switch
      case mchoice = "Maintenance" :
        edit "Sales"
        wait table message "Press F2 to return to the menu..."
          until "F2"
        do_it!
        clearimage
      case mchoice = "Report" :
        clear                                                                  ◆
        @ 10,10                                                                ◆
        ?? "Printing territory reports - Please Wait..."                       ◆
        sort "Sales" on "salesperson"                                          ◆
        report "Sales" "R"
        sort "Sales" on "state"                                                ◆
        report "Sales" "R"                                                     ◆
        clearall                                                               ◆
      case mchoice = "Esc" :
        quitloop
    endswitch
endwhile
;end sales.sc
```

6. Press **F10** (Scripts Menu), select the Go option, and select the Report option. Notice that the report prints twice. The first report is in order by the salesperson's name. The second report is in state order. They resemble the following report samples.

```
7/06/89                 Standard report              Page 1

State   Salesperson
-----   ---------------

Ok      James Free
Ak      Martin Davis
Tx      Mary Roberts
La      Sherry Jones
```

~~~~~~

```
7/06/89                 Standard report              Page 1

State   Salesperson
-----   ---------------

Ak      Martin Davis
La      Sherry Jones
Ok      James Free
Tx      Mary Roberts
```

7. When the application menu returns to the screen, press **Esc** to exit the application.
8. Turn to Module 38 to continue the recommended learning sequence.
~~~~~~

Module 93
STYLE

DESCRIPTION

When you use the TEXT, ?, and ?? commands in your scripts, the information displayed is often difficult to locate. To control the appearance of the information, use the STYLE command before the TEXT, ?, or ?? commands. There are three forms of the STYLE command. Use one or more of the functions that are enclosed with the << and >> symbols as follows.

```
STYLE <<REVERSE>>
      <<BLINK>>
      <<INTENSE>>

STYLE ATTRIBUTE <attribute code>

STYLE
```

Include the REVERSE option when you want reverse video. The information is displayed in a different shade or color. Use the BLINK option when you want the information to flash on and off. The INTENSE option causes brighter shades or colors (high intensity).

The STYLE ATTRIBUTE form lets you specify an ASCII code (an integer between 0 and 255, inclusive) that changes the color combinations on the screen. For example, if you have an IBM color graphics card and monitor, STYLE ATTRIBUTE 78 causes a red background and yellow foreground (yellow letters on red). Such a bright combination will get the user's attention. However, there are many other choices. IBM monochrome screens are able to use the same codes; the choices are reverse video, high intensity, underline, normal, and blank (non-display).

After the STYLE command is encountered, all information sent to the screen by the TEXT, ?, and ?? commands is subject to the new specifications. The existing information on the screen is not changed — only the new information.

When the third form of the STYLE command is performed, the specifications are returned to normal. New information is displayed as though the screen specifications were never changed.

APPLICATIONS

Use the STYLE command to change the appearance of new information that is displayed on the screen. For example, a message that blinks is noticeable. The user does not have to search the entire screen for it.

Choose a special color for each type of message. For example, present error messages in a blinking red, warning messages in green, and instructions in white. After the information is displayed on the screen, return the screen specifications to normal.

Once you decide on a color scheme, always conform to it when you write a script. It is easier for you and the users.

TYPICAL OPERATION

This example shows you how to use the STYLE command.

1. Edit the Weekcalc script.
2. Change the script so that when you are asked if you want to do another, the "(Y/N)" blinks. The end of the script resembles the one in the following display.

```
Changing script C:\paradox3\weekcalc                                  Script Ins

....+...10....+...20....+...30....+...40....+...50....+...60....+...70....+...80
    endwhile
    message "There are ",count," weeks between ",fromdate," thru ",todate
  else
    beep beep beep
    @ 21,05
    ?? "A valid ending date was not entered..."
  endif
endif
@ 23,05
?? "Do you want to do another "                                                ◆
style blink                                                                    ◆
?? "(Y/N)"                                                                     ◆
style                                                                          ◆
?? "? "                                                                        ◆
accept "A1" picture "&" to ans
endwhile
```

3. Press **F10** (Scripts Menu) and select the Go option.
4. Type **060189** and **061589** as the beginning and ending dates.
5. When you are asked if you want to do another, notice that part of the line is blinking. Type **N** and press **Enter**.
6. Change the Weekcalc script again. This time present the error messages in red on a black background. (If you have a color monitor.)

```
Changing script C:\paradox3\weekcalc                                   Script Ins

....+...10....+...20....+...30....+...40....+...50....+...60....+...70....+...80
if fromdate <01/01/88 and fromdate <> blankdate ()
  then
  beep beep beep
  @ 21,05                                                                       ◆
  style attribute 4                                                             ◆
  ?? "The beginning date is earlier than 01/01/88..."                           ◆
  style
  sleep 3000
  loop
endif
if fromdate <> blankdate ()
  then
  @ 12,10
  ?? "Enter the ending date "
  accept "D" picture "##/##/##" to todate
  if todate > 01/01/92 and todate <> blankdate ()
    then
    beep beep beep
    @ 21,05                                                                     ◆
    style attribute 4                                                           ◆
    ?? "The ending date is later than 01/01/92..."                              ◆
    style                                                                       ◆
    sleep 3000
    loop
  endif
  if todate <> blankdate ()
    then
    count = 0
    tdate = fromdate
    while tdate <= todate
      if todate - tdate >= 7
        then
        count = count + 1
      endif
      tdate = tdate + 7
    endwhile
      message "There are ",count," weeks between ",fromdate," thru ",todate
    else
    beep beep beep
    @ 21,05
    style attribute 4
    ?? "A valid ending date was not entered..."
    style
  endif
endif
@ 23,05
?? "Do you want to do another "
style blink
?? "(Y/N)"
style
?? "? "
accept "A1" picture "&" to ans
endwhile
```

7. Press **F10** (Scripts Menu) and type **G** to play the changed script.
8. Test the script for each possible combination. Notice that when the error is displayed, it is easy to locate.
9. When all testing is complete, you are asked if you want to do another. Type **N** and press **Enter**.
10. Turn to Module 88 to continue the recommended learning sequence.

Module 94
SUBTRACT

DESCRIPTION

This command lets you remove records from one table when they exist in another table. It is a quick way to delete a batch of records from a table. The format for the SUBTRACT command follows.

```
SUBTRACT <source table> <destination table>
```

Replace <source table> and <destination table> with the names of two tables that exist on the data disk. A source and a destination table name must be specified in this command line. Also, the structures of both tables must be the same, except for key field identifiers. Otherwise, a script error occurs when Paradox encounters the SUBTRACT command.

The <source table> contains the records to be deleted from the <destination table>. If either table is keyed, Paradox looks for matching key values during the subtract operation. When the same value exists in a record in both tables, Paradox deletes the record in the destination table. If a record in the source table is not found in the destination table, the deletion operation continues with the next record in the source table.

If keys are not used in either table, Paradox uses all fields in the structure to select deletion records in the destination table. Since all fields must be provided to match the record in the destination table, batch processing loses some of its appeal for non-keyed tables.

After the SUBTRACT operation is complete, the records remain in the source table. Use the EMPTY command to remove all records from the source table and avoid repeating the operation.

The SUBTRACT command is an abbreviated form of several menu options that are available through the Paradox menu-driven system. By including the following command line in the script instead of the SUBTRACT "Delrecs" "Mailtx" command line, you achieve the same results.

```
Menu {Tools} {More} {Subtract} {Delrecs} {Mailtx}
```

The updated destination table remains on the workspace after Paradox performs the SUBTRACT command. Include the ClearAll special keycode in the script to clear the table from the screen.

APPLICATIONS

Use this command in your application when you need to do batch deletions from the master table. Paradox removes the records from the destination table when they are found in both tables specified in the SUBTRACT command line.

For example, three people enter data for the Mail List application. Write a separate application for these people so that they type key values into a table called Delrecs. At the end of the day, use each floppy disk to update the Mailtx table.

When the key values match, the records are removed from the destination table. The source table is not changed by the SUBTRACT command.

TYPICAL OPERATION

This example shows you how to use the SUBTRACT command.

1. Type **C** to select the Create option from the Main Menu. When asked for the name of the new table, type **Delrecs** and press **Enter**. An empty structure form appears on the screen.
2. Press **F10** (Menu) and select the Borrow option by typing **B**. When asked for the name of the table structure to borrow, type **Mailtx** and press **Enter**.
3. Press **F2** (DO-IT!) to save the new table structure. The Main Menu returns to the screen.
4. Select the Modify/DataEntry menu options. When asked for the name of the table, type **Delrecs** and press **Enter**.
5. An empty table form appears on your screen. Press **F7** (Forms Toggle) to change to the Forms View. Type **Appleby Shirley Lynn** for the last, first, and middle names in the first record.
6. Type **Chadwick Arnold** for the last and first names in the second record.
7. Press **F2** (DO-IT!) to save the table on disk. Press **F8** (Clear Image) to remove the table from the workspace.
8. Edit the Mainmenu script. Change the Update option so that it matches the one in the following display.

```
Changing script C:\paradox3\mainmenu                                    Script Ins

....+...10....+...20....+...30....+...40....+...50....+...60....+...70....+...80
  case mchoice = "Update" :
    if isfile("Delrecs.db")                                                    ◆
      then                                                                     ◆
      clear                                                                    ◆
      @ 10,10                                                                  ◆
      ?? "Deleting customers - Please Wait..."                                 ◆
      subtract "Delrecs" "Mailtx"                                              ◆
    endif                                                                      ◆
    if isfile("Addrecs.db")                                                    ◆
      then                                                                     ◆
      clear                                                                    ◆
      @ 10,10                                                                  ◆
      ?? "Adding customers - Please Wait..."                                   ◆
      add "Addrecs" "Mailtx"
    endif                                                                      ◆
    clearall
  case mchoice = "Configure" :
    @ 10,10
    ?? "Configure..."
    sleep 2000
  case mchoice = "Weekcalc" :
    play "weekcalc"
```

9. Press **F10** (Scripts Menu) and select the Go option. When the application menu appears, select the Update option by typing **U**.

10. When the application menu returns to the screen, type **V** to select the View option. Press **Enter** twice to list all records in the table. Your screen lists three records as in the following display.

11. Press **Esc** to end the application.

12. Type **V** to select the View option from the Main Menu line. When asked for the name of the table, type **Mailtx** and press **Enter**.

13. Review the table until you are convinced that it was updated properly from the Delrecs and Addrecs tables.
14. Press **F8** (Clear Image) to remove the table from the workspace.
15. View the Delrecs table to verify that the records used to update Mailtx remained in the source table. Then clear the screen.
16. Turn to Module 29 to continue the recommended learning sequence.

Module 95
SWITCH, ENDSWITCH

DESCRIPTION

The SWITCH, ENDSWITCH command combination is similar to the IF, ENDIF command combination. The SWITCH command identifies the beginning and the ENDSWITCH marks the end of the conditional CASE commands. The format for the SWITCH, ENDSWITCH command combination follows. Substitute a number greater than zero for "-n."

```
SWITCH
  CASE <condition-1> : <commands-1>
   .       .                 .
   .       .                 .
  CASE <condition-n> : <commands-n>
<<OTHERWISE> : <commands>>
ENDSWITCH
```

Using the CASE command is like using the IF command. Replace <condition-1> through <condition-n> with a logical statement that, when evaluated, is true or false. For example, include one CASE command that checks the value of <variable> for each menu option as though it were in an IF command line.

Each CASE command performs one or more command lines when the condition is evaluated as true. When more than one command line is needed, type them on separate lines. Replace <commands-1> through <commands-n> with those command lines. Remember that the condition must be separated from its command lines by a colon (:).

Each CASE command line within the SWITCH and ENDSWITCH commands is evaluated in sequence (top to bottom). When one is evaluated as true, its command lines are performed. Then Paradox skips the remaining CASE command lines and processes the rest of the script beginning with the command line that follows the ENDSWITCH command.

The OTHERWISE clause is optional. Remember that it is matched to the SWITCH command instead of the CASE commands. When used, only one OTHERWISE command is allowed although there are several CASE commands included in the SWITCH, ENDSWITCH command combination.

When the OTHERWISE command is included in a SWITCH, ENDSWITCH command set, <commands> tells Paradox what to do when all CASE conditions are evaluated as false. Replace <commands> with one or more command lines. When more than one command line is needed, type them on separate lines. Remember that the OTHERWISE command must be separated from its command lines by a colon (:).

If all CASE statements are evaluated as false and an OTHERWISE clause is omitted, Paradox plays the rest of the script. It begins with the line that follows the ENDSWITCH command.

The following command lines display a menu on the screen. Then a SWITCH, ENDSWITCH command set evaluates the user's choice.

```
showmenu "Maintenance" : "Maintains table data.", "Labels" :
  "Print mailing labels.", "Configure" :
  "Change application configuration.", "Weekcalc" :
  "Count the number of weeks between two dates."
default "Maintenance" to mchoice switch
  case mchoice = "Maintenance" :
    @ 10,10
    ?? "Maintenance..."
    sleep 2000
  case mchoice = "Labels" :
    @ 10,10
    ?? "Labels..."
    sleep 2000
  case mchoice = "Configure" :
    @ 10,10
    ?? "Configure..."
    sleep 2000
  case mchoice = "Weekcalc" :
    @ 10,10
    ?? "Weekcalc..."
    sleep 2000
  case mchoice = "Esc" : quit
  otherwise :
    clear
    @ 10,10
    ?? "The requested option is not available from this menu..."
    sleep 2000
endswitch
```

The SWITCH and ENDSWITCH commands include CASE commands. Each CASE command evaluates the variable. When true, the command lines between the colon and the next CASE command are performed. When all CASE commands are evaluated as false, Paradox continues playing the script. It begins with the command line that follows the ENDSWITCH command.

This command set may be replaced by a nested IF, ELSE, ENDIF command combination. Since only one set of commands is performed, and all others are skipped, processing the following script lines is the same as the previous example.

```
showmenu "Maintenance" : "Maintains table data.", "Labels" :
  "Print mailing labels.", "Configure" :
  "Change application configuration.", "Weekcalc" :
  "Count the number of weeks between two dates."
default "Maintenance" to mchoice
if mchoice = "Maintenance"
  then
  @ 10,10
  ?? "Maintenance..."
  sleep 2000
else
  if mchoice = "Labels"
    then
    @ 10,10
    ?? "Labels..."
    sleep 2000
  else
    if mchoice = "Configure"
      then
      @ 10,10
      ?? "Configure..."
      sleep 2000
    else
      if mchoice = "Weekcalc"
        then
        @ 10,10
        ?? "Weekcalc..."
        sleep 2000
      else
        if mchoice = "Esc"
          then
          quit
        else
          clear
          @ 10,10
          ?? "The requested option is not available from
this menu..."
          sleep 2000
        endif
      endif
    endif
  endif
endif
```

The value of mchoice is compared to "Maintenance." If evaluated as true, "Maintenance . . ." is displayed on the screen, and the rest of the nested loop is skipped. However, if the comparison is evaluated as false, mchoice is then compared to "Labels." If that comparison is also false, the next IF command line is evaluated. When all IF conditions are evaluated as false, Paradox performs the ELSE command set.

A SWITCH, ENDSWITCH command set may be replaced only by a nested IF, ELSE, ENDIF command set to achieve the same processing. A series of IF, ENDIF command combinations are used in the following script lines.

```
showmenu "Maintenance" : "Maintains table data.", "Labels" :
  "Print mailing labels.", "Configure" :
  "Change application configuration.", "Weekcalc" :
  "Count the number of weeks between two dates."
default "Maintenance" to mchoice
if mchoice = "Maintenance"
  then
  @ 10,10
  ?? "Maintenance..."   sleep 2000
endif
if mchoice = "Labels"
  then
  @ 10,10
  ?? "Labels..."
  sleep 2000
endif
if mchoice = "Configure"
  then
  @ 10,10
  ?? "Configure..."
  sleep 2000
endif
if mchoice = "Weekcalc"
  then
  @ 10,10
  ?? "Weekcalc..."
  sleep 2000
endif
if mchoice = "Esc"
  then
  quit
else
  clear
  @ 10,10
  ?? "The requested option is not available from this menu..."
  sleep 2000
endif
```

Paradox evaluates each IF condition even when a previous one was true. Everytime an option other than "Esc" is selected, "The requested option is not available from this menu. . ." appears on the screen.

For example, if the "Maintenance" option is selected, "Maintenance. . ." is displayed on the tenth line of the screen. As soon as it disappears, you are told that the option is not available. Since you do not want to confuse the user, change the script so that this does not happen.

APPLICATIONS

Use the SWITCH, ENDSWITCH command set when you want the script to make a decision. Depending on the value of a variable, field, or array element, only one set of command lines, if any, must be performed.

For example, this command combination is often used to evaluate the variable from the SHOWMENU command. However, it may be used anytime an IF, ELSE, ENDIF command set is applicable.

TYPICAL OPERATION

This example shows you how to use the SWITCH, ENDSWITCH command combination.

1. Edit the Mainmenu script.
2. Insert the ELSE command set in the last IF, ENDIF command set so that it matches the one in the following display.

```
Changing script C:\paradox3\mainmenu                              Script Ins

....+...10....+...20....+...30....+...40....+...50....+...60....+...70....+...80
    then
    @ 10,10
    ?? "Configure..."
    sleep 2000
  endif
  if mchoice = "Weekcalc"
    then
    @ 10,10
    ?? "Weekcalc..."
    sleep 2000
  endif
  if mchoice = "Esc"
    then
    quit
  else                                                                          ◆
    clear                                                                       ◆
    @ 10,10                                                                     ◆
    ?? "The requested option is not available from this menu..."                ◆
    sleep 2000                                                                  ◆
  endif
endwhile
```

3. Press **F10** (Scripts Menu) and select the Go option by typing **G**.

4. Type **L** to select the Labels option. The screen clears and "Labels. . ." appears on the tenth line. After a couple of seconds, "The requested option is not available from this menu. . ." is displayed. The same message appears after each of the valid options are selected.
5. When the menu of options appears, press **Esc** to stop the script and return to the Paradox Main Menu screen.
6. Change the script again. Replace all of the IF, ENDIF commands to a SWITCH, ENDSWITCH command set as in the following display.

```
Changing script C:\paradox3\mainmenu                                    Script Ins

....+...10....+...20....+...30....+...40....+...50....+...60....+...70....+...80
  default "Maintenance" to mchoice
  switch                                                                       ◆
  case mchoice = "Maintenance" :                                               ◆
    @ 10,10
    ?? "Maintenance..."
    sleep 2000
  case mchoice = "Labels" :                                                    ◆
    @ 10,10
    ?? "Labels..."
    sleep 2000
  case mchoice = "Configure" :                                                 ◆
    @ 10,10
    ?? "Configure..."
    sleep 2000
  case mchoice = "Weekcalc" :                                                  ◆
    @ 10,10
    ?? "Weekcalc..."
    sleep 2000
  case mchoice = "Esc" : quit                                                  ◆
  otherwise :                                                                  ◆
    clear
    @ 10,10
    ?? "The requested option is not available from this menu..."
    sleep 2000
  endswitch                                                                    ◆
endwhile
```

7. Press **F10** (Scripts Menu) and select the Go option.
8. Since the cursor is already positioned, press **Enter** to select the Maintenance option. The screen clears and then displays "Maintenance. . ." on the tenth line. After a couple of seconds, the menu of options is returned to the top of your screen.
9. Type **J**. The computer beeps because none of the options begin with the letter "J." The SHOWMENU command accepts only valid menu options. Therefore, the message about valid options is never performed.
10. When the menu returns, select each of the other options in the menu.
11. When you are convinced that the script is playing correctly, press **Esc** to return to Paradox's Main Menu screen.
12. Turn to Module 51 to continue the recommended learning sequence.

Module 96
SYNCCURSOR

DESCRIPTION

The SYNCCURSOR positions the PAL canvas cursor at the same position as the workspace cursor.

NOTE: The SYNCCURSOR command is available in Paradox versions 2.0 and higher.

APPLICATIONS

The SYNCCURSOR command is useful when switching between the PAL canvas and the workspace. Use this command to keep the cursor aligned while switching between the two areas.

TYPICAL OPERATION

This illustration shows you how to use the SYNCCURSOR command.

1. Type **SEW** to write a new script. When asked for the name, type **DEMOSYNC** and press **Enter**.
2. Type the script so it matches the following command lines.

```
Designing script C:\paradox3\demosync                              Script

....+...10....+...20....+...30....+...40....+...50....+...60....+...70....+...80
; demosync.sc - demos synccursor command
edit "mailtx"
pickform "2"
moveto [first name]
CtrlBackspace
synccursor
clearall
accept "a15" to mans
[first name] = mans
do_it!
clearall
; end demosync.sc
```

3. Press **F2** to save the script.
4. Type **SS** to select the Script and ShowPlay options.

5. When asked for the name of the script, type **DEMOSYNC** and press **Enter**.
6. When asked if you want to play the script fast or slow, type **S** to select the slow option. The script opens the Mailtx table using the selected pickform and removes the value from the first name field of the first record. Then, it blanks the screen but leaves the cursor in the same position as though the pickform were still on the screen.
7. Type **Charles** and press **Enter** to place a value in the first name field of the current record.
8. Turn to Module 50 to continue the recommended learning sequence.

Module 97
TEXT, ENDTEXT

DESCRIPTION

The TEXT, ENDTEXT command combination lets you display a screenful of comments (text). Variables, fields, and array elements are not allowed in the text.

For example, the user needs a screen that provides helpful hints about the application. Instead of using the ? and ?? commands, the TEXT, ENDTEXT command combination is a better choice. The format of the TEXT, ENDTEXT command combination follows.

```
TEXT
  <text>
ENDTEXT
```

The TEXT command marks the beginning of the text (messages or comments). For every TEXT command, there must be an ENDTEXT command in the script. They are used as a pair. The ENDTEXT command marks the end of the screen's text.

Replace <text> with anything you need to be displayed. Whatever exists between the TEXT and ENDTEXT commands appears on the screen literally. When a blank line is included in <text>, Paradox skips a line on the screen. The following command lines tell the user who must be called if a problem is encountered while working with the application.

```
@ 1,01
TEXT
  If you have questions or problems with the Mailing List
System,
  please call:

                    Name            Ext.
                    ====            ===

                 Mary Roberts       455
                 Jerry Baily        323

ENDTEXT
SLEEP 5000
```

Use the @ command to position the cursor on the screen where you want to begin the first line of the text. Otherwise, the text begins at the current cursor position.

The TEXT, ENDTEXT command combination tells Paradox to display the text on the screen. Include a SLEEP command after the ENDTEXT command line so that the message stays on the screen long enough to be read.

If you want to send the text to the printer, use the PRINTER ON command before the TEXT line. Be sure to include the PRINTER OFF command after the ENDTEXT line. Otherwise, everything that you meant to display on the screen is echoed to the printer.

APPLICATIONS

Use this command combination when you have a lot of information for the user. It is easier to use the TEXT, ENDTEXT command combination than using many ? and ?? commands in the script.

There are times when lengthy instructions are more helpful to the user than a brief message. For example, when an error occurs, describe the problem and provide suggestions for solving it.

Make a habit of positioning script messages carefully. Set your own rules and then follow them consistently. For example, display error messages in the lower right corner. Center long messages. By following such standards, you relieve the user of having to look all over the screen to find your message.

TYPICAL OPERATION

This example shows you how to use the TEXT, ENDTEXT command combination.

1. Type **SEE** to select the Scripts, Editor, Edit options.
2. When asked for the name of the script, type **Weekcalc** and press **Enter**. The script appears on your screen.
3. Press **Up Arrow**, if necessary, to position the cursor on the first letter of the first line. Press **Ins** until "Ins" appears in the right top corner of your screen.
4. Press **Enter**. A blank line is inserted at the top of the script but the cursor is on the second line. Press **Up Arrow** so that the cursor is positioned on the blank line.
5. Type the changes on the lines indicated by diamonds so that your screen resembles the one in the following display.

```
Changing script C:\paradox3\weekcalc                              Script Ins

....+...10....+...20....+...30....+...40....+...50....+...60....+...70....+...80
clear                                                                        ◆
text                                                                         ◆
  This option counts the number of weeks between two dates. The results      ◆
  are displayed at the bottom of the screen.                                 ◆
                                                                             ◆
  Under the results line is an option. Type 0 (zero) to do another           ◆
  calculation. Do this as often as necessary.                                ◆
                                                                             ◆
  When ready to return to the previous menu, type any number except zero.    ◆
endtext                                                                      ◆
sleep 5000                                                                   ◆
for tcontinue from 0 to 1
  clear
fromdate = today()
todate = today()
@ 10,10
?? "Enter the beginning date "
accept "D" picture "##/##/##" to fromdate
@ 12,10
?? "Enter the ending date "
accept "D" picture "##/##/##" to todate
count = 0
```

6. Press **F10** (Scripts Menu) and type **G** (Go). Your screen resembles the following display.

```
  This option counts the number of weeks between two dates. The results
  are displayed at the bottom of the screen.

  Under the results line is an option. Type 0 (zero) to do another
  calculation. Do this as often as necessary.

  When ready to return to the previous menu, type any number except zero.
```

7. When the calc screen appears, type two dates. When the result is displayed, type **3** and press **Enter** to redisplay the Main Menu.

8. Now, edit the script again to position the information on the screen. Place the cursor on the second line of the script and press **Ins**. Press **Enter** to insert a blank line in the script. Then press **Up Arrow** to move the cursor to the blank line and type **@ 8,0**. To center the information on the screen when the script is played, type the information between the TEXT and ENDTEXT commands again so that it resembles the one in the following display.

```
Changing script C:\paradox3\weekcalc                                    Script Ins

....+...10....+...20....+...30....+...40....+...50....+...60....+...70....+...80
clear
@ 8,0                                                                          ◆
text
                   This option counts the number of weeks                      ◆
                   between two dates. The results are                          ◆
                   displayed at the bottom of the screen.                      ◆
                                                                               ◆
                   Under the results line is an option. Type                   ◆
                   0 (zero) to do another calculation.                         ◆
                   Do this as often as necessary.                              ◆
                                                                               ◆
                   When ready to return to the previous menu,                  ◆
                   type any number except zero.                                ◆
endtext
sleep 5000
for tcontinue from 0 to 1
  clear
fromdate = today()
todate = today()
@ 10,10
?? "Enter the beginning date "
accept "D" picture "##/##/##" to fromdate
```

9. Press **F10** (Scripts Menu) and select the Go option by typing **G**. This time the text begins on line eight of your screen.

```
                   This option counts the number of weeks
                   between two dates. The results are
                   displayed at the bottom of the screen.

                   Under the results line is an option. Type
                   0 (zero) to do another calculation.
                   Do this as often as necessary.

                   When ready to return to the previous menu,
                   type any number except zero.
```

10. Press **Ctrl-Break** to stop script play and type **C** to cancel it.
11. Turn to Module 75 to continue the recommended learning sequence.

Module 98
TYPEIN

DESCRIPTION

One of the ways to help the user is to write scripts that accept input with minimum time and effort. For example, data entry is accomplished faster if all Texas data is entered in the Mailtx table. Then all the Oklahoma data is entered in the Mailok table during another session.

It is even better when the user is presented a screen before the script accesses the table. The user provides information that is similar among a sequence of input documents. For example, all the cities and states are the same. If the input documents are arranged properly, the user's input time is shorter than if the documents are not organized.

The TYPEIN command supplies the values from the setup screen to the data file automatically before the record is displayed on the screen. The user is able to change the data to accomodate a document that is out of sequence. Otherwise, pressing Enter for the field leaves the value in the field.

APPLICATIONS

Use the TYPEIN command in scripts that accept data from the user. If a field is usually filled with a certain value, the TYPEIN command provides it instead of the user.

For example, the Mailtx table always needs the value "Tx" in the State field. Instead of the user typing it for each record, the TYPEIN command does it automatically.

TYPICAL OPERATION

This example shows you how to use the TYPEIN command.

1. Edit the Test1 script. Change the script so that it matches the following script.

```
Changing script C:\paradox3\test1                              Script Ins

....+...10....+...20....+...30....+...40....+...50....+...60....+...70....+...80
clear
@ 10,10
?? "Enter the name of the table "
accept "A8" picture "&*&" to mfile
mstate = substr(mfile,5,2)                                              ◆
@ 12,10                                                                 ◆
?? "Enter the city "                                                    ◆
accept "A20" picture "@*@" to mcity                                     ◆
```

```
mstate = substr(mfile,5,2)
@ 12,10
?? "Enter the city "
accept "A20" picture "@*@" to mcity
edit mfile
formkey
while (true)
  end
  PgDn
  moveto [City]
  typein mcity
  moveto [State]
  typein mstate
  moveto [Last Name]
  wait record message "Leave Last Name blank when ready to quit..." until "F2"
  if isblank([Last Name])
    then
    del
    quitloop
  endif
endwhile
do_it!
clearall
release vars mfile,mcity,mstate
```

2. Press **F10** (Scripts Menu) and select the Go option.
3. Type **Mailok** and press **Enter** for the filename.
4. Then type **Oklahoma City** and press **Enter** for the city. A new record appears on the screen. All fields except the City and State are blank. Your screen resembles the following display.

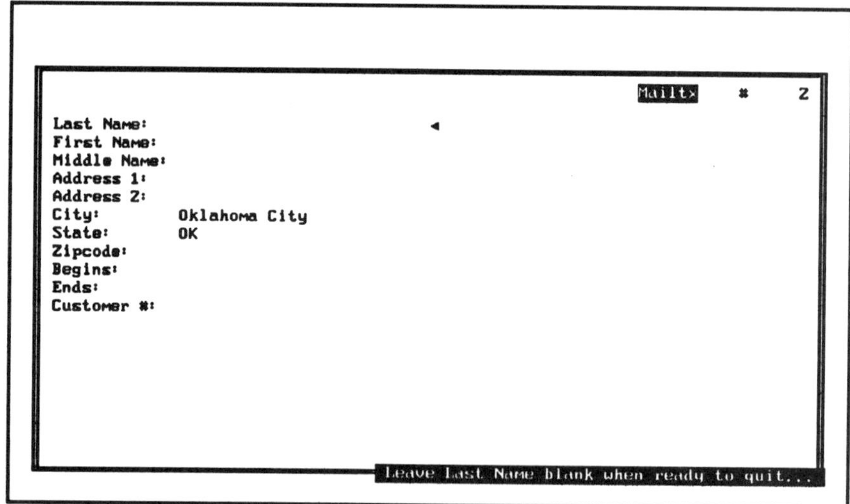

5. Press **F2** to end the script.
6. Turn to Module 40 to continue the recommended learning sequence.

Module 99
UNPASSWORD

DESCRIPTION

When a valid password is provided for a protected table, the table status is changed to unprotected until the end of the Paradox session or the UNPASSWORD resets its status. This command format is similar to the PASSWORD command. Substitute "-n" with a number greater than 1 in the following format.

```
UNPASSWORD <password-1>,...,<password-n>
```

Replace <password-1> through <password-n> with at least one of the passwords included in the PASSWORD command that was performed to allow the script to use the protected table. If a few of the tables are still needed, do not include their passwords in the UNPASSWORD command line.

APPLICATIONS

Use the UNPASSWORD command at the end of a script that has finished its work with protected tables. For example, the PASSWORD command provides the valid password for the protected Mailfile table. Unless the UNPASSWORD command is encountered before the application ends, the user is allowed access to the table until the end of the current Paradox session.

TYPICAL OPERATION

This example shows you how to use the UNPASSWORD command.

1. Play the Mainmenu script. Select the Utilities option and then the Passfile option. Type **DLS1** and press **Enter** when asked for an identification code.
2. When the table is displayed, press **F2** to return to the application menu.
3. Press **Esc** twice to end the application.
4. When the Main Menu screen returns, type **V** (View), then type **Mailfile** and press **Enter** to view the Mailfile table. You are not asked for the password since the Idcheck procedure provided it while playing the Mainmenu script.
5. Press **F8** (Clear Image) to remove the script from the workspace.

6. Edit the Maillist script. Insert the UNPASSWORD command in the Idcheck procedure. Then insert the Editpass procedure before the WRITELIB command line as shown in the following display. The dots indicate that lines in the script are omitted in the display. Do not change those lines.

```
Changing script C:\paradox3\maillist                              Script Ins

....+...10....+...20....+...30....+...40....+...50....+...60....+...70....+...80
copytoarray passes
clearall
unpassword "LevelCodes"                                                         ◆
clear
.
.
.
endif
endproc
; end idcheck
; editpass - allows changes to Mailfile table                                   ◆
proc editpass()                                                                 ◆
  password "LevelCodes"                                                         ◆
  edit "Mailfile"                                                               ◆
  formkey                                                                       ◆
  wait table message "Press F2 to return to the menu..." until "F2"             ◆
  do_it!                                                                        ◆
  clearall                                                                      ◆
  unpassword "LevelCodes"                                                       ◆
endproc                                                                         ◆
; end editpass                                                                  ◆
writelib "Maillist" Idcheck, editpass                                           ◆
@ 20,10
?? "Size of the Maillist procedure library = "
?? filesize("Maillist.lib")
sleep 2500
infolib "Maillist"
; end maillist
```

7. Press **F10** (Scripts Menu) and select the Go option. This script must be played so that the changed Idcheck procedure is saved in the procedure library.
8. The procedure library contains two procedures. Press **F8** (Clear Image) to remove the list of procedures from the workspace.
9. When the Main Menu screen returns, edit the Passfile option of the Utility script. Delete lines and insert the command line that plays the Editpass procedure as shown in the following display.

```
Changing script C:\paradox3\utility                                   Script

....+...10....+...20....+...30....+...40....+...50....+...60....+...70....+...80
    case mutility = "Passfile" :
      x = idcheck()
      if x = "9"
        then
        editpass()                                                         ◆
      else
        message "You have typed an invalid ID code..."
        sleep 2000
        clearall
      endif
      savevars all
      if isfile("Passes.sc")
        then
        Menu {Tools} {Rename} {Script} {Savevars} {Passes} {Replace}
      else
        Menu {Tools} {Rename} {Script} {Savevars} {Passes}
      endif
      release vars idcode, x
    case mutility = "Esc" :
      return
    otherwise :
      clear
```

10. Save the script with the DO-IT! option of the Scripts Menu.

11. Change the READLIB command in the Mainmenu script so that it matches the one shown in the following display.

```
Changing script C:\paradox3\mainmenu                                  Script

....+...10....+...20....+...30....+...40....+...50....+...60....+...70....+...80
readlib "Maillist" Idcheck, editpass                                       ◆
while (true)
  clear
  showmenu
    "View" : "Find and review customer information.",
    "Maintenance" : "Maintains table data.",
    "Report" : "Print the columnar report.",
    "Labels" : "Print mailing labels.",
    "Update" : "Batch update master table from a floppy disk.",
    "Summary" : "Provide statistics on subscription preferences.",
    "Configure" : "Change application configuration.",
    "Utilities" : "Perform various tasks for the Mail List application."
  default "View" to mchoice
  switch
  case mchoice = "View" :
    play "Custview"
  case mchoice = "Maintenance" :
    x = Idcheck()
    if x > "0" and x < "10"
      then
      play "Custmnt"
    endif
```

12. Play the Mainmenu script again by selecting the Go option from the Scripts Menu. Select the Utilities option and then the Passfile option. Use the DLS1 identification code.

13. Press **F2** to return to the Utilities submenu. Press **Esc** twice to end the application.

14. Select the View option from the Main Menu line. When asked for the name of the table, type **Mailfile** and press **Enter**. You are asked for the password. This tells you that the status for the table is protected even after playing the Passfile option.
15. Press **Esc** twice to return to the Main Menu screen.
16. Turn to Module 37 to continue the recommended learning sequence.

Module 100
VIEW

DESCRIPTION

This command is similar to the EDIT command since it makes the specified table available on the workspace. However, the table is not available for changes to the data. The format for this command follows.

```
VIEW <table name>
```

Replace <table name> with the name of the table you want to see on the workspace. Unless provided in a variable, enclose <table name> with quotation marks. For example, when the command line VIEW "Mailtx" is encountered in a script, Paradox reads the Mailtx table from the disk and displays it on the screen.

If the table is not found on the disk, Paradox displays a script error in the lower right corner of the screen. To avoid a possible error, use the ISFILE( ) function to verify that the table is available on the disk.

The VIEW command in a script is an abbreviated form of several menu options. By including the following command line in the script instead of the VIEW "Mailtx" command line, you achieve the same results.

```
Menu {View} {Mailtx}
```

When the VIEW command line is encountered, Paradox automatically provides the data in Table View. This form presents several records down the screen. However, only a few fields are visible across the screen as in the following display.

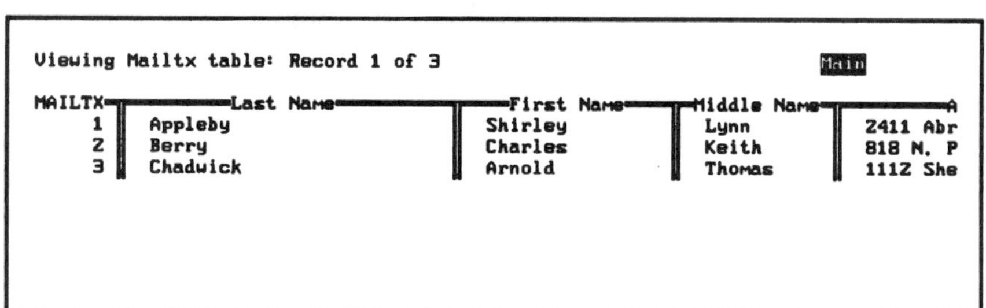

When the Table View is displayed on the screen, the cursor is positioned on the first record. To move the cursor to other records while in Table View, just press Up Arrow or Down Arrow. Other fields are made available by pressing Left Arrow or Right Arrow.

Paradox also provides a Forms View automatically that presents only one record per screen. The fields are listed down the screen as in the following display.

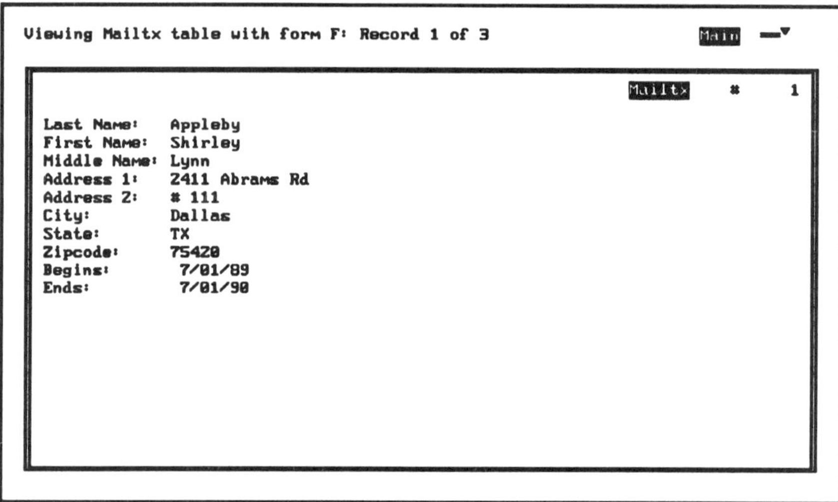

Press Up Arrow or Down Arrow to move the cursor from one field to another. If there are more than 20 fields, pressing Down Arrow moves the cursor to the second screen of fields.

If neither of the forms that are provided automatically by Paradox is sufficient, design and save your own forms. These are called *custom forms*. Design these forms by using the Forms option on the Main Menu screen of the Paradox menu-driven system.

Custom forms provide several advantages. For example, the user sees only the fields you include in the form. Also, the positioning of the information on the screen is under your control.

When a form is created, it is saved on disk so that it is available when the table is used. A maximum of ten forms may exist for each table. Replace the two automatic Paradox forms or make your forms available as part of the other eight forms that are allowed for the specified table.

Since the VIEW command automatically presents the data in Table View, the script must specify the desired form. The following command lines tell Paradox to display the first record of Mailtx in the Form View that was created automatically.

```
view "mailtx"
formkey
{Image} {Pickform} {F}
```

When the user presses the PgUp or PgDn keys, the previous or next record (respectively) is displayed on the screen. Press the Home key to move the cursor to the first record in the table. The End key tells Paradox to move the cursor to the last record in the table.

When the table is available on the screen, press F7 (FormKey) to switch between Forms View and Table View. For example, use the Table View to move the cursor to the desired record. Then press F7 (FormKey) again to return to the Forms View. To remove the table from the workspace, press F8 (Clear Image).

If the table contains a large number of records, do not force the user to look for the desired record. Write your application so that the user is asked for the key value of that record (e.g., "Smith"). Then use the LOCATE command or the QUERY, ENDQUERY command combination to search the table. When the record is found, make it available to the user. Otherwise, present a message that tells the user that the script was unable to locate the record.

Each time the VIEW command line is encountered in the script, the specified table is displayed on the workspace. If a table already exists on the screen, the most recent table is stacked under the existing image. Press F3 (Up Image) and F4 (Down Image) to move the cursor among the table images on the screen. To remove all images from the workspace, press Alt-F8 (Clear All Images).

APPLICATIONS

Use the VIEW command to display table data to the user. Remember that the data is not made available for changes from the VIEW command. Include the EDITKEY special keycode after the VIEW command line to tell Paradox to allow changes to the data.

The LOCATE command is usually included in scripts that display table data on the screen. The user must provide specific field values that are included in the desired record (e.g., "Smith, John"). This information is used by the LOCATE command to quickly find the record in the table. When found, the record is displayed on the screen for the user. Otherwise, display an appropriate message to the user before continuing the script play.

TYPICAL OPERATION

This example shows you how to use the VIEW command.

1. Edit the Mainmenu script. Change the menu so that it includes a View option as shown in the following display.

```
Changing script C:\paradox3\mainmenu                                    Script Ins

....+...10....+...20....+...30....+...40....+...50....+...60....+...70....+...80
while (true)
  clear
  showmenu
    "View" : "Find and review customer information.",                          ◆
    "Maintenance" : "Maintains table data.",
    "Report" : "Print the columnar report.",
    "Labels" : "Print mailing labels.",
    "Configure" : "Change application configuration.",
    "Weekcalc" : "Count the number of weeks between two dates."
  default "View" to mchoice                                                    ◆
  switch
  case mchoice = "View" :                                                      ◆
    play "Custview"                                                            ◆
  case mchoice = "Maintenance" :
    play "idcheck"
    if retval
      then
      play "Custmnt"
    endif
  case mchoice = "Report" :
    @ 10,10
    ?? "Printing the columnar report - Please Wait..."
```

2. Press **F10** (Script Menu) and select the DO-IT! option.
3. Type **SEW** to write a new script called Custview.
4. Write the script so that it matches the following display.

```
Designing script C:\paradox3\custview                                   Script Ins

....+...10....+...20....+...30....+...40....+...50....+...60....+...70....+...80
; custview - view customer data
view "Mailtx"
formkey {Image} {Pickform} {F}
while (true)
  clear
  @ 21,05
  ?? "To return to the menu, leave customer name blank..."
  @ 10,10
  ?? "Enter Last Name "
  accept "A30" to lastname
  @ 12,10
  ?? "Enter First Name "
  accept "A20" to firstname
  if lastname > "    " and firstname   > "    "
    then
    locate lastname, firstname
    if (retval)
      then
      while not atlast()
        wait record message "Esc=menu, F2=find another customer, PgDn=continue search"
          until "Esc", "F2", "PgDn"
        if retval = "Esc"
          then
          clearimage
          return
        else
          if retval = "F2"
            then
            quitloop
          else
            if retval = "PgDn"
              then
              PgDn
              locate next lastname, firstname
              if not (retval)
                then
                beep beep beep beep
                message "No other records were found in the table for that customer..."
```

```
                sleep 2000
              endif
            else
              end
            endif
          endif
        endif
      endwhile
    else
      @ 21,05
      beep beep beep beep
      ?? "Requested Customer name not found in table..."
      sleep 2000
    endif
  else
    quitloop
  endif
endwhile
clearimage
; end custview
```

5. Press **F10** (Script Menu) and select the DO-IT! option. The Main Menu returns to the screen.
6. Play the Mainmenu script.
7. Type **V** to select the View option. Then type **Berry** and press **Enter** for the Last Name field.
8. Type **Charles** and press **Enter** for the First Name. Your screen resembles the following display.

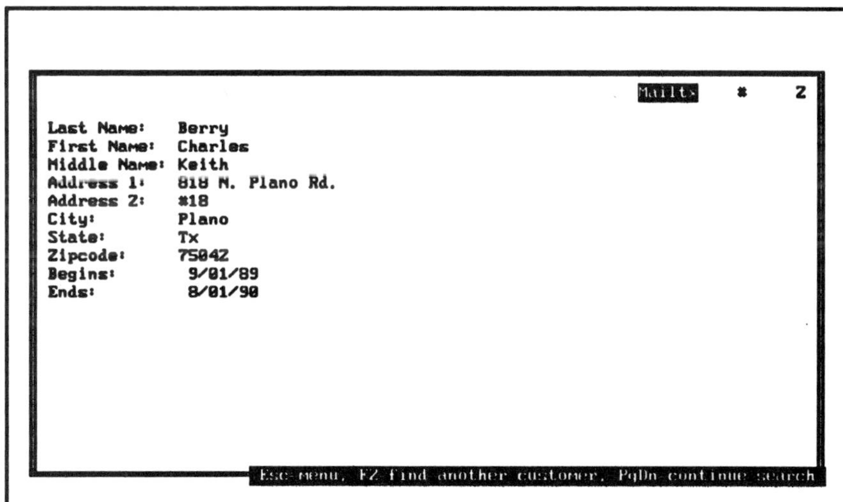

9. Press **Esc** to return to the application menu. Select the View option and type the same customer name again.

10. Press **F2** to enter another customer name. This time, type **Appleby** for the Last Name and type **Shirley** for the First Name.
11. When the record appears on the screen, press **PgDn** to continue the search. The computer beeps and a message appears telling you that no other records are found for the customer.
12. When the cursor returns to the record, press **Esc** to clear the screen and return to the application menu. Press **Esc** again to exit the application.
13. Turn to Module 50 to continue the recommended learning sequence.

Module 101
WAIT

DESCRIPTION

This command tells Paradox to wait for the user to respond to the record presented in the edit mode. By including the WAIT command in scripts that allow the user to change data in the table, the script gives the user limited control. Though similar, there are three forms of the WAIT command.

```
WAIT FIELD << PROMPT <prompt-1> <<, <prompt-2> >> >>
           << MESSAGE <message> >> UNTIL <keycodes>

WAIT RECORD << PROMPT <prompt-1> <<, <prompt-2> >> >>
            << MESSAGE <message> >> UNTIL <keycodes>

WAIT TABLE << PROMPT <prompt-1> <<, <prompt-2> >> >>
           << MESSAGE <message> >> UNTIL <keycodes>
```

Use the WAIT FIELD form when you want the script to allow changes to one field. Include a LOCATE and a MOVETO command line before the WAIT command. The LOCATE command finds the specified record in the table. The MOVETO command positions the cursor in the field to be changed. The cursor is not allowed to move from that field. Pressing Up Arrow, Home, or any of the cursor movement keys causes the computer to beep.

The WAIT RECORD form allows changes to the current record. Include a LOCATE command line before the WAIT command so that the record to be changed is found for the user. Moving the cursor to another record by pressing the PgUp, PgDn, Home, and End keys is not allowed. These keystrokes cause the computer to beep.

Use the WAIT TABLE form to allow the user to change any record in the table. Records may be changed or deleted. Also, this form of the WAIT command allows the user to add new records to the table.

The PROMPT clause is optional. When used, replace <prompt-1> with information for the user. It is displayed on the top line of the workspace. For example, the PROMPT "Record # = "+strval(recno( )) clause tells the user the current record number at the top of the screen. If <prompt-2> is included in the PROMPT clause, separate it from <prompt-1> with a comma. The <prompt-2> information is displayed on the second line.

Since the MESSAGE <message> clause is optional, use it only when you want to display a message in the lower right corner of the workspace during the edit activity. For example, tell the user to press F2 (DO-IT!) when ready to end the edit session.

The UNTIL <keycodes> clause must be included in the WAIT command line. Replace <keycodes> with one or more keys that you want the application to accept from the user to stop the Edit mode. For example, the clause UNTIL "F1," "F2," "Q" tells Paradox to stop the edit session when the user types Q or presses F1 (Help) or F2 (DO-IT!).

Even when the F2 (DO-IT!) key is pressed by the user (as required by the UNTIL clause), the record remains available for changes. The keystroke told Paradox to end the WAIT command and continue playing the script. Include the special keycodes (see Appendix B) in the script to end the editing session (DO-IT!) and clear the screen (Clear Image). When a special keycode is encountered in the script, the effect is the same as when the user presses the key.

The Paradox variable called Retval is set automatically to the value of the key typed by the user to exit the WAIT command. When more than one key is specified in the UNTIL <keycodes> clause, write the script so that Retval is evaluated and certain tasks are performed according to its value.

APPLICATIONS

A script that lets users change table data must be written carefully. While allowing changes, it must also protect the data.

Some control of the editing session is achieved by using a custom form. It is like a pattern for the screen. Paradox uses the form to place specific fields on the screen. It also tells Paradox to allow or prohibit changing the field value.

Further control of the editing session is achieved when the WAIT command is included in the script. It restricts or allows cursor movement among the records in the table.

For example, a WAIT RECORD command line in a script restricts the user to changing the record that appears on the screen. This command makes the computer beep when the PgUp, PgDn, Home, and End keys are pressed. The cursor is not allowed to move to another record within the table.

TYPICAL OPERATION

This example shows you how to use the WAIT command.

1. Edit the Custmnt script and change it until it matches the one in the following display.

```
Changing script C:\paradox3\custmnt                                     Script Ins

....+...10....+...20....+...30....+...40....+...50....+...60....+...70....+...80
;custmnt - customer maintenance script
clear
@ 10,10
?? "Enter the name of the table "
accept "a8" picture "&*&" to fileans
if not isblank(fileans)
  then
  if isfile(fileans+".db")
    then
    edit fileans
    formkey {Image} {PickForm} {F}
    wait record message "Press F2 when ready to return to the menu..."          ◆
    until "F2"                                                                  ◆
  else
    beep beep beep beep
    message "Table "+fileans+".db is not on the current data disk."
    sleep 2000
  endif
endif
; end custmnt
```

2. Press **F10** (Scripts Menu) and select the DO-IT! option by typing **D**. The Main Menu returns to your screen.
3. Type **SP** to play an option. Type **Mainmenu** for the name of the script and press **Enter**.
4. Type **M** to select the Maintenance option. Type **DLS1** and press **Enter** when asked for the ID. When asked for the name of the table, type **Mailtx** and press **Enter**. Your screen resembles the following display.

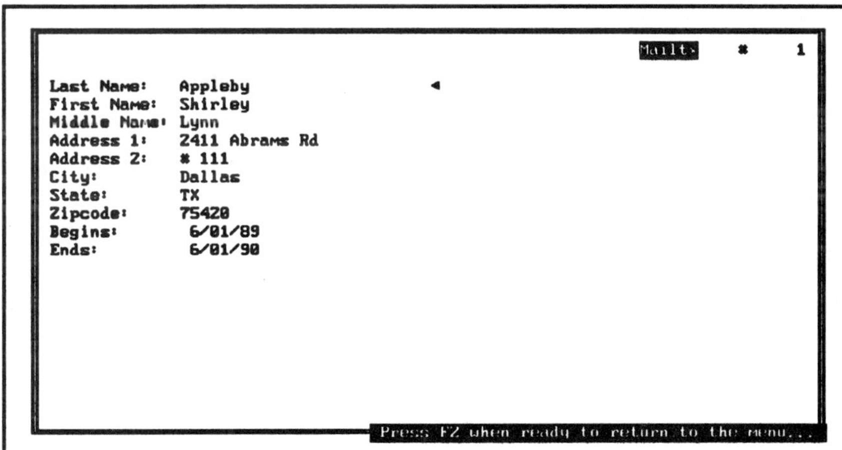

5. Press **End** to move to the last record in the table. The computer beeps and the first record remains on the screen.
6. Press **Down Arrow** for every field on the screen. While the cursor is positioned on the Ends field, each time you press Enter or Down Arrow, the computer beeps.

7. Press **F2** (DO-IT!) as instructed by the message at the bottom of the screen. The application menu returns to the workspace.

8. Press **Esc**. The record is displayed on the screen in editing mode. Press **F2** (DO-IT!) to end the editing session. Then press **F8** (Clear Image) to remove the record from the screen and return to the Main Menu.

9. Return to the Scripts Editor and change the WAIT command in Custmnt. Also, add the keycodes to end the editing session and clear the screen. The script must match the following display.

```
Changing script C:\paradox3\custmnt                                  Script Ins

....+...10....+...20....+...30....+...40....+...50....+...60....+...70....+...80
;custmnt - customer maintenance script
clear
@ 10,10
?? "Enter the name of the table "
accept "a8" picture "&*&" to fileans
if not isblank(fileans)
  then
  if isfile(fileans+".db")
    then
    edit fileans
    formkey {Image} {PickForm} {F}
    wait field message "Press F2 when ready to return to the menu..."      ◆
      until "F2"                                                            ◆
    do_it!                                                                  ◆
    clearimage                                                              ◆
  else
    beep beep beep beep
    message "Table "+fileans+".db is not on the current data disk."
    sleep 2000
  endif
endif
; end custmnt
```

10. Save the script and play Mainmenu again. Choose the Maintenance option and return to the Mailtx table. The cursor is positioned on the Last Name field.

11. Press **Enter** to move the cursor to the First Name field. The computer beeps. Press **PgDn**. Press **End**. The computer beeps for each keystroke.

12. Press **F2** (DO-IT!). Then press **Esc** to exit the application.

13. Change the WAIT command in Custmnt again. This time, change the word FIELD to TABLE in the WAIT command line. Then save the changed script.

14. Play Mainmenu again. Return to the first record of Mailtx. Press **PgDn**. The second record appears on the screen.

15. Press **Enter** for all the fields until the third record appears on the screen. Press **Home** so that the first record is available for changes.

16. Press **F2** (DO-IT!) to return to the application menu. Then press **Esc**.

17. Turn to Module 28 to continue the recommended learning sequence.

Module 102
WHILE, ENDWHILE

DESCRIPTION

Looping is one of the best techniques available for making your scripts shorter and thus more efficient. It allows you to write a set of command lines once and perform them until a condition is met.

The WHILE, ENDWHILE command combination is one way to set up a loop. The format for using these commands follows.

```
WHILE <condition>
  <commands>
ENDWHILE
```

The WHILE command marks the beginning of the loop. The ENDWHILE identifies the end of the loop. When you use the WHILE command in a script, there must always be an ENDWHILE command to match it. The two commands are used as a pair.

Replace <condition> with an expression that Paradox evaluates as true or false. This is called a *logical expression*. For example, the command line "WHILE n < tlimit" is the same as saying "Do this loop while the value of n is less than the value of tlimit."

The < symbol is the algebraic symbol for "less than." Paradox recognizes the following comparison operators.

<	less than
>	greater than
=	equal to
<=	less than or equal
>=	greater than or equal
<>	not equal

As long as the logical expression is true, Paradox continues to process the loop. When the condition is evaluated as false, the looping activity is stopped, and Paradox continues to play the rest of the script beginning with the next line after the ENDWHILE command.

Two or more logical expressions may also replace <condition>. This is done by including a *logical operator* OR, NOT, or AND.

The AND connector is used to specify that both logical expressions must be true. An example of a WHILE command line using the AND connector follows.

```
while n < tlimit and tlimit <> 0
```

Use OR to specify that either of the two expressions must be true. The following example shows you how to use the OR connector.

```
while city = "Dallas" or city = "Ft. Worth"
```

The NOT operator is used to specify the negative of the expression. Use the <> (not equal) symbol, when possible, to accomplish the same thing. For example, the following examples are interchangeable.

```
while city not = "Dallas" and city not = "Ft. Worth"
while city <> "Dallas" and city <> "Ft. Worth"
```

NOTE

Never use NOT and OR in the same WHILE command line. The computer does not evaluate the command line as you expect.

Replace <commands> with one or more command lines that you want performed each time the loop is processed. For example, include the command lines that print a sample label and then asks the user if another sample is needed. The user's answer controls the looping process.

There are times when you need to include at least one WHILE, ENDWHILE command combination as part of <commands>. When a loop exists within another loop, it is called a *nested loop*. Use as many loops as you need but make sure all the <condition> phrases are met eventually.

If the QUITLOOP command is performed within a WHILE, ENDWHILE loop, the looping activity is stopped immediately. Paradox then performs the line following the ENDWHILE command and finishes playing the rest of the script.

If the LOOP command is performed within a WHILE, ENDWHILE loop, all command lines between the LOOP and ENDWHILE commands are not performed. The variable that controls the loop is evaluated to determine if the specified criteria is met. If not, the looping activity is continued. If the criteria is met, processing continues with the command line that follows the ENDWHILE command.

Be careful that the condition is met eventually. Otherwise, your application may get stuck and run longer than expected.

If you suspect that this has happened, press Ctrl-Break to stop the script and access the Debugger. Before cancelling the script's play, use the Debugger to verify that the values of variables and fields are changing in each occurrence of the loop. If so, edit the script and play it again.

APPLICATIONS

Use the WHILE, ENDWHILE command combination to enclose command lines that need to be performed if, and when, a condition is met. For example, the following command lines count every record in the current table.

```
count = 0
while not eot( )
  count = count + 1
  skip
endwhile
```

The loop continues as long as the end of the table is not encountered. Refer to Appendix D for PAL functions like EOT( ) that may be included in <condition>.

Like the FOR, ENDFOR command combination, the values for <condition> may be *hardcoded* in the WHILE command line. However, the line in the script must be edited each time that one of the specific values change. Instead of changing the script, let the user or the table provide the values in a variable or field. For example, the following command lines use variables to control the loop. The dots indicate omitted command lines.

```
while accept <> "N"
  .
  .
  .
  @ 21,05
  ?? "Do you want to do another (Y/N)? "
  accept "A1" picture "&" to ans
endwhile
```

The user must type an "N" to stop the loop and continue playing the rest of the script. If any other letter is typed, the loop is processed again. By writing the script this way, you let the user control the looping activity.

Always look for ways to make your scripts more efficient. The quality and speed of your application benefits you and the user. Use a loop as often as possible to make your scripts short, effective, and easy to change.

TYPICAL OPERATION

This example shows you how to use the WHILE, ENDWHILE command combination.

1. Edit the Weekcalc script.
2. Delete the EXIT command from the script. Then, change the outer loop of the script so that it matches the one in the following display.

```
Changing script C:\paradox3\weekcalc                                  Script Ins

....+...10....+...20....+...30....+...40....+...50....+...60....+...70....+...80
                      When ready to return to the previous menu,
                      type any number except zero.
endtext
sleep 5000
ans = "Y"                                                                      ◆
while ans = "Y"                                                                ◆
clear
fromdate = today()
todate = today()
.
.
.
endfor
@ 21,05
?? "There are "+strval(count)+" weeks between "
?? fromdate
?? "thru"
?? todate
@ 23,05
?? "Do you want to do another (Y/N) "                                          ◆
accept "A1" picture "&" to ans                                                 ◆
endwhile                                                                       ◆
```

3. Press **F10** (Scripts Menu) and select the Go option. After the text is displayed, you are asked for the beginning date.
4. Type two dates so that the number of weeks are calculated. When asked if you want to do another, type **Y** and press **Enter**.
5. Type two dates. Then, type **1**. The computer beeps because the picture in the ACCEPT command requires a letter.
6. Type **B** and press **Enter**. Since a "Y" was not typed, the Main Menu returns to the workspace.
7. Change the script again. This time the inner loop is changed from a FOR, ENDFOR command combination to a WHILE, ENDWHILE loop as in the following display.

```
Changing script C:\paradox3\weekcalc                                  Script Ins

....+...10....+...20....+...30....+...40....+...50....+...60....+...70....+...80
?? "Enter the beginning date "
accept "D" picture "##/##/##" to fromdate
@ 12,10
?? "Enter the ending date "
accept "D" picture "##/##/##" to todate
count = 0
tdate = fromdate                                                               ◆
while tdate <= todate                                                          ◆
  count = count + 1
  tdate = tdate + 7                                                            ◆
endwhile                                                                       ◆
@ 21,05
?? "There are "+strval(count)+" weeks between "
?? fromdate
?? "thru"
?? todate
@ 23,05
?? "Do you want to do another (Y/N) "
accept "A1" picture "&" to ans
endwhile
```

8. Press **F10** (Scripts Menu) and select the Go option so that the script is played.
9. Type two dates to prove that the WHILE, ENDWHILE loop is working just like the FOR, ENDFOR loop. When you are convinced that the calculations are correct, type **N** and press **Enter** to end the script's play. The Main Menu returns to the workspace.
10. Turn to Module 36 to continue the recommended learning sequence.

Module 103
WRITELIB

DESCRIPTION

This one command reads procedures that currently exist in memory, makes them unreadable (like compiled programs), and writes them to the specified procedure library on disk. Use the READLIB command in an application script to read them into memory and the RELEASE PROCS command to remove them.

The procedures are available on disk so that the script is able to play them. However, they are protected from unauthorized changes. They are smaller so that they occupy less disk and memory space. Also, their size causes them to be performed faster by the application.

The format for this command follows. Substitute a number greater than 1 for "-n."

```
WRITELIB <library name> <procname-1>,...,<procname-n>
```

Use <library name> to supply the filename for the procedure library. Unless provided in a variable, enclose <library name> with quotation marks. The specified library must exist on the disk before the script performs the WRITELIB command. Otherwise, the script encounters a script error.

Replace <procname-1> through <procname-n> with at least one procedure name that is available in memory. Include at least one procedure name in this command line and separate each name with a comma.

When this line is performed, the specified procedure is read from memory, made unreadable, and saved to the <library name> file. If the same procedure name exists in the library before this command is performed, the existing version is flagged as unusable and the new version is saved in the library. Otherwise, the procedures included in <procname-1> through <procname-n> are added to the library with the existing procedures.

If you need to delete a procedure from the library to regain disk space, you must recreate the library from scratch with the CREATELIB command. Then use the WRITELIB command to reload the library with all of the valid scripts.

Remember that the procedure and its fully qualified name (e.g., a:\procs\maillist) are stored in the library when Paradox performs the WRITELIB command. If changes are needed in a stored procedure, be sure that the readable procedure is available in the same drive and directory that was used the first time.

APPLICATIONS

Using the WRITELIB command is the only way to save a cryptic (unreadable) version of procedures in a specified library on disk. Since they are smaller files, they perform tasks faster and occupy less memory while running the application.

For example, write and play a script that includes the PLAY "MAILLIST" command line. It plays the original Maillist procedure file from the disk so that the procedures are saved in memory. Then include the WRITELIB "MAILLIST" IDCHECK, UTILITY command line in this script. The two procedures are saved in the Maillist procedure library.

TYPICAL OPERATION

This example shows you how to use the WRITELIB command.

1. Type **SEE** to use the editor. Type **Maillist** and press **Enter** for the name of the script. Add the WRITELIB command to the end of the script so that it matches the one in the following display. The dots indicate that lines in the script are omitted in the display. Do not change those lines in your script.

```
Changing script C:\paradox3\maillist                              Script Ins

....+...10....+...20....+...30....+...40....+...50....+...60....+...70....+...80
; maillist - prodedures for the Mail List application                          ◆
clear                                                                          ◆
@ 05,10                                                                        ◆
?? "Size of the Maillist procedure library = "                                 ◆
?? filesize("Maillist.lib")                                                    ◆
proc idcheck()
  private passes, idcode, x
view "Mailfile"
copytoarray passes
.
.
.
endif
endproc
; end idcheck
writelib "Maillist" Idcheck                                                    ◆
@ 20,10                                                                        ◆
?? "Size of the Maillist procedure library = "                                 ◆
?? filesize("Maillist.lib")                                                    ◆
sleep 2500                                                                     ◆
; end maillist                                                                 ◆
```

2. Press **F10** (Scripts Menu) and select the Go option. The size of the Maillist library is displayed before and after performing the WRITELIB command.
3. Play the Maillist script again. The library size increases because the previously saved version of Idcheck is flagged as unusable and the new version is added to the library.
4. To regain the disk space, recreate the procedure library and reload it with the procedures. Edit the Maillist script and insert a CREATELIB command line at the top of the script so that it matches the one shown in the following display.

```
Changing script C:\paradox3\maillist                              Script Ins

....+...10....+...20....+...30....+...40....+...50....+...60....+...70....+...80
; maillist - prodedures for the Mail List application
clear
@ 05,10
?? "Size of the Maillist procedure library = "
?? filesize("Maillist.lib")
createlib "Maillist"                                                           ◆
proc idcheck()
  private passes, idcode, x
view "Mailfile"
copytoarray passes
clearall
clear
@ 10,10
?? "Enter your identification code "
accept "A4" picture "&&&*" to idcode
x = 2
while x < 12
  if idcode <> passes[x]
    then
    x = x + 2
  else
    quitloop
```

5. Press **F10** (Scripts Menu) and select the Go option. The Maillist library size is displayed before and after performing the CREATELIB and WRITELIB commands. This time the script decreased the amount of diskspace occupied by the procedure library.
6. Turn to Module 39 to continue the recommended learning sequence.

Appendix A
TERMS AND DEFINITIONS

Term	*Definition*
Access	The manner used by the computer to reference files on disk.
Alphanumeric Character	A letter (A through Z), number (0 through 9), or special character (e.g., @, %, $, (,), etc.).
Application	A set of procedures used to perform a task.
Array	A series of items (variables) that are combined under one variable name.
Array Element	A piece of an array that contains a value. It is like a variable that is referenced by the array name and a subscript.
Arithmetic Expression	A formula containing a combination of data names and numeric literals joined together by one or more arithmetic operators (+, –, *, /) to calculate a number.
Ascending Order	The sequence of data which is sorted (sequenced) on the key values from the lowest to the highest value.
ASCII	American Standard Code for Information Interchange. A standard set of 128 characters used in computers.
Band	A horizontal section of a report form. Each band serves special services. For example, the information in the top part of the report band is printed at the beginning of a report and the information in the bottom part of the report band is printed at the end of a report.
Blank Field	A field which contains no value.
Block	Computers can handle a group of characters or records at one time. It moves each group into and out of the computer memory instead of one record at a time.
Borrow	To copy an existing table structure to another table name. This provides a starting point for a new table structure which may be used with or without modifications.
Byte	An area of memory which can hold one letter, number, or special character.

Term	*Definition*
Calc Operators	Using the combination of the calc keyword and a formula to manipulate field information. For example, calculate the average value of selected records within a table.
Cancel	An option on many menus which stops an operation and returns the Main Menu.
Character	A number, letter, or symbol (including blanks) which appears in the workspace.
Concatenated Key	A key for a table which is created by connecting two or more fields with the plus symbol (+).
Conditional Statement	A comparison which is evaluated for a true or false situation.
Cursor	A blinking underline or bright box that marks your location on the workspace.
Data Item	A unit of information that can be identified by a symbolic name or by a combination of names and subscripts.
Data Name	A name assigned by the programmer to an area of memory. The name must contain at least one alphabetic letter.
Database	Information that is organized and saved on the computer for later retrieval. The type and amount of information you keep, as well as the way it is organized is up to you. For example, a class of students and their grades could be kept in a database.
Debug	The process of testing and changing a script or PAL program until it runs successfully.
Default	A standard or preset value.
Descending Order	The sequence of data which is sorted (sequenced) on the key values from the highest to the lowest value.
Directory	An area on the disk which contains saved files. All information about those files is stored in a directory file.
Example	The characters in a query which are shown in reverse video and specify how a field in one table must match a field in another table.
Execution	The computer performs each statement of a program. This processing is called program execution.
Export	Transferring the information in a Paradox table to a format which may be read by another program. For example, exporting a Paradox table to a dBASE III table (file).
Expression	A valid series of constants, variables, and/or functions.

Term	*Definition*
Family	A Paradox table and its set of related reports, scripts, forms, queries, and indexes.
Field	A unit of information that can be identified by a symbolic name or by a combination of names and subscripts. These areas are described in the DATA DIVISION. Each one is often called a "data item."
Field Type	The information in a structure which identifies a field as alphanumeric, date, dollar, or numeric (A, D, $, N).
File	A collection of information which is saved on a disk and identified by a specified name.
Filename	A name assigned to a set of input data or output data. A filename can only be eight positions in length and must include at least one letter.
Form View	The workspace displays only one record at a time and is arranged as specified by the selected image. The Table View displays many records on each screen.
Group	A set of records that meet specified criteria. For example, they contain the same value in one or more fields.
Image	The appearance of a table on the workspace. The Table View is the default image for a table. One or more forms may be created, saved, and used to rearrange or remove the table information for viewing.
Import	Transferring the information (data) from another program format to one which may be read by Paradox. For example, import a dBASE III table (file) to a Paradox table.
Index	A file created by the QuerySpeedup option which helps Paradox locate records faster for a specific query.
Instant Report	The report form which is identified as the default report (R) for the table on the workspace. The default report is printed immediately by pressing Alt-F7.
Join	The linking of two or more tables in a query by specifying criteria (examples) for data selection.
Key	One or more data items used to order or sequence the data in the table.
Key Word	A reserved word which is essential to the meaning and structure of a Paradox command.
Literal	A character string whose value is obvious. For example, "DALLAS," "John Davis," 832, and 21.444 are called literals.

Term	*Definition*
Mask	A picture which specifies a field's position, type, and format. For example, "999.99" is a picture that forces numeric fields to appear as six characters in length with two decimal positions (hundredths).
Message Window	The bottom right corner of the workspace where Paradox messages are displayed.
Output	Results of a script that is sent to the screen, printer, or disk file.
PAL	An abbreviation for the programming language which is included in the Paradox software package. It is an abbreviation for Paradox Application Language.
Password	A set of characters which must be typed before access to a protected table or script is allowed.
Pattern	A model (example) using @ or .. to identify specific criteria for a Paradox query. For example, typing A.. in a field of the query tells Paradox to retrieve the records which begin with A.
Procedure	A special script that is stored in memory before being performed by the script.
Process	Any operation or combination of operations upon data.
Program	A collection of Paradox functions that is kept and performed consecutively by the computer.
Query	Asking Paradox to retrieve the records which meet specified criteria from one or more tables.
Query Form	An empty Table View which is presented on your workspace for the requested table. Supply the criteria which must be met, and press F2 (DO-IT!) to tell Paradox to begin the search.
Record	By combining related fields of information, you create a record. For example, a person's name, address, and phone number fields are called a record.
Routine	A sequence of instructions that perform a specific task.
Run	Performing the command lines in a script or program. RUN is also a Paradox command.
Script	A Paradox program. A collection of keystrokes and/or PAL commands that performs specified tasks when played (executed or run). For example, create and save a script to open a table, select a report form, print the information on paper, and return to the Main Menu screen.
Short Number	A numeric field type which allows only whole numbers. A number with a decimal point is not allowed (e.g., 29.82).

Term	*Definition*
Sort	Arrange the records in a table in ascending or descending order.
Structure	The layout of a table. It contains the name, type, and length of each field. Also, key fields are identified in the table structure.
Submenu	A set of options which is made available only when an option from a previous menu is selected. It is a lower-level menu.
Subscript	A number or a numeric variable that specifies a field included in an array. For example, x[1] specifies the first element in the array.
Syntax	The rules governing command structure (format).
Table	A collection of information which is saved on disk for later retrieval. It is a Paradox database.
Table View	The workspace displays many records on each screen. They are arranged in columns across and rows down the workspace. The Form View displays only one record on each screen and is arranged according to the selected image.
Temporary Table	A scratchpad area which is reserved for Paradox to write information. Each time the scratchpad is used, any existing information is erased. For example, records are written to this area when a query is performed.
Toggle	Switch from one situation to another. For example, pressing F7 (Form Toggle) switches you (toggling) from Table View to Form View.
Validity Check	When data must meet specified criteria for correctness, a validity check is performed.
Variable	A variable is used for temporary storage of a value in a PAL script (program). Each one is assigned a name when it is created with the = command and is used as needed. The value of a variable may be changed at any time. Use the RELEASE command to delete the variable.
Workspace	The area below the menu line where tables, scripts, forms, etc. are displayed.

Appendix B
SPECIAL KEYS

Pal Command	*Keyboard Sequence*	*Result*
Alternate	Alt	Changes effect of other keys
Backspace	Backspace	Moves cursor left and delete character
Check	F6	Selects field to appear in query Answer table (excluding duplicate values)
CheckDescending	Ctrl-F6	Sorts current field in descending order
Checkplus	Alt-F6	Selects field to appear in query Answer table (including duplicate values)
Clearall	Alt-F8	Removes all images from workspace
Clearimage	F8	Removes image identified by cursor from workspace
Coeditkey	Alt-F9	Enters Coedit mode
CrossTabKey	Alt-X	Crosstabulates current table
Ctrl (Control)		Changes effect of other keys
CtrlBackspace	Ctrl-Backspace	Erases current field
CtrlBreak	Ctrl-Break	Stops current task
CtrlEnd	Ctrl-End	Moves cursor to last character of current field
CtrlHome	Ctrl-Home	Presses Ctrl Home
CtrlLeft	Ctrl-Left	Presses Ctrl <—
CtrlPgdn	Ctrl-PgDn	Presses Ctrl PgDn
CtrlPgup	Ctrl-PgUp	Presses Ctrl PgUp
CtrlRight	Ctrl-Right	Presses Ctrl —>
Del	Del	Presses the Delete key
Deleteline	Ctrl-Y	Deletes from cursor to End of line
Ditto	Ctrl-D	Fills field with previous record's value
Do_it!	F2	Ends or performs an operation
Dos	Ctrl-O	Suspends Paradox and accesses DOS
Dosbig	Alt-O	Suspends Paradox and accesses DOS with maximum memory available
Down	Down-Arrow	Presses Down Arrow
Downimage	F4	Moves down one image
EditKey	F9	Enters Edit mode

Pal Command	*Keyboard Sequence*	*Result*
End	End	Presses End
Enter	Enter	Presses Enter key
Esc	Esc	Presses the Escape key
Example	F5	Enters an example query element
FieldView	Alt-F5	Enters Field View
Formkey	F7	Switches between Table and Form View
GraphKey	Ctrl-F7	Graphs current table
GroupBy	Shift-F6	For set queries to group records by current query field without displaying it
Help	F1	Enters Help subsystem
Home	Home	Presses the Home key
Ins	Ins	Presses the Insert key
Instantplay	Alt-F4	Plays an instant script
Instantreport	Alt-F7	Prints an instant report
Keylookup	Alt-K	Displays records with duplicate keys
Left	Left-Arrow	Presses Left Arrow key
LockKey	Alt-L	Locks or unlocks current record
Menu	F10	Presses menu key
PgDn	PgDn	Presses page down key
PgUp	PgUp	Presses page up key
Refresh	Alt-R	Updates screen images
ReverseTab	Shift-Tab	Moves to previous field
Right	Right-Arrow	Presses Right Arrow key
Rotate	Ctrl-R	Moves current field to end of record
Tab	Tab	Moves to next field
Up	Up-Arrow	Presses Up Arrow
UpImage	F3	Moves up one image on the workspace
VerticalRuler	Ctrl-V	Turns ruler on and off screen
Zoom	Ctrl-Z	Moves to 1st record with specific value
ZoomNext	Alt-Z	Moves to next record with specific value

Appendix C
QUERY OPERATORS

Category	*Operator*	*Definition*
Reserved Words	✓	Display this field in Answer table
	✓+	Display this field including duplicates in Answer table
	calc	Include calculated field in Answer table
	insert	Insert new records in a table
	delete	Delete selected records from a table
	changeto	Change values in selected fields
	find	Locate selected records in table
	like	Match on any similar value (Ex. like Smith would extract records whose value matches both Smith and Smyth)
	not	Exclude these records from Answer table
	blank	Match on blank values
	today	Today's date
	average	Average of the values
	count	Count of the values
	max	Highest value
	min	Lowest value
	sum	Total of the values
Arithmetic Symbols	+	Addition or concatenation (combine A Alphanumeric fields)
	–	Subtraction
	*	Multiplication
	/	Division
	( )	Group operator together
Range Symbols	=	Equal to (exact match)
	>	Greater than
	<	Less than
	>=	Greater than or equal to
	<=	Less than or equal to
Pattern Symbols	..	Wild card match on any group of characters
	@	Wild card match on a single character

Appendix D
PAL FUNCTIONS

ABS(Number)

DESCRIPTION — Strips the sign from a number.
ARGUMENTS — Number — Any numerc expression between +–10 –307 and +–10 308.
RETURNS — Numeric value (always positive).

ACOS(Number)

DESCRIPTION — ACOS returns the arc cosine of a number.
ARGUMENTS — Number — Must be a numeric expression between –1 and 1.
RETURNS — A numeric value between – and pi expressed in radians or the string "Error" if an illegal or invalid argument is passed.
WARNINGS — Always check for a returned value of "Error" before using the result of ACOS.

ARRAYSIZE(Array)

DESCRIPTION — Returns a value indicating the number of elements an array can hold.
ARGUMENTS — Array — An array name.
RETURNS — Numeric value indicating the number of elements in the array or zero if the array has not been declared or an illegal entry is passed.
WARNINGS — Check for zero return value before using return value of ARRAYSIZE function.

ASC(Char)

DESCRIPTION — Returns ASCII value of a character string.
ARGUMENTS — Char — A PAL keycode expression.
RETURNS — ASCII code for Char in numeric form.

ASIN(Number)

DESCRIPTION — Returns arc sine of a number.
ARGUMENTS — Number is a numeric expression between –1 and 1.
RETURNS — Numeric value between –pi/2 and pi/2 expressed in radians or zero if an invalid argument is passed.

ATAN(Number)

DESCRIPTION — Returns the 2-quadrant arctangent of a number.
ARGUMENTS — Number — A numeric expression representing the tangent of an angle.
RETURNS — Numeric value between –pi/2 and pi/2 expressed in radians.

ATAN2(Number1, Number2)

DESCRIPTION — Returns the 4-quadrant arctangent of a number.
ARGUMENTS — Number1 and Number2 are numeric expressions representing a cosine and a sine of an angle.
RETURNS — Numeric value expressed in radians.

ATFIRST( )

DESCRIPTION	Tests to see if current record is the first record.
ARGUMENTS	None
RETURNS	Returns True or False.

ATLAST( )

DESCRIPTION	Tests to see if current record is the last record.
ARGUMENTS	None
RETURNS	True or False.

BANDINFO( )

DESCRIPTION	Returns the name of the band the cursor is on in the report generator.
ARGUMENTS	None
RETURNS	String value representing the current band indicator in the report generator.

BLANKDATE( )

DESCRIPTION	Returns a blank date value.
ARGUMENTS	None
RETURNS	A blank date value.

BLANKNUM( )

DESCRIPTION	Returns a blank number.
ARGUMENTS	None
RETURNS	A blank numeric number (not zero).

BOT( )

DESCRIPTION	Test for a move beyond the beginning of the current table.
ARGUMENTS	None
RETURNS	Logical value (True/False)

CAVERAGE(TableName, FieldName)

DESCRIPTION	Returns the average of a numeric column of a table.
ARGUMENTS	TableName — String representing the table to use.
	FieldName — String representing the field to use.
WARNINGS	FieldName must be numeric or an error will occur.
RETURNS	Numeric value representing the average of FieldName.

CCOUNT(TableName, FieldName)

DESCRIPTION	Returns the number of non-blank values in FieldName.
ARGUMENTS	TableName — String representing the table to use.
	FieldName — String representing the field to use.
WARNINGS	FieldName must be numeric or an error will occur.
RETURNS	Numeric value representing the count of FieldName.

CHARWAITING( )

DESCRIPTION	Tests whether a character is waiting to be read.
ARGUMENTS	None
RETURNS	True/False

CHECKMARKSTATUS( )
DESCRIPTION Tests a field in a query form to see if it is checked.
ARGUMENTS None
RETURNS "Null" if the field is not checked, "Check" if it is marked.

CHR(Number)
DESCRIPTION Converts an ASCII code to a one-character string.
ARGUMENTS Number — Must be numeric between 1 and 255.
RETURNS One-character string containing the ASCII character representing Number.

CMAX(TableName, FieldName)
DESCRIPTION Returns the largest value in FieldName (must be a numeric field).
ARGUMENTS TableName — String representing the table to use.
FieldName — String representing the field to use.
WARNINGS FieldName must be numeric or an error will occur.
RETURNS Numeric value representing the largest value in FieldName.

CMIN(TableName, FieldName)
DESCRIPTION Returns the smallest value in FieldName (must be a numeric field).
ARGUMENTS TableName — String representing the table to use.
FieldName — String representing the field to use.
WARNINGS FieldName must be numeric or an error will occur.
RETURNS Numeric value representing the smallest value in FieldName.

CNPV(TableName, FieldName, Number)
DESCRIPTION Calculates the net present value of a series of cash flows in FieldName (must be a numeric field).
ARGUMENTS TableName — String representing the table to use.
FieldName — String representing the field to use.
Number — Numeric value representing the interest rate or discount as a decimal value (example .12).
RETURNS Net present value of the non-blank entries in FieldName.

COL( )
DESCRIPTION Returns the column position of the PAL cursor.
ARGUMENTS None
RETURNS Integer value between 0 and 79.

COLNO( )
DESCRIPTION Returns the current column number on the workspace.
ARGUMENTS None
RETURNS Integer value representing the current column number.

COS(Number)
DESCRIPTION Returns the cosine of an angle.
ARGUMENTS Number — Numeric value representing an angle, expressed in radians.
RETURNS Returns a numeric value between –1 and 1.

CSTD(TableName, FieldName)

DESCRIPTION	Returns the standard deviation of entries in a numeric column.
ARGUMENTS	TableName — String representing the table to use. FieldName — String representing the field to use.
RETURNS	Numeric value equal to standard deviation of the values in FieldName. "Error" if the field has no non-blank entries.

CSUM(TableName, FieldName)

DESCRIPTION	Returns the sum of the entries in FieldName.
ARGUMENTS	TableName — String representing the table to use. FieldName — String representing the field to use.
RETURNS	Numeric value equal to the sum of the entries in FieldName or "Error" if FieldName has no non-blank entries.

CURSORCHAR( )

DESCRIPTION	Determines the character at the cursor on the Paradox workspace.
ARGUMENTS	None
RETURNS	One character string containing the character under the cursor.
VERSION	Paradox 1.1 and above

CURSORLINE( )

DESCRIPTION	Determines the line of text on the Paradox workspace as a string.
ARGUMENTS	None
RETURNS	String that holds the current line of text in Form and Report mode and in the Script editor.

CVAR(TableName, FieldName)

DESCRIPTION	Calculates the population variance in a numeric column.
ARGUMENTS	TableName — String representing the table to use. FieldName — String representing the field to use.
RETURNS	Number equal to the population variance of the non- blank entries in FieldName. "Error" if FieldName has no non-blank entries.

DATEVAL(String)

DESCRIPTION	Converts a string to a date.
ARGUMENTS	String — Must be in a valid Paradox date format.
RETURNS	Date value equal to string. "Error" if string does not contain a valid date.

DAY(Date)

DESCRIPTION	Gets the day of the month from a date string.
ARGUMENTS	Date — A valid date expression.
RETURNS	Integer value between 1 and 31.

DIRECTORY

DESCRIPTION	Gets the name of the current working directory.
ARGUMENTS	None
RETURNS	String containing the DOS pathname.

DIREXISTS(DOSPath)

DESCRIPTION	Verifies the existence of the specified directory.
ARGUMENTS	DOSPath — String containing the DOS path of a directory.
RETURNS	Numeric value, 1 if the directory exists and 0 if it doesn't exist.
VERSION	Paradox 2.0 and above

DOW(Date)

DESCRIPTION	Gets the day of the week from a date expression.
ARGUMENTS	Date — A valid date expression.
RETURNS	Three-letter string that represents the day of the week for the date expression (Example "Mon," "Wed," etc.).

DRIVESPACE(String)

DESCRIPTION	Number of bytes of free space on a disk.
ARGUMENTS	String — A single-letter string that contains a valid drive name
RETURNS	Numeric value representing the number of bytes of free space or –1 if the drive is not ready.

DRIVESTATUS(String)

DESCRIPTION	Tests to see if a disk drive is ready.
ARGUMENTS	String — A single-letter string that contains a valid drive name.
RETURNS	True if it is ready, False if it is not (or if String is a valid name but doesn't exist).

EOT( )

DESCRIPTION	Test for a move beyond the end of the current table.
ARGUMENTS	None
RETURNS	Logical value (True/False)
VERSION	Paradox 1.1 and above

ERRORCODE( )

DESCRIPTION	Returns the category code for the most recent run error.
ARGUMENTS	None
RETURNS	

Code	Meaning
0	no error (record was not changed etc.)
File/Directory Errors	
1	Drive not ready.
2	Directory not found.
3	Table in use by another user.
4	Full lock placed on table by another user.
5	File not found.
6	File corrupted.
7	Index File corrupted.
8	Object version mismatch.
9	Record locked by another user.
10	Directory in use by another user.
11	Directory in private directory of another user.
12	No access to directory at operating system level.
13	Index inconsistent with sort order.
General Script Errors	
20	Invalid context for operation.

21 Insufficient password rights.
22 Table is write protected.
23 Invalid field value.

Argument Errors

30 Data type mismatch.
31 Arguments out of range.
32 Wrong number of arguments.
33 Invalid argument.
34 Variable or procedure not assigned.
35 Invalid menu selection.

Resource Errors

40 Not enough memory to complete operation.
41 Not enough disk space to complete operation.
42 Not enough stack space to complete operation.
43 Printer not ready.

Record-Oriented Operation Errors

50 Record was deleted by another user.
51 Record was changed by another user.
52 Record was inserted by another user.
53 Record with that key already exists.
54 Record or table was not locked.
55 Record is already locked by you.
56 Lookup key not found.

(Note: Use ERRORUSER( ) to find who caused the error when you get an error code 3, 4, 9, or 11.)

VERSION Paradox 2.0 and above

ERRORMESSAGE( )

DESCRIPTION Returns the most recent error message.
ARGUMENTS None
RETURNS String value containing the message displayed by the most recent run error or error condition.
A blank string if no error has been encountered.
VERSION Paradox 2.0 and above

ERRORUSER( )

DESCRIPTION Gets the Paradox user who has placed a lock on an object.
ARGUMENTS None
RETURNS A string containing the users name. (Note: Use ERRORUSER( ) to find who caused the error when you get an error code of 3, 4, 9, or 11.)
VERSION Paradox 2.0 and above

EXP(Number)

DESCRIPTION Calculates the exponential (base e) of a number.
ARGUMENTS Number — A numeric expression.
RETURNS Numeric expression equal to the exponential of Number.

FAMILYRIGHTS(TableName, String)

DESCRIPTION Tests to see if a user has rights to create or modify objects in a family's table.
ARGUMENTS TableName — String representing the table to use.
String — Single-letter string ("F" - form, "R" - report, "S" - image setting, "V" - validity check).
RETURNS True/False
VERSION Paradox 2.0 and above

FIELD()

DESCRIPTION Gets the name of the current field.
ARGUMENTS None
RETURNS String with the name of the current field in the current image.

FIELDINFO()

DESCRIPTION Gets the current contents of the field indicator as a string.
ARGUMENTS None
RETURNS String value that holds the current contents of the Form or Report mode field indicator.

FIELDNO(FieldName, TableName)

DESCRIPTION Gets the position of a field in a table.
ARGUMENTS FieldName — String value that holds a valid field name.
TableName — String value that holds the name of the table.
RETURNS Numeric value representing the position of the field.

FIELDRIGHTS(TableName, FieldName, String)

DESCRIPTION Lets you know if a user has the right to read or modify a field in a table.
ARGUMENTS TableName — String value that holds the name of the table.
FieldName — String value that holds the name of the field.
String — String value ("ReadOnly" | "All").
RETURNS True/False
VERSION Paradox 2.0 and above

FIELDSTR()

DESCRIPTION Gets the contents of the current field as a string.
ARGUMENTS None
RETURNS String that holds the contents of the current field or Null if the field is blank.
VERSION Paradox 2.0 and above

FIELDTYPE()

DESCRIPTION Gets the field type of the current field.
ARGUMENTS None
RETURNS A field type string. (A [string length of n], "D", "N", "S", "$" or a script error occurs if no images are present on the workspace.)
VERSION Paradox 2.0 and above

FILESIZE(FileName)

DESCRIPTION Gets the size of a file in bytes.
ARGUMENTS FileName — A character expression that represents an existing filename.
RETURNS Numeric value that represents the number of bytes in the file (including unoccupied space).

FILL(Expression, Number)

DESCRIPTION Returns a string containing repeated instances of a character.
ARGUMENTS Expression is any PAL expression or Number — Numeric integer expression between 0 and 255.
RETURNS A string filled with the first character of Expression repeated Number times or zero if Number is zero.

FORM( )

DESCRIPTION Returns the name of the active form for the current table.
ARGUMENTS None
RETURNS String value containing name of current form.
VERSION Paradox 3.0 and above

FORMAT(FormatSpec, String)

DESCRIPTION Formats an expression for display or printing.
ARGUMENTS FormatSpec — String expression containing one or more format specifications.
String — Character string to be formatted.
Format Data Types

Type	*Specification*		*Applied to*
Width	Wn	allowable width	all
	Wn.m	width and decimal places	N,$
Alignment	AL	left justify	all
	AR	right justify	all
	AC	center within width	all
Case	CU	make uppercase	all
	CL	make lowercase	all
	CC	initial caps only	all
Edit	E$	floating $ sign	N,S,$
	EC	use separators between every 3 whole digits	N,S,$
	EZ	print leading zeros	N,S,$
	EB	blank leading zeros	N,S,$
	E*	"*" for leading zeros	N,S,$
	EI	international format	N,S,$
	ES	print in sientific notation	N,S,$
Sign	S+	print leading + or – sign	N,S,$
	S–	print leading – sign	N,S,$
	SP	print negative in ( )	N,S,$
	SD	print DB or CR notation	N,S,$
	SC	print CR after negative num.	N,S,$
Date	D1	use mm/dd/yy format	D
	D2	use Month dd,yyyy format	D
	D3	use mm/dd format	D
	D4	use mm/yy format	D
	D5	use dd-Month format	D
	D6	use Mon yy format	D
	D7	use dd-Mon-yyyy format	D
	D8	use mm/dd/yyyy format	D
	D9	use dd.mm.yy format	D
	D10	use dd/mm/yy format	D

FORMAT(FormatSpec, String) (Cont.)

Type	*Specification*		*Applied to*
	D11	use yy-mm-dd format	D
Logical	LY	use Yes/No for True/False	L
	LO	use On/Off for True/False	L

Note: Data types:
- N = number
- S = short number
- $ = currency
- D = date
- L = logical

RETURNS A formatted string.
VERSION Edit types EI and data types D9-D11 were added in Paradox 2.0.

FV(Number1, Number2, Number3)
DESCRIPTION Returns the future value of a series of equal payments.
ARGUMENTS Number1 — Numeric expression representing the periodic payment.
Number2 — Numeric interest rate expressed as a decimal number.
Number3 — Numeric expression representing the number of periods.
RETURNS Future value of a series of n equal payments of amount p, invested at rate r.

GETCHAR( )
DESCRIPTION Reads a character from the keyboard.
ARGUMENTS None
RETURNS Numeric value representing the next key pressed.

GRAPHTYPE( )
DESCRIPTION Returns the current graph type.
ARGUMENTS None
RETURNS String value containing current graph type.
VERSION Paradox 3.0 and above

HELPMODE( )
DESCRIPTION Notifies you whether help is being displayed and its type.
ARGUMENTS None
RETURNS A string value of "Help," "LookupHelp," or "None."
VERSION Paradox 2.0 and above

IMAGECAVERAGE( )
DESCRIPTION Averages the entries in the current column of the current image.
ARGUMENTS None
RETURNS Numeric value of the average described above.
VERSION Paradox 3.0 and above

IMAGECCOUNT( )
DESCRIPTION Counts the number of non-blank entries in the current column of the current table.
ARGUMENTS None
RETURNS Numeric value of the count described above.
VERSION Paradox 3.0 and above

IMAGECMAX( )

DESCRIPTION	Finds the largest entry in the current column of the current table.
ARGUMENTS	None
RETURNS	Numeric value that represents the largest entry.
VERSION	Paradox 3.0 and above

IMAGECMIN( )

DESCRIPTION	Determines the smallest entry in the current column of the current table.
ARGUMENTS	None
RETURNS	Numeric value that represents the smallest entry.
VERSION	Paradox 3.0 and above

IMAGECSUM( )

DESCRIPTION	Calculates the sum of the current column of the current image.
ARGUMENTS	None
RETURNS	Numeric value representing the calculated sum.
VERSION	Paradox 3.0 and above

IMAGENO( )

DESCRIPTION	Returns the position of the current image on the workspace.
ARGUMENTS	None
RETURNS	Numeric value that holds the position of the current image on the workspace.

IMAGETYPE( )

DESCRIPTION	Returns the type of image the cursor is in.
ARGUMENTS	None
RETURNS	A String value; "Display" - if image is a display image, "Query" - if image is a query form, "None" - if no images are present.

INT(Number)

DESCRIPTION	Gets the integer part of a number.
ARGUMENTS	Number — Numeric expression.
RETURNS	Integer portion of a number.

ISASSIGNED(String)

DESCRIPTION	Tests whether a variable or array element has been given a value.
ARGUMENTS	String — A character expression that holds a variable name or array element.
RETURNS	True/False

ISBLANK(Expression)

DESCRIPTION	Tests an expression for a blank value.
ARGUMENTS	Expression — Any valid PAL expression.
RETURNS	True/False

ISBLANKZERO( )

DESCRIPTION	Tests to see if blank values are treated as zero.
ARGUMENTS	None.
RETURNS	True/False
VERSION	Paradox 3.0 and above

ISEMPTY(TableName)

DESCRIPTION	Tests to see if a table has any records.
ARGUMENTS	TableName — A string expression that holds a valid table name.
RETURNS	True/False

ISENCRYPTED(TableName)

DESCRIPTION	Tests to see if a table is encrypted.
ARGUMENTS	TableName — A string expression that holds a valid table name.
RETURNS	True/False
VERSION	Paradox 2.0 and above

ISFIELDVIEW( )

DESCRIPTION	Tests to see if field view has been selected.
ARGUMENTS	None
RETURNS	True/False

ISFILE(String)

DESCRIPTION	Tests to see whether a file exists.
ARGUMENTS	String — Contains a valid DOS filename (including extension). Note: If string does not include drive and path specification, the current working directory is used.
RETURNS	True/False

ISFORMVIEW( )

DESCRIPTION	Tests to see if the current table image is in form view.
ARGUMENTS	None
RETURNS	True/False

ISINSERTMODE( )

DESCRIPTION	Tests to see if Paradox is in insert mode.
ARGUMENTS	None
RETURNS	True/False

ISLINKLOCKED( )

DESCRIPTION	Used to test whether the current table is link locked.
ARGUMENTS	None
RETURNS	True/False
VERSION	Paradox 3.0 and above

ISMULTIFORM(TableName, FormName)

DESCRIPTION	Tests to see if a form has multiple tables.
ARGUMENTS	String value representing table name and string value representing form name.
RETURNS	True/False
VERSION	Paradox 3.0 and above

ISMULTIREPORT(TableName, ReportName)

DESCRIPTION	Tests whether a report has lookup tables.
ARGUMENTS	String value representing table name and string value representing report name.
RETURNS	True/False
VERSION	Paradox 3.0 and above

ISRUNTIME( )

DESCRIPTION	Tests to see if the current script is being run under the Runtime version of Paradox.
ARGUMENTS	None
RETURNS	True/False
VERSION	Paradox 2.0 and above

ISSHARED(TableName)

DESCRIPTION	Tests to see if a table is in a shared network directory other than your current private directory.
ARGUMENTS	TableName — String expression that holds a valid table name.
RETURNS	True/False
VERSION	Paradox 2.0 and above

ISTABLE(TableName)

DESCRIPTION	Tests to see if a table exists.
ARGUMENTS	TableName — String expression that holds a valid table name.
RETURNS	True/False

ISVALID( )

DESCRIPTION	Tests the validity of a field.
ARGUMENTS	None
RETURNS	True/False
VERSION	Paradox 2.0 and above

LEN(Expression)

DESCRIPTION	Calculates the length of a string.
ARGUMENTS	Expression — Any valid PAL expression.
RETURNS	Numeric value that holds the length of expression.

LINKTYPE( )

DESCRIPTION	Used to determine the type of link between tables on a multi-table form.
ARGUMENTS	None
RETURNS	String value containing a link type: 1-1 Group — One to one relationship 1-M Group — One to many relationship Group — Many to many relationship None — No multi-user form
VERSION	Paradox 3.0 and above

LN(Number)

DESCRIPTION	Calculates the natural logarithm of a number.
ARGUMENTS	Number — Positive numeric expression.
RETURNS	Numeric value equivalent to the natural logarithm of Number.

LOCKSTATUS(TableName, LockType)

DESCRIPTION	Calculates the number of times a specified type of lock has been placed on a table.
ARGUMENTS	TableName — A string expression that holds a valid table name.
	LockType — A string value that holds a valid lock type. Valid lock types are: "FL," "WL," "PWL," "PFL," "ANY."
RETURNS	Numeric value that holds the number of times the specified lock type has been used.
VERSION	Paradox 2.0 and above

LOWER(Expression)

DESCRIPTION	Converts a string to lowercase.
ARGUMENTS	Expression — Any expression.
RETURNS	String equivalent to Expression converted to lowercase.

MATCH(String, PatternString, [VarNameList])

DESCRIPTION	Compares a string with a pattern.
ARGUMENTS	String — The string to be searched.
	PatternString — Matching string.
	VarNameList — List of variables to which the matching portions will be assigned.
RETURNS	True/False — VarNameList will be assigned the matching strings (if present).

MAX(Number1, Number2)

DESCRIPTION	Returns the larger of two numbers.
ARGUMENTS	Number1 — Numeric expression to compare.
	Number2 — Numeric expression to compare.
RETURNS	Numeric value equal to the larger of Number1 and Number2.

MEMLEFT( )

DESCRIPTION	Calculates the free memory left to Paradox.
ARGUMENTS	None
RETURNS	Numeric valuc rcprcsenting free RAM.

MENUCHOICE( )

DESCRIPTION	Gets the current menu selection.
ARGUMENTS	None
RETURNS	String value that holds the current menu selection.
	"Error" if a menu is not displayed.

MIN(Number1, Number2)

DESCRIPTION	Returns the smaller of two numbers.
ARGUMENTS	Number1 — Numeric expression to compare.
	Number2 — Numeric expression to compare.
RETURNS	Numeric value equal to the smaller of Number1 and Number2.

MOD(Number1, Number2)

DESCRIPTION	Returns remainder when one number is divided by another.
ARGUMENTS	Number1 — Numeric expression to compare.
	Number2 — Numeric expression to compare.
RETURNS	Modulus of Number1/Number2 or zero if Number2 is 0.

MONITOR
DESCRIPTION Gets the currently-set monitor type.
ARGUMENTS None
RETURNS String value containing the current monitor type ("Mono,""B&W," and "Color").

MONTH(Date)
DESCRIPTION Extracts the month from a date expression.
ARGUMENTS Date — A valid date expression.
RETURNS Integer value between 1 and 12.

MOY(Date)
DESCRIPTION Extracts a character month from a date expression.
ARGUMENTS Date — A valid date expression.
RETURNS Three character string ("Jan," "Oct," etc.).

NETTYPE( )
DESCRIPTION Determine the network type.
ARGUMENTS None
RETURNS String value of: "Novell," "3COM," "IBM," "Torus," "AT&T Starlan," "Banyan," "Other," or "SingleUser."
VERSION Paradox 2.0 and above

NFIELDS(TableName)
DESCRIPTION Gets the number of fields in a table.
ARGUMENTS TableName — String expression that contains the name of a table.
RETURNS Numeric value equal to the number of fields in TableName.

NIMAGERECORDS
DESCRIPTION Determines the number of linked or unlinked records in the current image.
ARGUMENTS None
RETURNS Numeric value representing number of records in the current image.
VERSION Paradox 3.0 and above

NIMAGES( )
DESCRIPTION Returns the number of images on the workspace.
ARGUMENTS None
RETURNS Numeric value equal to the number of images on the workspace.

NKEYFIELDS(TableName)
DESCRIPTION Gets the number of key fields in a table.
ARGUMENTS TableName — String expression that contains the name of a table.
RETURNS Numeric value equal to the number of key fields in TableName.

NPAGES( )
DESCRIPTION Gets the number of pages in the current form or report specification.
ARGUMENTS None
RETURNS Numeric value equal to the number of pages in the current form or report specification.

NRECORDS(TableName)
DESCRIPTION Gets the number of records in a table.
ARGUMENTS TableName — String expression that contains the name of a valid table.
RETURNS Numeric value equal to the number of records in TableName.

NROWS( )
DESCRIPTION Gets the number of rows in the current image or report specification.
ARGUMENTS None
RETURNS Numeric value equal to the number of rows in the current image or report specification.

NUMVAL(String)
DESCRIPTION Converts a string to a number.
ARGUMENTS String — A valid string expression.
RETURNS Numeric value that is equal to String.

PAGENO( )
DESCRIPTION Gets the current page number in a form or report specification.
ARGUMENTS None
RETURNS Numeric value equal to the current page number.

PAGEWIDTH( )
DESCRIPTION Gets the page width of the current report.
ARGUMENTS None
RETURNS Numeric value equal to the report width.

PI
DESCRIPTION Returns the constant PI.
ARGUMENTS None
RETURNS Numeric constant value = 3.14159265.

PMT(Number1, Number2, Number3)
DESCRIPTION Calculates the periodic payment required to pay off a loan.
ARGUMENTS Number1 — Numeric expression - Principal
Number2 — Numeric expression - Interest expressed as a decimal number (.12, etc.).
Number3 — Number of periods.
RETURNS Numeric value — Payment.

POW(Number1, Number2)
DESCRIPTION Raises a number to a power.
ARGUMENTS Number1 — Numeric expression representing number to be raised.
Number2 — Numeric expression representing the power to raise Number1 to.
RETURNS Numeric value — Number1 raised to the Number2 power.

PRINTERSTATUS( )
DESCRIPTION Tests to see if the printer is ready.
ARGUMENTS None
RETURNS True/False

PRIVDIR( )

DESCRIPTION	Gets the name of the user's private directory.
ARGUMENTS	None
RETURNS	String value that contains the users private directory name.
VERSION	Paradox 2.0 and above

PV(Number1, Number2, Number3)

DESCRIPTION	Determines the value of payments.
ARGUMENTS	Number1 — Numeric value representing periodic payment. Number2 — Numeric Value representing interest rate per period expressed as a decimal. Number3 — Numeric expression representing number of payments.
RETURNS	Numeric value representing present value of a series of equal payments.

QUERYORDER( )

DESCRIPTION	Determines the default order for fields in an answer table.
ARGUMENTS	None
RETURNS	String value containing "TableOrder" or "ImageOrder" depending on how query fields are ordered.
VERSION	Paradox 3.0 and higher

RAND( )

DESCRIPTION	Generates a random number between 0 and 1.
ARGUMENTS	None
RETURNS	Numeric value from 0 up to but not including 1.

RECNO( )

DESCRIPTION	Gets the current record number.
ARGUMENTS	None
RETURNS	Numeric value representing the current record number of the current image.

RETRYPERIOD( )

DESCRIPTION	Gets the duration of the current retry period.
ARGUMENTS	None
RETURNS	Numeric integer value representing the currently set retry period.
VERSION	Paradox 2.0 and above

ROUND(Number1, Number2)

DESCRIPTION	Rounds a number to a specified number of digits.
ARGUMENTS	Number1 — Numeric expression to be rounded. Number2 — Numeric expression representing number of digits to round.
RETURNS	Numeric value which has been rounded.

ROW( )

DESCRIPTION	Gets the row position of the cursor on the PAL canvas.
ARGUMENTS	None
RETURNS	Integer value between 0 and 24.

ROWNO( )

DESCRIPTION	Gets the number of the current row in the current image, report, or form.
ARGUMENTS	None
RETURNS	Integer value between 1 and 22.

SDIR( )

DESCRIPTION	Gets the full pathname of the current script.
ARGUMENTS	None
RETURNS	String value that contains the DOS Pathname of the script being executed.

SEARCH(Substring, String)

DESCRIPTION	Gets the position of one string in another.
ARGUMENTS	Substring — String expression containing the substring you want to search for. String — String expression to search.
RETURNS	Numeric value that contains the starting position of Substring in String, or zero if not found.

SIN(Number)

DESCRIPTION	Calculates the sine of an angle.
ARGUMENTS	Number — Numeric expression representing an angle expressed in radians.
RETURNS	Numeric value between –1 and 1.

SORTORDER( )

DESCRIPTION	Gets the sort order being used by Paradox.
ARGUMENTS	None
RETURNS	Character string containing the installed sort order.
VERSION	Paradox 2.0 and higher

SPACES(Number)

DESCRIPTION	Returns a string of Number spaces in length.
ARGUMENTS	Number — A numeric expression between 0 and 255.
RETURNS	A string value filled with spaces of Number length.

SQRT(Number)

DESCRIPTION	Calculates the square root of a number.
ARGUMENTS	Number — Non-negative numeric expression.
RETURNS	Numeric value equal to the positive square root of Number.

STRVAL(Expression)

DESCRIPTION	Converts a value of any type to a string.
ARGUMENTS	Expression — Any type of expression.
RETURNS	String value that contains the expression.

SUBSTR(String, Number1, Number2)

DESCRIPTION	Returns a substring of a number.
ARGUMENTS	String — String to take apart. Number1 — Integer expression containing starting offset. Number2 — Integer expression containing extract length.
RETURNS	Character string representing the substring of String.

SYSCOLOR Number

DESCRIPTION Determines the color attribute of a Paradox screen element.

ARGUMENTS Integer expression representing Paradox screen element.

Number	*Element*	*Description*
General		
0	TopTwoLines	Top two lines and menu selection.
2	CurrentSelection	Current menu selection.
4	Annotation	Annotation line that describes the current menu selection.
5	ModeIndicator	Mode indicator at top right of screen.
8	WorkSpace	Empty workspace areas; literals in the report generator.
19	QueryElements	Checkmarks and example elements in a query image.
Image Display		
6	NoncurrentImage	Non-current image(s) on the workspace.
9	Current Image	Current image on the workspace.
Field Display		
11	FieldView	Cursor in field view; edit marker when record is locked.
17	FieldValues	Field values in table and form view; field symbols in report generator.
18	NegativeValues	Negative values in numeric or currency fields.
Message/Status Display		
3	Messages	Messages display in bottom left corner; current line in = PAL debugger.
16	DebuggerStatus	Status of PAL debugger.
Help/Protection Generator		
12	Border	Border of systems forms.
13	NormalText	Text of system forms.
15	Highlight	"Reverse-video" text.
21	RegularText	Text of the Help Index
22	Lines	Graphic and bold characters of the Help index.
23	Bold	"Reverse-Video" text of the Help Index.
Report		
24	VertiRuler	Vertical ruler and page-width edge marker in Report Generator = and PAL editor.
25	BandLines	Band lines in the report generator.
Form		
7	FormArea	Edge marker of an area in the form designer.
28	ReverseVideo	Reverse video mapping in the form designer on B&W monitors.
27	ReverseVideo/HI	High intensity and reverse video mapping in the form designer on B&W monitors.
29	High Intensity	High intensity mapping in the form designer on B&W monitors.

RETURNS Attribute value representing screen element current color.

VERSION Paradox 3.0 and higher

SYSMODE( )

DESCRIPTION Gets the current Paradox mode.
ARGUMENTS None
RETURNS Character string that contains the current mode: "Main," "Create," "DataEntry," "Edit," "Coedit," "Form," "Password," "Report," "Restructure," "Script," "Sort."

TABLE( )

DESCRIPTION Gets the name of the current table as a string.
ARGUMENTS None
RETURNS String value containing the name of the current display or query image.

TABLERIGHTS(TableName, String)

DESCRIPTION Tells you whether you have right to perform certain operations on a table.
ARGUMENTS TableName — Character string that contains a valid table name.
String — Character string describing rights. Valid arguments are: "ReadOnly," "Update," "Entry," "InsDel," "All."
RETURNS True/False
VERSION Paradox 2.0 and above

TAN(Number)

DESCRIPTION Returns the tangent of a number.
ARGUMENTS Number is a numeric expression representing an angle expressed in radians.
RETURNS Numeric value equal to the tangent of a number.

TIME( )

DESCRIPTION Gets the time of day as a string.
ARGUMENTS None
RETURNS Character string containing the current time in 24-hour format.

TODAY( )

DESCRIPTION Gets today's date.
ARGUMENTS None
RETURNS A date value containing the current system date.

TYPE(Expression)

DESCRIPTION Returns the type of an expression.
ARGUMENTS Expression — Any expression.
RETURNS "An" - Character of n length, "N" - numeric, "D" - Date, "S" - Short number, "$" - Dollars and Cents, "L" - Logical (True/False).

UPPER(Expression)

DESCRIPTION Converts a string to uppercase.
ARGUMENTS Expression — Any expression.
RETURNS Expression converted to uppercase.

USERNAME( )

DESCRIPTION Gets the name of the current user as a string.
ARGUMENTS None
RETURNS String expression stored as the user name.
VERSION Paradox 2.0 and above

VERSION( )

DESCRIPTION	Returns the Paradox version number.
ARGUMENTS	None
RETURNS	Numeric value containing the version number.
VERSION	Paradox 1.1 and above

WINDOW( )

DESCRIPTION	Returns a string containing the current contents of the Paradox message window.
ARGUMENTS	None
RETURNS	String value with the message text or a blank string if no window is present.

YEAR(Date)

DESCRIPTION	Extracts the year from a Date.
ARGUMENTS	Date — A valid date expression.
RETURNS	A numeric value representing the year (1988, 1982, etc.).

Appendix E
PAL RESERVED WORDS

=
?
??
DD
ALL
ARRAY
ARRAYSIZE
ASC
ASIN
ATAN
ATAN2
ATFIRST
ATLAST
ATTRIBUTE
AUTOLIB

BACKGROUND
BACKSPACE
BANDINFO
BEEP
BLANKDATE
BLANKNUM
BLINK
BORDER
BOT

CANCELEDIT
CANVAS
CASE
CAVERAGE
CCOUNT
CHARWAITING
CHECK
CHECKDESCENDING
CHECKMARKSTATUS
CHECKPLUS
CHR
CLEAR
CLEARALL
CLEARIMAGE
CLOSE
CLOSED
CMAX
CMIN
CNPV
COEDIT
COEDITKEY
COL
COLNO
COPY
COPYFORM
COPYFROMARRAY
COPYREPORT
COPYTOARRAY
COS
CREATE
CREATELIB
CROSSTABKEY
CSTD
CSUM
CTRLBACKSPACE
CTRLBREAK
CTRLEND
CTRLHOME
CTRLLEFT
CTRLPGDN
CTRLPGUP
CTRLRIGHT
CURRENCY
CURSOR
CURSORCHAR
CURSORLINE
CVAR

D
DATEVAL
DAY
DEBUG
DEFAULT
DEL
DELETE
DELETELINE
DIRECTORY
DIREXISTS
DITTO
DO_IT!
DOS
DOSBIG
DOW
DOWN
DOWNIMAGE
DRIVESPACE
DRIVESTATUS

ECHO
EDIT
EDITKEY
EDITLOG
ELSE
EMPTY
END
ENDFOR
ENDIF
ENDPROC
ENDQUERY
ENDSCAN
ENDSWITCH
ENDTEXT
ENDWHILE
ENTER
EOL
EOS
EOT
ERRORCODE
ERRORMESSAGE
ERRORPROC
ERRORUSER
ESC
EXAMPLE
EXECPROC

EXECUTE
EXIT
EXP

FAMILYRIGHTS
FAST
FIELD
FIELDINFO
FIELDNO
FIELDRIGHTS
FIELDSTR
FIELDTYPE
FIELDVIEW
FILE
FILESIZE
FILL
FIRSTSHOW
FOR
FORM
FORMAT
FORMKEY
FORMTABLES
FROM
FV

GETCHAR
GRAPHKEY
GRAPHTYPE
GROUPBY

HELP
HELPMODE
HOME

IF
IMAGECAVERAGE
IMAGECCOUNT
IMAGECMAX
IMAGECMIN
IMAGECSUM
IMAGENO
IMAGEORDER
IMAGERIGHTS
IMAGETYPE
INDEX
INFOLIB
INS
INSTANTPLAY
INSTANTREPORT
INT
INTENSE
ISASSIGNED
ISBLANK
ISBLANKZERO
ISDIRNAME
ISEMPTY
ISENCRYPTED
ISFIELDVIEW
ISFILE
ISFORMVIEW
ISINSERTMODE
ISLINKLOCKED
ISMULTIFORM
ISMULTIREPORT
ISPRIVATE
ISRUNTIME
ISSHARED
ISVALID
ISTABLE

KEYLOOKUP
KEYPRESS
KEYTO

LEFT
LEN
LIKE
LINKTYPE
LN
LOCATE
LOCK
LOCKKEY
LOCKRECORD
LOCKSTATUS
LOG
LOOKUP
LOOP
LOWER

MARK
MATCH
MAX
MEMLEFT
MENU
MENUCHOICE
MESSAGE
MIN
MOD
MONITOR
MONTH
MOVETO
MOY

NETTYPE
NEXT
NFIELDS
NIMAGERECORDS
NIMAGES
MKEYFIELDS
NOEXT
NOREFRESH
NORESTORE
NORMAL
NPAGES
NRECORDS
NROWS
NUMERIC
NUMVAL

OFF
ON
OPEN
OTHERWISE

PAGENO
PAGEWIDTH
PAINTCANVAS
PALMENU
PASSWORD
PATTERN
PERMANENT
PGDN
PGUP
PI
PICKFORM
PICTURE
PLAY
PMT
POW
PRINT
PRINTER
PRINTERSTATUS
PRIVATE
PRIVDIR
PRIVTABLE
PROC
PROCS

PROMPT
PROTECT
PV

QUERY
QUERYORDER
QUIT
QUITLOOP

RAND
READLIB
READONLY
RECNO
RECORD
REFRESH
REFRESHKEY
RELEASE
RENAME
REPORT
REPORTTABLES
REQUIRED
REQUIREDCHECK
RESET
RETRYPERIOD
RETURN
RETVAL
REVERSE
REVERSETAB
REVERT
RIGHT
ROTATE
ROUND
ROW
ROWNO
RUN

SAVEVARS
SCAN
SDIR
SEARCH
SELECT
SETDIR
SETKEY
SETMARGIN
SETMAXSIZE
SETNEGCOLOR
SETPRINTER
SETPRIVDIR
SETQUERYORDER
SETRECORDPOSITION
SETRESTARTCOUNT
SETRETRYPERIOD
SETSWAP
SETUSERNAME
SHOWARRAY
SHOWFILES
SHOWMENU
SHOWTABLES
SIN
SKIP
SLEEP
SLOW
SORT
SORTORDER
SPACES
SQRT
STEP
STRVAL
STYLE
SUBSTR
SUBTRACT
SWITCH
SYNCCURSOR
SYSCOLOR
SYSMODE

TAB
TABLE
TABLEORDER
TABLERIGHTS
TAN
TEXT
THEN
TIME
TO
TODAY
TYPE
TYPEIN

UNIQUE
UNLOCK
UNLOCKRECORD
UNPASSWORD
UNTIL
UP
UPDATE
UPIMAGE
UPPER
USERNAME
USEVARS

VARS
VERSION
VERTRULER
VIEW

WAIT
WHILE
WINDOW
WRITELIB

YEAR

ZOOM
ZOOMNEXT

Appendix F
PARADOX MENU OPTIONS

The menu options are listed as they appear on the Main Menu. Each submenu option is indented under the option which allows access to it.

- View
- Ask
- Report
  - Output
  - Design
    - Tabular
      - Field
      - TableBand
      - Group
      - Output
      - Setting
      - Help
      - DO-IT!
      - Cancel
    - Free-form
      - Field
      - Group
      - Output
      - Setting
      - Help
      - DO-IT!
      - Cancel
  - Change
  - RangeOutput
  - SetPrinter
- Create
  - Borrow
  - Help
  - DO-IT!
  - Cancel
- Modify
  - Sort
  - Edit
  - Coedit
  - DataEntry
  - MultiEntry
  - Restructure
- Image
  - TableSize
  - ColumnSize
  - Format
  - Zoom
  - Move
  - PickForm
  - KeepSettings
  - Graph
    - Modify
      - Type
      - Overall
        - Titles
        - Colors
        - Axes
        - Grids
        - Printer Layout
        - Device
        - Wait
      - Series
      - Pies
      - ViewGraph
      - Help
      - DO-IT!
      - Cancel
    - Load
    - Save
    - Reset
    - Crosstab
    - ViewGraph
- Forms
  - Design
    - Field
    - Area
    - Border
    - Page
    - Style
    - Multi
    - Help
    - DO-IT!
    - Cancel
  - Change
    - Field
    - Area
    - Border
    - Page
    - Style
    - Multi
    - Help
    - DO-IT!
    - Cancel
- Tools
  - Rename
  - QuerySpeedup
  - ExportImport
    - Export
      - Quattro
      - 1-2-3
      - Symphony
      - dBASE
      - pfs
      - Reflex
      - Visicalc
      - ASCII

Tools (Cont.)
- Import
  - Quattro
  - 1-2-3
  - Symphony
  - dBASE
  - pfs
  - Reflex
  - Visicalc
  - ASCII
- Copy
  - Table
  - Form
  - Report
  - Script
  - JustFamily
  - Graph
- Delete
  - Table
  - Form
  - Report
  - Script
  - QuerySpeedUp
  - KeepSet
  - ValCheck
  - Graph
- Info
  - Structure
  - Inventory
  - Family
  - Who
  - Lock

Tools (Cont.)
- Net
  - Lock
  - PreventLock
  - SetPrivate
  - UserName
  - AutoRefresh
- More
  - Add
  - MultiAdd
  - FormAdd
  - Subtract
  - Empty
  - Protect
  - Directory
  - ToDOS

Scripts
- Play
- BeginRecord
- QuerySave
- Showplay
- RepeatPlay
- Editor
  - Write
    - Read
    - Go
    - Print
    - Help
    - DO_IT!
    - Cancel

Scripts (Cont.)
- Edit
  - Read
  - Go
  - Print
  - Help
  - DO_IT!
  - Cancel

Help
- Basics
- GettingAround
- Keys
- MenuChoices
- Index
- Scripts/PAL
- Paradox

Exit
- No
- Yes

Appendix G
PARADOX NETWORK OVERVIEW

Paradox can be installed and used on many kinds of local area networks and is easy to use in single and multi-user environments. In a multi-user environment, Paradox automatically locks all objects as required. An object in Paradox terminology is any form, table, or report. If you want to take advantage of Paradox's multi-user capabilities to share data, however, any shared objects must be stored in a network *shared* directory. A shared directory is a special network directory used to store objects you wish to share with other users.

Each Paradox network user also has a special *private directory*. Paradox uses this directory to store tempory objects (Answer, Changed, Deleted, Inserted, Problems and Keyviol tables) that you don't want to share with other users. In some situations, you might not want to clutter up your personal private directory with the results of queries and reports. Use the PRIVDIR command to temporarily change your private directory while a PAL script is running.

You can control access to Paradox objects with the LOCK and UNLOCK commands. Paradox locks types are:

FULL LOCK	Gives you exclusive use of a table on a network.
WRITE LOCK	Stops other users attempting to change a record in a table and stops them from locking a table.
PREVENT FULL LOCK	Stops other users attempting to place a full lock on a table.
PREVENT WRITE LOCK	Stops other users attempting to place a write lock on a table.
FAMILY LOCK	Stops other users attempting to change objects in a table (forms, reports).
RECORD LOCK	Stops other users from changing a specific record in a table.

Sec the LOCK and UNLOCK commands for more details.

The Paradox EDIT command *F9* is used to make changes to tables. When you *EDIT* a table, all other users of that table are locked out with a WRITE LOCK and can't make changes to records until you unlock the table.

A special form of the EDIT command, the COEDIT command, allows more than one user to make simultaneous changes to Paradox tables on a record level. In COEDIT mode, when a user attempts to change a record, it is automatically locked and no other user can make any changes to that record while it is locked. If you attempt to change a record locked by another user, Paradox will not change it. However, it will supply the user name that has the record locked.

If a record is changed while in COEDIT mode, the screens of all network users currently coediting the same table will be automatically updated to reflect the changes. You can also force a refresh of your screen at any time with the REFRESH Alt-R command.

If other users are performing queries on a coedited table, their queries will restart each time the contents of a record is changed. This can cause a query to run for a very long time. The SETRESTART command can be used to control the number of times Paradox restarts a query. If the count is set to OFF, Paradox will continue to restart the query until it can successfully gather the data. If you set the restart count to any number, Paradox will restart the query a maximum of that number of times. If you specify a restart count, remember that records may have changed since you started your query.

Paradox uses a special user name (usually assigned by network administrator) to identify each network user. On many local area networks, the network administrator assigns user names according to some internal coding scheme, such as department or function. In many cases, users are often given a very cryptic name like ACCT-01, PURCH-21, or ADMIN-DAL. Fortunately, you can reassign the network name (at least as far as Paradox is concerned) with the menu option, Tools/Network/UserName. Remember, when you have locked an object or record, other users are given your network name unless you reset it.

Paradox has built-in password access control features that allow network users to protect their data from unauthorized use. Paradox has two different kinds of passwords, OWNER and AUXILLIARY. OWNER passwords give a user full control of a table.

Remember, *any* user that knows the owner password for a table has *complete* access including read, update, empty, and yes, even the right to delete the table. It is important to keep your owner passwords confidential. An AUXILLIARY password can be given to other network users to limit their actions. AUXILLIARY password options are:

All	Complete access to the table (just like an owner password).
Entry	Enter new records, change non-key fields but can't delete records or empty a table (delete all records).
InsDel	Grant a user all privilages but restructure and table delete privileges).
ReadOnly	Read privilages only.

For more information on PAL network commands, see the following modules: COEDIT, IMAGERIGHTS, KEYLOOKUP, LOCK, LOCKKEY, LOCKRECORD, PASSWORD, PRIVTABLES, SETPRIVDIR, SETRESTARTCOUNT, SETRETRYPERIOD, SETUSERNAME, UNLOCK, UNLOCKRECORD UNPASSWORD.

The following functions are used to control access to data on a local area network: FAMILYRIGHTS, FIELDRIGHTS, ISENCRYPTED, ISSHARED, LOCKSTATUS, NETTYPE, PRIVDIR, RETRYPERIOD, TABLERIGHTS, USERNAME.

Appendix H
PARADOX EXERCISES

1. About This Book
   a. What hardware requirements must be met to run Paradox?
   b. What should you know before you begin a Paradox session?
2. An Overview of Paradox
   a. What are the two modes of Paradox?
   b. Briefly describe the difference between the two modes of Paradox.
   c. What is PAL?
3. Sample Session
   a. Where is the Main Menu located, and how do you select options from it?
   b. How do you end the current Paradox session?
4. Game Rules
   a. Briefly describe the Paradox menu-driven system.
   b. How do you begin a Paradox session?
   c. List five special keys and briefly describe their use.
   d. How are PAL and Paradox related?
5. =
   a. What is a variable, and how is it used?
   b. How do you tell Paradox that the value for the variable is numeric or alphanumeric?
   c. Where are variables stored?
6. @, ?, ??
   a. Briefly describe the uses of these three commands.
   b. What happens if the @ command is not included before the ?? command?
7. ACCEPT
   a. List four optional clauses available for the ACCEPT command.
   b. List and briefly describe two of the symbols available for the PICTURE clause.
   c. When is the ACCEPT command included in a script?
8. ADD
   a. Briefly describe the ADD command.
   b. What menu options perform the same results as the ADD command?
   c. Briefly describe "batch processing."
   d. What happens to the source table after Paradox performs the ADD command?

9. ARRAY
   a. Briefly describe an array.
   b. Why is a subscript necessary when referencing an array element?
   c. When the array is created, what values are stored in the elements?
   d. List two ways to remove arrays from memory.
10. BEEP
    a. Why is the BEEP command often included in scripts?
    b. How many BEEP commands are allowed in a script?
11. CANCELEDIT
    a. Briefly describe the effect of the CANCELEDIT command.
    b. If a blank record is added to the open table, what must be done before the CANCELEDIT command is encountered?
    c. When the CANCELEDIT command is performed, what is displayed on the screen?
12. CANVAS
    a. What are the options for the CANVAS command?
    b. Briefly describe the effect of performing the CANVAS command.
13. CLEAR
    a. List the three forms of the CLEAR command and briefly describe each one.
    b. What happens when the CLEAR command is not included in a script that displays information to the screen?
    c. Is the CLEAR command useful when a table is displayed on the screen? If not, how is the table removed from the workspace?
14. COEDIT
    a. Briefly describe the effect of performing the COEDIT command.
    b. What is the difference between the EDIT and COEDIT commands?
15. COPY
    a. Briefly describe the effect of the COPY command.
    b. What happens to the source table after the script performs the COPY command?
    c. List the menu options that achieve the same results as the COPY command.
    d. What happens if the new table name already exists on the disk when the COPY command is encountered in the script?
16. COPYFORM
    a. Briefly describe the effect of performing the COPYFORM command.
    b. What happens if the form number of the receiving table is already used?
    c. Must the sending and receiving table structures match?
17. COPYFROMARRAY
    a. Briefly describe the results of using the COPYFROMARRAY command.
    b. What happens if the array does not exist in memory?
    c. Is an array always used to collect information for a table record?

18. COPYREPORT
    a. Briefly describe the effect of performing the COPYREPORT command.
    b. What happens if the report number of the receiving table is already used?
    c. Must the sending and receiving table structures match?
19. COPYTOARRAY
    a. Briefly describe the results of using the COPYTOARRAY command.
    b. What is the value in the first element of the array?
    c. What happens if the array does not exist in memory before the script performs the COPYTOARRAY command?
    d. Must the specified name of the array be enclosed in quotation marks?
20. CREATE
    a. What is a table structure?
    b. List three valid data types for describing the table's fields.
    c. What menu option line performs the same results as the CREATE command?
    d. Is it possible to borrow the structure from an existing table?
21. CREATELIB
    a. Briefly describe the use of the CREATELIB command.
    b. Where is the library saved and what does it contain?
    c. List two reasons for using libraries.
22. CURSOR
    a. What are the four cursor options?
    b. Why would you turn the cursor off?
23. DEBUG
    a. Briefly describe the debugging process.
    b. What happens when the DEBUG command is encountered?
    c. List and describe two special keycodes using the Ctrl key that affect the debugger.
    d. When using the debugger, what is displayed on the last line of the screen?
24. DELETE
    a. When the DELETE command is performed, what file(s) are deleted?
    b. What happens if the specified table name already exists on the disk?
    c. When is the DELETE command useful?
25. DOS, DOSBIG
    a. Briefly describe what happens when a script performs the DOS command.
    b. Why is the DOS command useful?
26. ECHO
    a. What are the three forms of the ECHO command?
    b. List two reasons for including the ECHO command in a script.
27. EDIT
    a. Briefly describe what happens when a script performs the EDIT command.
    b. What happens when you press Ctrl-Backspace while in an edit mode?
    c. List the menu options necessary to achieve the same results as the EDIT command.

28. EDITLOG
    a. When is the EDITLOG command useful?
    b. What are the four options for the EDITLOG command?
    c. Is the EDITLOG command available to linked tables on a multi-table form?
29. EMPTY
    a. When is the EMPTY command included in a script?
    b. List the menu options necessary to achieve the same results as the EMPTY command.
    c. Is there a way to return the records after performing the EMPTY command?
30. EXECPROC
    a. Briefly describe the advantage of using the EXECPROC command.
    b. Which Paradox version includes the EXECPROC command?
31. EXECUTE
    a. What does Paradox do when the EXECUTE command is encountered in a script?
    b. How does the EXECUTE command help you write flexible applications?
32. EXIT
    a. What is seen on the screen after a script performs the EXIT command?
    b. Briefly describe the difference between the EXIT command and the QUIT command.
    c. Is the user given the chance to abort the operation when the script performs the EXIT command?
33. FIRSTSHOW
    a. Briefly describe the effect of performing the FIRSTSHOW command.
    b. What options are available for this command?
34. FOR, ENDFOR
    a. Briefly describe the use of the FOR, ENDFOR command combination.
    b. What is a "loop?"
    c. List and briefly describe two optional clauses available for the FOR, ENDFOR command combination.
    d. Briefly describe a "nested loop."
    e. What command is often used to end a loop?
35. FORMTABLES
    a. What information is provided when the FORMTABLES command is performed?
    b. Must an array be declared before issuing the FORMTABLES command?
    c. Briefly describe the use of the ISMULTIFORM( ) function.
36. IF, ENDIF
    a. Briefly describe "conditional processing."
    b. What happens when the command combination does not include THEN?
    c. When is the IF, ENDIF command combination useful?
37. IMAGERIGHTS
    a. Briefly describe the effect of the IMAGERIGHTS command.
    b. What are the two options of the IMAGERIGHTS command?

38. INDEX
    a. What is an index and how is it used?
    b. Is a script allowed to specify an index for a table?
    c. Briefly describe why indices help the LOCATE command and the QUERY, ENDQUERY command combination.
    d. What is the extension assigned to index files?
39. INFOLIB
    a. What happens when the script performs the INFOLIB command?
    b. Is there another way to obtain the information provided by the INFOLIB command?
    c. What kind of error occurs if the specified library does not exist on the disk?
40. KEYPRESS
    a. Briefly describe the use of the KEYPRESS command.
    b. When should the SELECT command be used instead of the KEYPRESS command?
41. LOCATE
    a. Briefly describe why the LOCATE command is often included in a script.
    b. What happens when NEXT is included in the LOCATE command?
    c. Does the LOCATE command use indices that exist for the current table?
42. LOCK, UNLOCK
    a. When is the LOCK command useful?
    b. Why should you use the UNLOCK command?
    c. List and briefly describe the four lock types.
43. LOCKRECORD, UNLOCKRECORD
    a. When is the LOCKRECORD command useful?
    b. Why should you use the UNLOCKRECORD command?
44. LOOP
    a. Briefly describe what happens when a script performs the LOOP command.
    b. What command combination(s) are affected by the LOOP command?
    c. Must the LOOP command be controlled by another command combination?
45. MESSAGE
    a. Briefly describe when the MESSAGE command is included in a script.
    b. Where does Paradox display the information provided by the MESSAGE command?
    c. List three reasons that the MESSAGE command is preferred over the @, ?, and ?? commands.
46. MOVETO
    a. What happens when the script performs the MOVETO command?
    b. List three formats for the MOVETO command.
    c. How are table fields specified when using them in the MOVETO command?
    d. Is the MOVETO command helpful when multiple images are displayed on the workspace?
47. OPEN PRINTER, CLOSE PRINTER
    a. Briefly describe the effect of the OPEN PRINTER and CLOSE PRINTER commands.
    b. When are these commands useful?

48. PAINTCANVAS
    a. When is the PAINTCANVAS command useful?
    b. What number in the ATTRIBUTE clause causes black letters on a red background?
    c. What function does the FILL clause provide in the PAINTCANVAS command line?

49. PASSWORD
    a. Is the PASSWORD command used to assign passwords to tables or scripts?
    b. Briefly describe why the PASSWORD command is often included in a script.

50. PICKFORM
    a. Briefly describe the use of the PICKFORM command in a script.
    b. What mode must exist when using the PICKFORM command?
    c. List the menu options that achieve the same results as the PICKFORM command.

51. PLAY
    a. Why is it better for scripts to be small and task oriented?
    b. What happens when the script performs the PLAY command?
    c. If the specified script does not exist, what is the result?
    d. List the menu options that perform the same results as the PLAY command.

52. PRINT
    a. When is the PRINT command useful?
    b. How is the PRINT command different from the PRINTER command?

53. PRINTER
    a. What happens when a script performs the PRINTER command?
    b. Why is the PRINTER command often included in scripts?
    c. List three commands that are often used with the PRINTER command.

54. PRIVTABLES
    a. When is the PRIVTABLES command necessary?
    b. Must the tables exist before issuing the PRIVTABLES command?
    c. Is this command effective for a single-user system?

55. PROC, ENDPROC
    a. How is a procedure different from a script?
    b. List two advantages of using procedures in an application.
    c. How is a procedure played by a script?
    d. Where are procedures stored?

56. PROMPT
    a. Briefly describe the use of the PROMPT command in a PAL script.
    b. Which lines on the screen are affected by the PROMPT command?
    c. Can the prompt values be provided by variables?

57. PROTECT
    a. Briefly describe the effect of performing the PROTECT command.
    b. List the menu options that achieve the same results as the PROTECT command.
    c. Which Paradox files need to be protected?
    d. Can a protected file be unprotected?

58. QUERY, ENDQUERY
    a. Briefly describe queries.
    b. What type of information is provided by the QUERY, ENDQUERY command combination?
    c. How is a query created and saved?
    d. After the query is performed, where are the results stored?

59. QUIT
    a. Describe the difference between the QUIT command and the EXIT command.
    b. If a message is included in the QUIT command line, where is it displayed?
    c. What is seen on the screen after the script performs the QUIT command?

60. QUITLOOP
    a. What happens when a script performs the QUITLOOP command?
    b. Is the QUITLOOP command valid for loops only?
    c. Which command combination is usually included in the script to control the QUITLOOP command?
    d. What is an alternative method of ending looping activity?

61. READLIB
    a. How does the READLIB command affect procedures?
    b. Which scripts should include the READLIB command?
    c. If the specified library or procedures do not exist when the script performs the READLIB command, what is the result?

62. RELEASE
    a. Why should a form of the RELEASE command be used often in scripts?
    b. What is the result of the RELEASE command?
    c. What happens when a RELEASE VARS ALL command is performed in a script?

63. RENAME
    a. What happens when a script performs the RENAME command?
    b. If the new table name exists when the RENAME command is encounterd, what happens?
    c. Can the RENAME command be used to rename scripts?

64. REPORT
    a. What happens when a script performs the REPORT command?
    b. Is it possible to use the REPORT command to create a file of output?
    c. List the menu options required to achieve the same results as the REPORT command.
    d. What happens if the specified table is not available when the script encounters the REPORT comm

65. REPORTTABLES
    a. What information is provided when the REPORTTABLES command is performed?
    b. Must an array be declared before issuing the REPORTTABLES command?
    c. Briefly describe the use of the ISMULTIREPORT( ) function.

66. REQUIREDCHECK
    a. Briefly describe the effect of issuing the REQUIREDCHECK command.
    b. When is this command useful?
67. RESET
    a. When should the RESET command be included in a script? Why?
    b. Is the computer memory cleared of variables, arrays, and procedures when the script performs the RESET command?
68. RETURN
    a. Briefly describe the results of performing the RETURN command.
    b. When should the RETURN command be included in a script?
    c. Is the RETURN command available for procedures?
69. RUN
    a. Why would you include the RUN command in a script?
    b. What type of operations are available for the RUN command?
    c. What happens when the SLEEP clause is not included in the RUN command?
70. SAVEVARS
    a. What is the effect of including the SAVEVARS command in a script?
    b. What is the name of the file created by the SAVEVARS command?
    c. Once created, how is the file used?
    d. Can you rename this file? If so, how?
71. SCAN, ENDSCAN
    a. How is the SCAN, ENDSCAN command combination different from the WHILE, ENDWHILE command combination?
    b. Can you use the SCAN, ENDSCAN command combination to affect only certain records in the table?
    c. Is the QUITLOOP command valid with the SCAN, ENSCAN command combination?
72. SELECT
    a. What happens when a script performs the SELECT command?
    b. When should the SELECT command be used instead of the KEYPRESS command?
73. SETDIR
    a. Briefly describe the effect of performing the SETDIR command.
    b. If the drive or directory do not exist, what happens?
    c. Why should you consider using different subdirectories for an application?
74. SETKEY
    a. List two advantages to using the SETKEY commands in a script.
    b. When keys are changed from their normal status with the SETKEY command, how is their status returned?
75. SETMARGIN
    a. What is the effect of issuing the SETMARGIN command with a number?
    b. What happens when the SETMARGIN OFF command line is performed in a script?

76. SETMAXSIZE
    a. Briefly describe the effect of the SETMAXSIZE command.
    b. List the four options of this command.
    c. What happens when the number in the SETMAXSIZE command is not one of the valid options?
77. SETNEGCOLOR
    a. When is the SETNEGCOLOR command useful?
    b. List the valid options of the SETNEGCOLOR command.
    c. What is the default color for negative numbers?
78. SETPRINTER
    a. Briefly describe the effect of the SETPRINTER command.
    b. List four of the valid options for this command.
    c. What is the Paradox default destination?
79. SETPRIVDIR
    a. When is the SETPRIVDIR command useful?
    b. When providing the subdirectory path, what must be done to provide backslashes in the command line?
80. SETQUERYORDER
    a. Briefly describe the effects of the SETQUERYORDER command.
    b. What is the difference between the TABLEORDER and IMAGEORDER options?
81. SETRECORDPOSITION
    a. When is the SETRECORDPOSITION command useful?
    b. Briefly describe the necessary steps for using this command.
    c. Is this command effective for single-record forms?
82. SETRESTARTCOUNT
    a. Briefly describe the effect of issuing the SETRESTARTCOUNT command.
    b. What happens when you include the OFF option in this command line?
    c. What happens when you include a number in this command line?
83. SETRETRYPERIOD
    a. Briefly describe the effect of issuing the SETRETRYPERIOD command.
    b. What does the number provide this command?
84. SETSWAP
    a. What happens when this command is included in a script?
    b. When is this command useful?
85. SETUSERNAME
    a. What is the effect of issuing the SETUSERNAME command?
    b. What Paradox menu selections allow you to change the user name?
86. SHOWARRAY
    a. Briefly describe the effects of issuing the SHOWARRAY command.
    b. What does <array1> provide this command?
    c. What does <array2> provide this command?

87. SHOWFILES
    a. When is the SHOWFILES command useful?
    b. Briefly describe the effects of the SHOWFILES command.
    c. What is the effect of the NOEXT command?

88. SHOWMENU
    a. What is the effect of the SHOWMENU command?
    b. Why is the SHOWMENU command often used in scripts?
    c. Briefly describe the use of the optional DEFAULT clause.

89. SHOWTABLES
    a. Briefly describe the effects of the SHOWFILES command.
    b. When is this command useful?
    c. What does the variable in the TO clause provide?

90. SKIP
    a. What happens when the SKIP command is performed?
    b. Can negative as well as positive numbers be used in the SKIP command?
    c. What function is used to determine if the end of the table has been encountered?

91. SLEEP
    a. How does the SLEEP command help the user?
    b. Briefly describe an example where the SLEEP command might be used in a script.

92. SORT
    a. Why include the SORT command in a script?
    b. Does the SORT command always create a new table?
    c. Is it possible to sort the data on multiple keys?

93. STYLE
    a. How do scripts that use the STYLE command help the user?
    b. List two of the style options.
    c. What command is necessary to reset the screen to its normal status?

94. SUBTRACT
    a. Briefly describe what happens when a script plays the SUBTRACT command.
    b. Does the SUBTRACT command perform differently if the specified tables are non-keyed?
    c. Describe a situation when the SUBTRACT should be used in a script.

95. SWITCH, ENDSWITCH
    a. Which Paradox command combination is similar to the SWITCH, ENDSWITCH?
    b. How many CASE statements are included in the SWITCH, ENDSWITCH command combination?
    c. What happens if all CASE statements are evaluated as False and the OTHERWISE clause is omitted?
    d. Describe a situation where the SWITCH, ENDSWITCH command combination applies.

96. SYNCCURSOR
    a. Briefly describe the effects of the SYNCCURSOR command.
97. TEXT, ENDTEXT
    a. Briefly describe the use of the TEXT, ENDTEXT command combination.
    b. How does the TEXT, ENDTEXT command differ from the ? and ?? commands?
98. TYPEIN
    a. Briefly describe the use of the TYPEIN command.
    b. Does including the TYPEIN command in a script help the user? If so, how?
99. UNPASSWORD
    a. Briefly describe the effects of a script performing the UNPASSWORD command.
    b. When using the UNPASSWORD command, must all passwords be provided or just a few?
100. VIEW
    a. What other information must be provided when using the VIEW command in a script?
    b. Can a table be edited when the VIEW command is performed from a script?
    c. What happens if the F7 function key is pressed after the VIEW command is performed?
101. WAIT
    a. Why should the WAIT command be included in a script that accesses a table in edit mode?
    b. Briefly describe the difference between the Field, Record, and Table options.
    c. Where are the PROMPT messages displayed on the screen?
    d. When the WAIT command is performed by a script, what value is stored in the Retval variable?
102. WHILE, ENDWHILE
    a. What happens when the WHILE command is encountered in a script?
    b. List two logical operators that may be included in the conditional expression.
    c. When the WHILE, ENDWHILE command combination is used to evaluate each record in the current table, what happens if the WHILE command does not include the EOT( ) function?
103. WRITELIB
    a. Briefly describe the use of the WRITELIB command.
    b. When is the WRITELIB command included in a script?
    c. What happens if the specified library does not exist on the disk?
    d. Are the procedures in memory affected by the WRITELIB command?

Index

?, ??, 143, 158, 165, 180, 187, 310
Accept, 26-32, 143
Alt, 12
array, 17-19, 22, 37-39, 64-67, 70-73, 288-289
Ask, 8, 203-210
attribute, 167, 310

Backspace, 12
bar, 82
batch update, 34
beep, 41-42
blink, 310
bot( ), 298
box, 82

cancel, 43-46
canvas, 47-48, 167-169
case, 317
Check, 204
CheckPlus, 204
clear, 49-51
close printer, 165
close tables, files, 240
coedit, 52-54, 151-153
conditions, 128-132, 317-322
copy, 58-61
copyform, 62-63
copyreport, 68-69
Create, 8, 74-78, 205
Createlib, 79-81, 139, 350
Ctrl, 12
Ctrl-Break, 12, 211
Ctrl-D, 12
Ctrl-E, 12
Ctrl-F, 12
Ctrl-R, 12
Ctrl-V, 12
Ctrl-Y, 12
cursor, 82-83
custom forms, 99

data type, 18, 26, 75
debug, 12, 84-91
Default, 28
Del, 12
delete, 90-92, 108-109
DOS, 93-94
Down Arrow, 12

echo, 94-97
edit, 11, 43, 52-54, 84-89, 98-104
editlog, 105-107
empty, 33, 108-109, 313
End, 12
EndProc, 195, 243
Endquery, 203
Enter, 12
eot( ), 299, 347
Error, 12
Errorcode( ), 151, 282
Esc, 14
Execproc, 110-111
Exit, 8, 114-116, 211, 242

F1 (Help), 14
F2 (DO-IT!), 14
F3 (Up Image), 14
F4 (Down Image), 14
F5 (Example), 14
F6 (Check Mark), 14
F7 (Form Toggle), 15
F8 (Clear Image), 15
F9 (Edit Mode), 15
F10 (Menu), 15
filesize( ), 139
fill, 167
For, Endfor, 119-124, 253, 347
forms, 8, 124-127, 172-176
Full lock, 148

Help, 8
Home, 15

image, 8, 117-118, 133-134
imageorder, 117-118, 276-279
imagerights, 133

index, 135-138
Infolib, 139-140
Ins, 15
Isfile( ), 224, 307, 335
ismultiform( ), 124-127
ismultireport( ), 233

key field, 75
keypress, 141

Left Arrow, 15
library, 79-81
Locate, 143-149, 255, 335-341
lock, 52-54, 148-150
Lockrecord, 151-153
Lookup, 28
looping, 119-123, 154-157, 253-256, 345-349

Max, 28
memleft( ), 286
memory, 219-221
menu driven, 4-5, 43
message, 158-160, 341-344
Min, 28
Modify, 8
Modify/Coedit, 52-54
Modify/Edit, 98-104
Moveto, 161-164, 341
multi-record forms, 280
multi-table forms, 124-127

Num Lock, 15

open printer, 165
Otherwise, 317
Out of memory, 219

Paintcanvas, 167-170
PAL (Paradox Application Language), 1, 3, 5, 10
password, 170-171, 201-203, 331-334
PgDn, 16
PgUp, 16
Pickform, 172-176
Picture, 26-32
Play, 177-179
Prevent Full Lock, 148
Prevent Write Lock, 148
Print, 180-184
printer, 21-22, 165-166, 185-192, 273-275
private directory, 274
privtable, 193-194
procedure, 38, 79-81, 110-111, 195-198, 217-223, 243, 350-352
prompt, 199-200, 341-344
Protect, 201-202

query, 203-210, 337
Quit, 210-213, 242
quitloop, 119-123, 214-216, 254

Readlib, 217-218, 350
recno( ), 280
release, 217, 219-223, 249-252, 350
rename, 224, 226, 250
report, 8, 68-69, 227-232
report tables, 233-237
Required, 28
requiredcheck, 238-239
reset, 240-241
retryperiod( ), 284-285
return, 242-246
retval, 148, 151, 243, 296
reverse, 310
Right Arrow, 16
run, 247-248

savevars, 249-252
Scan, 154-157, 214-216, 253-256
Scripts, 5, 9-10, 17, 26-32, 84-89, 177-179
Scripts/BeginRecord, 9
Scripts/Editor, 9
select, 141, 257-258
setdir, 259-262
setkey, 263-264
setmargin, 265-267
setmaxsize, 248-249
setnegcolor, 270-272
setprinter, 273-275
setprivdir, 274
setqueryorder, 276-279
setrecordposition, 280-281
setrestartcount, 282-283
setretryperiod, 284-285
setswap, 286
setusername, 287
showarray, 288-289
showfiles, 288-289

showmenu, 292-295
showtables, 296-297
skip, 253, 298-302
sleep, 245, 303-305
sort, 306-309
style, 310-313
Subtract, 313-316
Switch, Endswitch, 317-322
Synccursor, 323-324

Tab, 16
table, 74-78, 98-104, 117-118, 135-138, 296-297, 306-309, 335-340
tableorder, 276-279
temporary tables, 43
Text, Endtext, 265, 310, 325-328
ToDos, 247
Tools, 8
Tools/More/Add, 33
Tools/More/Empty, 33, 108-109
Typein, 329-330

Unlock, 53, 148
Unlockrecord, 151
Unpassword, 170-171, 331-334
Up Arrow, 16

Validitycheck, 328
variables, 17-19, 22, 26-31, 219-223
View, 52, 335-340

Wait, 341-344
While, Endwhile, 154-157, 214-216, 253, 345-349
Writelib, 350-352
Writelock, 148

Other Books From Wordware

Computer Books

dBASE III Plus
RUSSELL A. STULTZ
This complete guide to dBASE III Plus commands and functions provides a step-by-step tutorial for beginners and a quick reference for the familiar dBASE user. Easy-to-understand examples illustrate new commands, correct syntax, and file structures. Enter, manipulate, and retrieve large volumes of data and develop customized application programs. Create a filing system, then write procedures to store, retrieve, edit, and display on-screen menus and user-help information.
0-915381-92-3 • **$19.95**
softbound • 384 pages

dBASE IV
RUSSELL A. STULTZ
Grasp the power and flexibility of dBASE IV commands, functions, system memory variables, and SQL commands as you work through the hands-on examples contained in this clearly written book. Fully operational, annotated programs help you create and use menu bars, pop-ups, windows, macros, user-defined functions, and more. Practical development activities probe the Control Center, and WYSIWYG report, label, query, view and application generators. Explore the latest programming techniques of this top-selling database management program. This book is an in-depth reference for the dBASE IV developer.
1-55622-116-9 • **$21.95**
softbound • 450 pages

FoxBASE+ 2.01
BOB GRANILLO
This illustrated tutorial will guide the novice step-by-step through the FoxBASE+ software. Create professional looking windows and light bar menus, and learn to use data structures such as one- and two-dimensional arrays. Streamline record retrieval and reloading by using the GATHER and SCATTER commands. Programming tips and easy-to-understand examples make this book an excellent reference for the intermediate and advanced user and will add speed and flexibility to your applications.
1-55622-168-1 • **$21.95**
softbound • 352 pgs

Paradox 3.0 Volume I
Basic Menu Commands Edition
2nd Edition
DEBBIE and DOUG STONE
Explore the powerful capabilities of Paradox with the updated information found in this book. This excellent tutorial details Paradox rules, terms, techniques, keys, and menu options. Examples provide models to custom design application solutions. This book is a stand-alone reference to Paradox commands and an introductory to Volume II, the Paradox application language (PAL) tutorial.
1-55622-158-4 • **$21.95**
softbound • 416 pgs

MS/PC-DOS 4.0
Sixth Edition
RUSSELL A. STULTZ
This complete, timesaving reference contains all the significant updates to the world's most popular operating system. The novice-to-expert DOS user is led keystroke-by-keystroke through a sequence of exercises designed to provide hands-on experience. Use the new text-based DOSSHELL to initiate powerful DOS utilities. Each command is detailed in brief, easy-to-understand modules which make this book an indispensable reference.
1-55622-111-8 • **$21.95**
softbound • 272 pages

Novell NetWare 2.15
TIMOTHY K. McDONALD
Step-by-step techniques clearly demonstrate the fundamentals of this networking operating system from installation to operation. Master NetWare's user commands to effectively store, protect, and share company data and resources among personal computers. Learn to adapt essential software programs to NetWare's LAN for custom applications. Tips on a variety of security and printer options are included. A complete guide for effective communications between centralized personal computers. Reviewed for accuracy by Novell Corporation.
1-55622-065-0 • **$21.95**
softbound • 256 pgs

Business Professional Books

The Business Side of Writing
RUSSELL A. STULTZ
If you regard writing as a business rather than an art, this book can provide the reference information you need for a successful career in writing or publications management. These guidelines help organize and refine your approach to project planning, cost estimating, project research, financial control, development, and production. Mr. Stultz addresses the tools, techniques, methodologies, and processes to plan, manage, and automate publications development and production with emphasis on the bottom line.
1-55622-157-6 • **$15.95**
hardbound • 224 pages • 6 x 9

Innovation, Inc.
Unlocking Creativity in the Workplace
GROSSMAN, RODGERS, and MOORE
Unlock your hidden potential to reach a new plane of creative thinking. Seek new avenues of problem solving by elevating your ability to conceive ideas. Techniques and exercises in this book expand your creativity. The authors take you on a journey designed to spark confidence by reorganizing your thinking processes and patterns. Learn to use innovative thinking to inspire fresh ideas and formulate imaginative concepts.
1-55622-054-5 • **$14.95**
softbound • 256 pages • 6 x 9

Business Emotions
A New Business Concept
RICHARD M. CONTINO
Revolutionize your thinking, conditioning, and approach. Learn why emotions are a controlling factor in every success and failure situation. This practical book will guide you through the maze of hidden psychological issues in a simple and straightforward manner. Achieve predictable, positive, and immediate results. The author introduces unique concepts in and practical techniques for emotional awareness, self-analysis, and effective business functioning.
1-55622-058-8 • **$14.95**
softbound • 184 pages • 6 x 9

Steps to Strategic Management
A Guide for Entrepreneurs
DR. RICK MOLZ
This book will help the entrepreneur uncover opportunities for a more successful business. A fictitious person, business, and product illustrate how this system works. Nine key steps to strategic management are developed and followed by real-world business applications. This system is used worldwide by sophisticated organizations of all types and sizes. The case example approach and readable style make this strategic method easy to understand and apply.
1-55622-050-2 • **$13.95**
softbound • 184 pages • 6 x 9

Investor Beware
Investigating Investments and Scams
HENRY H. ROTHENBERG
Create your own luck with this book detailing the essentials for safe investments. Avoid shady, risky, and unsuccessful investments. Learn to anticipate and interpret various investment climates and analyze a business from financial statements. The average investor will find what he needs to know about economics, financing, taxes, operating entities, and types of investments. Discover the ramifications of diversified investments such as real estate, franchises, oil and gas, gold, tax shelters, and syndications.
1-55622-055-3 • **$14.95**
softbound • 464 pages • 6 x 9

Other Books from Wordware Publishing, Inc.

Artificial Intelligence
Illustrated VP-Expert

Business-Professional Books
Business Emotions
The Business Side of Writing
Consulting Handbook for the High-Tech Professional
Hawks Do, Buzzards Don't
How to Win Pageants
Innovation, Inc.
Investor Beware
MegaTraits
Occupying the Summit
Steps to Strategic Management

Computer Aided Drafting
Illustrated AutoCAD (Release 9)
Illustrated AutoCAD (Release 10)
Illustrated AutoLISP
Illustrated AutoSketch 2.0
Illustrated GenericCADD Level 3

Database Management
The DataFlex Developer's Handbook
Illustrated dBASE II (2nd Ed.)
Illustrated dBASE III Plus
Illustrated dBASE IV
Illustrated Paradox Volume I 3.0 (2nd Ed.)
Illustrated Paradox Volume II 3.0 (2nd Ed.)

Desktop Publishing
Achieving Graphic Impact with Ventura 2.0
Desktop Publisher's Dictionary
Illustrated PFS:First Publisher 2.0
Handbook of Desktop Publishing
Illustrated Interleaf
Illustrated PageMaker 3.0
Illustrated Ready, Set, Go! 4.5 (Macintosh)
Illustrated Ventura 2.0
Ventura Troubleshooting Guide

General Advanced Topics
Illustrated Dac Easy Accounting 3.0
Illustrated Dac Easy Accounting 4.0
Illustrated Harvard Graphics
Illustrated Novell NetWare 2.15
Novell NetWare: Advanced Techniques and Applications

Programming Languages
Illustrated C Programming (ANSI) (2nd Ed.)
Illustrated Clipper 5.0
The FOCUS Developer's Handbook
Illustrated FoxBASE+ 2.01
Illustrated QuickBASIC 4.0
Illustrated Turbo C
Illustrated Turbo Debugger 1.0
Illustrated Turbo Pascal 4.0
Illustrated Turbo Pascal 5.5

Spreadsheet/Integrated
Illustrated Enable/OA
Illustrated Framework III
Illustrated Lotus 1-2-3 2.01
Illustrated Lotus 1-2-3 Rel. 3.0
Illustrated Lotus 1-2-3 Rel. 2.2
Illustrated Microsoft Excel 2.10 (IBM)
Illustrated Microsoft Excel 1.5 (Macintosh)
Illustrated Microsoft Works 2.00
Illustrated Multiplan 2.0
Illustrated Q & A 3.0 (2nd Ed.)
Illustrated Quattro
Illustrated SuperCalc 5

Systems and Operating Guides
Illustrated Microsoft Windows 2.0
Illustrated MS/PC DOS 3.3
Illustrated MS/PC DOS 4.0 (6th Ed.)
Illustrated OS/2

Word Processing
Illustrated DisplayWrite 4
Illustrated Microsoft Word 5.0
Illustrated Microsoft Word for the Mac
Illustrated WordPerfect 1.0 (Macintosh)
Illustrated WordPerfect 4.2
Illustrated WordPerfect 5.0
Illustrated WordStar 3.3
Illustrated WordStar Professional (Rel. 5)
The New WordStar Customizing Guide 4.0
WordPerfect: Advanced Applications Handbook

Regional
This Dog'll Hunt
100 Days in Texas: The Alamo Letters
Exploring the Alamo Legends
Texas Wit and Wisdom
Forget the Alamo
Rainy Days in Texas Workbook